Jim B. and Josephine S. All

Purchased at Dallas Museum

WORKING AMONG *Flowers*

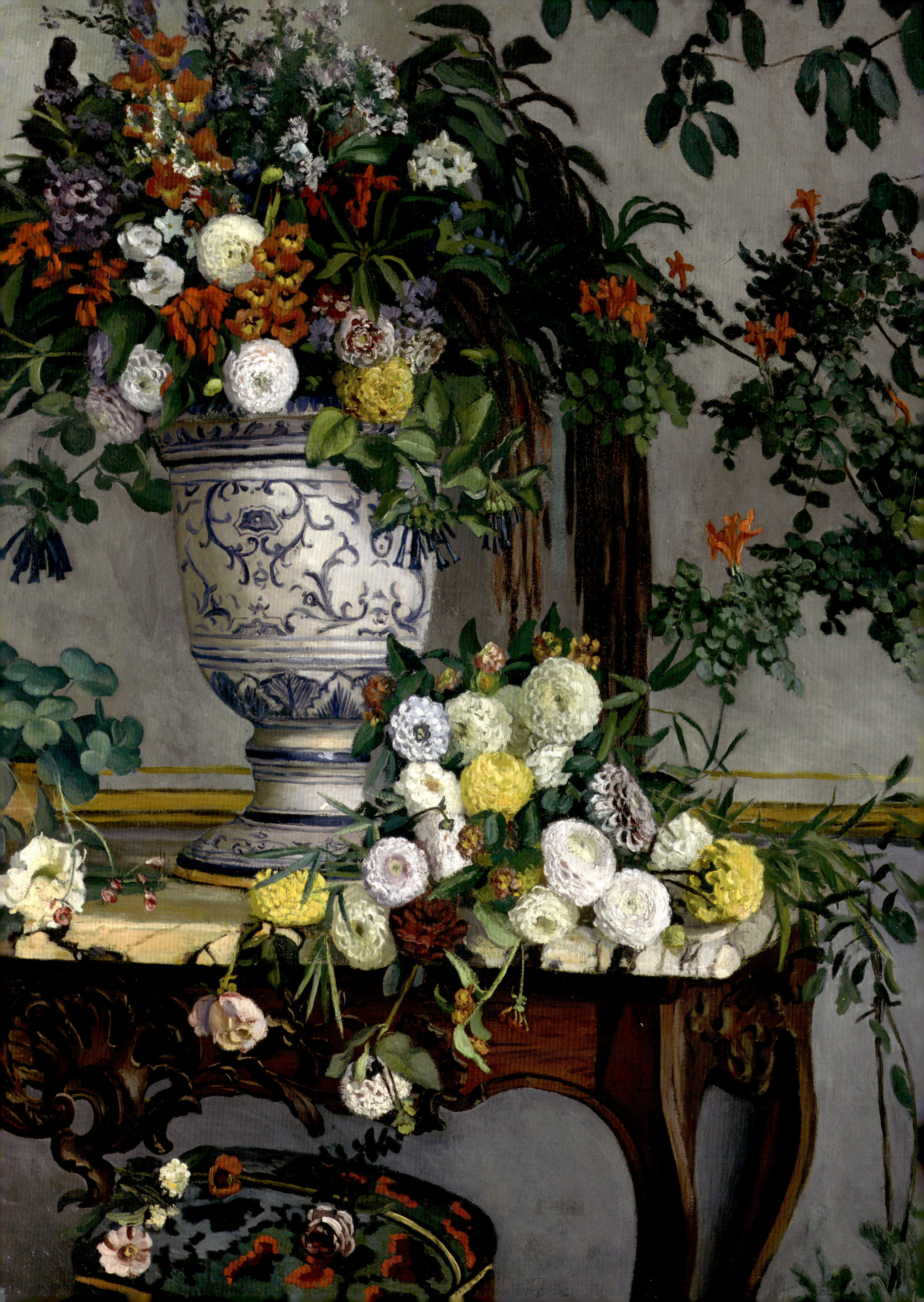

WORKING AMONG *Flowers*

Floral Still-Life Painting in Nineteenth-Century France

Heather MacDonald AND Mitchell Merling

WITH ESSAYS BY Audrey Gay-Mazuel, Olivier Meslay, AND Sylvie Patry

Dallas Museum of Art   Virginia Museum of Fine Arts

DISTRIBUTED BY Yale University Press, New Haven and London

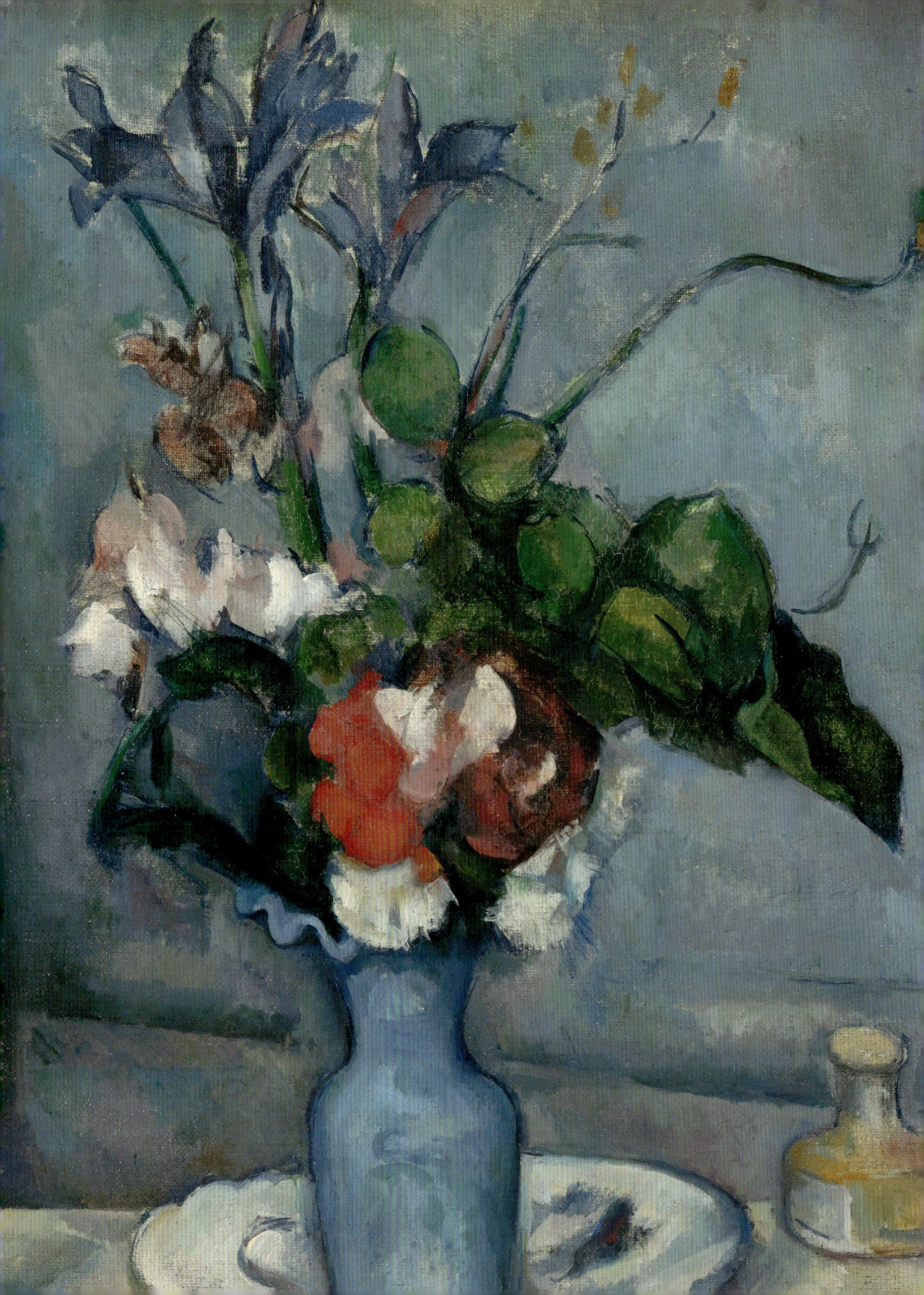

Contents

DIRECTORS' FOREWORD AND ACKNOWLEDGMENTS

THOUGH THE BEAUTY AND SENSUOUS APPEAL OF floral still-life paintings are undeniable, the significance of these works within the history of art has not been fully appreciated. This catalogue, which accompanies a traveling exhibition, reveals how a traditional genre—well established in France by the seventeenth century—was reinvented by nineteenth-century painters even at a time when modernism was radically transforming the art world.

The title *Working Among Flowers* is taken from a letter Vincent van Gogh wrote to his sister Willemien in 1888, in which he suggested that painting is similar to other artistic endeavors, including flower arranging:

> *The uglier, older, meaner, iller, poorer I get, the more I wish to take my revenge by doing brilliant colour, well arranged, resplendent. . . . And arranging colours in a painting to make them shimmer and stand out through their contrasts, that's something like arranging jewels or—designing costumes. You'll see now that by regularly looking at Japanese prints you'll enjoy making bouquets even more, working among flowers.*

Van Gogh himself, along with the many French artists featured here, began "working among flowers" both as a subject poised between nature and culture and as a source of painterly meditation. The commitment of these artists to the floral still life is mirrored in the curators' intention to reassess thoroughly a subject that is often dismissed at best as merely decorative, or at worst as primarily commercial. Artists who explored the floral still life, such as Henri Fantin-Latour and Gustave Courbet, were sometimes ambivalent about the genre and sought to explain or apologize for their work; however, the stunning and unquestionably ambitious paintings they produced need no excuses. While researching the catalogue and selecting works for the exhibition, the curators discovered a surprising variety of artistic purposes and achievement in this genre, which offers inspiration and nuance.

We congratulate the co-curators of the exhibition—Mitchell Merling, Paul Mellon Curator and Head of the Department of European Art at the Virginia Museum of Fine Arts, and Heather MacDonald, the Lillian and James H. Clark Associate Curator of European Art at the Dallas Museum of Art—for their productive collaboration and successful realization of this ambitious project. The catalogue has also benefited from the participation of the other scholars who contributed both advice and essays: Audrey Gay-Mazuel, Curator, Department of the Nineteenth Century at the Musée des Arts décoratifs, Paris; Olivier Meslay, Associate Director of Curatorial Affairs and the Barbara Thomas Lemmon Curator of European Art at the Dallas Museum of Art; and Sylvie Patry, Chief Curator of Impressionist and Post-Impressionist Paintings at the Musée d'Orsay, Paris.

The exhibition would not have been possible without the generosity of the lenders, whose willingness to part with some of their most prized paintings is much appreciated. We thank the directors and curators of the lending institutions, as well as the private lenders, for their exceptional cooperation. The support of an indemnity from the Federal Council on the Arts and Humanities has allowed the inclusion of many important loans from both North America and Europe. We also acknowledge the creative and supportive environment of the French Regional American Museum Exchange (FRAME), at whose meetings we initially conceived of the exhibition, confirmed the institutional partnership between Dallas and Richmond, discussed the Denver Art Museum as a venue for the tour, and agreed on many crucial loans. Of the numerous FRAME lenders, we particularly wish to thank the Musée des Beaux-Arts, Lyon, and its director, Sylvie Ramond, for making possible the presentation of the important history of Lyonnais flower painting with especially generous loans. We also thank the past and present FRAME directors and staff members in France and North America for their encouragement and support.

We are both very proud of the teams at each museum who together produced this landmark exhibition. At the Dallas Museum of Art, we wish to thank Olivier Meslay, Associate Director of Curatorial Affairs as well as a contributor to this catalogue; Tamara Wootton-Bonner, Associate Director for Collections and Exhibitions; Reagan Duplisea, Associate Registrar for Exhibitions; Anne Bergeron, DMA's former Associate Director for External Affairs; Jill Bernstein, Director of Communications; Joni Wilson-Bigornia, Exhibitions

Manager; Andrea Lesovsky, Exhibitions Assistant; Jessica Harden, Director of Exhibition Design; Mark Leonard, Chief Conservator; Nicole Stutzman, Chair of Learning Initiatives and Dallas Museum of Art League Director of Education; Andrea Vargas Severin, Interpretation Manager; Mandy Engleman, Director of Creative Services; Jacqui Allen, Director of Libraries and Imaging; Mary Leonard, former Librarian; Jenny Stone, Librarian; Martha MacLeod, Curatorial Administrative Assistant; and Michael Hartman, former McDermott Curatorial Intern for European Art.

At the Virginia Museum of Fine Arts, the exhibition has benefited greatly from the support and supervision of Sylvia Yount, former Chief Curator and Louise B. and J. Harwood Cochrane Curator of American Art; Robin Nicholson, former Deputy Director for Art and Education; Stephen Bonadies, Deputy Director for Collections and Facilities Management; and their respective departments: in Exhibitions, Aiesha Halstead, Project Coordinator; in Registration, Kelly Burrow, Exhibitions Registrar, and Karen Daly, Registrar of Exhibitions; and in Education, Celeste Fetta, Chief Educator, Art and Education Division, and Megan Liles, Youth and Family Studio Programs Coordinator. The staff of the Library, overseen by Director Lee Viverette, was especially helpful. Kristie Couser, Curatorial Assistant for the Paul Mellon Collections, ably carried out in-depth research and assisted with editorial production. Her contribution to the department was supplemented by Corey Piper, former Mellon Curatorial Associate; Sara Moriarty, former Mellon Curatorial Assistant; and interns Casey Nye, Owen Duffy, Thomas Daley, and Jamie Staples.

For the exhibition's presentation at the Denver Art Museum, we thank Christoph Heinrich, the Frederick and Jan Mayer Director, and his colleagues: Timothy Standring, Gates Foundation Curator of Painting and Sculpture; Angelica Daneo, Associate Curator of Painting and Sculpture; Lori Illif, Director of Exhibition and Collection Services; Andrea Kalivas Fulton, Deputy Director and Chief Marketing Officer; Melora McDermott-Lewis, Director of Education and Master Teacher for European and American Art; Molly Medakovich, Master Teacher for Western American Art; Jill Desmond, Associate Director of Exhibitions and Collections Services; Jennifer Pray, Assistant Project Manager/Assistant Registrar; Elen Woods, Curatorial Assistant, Painting and Sculpture; and Katie Ross, Associate Director of Marketing.

This catalogue has been guided at every stage of its development by Rosalie West, Editor in Chief at VMFA, and her talented colleagues: Stacy Moore and Sally Curran, Editors; Doug Fisher, Director of Design and Production; Sarah Lavicka, Chief Graphic Designer; and Howell Perkins, Image Rights Licensing Coordinator. Chris Miller provided lucid translations from French for three of the essays. At Yale University Press, the catalogue was shepherded by Patricia Fidler, and at Marquand Books, our partner in the catalogue's production, we owe special thanks to Adrian Lucia, Managing Director, and Leah Finger, Production Manager, for their patient oversight; Melissa Duffes, Managing Editor, and Diana George, Proofreader, for their attention to the text; and Design Director Jeff Wincapaw and Designers Susan E. Kelly, Ryan Polich, Jeremy Linden, and Marie Weiler for the elegant appearance of this publication.

To the teams in Dallas and Richmond—who have truly been working among flowers for the past several years to bring this project to fruition—we offer our sincere thanks for their perseverance and professional dedication.

Maxwell L. Anderson
THE EUGENE MCDERMOTT DIRECTOR,
DALLAS MUSEUM OF ART

Alex Nyerges
DIRECTOR, VIRGINIA MUSEUM OF FINE ARTS

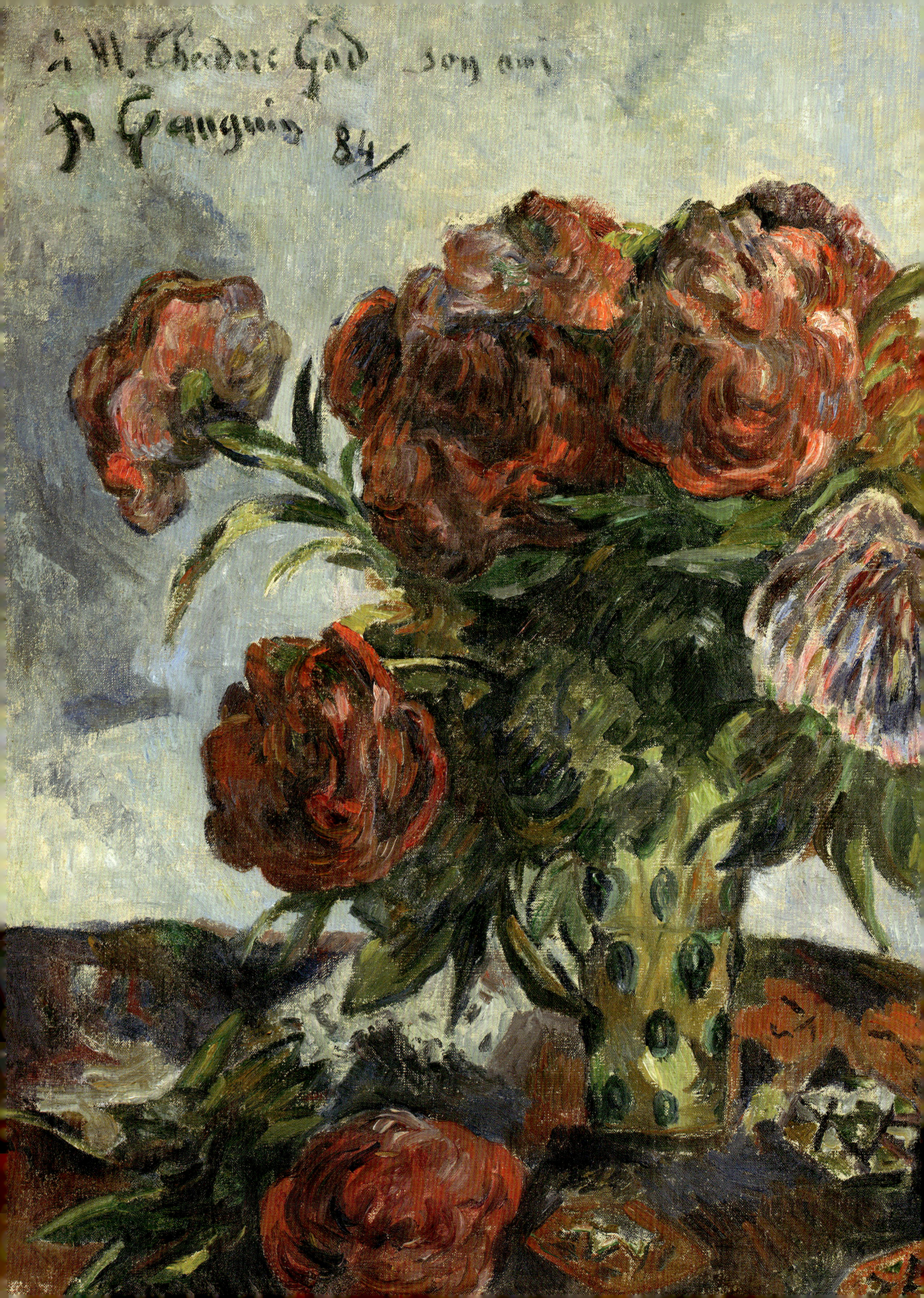
à M. Theodore Gad son ami
P Gauguin 84

LENDERS TO THE EXHIBITION

Albertina, Vienna, Batliner Collection

Brooklyn Museum, New York

Carnegie Museum of Art, Pittsburgh

Centre nationale des arts plastiques, France

The Cleveland Museum of Art

Dallas Museum of Art

Fine Arts Museums of San Francisco

The Fitzwilliam Museum, Cambridge, United Kingdom

High Museum of Art, Atlanta, Georgia

Indianapolis Museum of Art

The J. Paul Getty Museum, Los Angeles

Kelvingrove Art Gallery and Museum, lent by Glasgow Life (Glasgow Museums) on behalf of Glasgow City Council

The Lawrence J. Ellison Art Collection

The Metropolitan Museum of Art, New York

The Minneapolis Institute of Arts

Musée de Grenoble

Musée de l'Orangerie, Paris

Musée des Beaux-Arts de Lyon

Musée des Beaux-Arts de Rouen

Musée des Beaux-Arts de Tours

Musée d'Orsay, Paris

Musée du Louvre, Paris

Musée Fabre, Montpellier Agglomération

Musée National d'Art Moderne, Paris, on deposit at Musée des Beaux-Arts et d'Archéologie de Besançon

Musée national du château de Fontainebleau

Museum of Fine Arts, Boston

The Museum of Modern Art, New York

The National Gallery, London

National Gallery of Art, Washington, D.C.

National Gallery of Canada, Ottawa

The Nelson-Atkins Museum of Art, Kansas City

New Orleans Museum of Art

Ny Carlsberg Glyptothek, Copenhagen

Philadelphia Museum of Art

Saint Louis Art Museum

The San Diego Museum of Art

Scottish National Gallery, Edinburgh

Stedelijk Museum, Amsterdam

Triton Collection Foundation

Van Gogh Museum (Vincent van Gogh Foundation), Amsterdam

Virginia Museum of Fine Arts, Richmond

Anonymous lenders

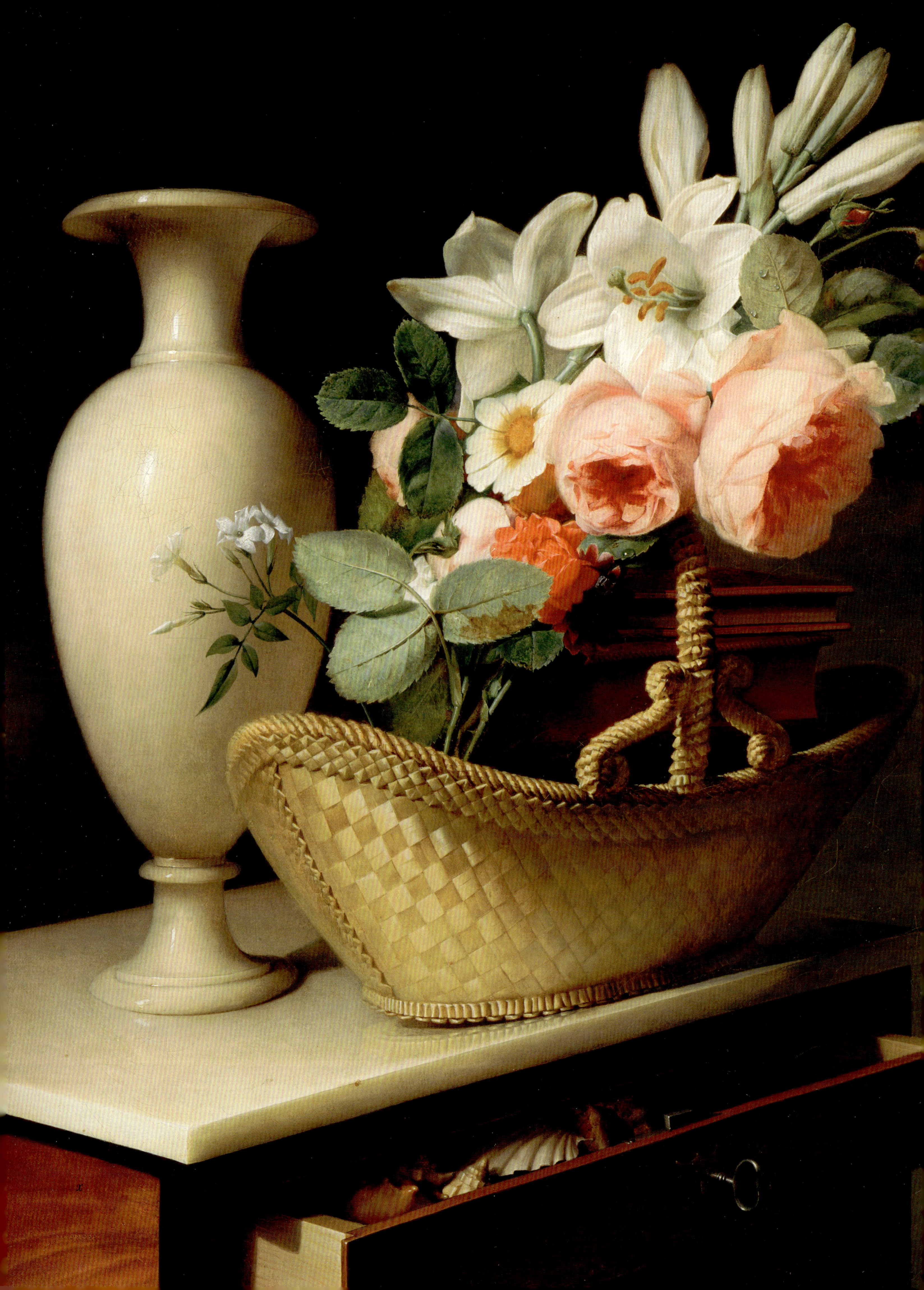

Introduction

IN AN 1860 ARTICLE DISCUSSING THE GREAT DUTCH still-life painters of the seventeenth century, the art historian and critic Théophile Thoré abruptly complains, "It is in vain that we struggle against this nasty appellation, 'nature morte.'"[1] Thoré's dislike of the French term for still life, which can be translated as "dead nature," prompted him to make a passionate case for reconsidering one of the genre's forms in particular, the flower painting. "Aren't flowers alive?" Thoré asks.

> *They have their breath and their health; they are gay and brilliant, or sad and dull; they are in constant motion, although it may be imperceptible, as they turn toward the light, separate to allow importunate branches to pass, droop in response to thirst, swell and spread in the caress of a beam of light. Flowers are not "nature morte." There is no such thing as a "nature morte." Everything is alive and moves, everything breathes in and exhales, everything is in a constant state of metamorphosis. Everything takes or gives something around itself, altering its surroundings as well as itself with irresistible persistence. Everything communicates with everything else and participates in the unity of life. There is no dead nature!*[2]

By the mid-nineteenth century, the status of still life in French critical judgment had been governed for nearly two hundred years by the "hierarchy of genres," an established formula that positioned still life at the lowest register of artistic production, below landscape, portraiture, or history painting. This system had been codified in 1667 by André Félibien, a theorist and historian of art, who explained it as a gradual movement from the base to the divine: "He who paints landscapes beautifully is above the artist who paints only fruits, flowers, or shells. He who paints living animals is worthy of more esteem than he who represents things that are dead and no longer moving. And since man himself is God's most perfect work on earth, it is certain that he who imitates God in painting the human figure is far more excellent than all the others."[3] The measure of nature's divinity was thus at the core of academic constructions of genre. If the depiction of humans—particularly in the midst of significant action—brought the artist closest to God, then the description of flowers or other elements of still life—dead, inert, and incapable of conveying heroism or moral example—kept the artist at the greatest remove.

In practice, though, still-life painters met with considerable approbation from both the market and critics. At the biennial Salon exhibitions sponsored by the French Academy (Académie royale de peinture et de sculpture), still-life painting competed successfully for the attention and praise of audiences and critics, even if the critical endorsement was often confined to the conventional formula of "more real than nature itself." Perhaps only with the responses of Denis Diderot and other critics to the extraordinary still-life paintings of Jean-Siméon Chardin in the mid-eighteenth century did a coherent challenge emerge to the formulaic understanding of still life as a fundamentally imitative art, concerned with mimesis rather than meaning.

During the same period, the cultural construction of nature was itself in flux; in the second half of the eighteenth century, nature assumed a new prominence and intellectual complexity that can be traced from the writings of Jean-Jacques Rousseau to the cult of nature that pervaded the rhetoric of the Revolution of 1789 to the protoromantic literary and visual culture that was well established in France by the turn of the nineteenth century. Nature was no longer understood as a more or less inert form of existence, remote from both human morality and the divine, but rather as a force constantly interacting with all other living beings and exerting a deep fascination for the human intellect and spirit. Thoré's reverie about the ineluctable vitality of flowers even suggests an emerging understanding, informed by contemporary science, of nature as an active system subject to constant transformation. His views also reflect the alternative seventeenth-century intellectual tradition of Jansenist philosopher Blaise Pascal, whose expression of the profound unity of nature exerted a powerful influence on many French artists and writers of the modern period.

By the middle of the nineteenth century, still life was increasingly visible in exhibitions and Salons; the unjuried "open" Salon that followed the Revolution of 1848 marked a high point for the prominence of still life in the Academy's annual exhibition. At the same time, critics more and more frequently expressed their frustration with the theoretical limitations of the Academy's increasingly fragile and irrelevant hierarchy. For Félibien in the mid-seventeenth century, the materials of still life were understood to be "dead and no longer moving," but for nineteenth-century artists and critics, the stuff of nature was not only unquestionably alive but also richly endowed with meaning.

During the 1860s, conservative academicians such as Charles Blanc continued to argue for the preservation of a fixed hierarchy in artistic subjects, from "the plant that vegetates, captive in the soil," to "man as the sum of all previous creations."[4] However, critics associated with the emerging modernist avant-garde were not simply rejecting the hierarchy but actively turning it on its head, particularly in their analysis of the works of Édouard Manet. Émile Zola described Manet's figure-painting technique as "like the approach to still life taught in art schools; I mean that he groups the figures before him a bit haphazardly, and then he is concerned only to fix them on the canvas just as he sees them, with the lively contrasts they produce by their juxtaposition."[5] Upping the ante, Thoré accused Manet of "pantheism" and marveled with mock astonishment that he "sometimes even accords more importance to a bouquet of flowers than to a woman's face, for instance in his famous painting of a *Black Cat*."[6] It is perhaps not surprising that contemporary cartoons satirizing Manet's controversial painting *Olympia* (Thoré's "*Black Cat*") exaggerate the importance of the bouquet, investing this incidental element in the painting's narrative with a looming presence. These satirists clearly recognized how Manet's "pantheistic" approach upset conventional expectations of the respective claim of the human figure and still life on the attention of the artist or the viewer.

THIS CATALOGUE, AND THE EXHIBITION IT ACCOMPANIES, originated with the aspiration to establish a broad artistic, cultural, and intellectual context for French floral still-life painting in the nineteenth century. To fulfill the scope of this ambition, it pursues the subject beyond those chronological boundaries, following the landmark developments in the genre across nearly two centuries, in eight sections arranged loosely chronologically.

The first section opens with Chardin in the mid-eighteenth century and explores the foundations for the experiments of the nineteenth century by looking closely at a group of works from the paradigmatic masters of ancien régime flower painting. The second section examines the important developments in floral still life in Lyon, a center of French textile production that nurtured a close collaboration between academic flower painting, the decorative application of still life, and the demands of mass production. In the third section, the brief but intense engagements with floral still life of Eugène Delacroix and Gustave Courbet are placed in the context of contemporary productions by artists of the Lyon school and the first stirrings of Impressionist floral still life in the paintings of the young Frédéric Bazille and Pierre-Auguste Renoir. In the fourth section, a diverse selection of paintings by the specialist Henri Fantin-Latour shows him taking up the intimate still-life tradition following the rediscovery of Chardin's work in the 1860s.

The fifth section turns to the place of floral still life in Impressionist practice, among the same artists who were championed by Thoré and Zola and whose work built upon Manet's provocative inversion of genre conventions. The sixth section looks more closely at modernist flower painting in the early 1880s, when both Manet and the Impressionists turned to the genre with a renewed intensity. The seventh section examines the years between the end of the Impressionist movement and the close of the nineteenth century, and as a coda, the final section investigates three artists—Odilon Redon, Pierre Bonnard, and Henri Matisse—whose long engagements with the floral still life form a bridge between the work of the late nineteenth-century avant-garde and early twentieth-century modernism.

Even within its strictest definition, there exists a surprising diversity in the genre, not only in terms of style but also in format and function. *Working Among Flowers* largely focuses on a particular cross-section of the floral still life: the traditional image of the bouquet presented in a domestic or, more rarely, landscape context. This is in distinction to garden imagery, which became an increasingly important outlet for modernist painters, culminating in Claude Monet's iconic paintings of his own garden at Giverny.[7] The traditional bouquet remained, though, a motif central to still-life practice throughout the nineteenth century, serving as a persistent touchstone for commentary on and dialogue with the genre's past. Floral still lifes made explicitly for decorative purposes, such as in painted interiors or paneling, or for use in the applied arts also lie outside the focus of the exhibition, although this traditional function of flower painting persisted and indeed flourished during the nineteenth century. The decorative adaptation of floral still life is discussed in the catalogue in relationship to the easel pictures—painted for display in public galleries as well as private interiors—featured in the exhibition.

The exhibition's focus was determined with attention to the work of past historians and with the intention of complementing and extending the existing scholarship on still life, particularly floral still life, in France. The foundational texts in the field include the mid-twentieth-century histories of still life by Charles Sterling and Michel Faré, as well as the influential but unpublished dissertation on French still life by John McCoubrey.[8] Numerous monographs and dictionaries of practitioners by Elisabeth Hardouin-Fugier, Étienne Grafe, and Peter Mitchell have greatly expanded fundamental knowledge of the careers of many floral still-life specialists, particularly Lyonnais artists.[9] Douglas Druick and Michel Hoog's landmark exhibition on Fantin-Latour transformed scholarly understanding of that pivotal floral still-life painter.[10] In the past generation, a series of sophisticated investigations of still life have created a richly historicized and theoretically informed context for interpreting the floral still life, and the unpublished 1995 dissertation of Jeannene Przyblyski has served as an essential source of ideas and information for later scholars.[11] A number of recent exhibitions—including George Mauner's *Manet: The Still-Life Paintings* (2000–2001), Eliza Rathbone and George Shackelford's *Impressionist*

Still Life (2001–2002), and Christophe Leribault's *Eugène Delacroix: Des Fleurs en Hiver* (2013)—have offered important models for scholarly exhibitions that expand our understanding of floral still life in nineteenth-century France.[12] In past accounts of the genre, floral symbolism has often played a predominant role in interpretation, but a turn away from this field of analysis to a broader historical and cultural understanding of the context for still-life painting has been apparent in a number of intellectually diverse publications, from Arthur Wheelock's 1999 exhibition catalogue reappraising the Northern flower painting tradition to Alison Syme's 2010 exploration of the multivalent signification of flowers in fin de siècle Britain.[13]

This catalogue builds on preceding literature in the field by drawing new attention to a set of concerns that have not previously been brought into close dialogue with the history of floral still life. The first section consists of essays that address a wide spectrum of topics: the epistemological and visual implications of floral still life's scientific roots in botanical illustration; the critical context for instruction in and reception of flower painting; the conflicted and poorly understood relationship between avant-garde flower painting and the market; the cultural meanings of the vases and ceramic vessels depicted by nineteenth-century still-life painters; and the literary context for flower painting within the French poetic tradition. There are, of course, innumerable other contexts for French floral still life that merit closer examination, work that we hope will be pursued by future researchers, drawing on the new information and ideas examined in this volume. The book's second section comprises a comprehensive annotated and illustrated catalogue of the exhibition.

Throughout the nineteenth century, nature remained a central subject of inquiry in literature, philosophy, and science as well as art. The genres that were privileged avenues for the expression of the cultural meanings of nature, particularly landscape and flower painting, were thereby endowed with a new urgency. At the same time, still life emerged as a genre of particular interest for artists precisely because of its perceived distance from significance and legible meaning, as those categories were conventionally constructed in the French Academy. By the beginning of the twentieth century, the floral still life had emerged as an established site of artistic meditation and as a subject matter that was both nature and culture, deeply traditional but unmistakably modern, apparently simple and infinitely various.

Heather MacDonald
THE LILLIAN AND JAMES H. CLARK
ASSOCIATE CURATOR OF EUROPEAN ART,
DALLAS MUSEUM OF ART

Mitchell Merling
PAUL MELLON CURATOR AND HEAD OF
THE DEPARTMENT OF EUROPEAN ART,
VIRGINIA MUSEUM OF FINE ARTS

1. Thoré 1860, 317, quoted in Mauner 2000, 37.
2. Thoré 1860, 317–18, quoted in Mauner 2000, 37–38.
3. Quoted in Bailey et al. 2003, 4.
4. Blanc 1867, 634.
5. Zola 1928, 259–60, quoted in Rathbone and Shackelford 2001, 28.
6. "Son vice actuel est une sorte de panthéisme qui n'estime pas plus une tête qu'une pantoufle; qui parfois accorde même plus d'importance à un bouquet de fleurs qu'à la physionomie d'une femme, par exemple dans son fameux tableau du *Chat noir*." Thoré 1870, 532. Authors' translation.
7. Willsdon 2004.
8. See Sterling 1952; Faré 1962 and his exhibition *Peintres de fleurs en France du XVIIe au XIXe siècles* (Paris: Musée du Petit Palais, 1979); and McCoubrey 1958.
9. See, for example, Hardouin-Fugier and Grafe 1979, 1980, and 1992. See also Hardouin-Fugier and Grafe 1989, as well as Mitchell 1973.
10. Druick and Hoog 1983.
11. Przyblyski 1995.
12. Mauner 2000; Rathbone and Shackelford 2001; Leribault et al. 2012.
13. Wheelock 1999; Syme 2010.

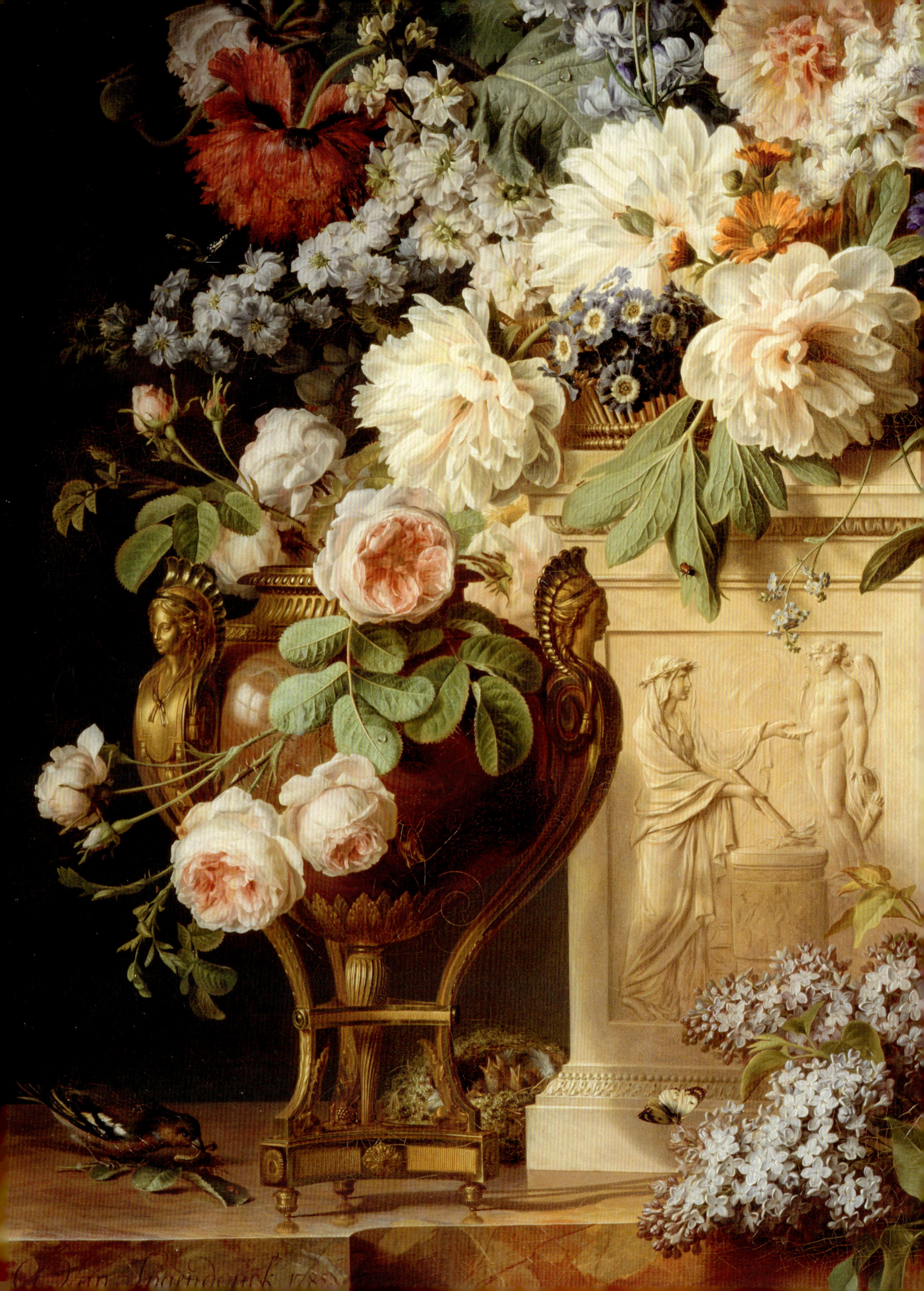

Information and Illusion: Botany and Painting at the Turn of the Nineteenth Century

Heather MacDonald

THE SALON OF 1785 IS BEST REMEMBERED FOR JACQUES-LOUIS DAVID'S groundbreaking painting *The Oath of the Horatii*, which became an immediate flash point for critics and artists alike. Its stylistic innovations and thematic radicalism are now seen as harbingers of the modernist turn in French painting during the nineteenth century. Elsewhere in the same Salon, however, another painting quietly testified to the remarkable power of the French Academy to sustain and renew visual convention. The artist, only two years David's senior, was Dutch-born painter Gerard van Spaendonck, miniaturist to Louis XVI. His royal commission at the 1785 Salon, however, was not a miniature; it was an imposing, life-size painting of flowers, the product of van Spaendonck's recent appointment as professor of flower painting at the Jardin du roi, the king's botanical gardens in Paris (fig. 1; cat. no. 4).

Van Spaendonck's informal bouquet combines humble garden flowers with showy specimens cascading from a shallow basket atop an alabaster pedestal. At left, a bronze and porphyry vase accentuates the setting's fashionable neo-classicism while featuring in its polished, convex surface a significant visual detail: the diminutive reflection of a mullioned window that bathes the flowers in light. This apparently "natural" light source embedded into the fiction of the painting is a subtle allusion to the Dutch and Flemish still-life tradition, which van Spaendonck claimed as his inheritance. Below the vase, among the leaves of a stray fallen branch, a small bird searches out a meal for its nest of hatchlings nearby. This quasi-narrative episode is a deliberate allusion to the importance of mimesis in the still-life genre and references a story by Greek historian Pliny about the artist Zeuxis, whose painting of grapes was so realistic that birds were drawn to peck at its surface.

In composition and style, van Spaendonck hewed closely to the tradition of Northern painters such as Jan Davidsz. de Heem, Rachel Ruysch, and Jan van Huysum, only lightly refreshing their formulas by incorporating references to contemporary tastes. For instance, the alabaster pedestal's bas-relief, which depicts a Roman priestess making offerings to Eros, was adapted from a modern marble by the fashionable neoclassical sculptor Clodion.[1] Van Spaendonck's facility in constructing a floral still life that visually narrates its own art historical pedigree, while also asserting its maker's status as the modern interpreter of that tradition, may have led viewers to underestimate the sheer artistic ambition of what is

FIG. 1 Gerard van Spaendonck, *Basket of Flowers on an Alabaster Pedestal* (detail), 1785, cat. no. 4

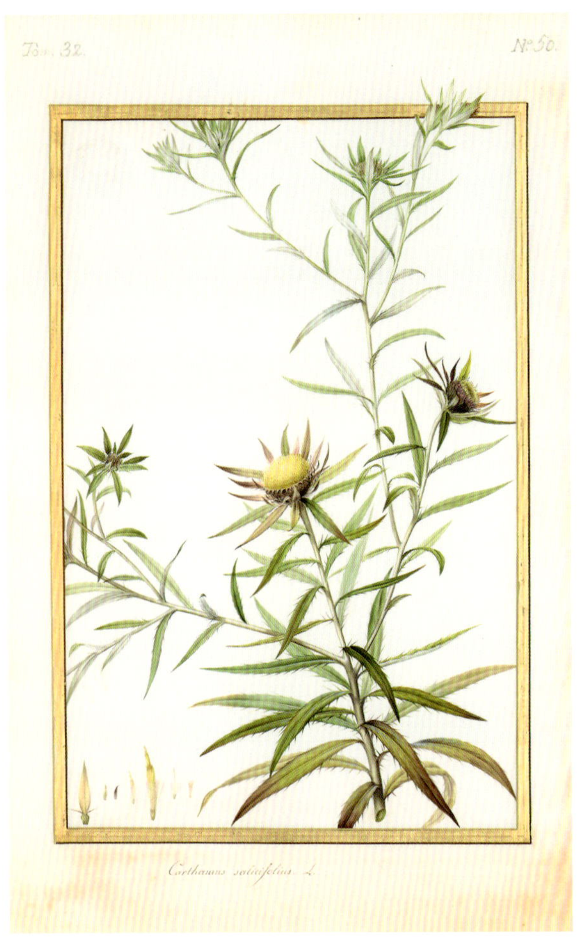

FIG. 2 Gerard van Spaendonck, *Carthamus (Safflower)*, from *Vélins du roi* (ca. 1780–93), watercolor on vellum. Muséum national d'Histoire naturelle, Paris

fundamentally a conservative painting. It may also distract from the fact that van Spaendonck's artistic identity in 1785 was that of not only a painter to the court of Louis XVI and a member of the French Academy but also, perhaps even primarily, a botanical illustrator.

Van Spaendonck arrived in Paris from Holland at age twenty and began a successful career as a miniaturist and decorative painter. By the 1780s, though, he was firmly established in the scientific milieu of the Jardin du roi, where in addition to holding the post as professor of flower painting, he also served as the premier botanical illustrator in France, responsible for the important royal series of botanical illustrations, the *Vélins du roi* (fig. 2). In his Salon painting, van Spaendonck drew on a range of source materials, weaving together the pictorial strategies of the Northern still-life tradition with up-to-date stylistic cues. His images present a seductive illusion of the natural world while also serving as objects of elite luxury consumption. The success with which he merges these potentially contradictory impulses testifies to van Spaendonck's artistic confidence and savoir-faire but also suggests flower painting's place in contemporary visual and scientific culture.

By the end of the nineteenth century, the French tradition of flower painting was often associated with a predilection for hermetic focus on states of interiority, both psychological and artistic. At its origins, though, it was an extension of the empirical sciences, fundamentally concerned with the representation and transmission of information about the natural world. For much of its history, the floral still life was coextensive with scientific illustration. Flower paintings and botanical illustrations may have been made for different purposes, patrons, and audiences, but whether intended for the Salon or the Jardin du roi, they were frequently created by the same artists, who drew on the same technical skills and visual traditions. To make sense of the emergence of the floral still life as a self-sufficient genre and a habitual site of artistic introspection in the nineteenth century, we must first understand something of its very different roots in early modern scientific inquiry.

Botanical illustrations resist our efforts to analyze them as visual representation. If anything, they are even more opaque to scrutiny than other forms of scientific imagery by virtue of their familiarity as easy visual stand-ins for the plants and flowers we encounter in the natural world or in our gardens. We approach these images with the assumption that we already know what they look like and how they go about recording the natural world. We expect them to do so without the intrusion of the stylistic markers that would distract us from their informational content or alert us to their status as manufactured works of human artifice. Martin Kemp has termed this effect "the rhetoric of the real," a mode of description that effaces its own stylistic conventions even as it puts them to work.[2]

Botanical illustration has its own art history, however, of slowly shifting visual conventions and stylistic evolution, which has been traced by scholars of the discipline.[3] Drawing on these foundations as well as more recent studies of the cultural and intellectual context for botanical science, this essay looks more closely at how representations of flowers, both scientific and artistic, make legible the ways in which late-eighteenth- and early-nineteenth-century observers understood emerging information about the natural sciences. Flower painting reflected, and was circumscribed by, artistic convention as well as the scientific givens of historical context. Images of plants were not simply a means of sharing knowledge about an expanding botanical world; making and collecting such images was also a way of giving form to new understandings of the organization and operations of nature.

Picturing Botany

The earliest Western account of botanical illustration, from Pliny's *Natural History* (77–79 CE), already noted the challenges that such visual representation posed for the artist. For the early botanical illustrators named by Pliny, the obstacles to the successful practice of their genre were legion:

> *Crateuas, Dionysius and Metrodorus adopted a most attractive method, though one which makes clear little else except the difficulty of employing it. For they painted likenesses of the plants and then wrote under them their properties. But not only is a picture misleading when the colours are so many, particularly as the aim is to copy Nature, but besides this, much imperfection arises from the manifold hazards in the accuracy of the copyists. In addition, it is not enough for each plant to be painted at one period only of its life, since it alters its appearance with the fourfold changes of the year.*[4]

The purpose of botanical illustration is not (primarily) the delectation of a pleasing image but rather the communication of useful information. The image is made to be reproduced and circulated, but in the process, its scientific value can be quickly dissipated with each error of transcription (including, of course, those resulting from the original drawing taken from nature). The addition of color, so vulnerable to the vagaries of subjective perception and the shortcomings of memory, can be a hindrance rather than an asset in conveying the true appearance of a specimen. The synchronic character of a single illustration is inadequate to our diachronic experience of nature; one image can never fully represent a plant, which changes in appearance with the seasons and stages of its growth. However, as Pliny cautioned, the image seduces with its apparently self-sufficient presence.

During the early modern period, botanical illustrators developed new modes of pictorial naturalism in their efforts to solve the challenges of representing the natural world. The genre remained vexed, however, by a tension between the evident utility of images to botanical study and the suspicion that the image's reliance on the imperfect eye and fallible hand of the artist eroded its value for scientific work. Botanist Leonhard Fuchs, author of one of the most influential herbals of the mid-sixteenth century, railed against the conventional wisdom that illustrations were inferior to textual descriptions. Fuchs allowed that the scientific value of images depended on the suppression of artistic "whims" but nonetheless defended the importance of botanical illustration.[5]

> *Though the pictures have been prepared with great effort and sweat we do not know whether in the future they will be damned as useless and of no importance and whether someone will cite the most insipid authority of Galen to the effect that no one who wants to describe plants would try to make pictures of them. But why take up more time? Who in his right mind would condemn pictures which can communicate information much more clearly than the words of even the most eloquent men?*[6]

The hundreds of large-scale woodcuts for his *De Historia Stirpium* (1542) were visually innovative (fig. 3). They were not copied from existing prototypes, nor did they employ the "warts and all" naturalism of immediate precedents such as the illustrations for Otto Brunfel's *Herbarum Vivae Eicones* (1530–36) prepared by Hans Weiditz, who documented the particularities and even the imperfections of each specimen he depicted.[7] Fuchs's illustrators sought instead to capture a scientifically ideal representation of each plant, smoothing out the specificity of the individual specimen to offer a composite portrait of a species.[8] The goal of this mode of botanical illustration was scientific completeness rather than ideal beauty, an image that provides more information about a species than is available in nature. This synthetic method also allowed the illustrators to show a plant in multiple stages of development, a manifestly unrealistic and potentially confusing solution that has nonetheless remained a useful fiction for botanical illustrators.

During the sixteenth and seventeenth centuries, Europe's knowledge of the botanical world rapidly expanded with the introduction of new species from around the globe. The unfamiliarity of these plants to European eyes, and European systems of plant classification, made observation and description a more pressing concern and complicated the task for botanists and artists alike. Illustrators of herbals could no longer rely on copying past examples, and their new subjects were not always easily cultivated in Europe. Images were more essential than ever in sharing new discoveries, but the genres of visual culture tasked with picturing the natural world struggled to keep pace.

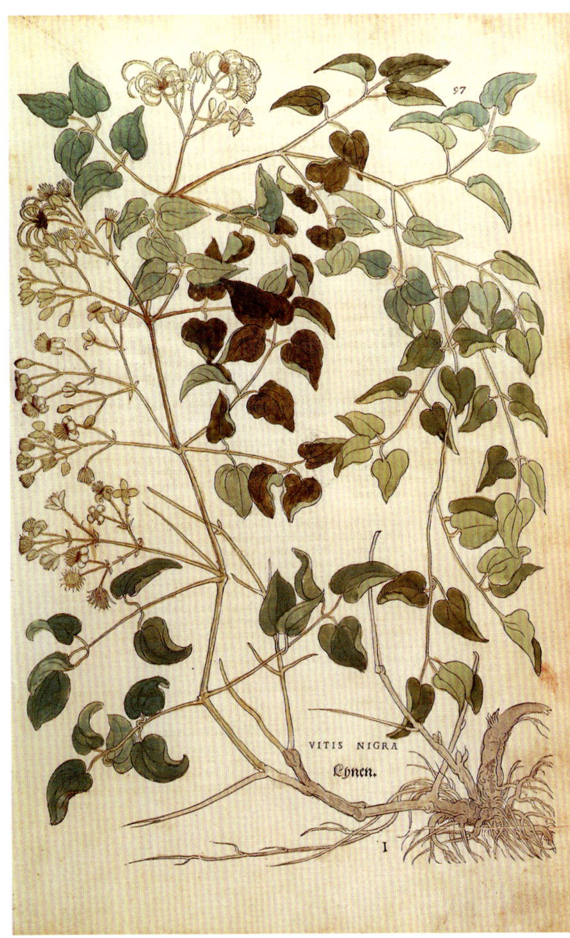

FIG. 3 *Old Man's Beard or Traveller's Joy*, from Leonhard Fuchs, *De Historia Stirpium* (1542), colored engraving. Biblioteca Nazionale, Turin

The need to give visual form to the expanding botanical world spurred a golden age of botanical illustration and, eventually, entirely new genres for representing flowers. Two of the most important were the floral still life and the florilegium, an illustrated botanical book featuring predominantly ornamental plants.[9] The floral still life, of course, persists as an independent genre today, while the florilegium was a short-lived phenomenon, though it offers an interesting study in the multiple, overlapping functions of natural imagery in early modern Europe. The florilegium differed from the traditional herbal in its emphasis on the image. It included only minimal text, such as captions; as with the floral still life, the hand of the artist took a primary role, no longer subservient to the scientific text. The florilegium was a hybrid genre, "which has no scientific purpose, no intent to analyze, classify or otherwise explore its subjects, no text, and no argument."[10] It often did double duty as a pattern book for decorative applications such as embroidery, which demanded attention to the details of botanical structure and habits of growth, and a botanical cabinet of curiosities, recording for example each species of exotic or ornamental plant cultivated in the garden of the patron who commissioned the book.

The new genres of floral imagery responded nimbly to an emerging set of demands. The still life and florilegium were fundamentally oriented toward the market, but they retained from more scientific models the expectation of providing a closely observed and persuasive representation that rendered the floral specimen visually present to the viewer. It is important to note that the rise of this novel floral imagery was not based on aesthetic considerations alone. These nascent genres took hold at a time when rapid expansion in the corpus of known plants was outpacing the ability of the older genres such as the herbal to collect and transmit current knowledge. For instance, while Fuchs's herbal had been the first to organize plant entries alphabetically rather than by medicinal or culinary application,[11] this innovation had been made impracticable within a generation by the proliferation of competing plant names.[12] The bounty of new botanical data reaching Europe in the early modern era collided with structures of knowledge inherited from antiquity, such as the herbal, that were ill equipped to absorb them. This confrontation not only gave rise to new genres of visual representation but also set the stage for a new system of botanic taxonomy.

A Flower-Centered Botany

In 1735, Swedish natural historian Carl Linnaeus, best remembered for creating the system of binomial nomenclature for plant and animal species still used today, published his *Systema naturae*, which introduced a new system

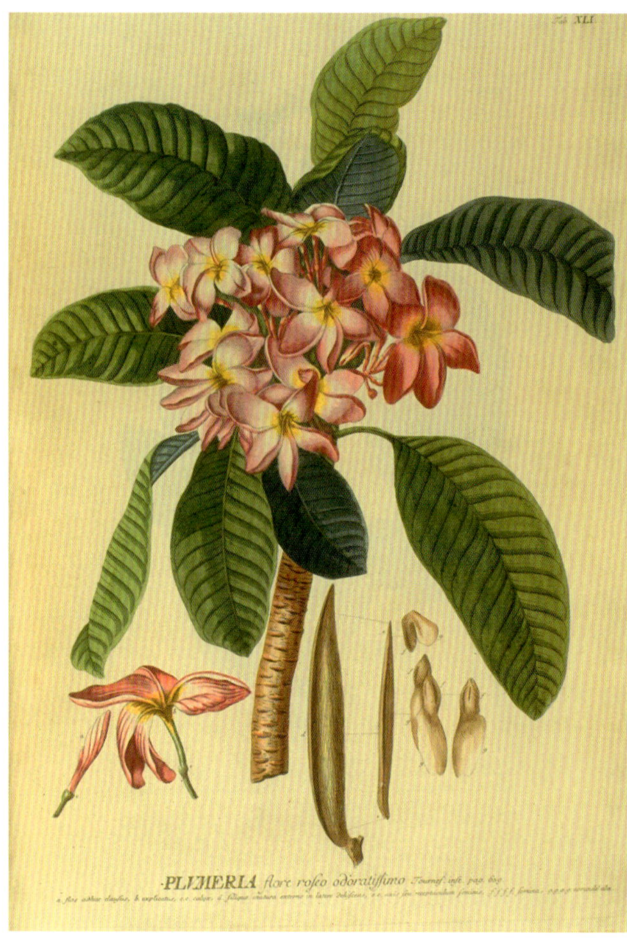

FIG. 4 Georg Dionysius Ehret, *Plumeria (Frangipani)*, from Christoph Jacob Trew and Georg Dionysius Ehret, *Plantae Selectae* (1750–73), colored copper engraving. Muséum national d'Histoire naturelle, Paris

of plant and animal classification. Linnaeus's taxonomy divided plants into twenty-four genera based on the number and arrangement of their stamens and pistils, effectively making the task of classifying even the most unfamiliar specimen as simple as examining its visible reproductive structures. The Linnaean "sexual system" held sway for the better part of a century, sweeping away past methodological accretions with its clarity and practicality.

Linnaeus's botanical publications had an enormous scientific and cultural impact during the second half of the eighteenth century and the first decades of the nineteenth century, not only for the novelty of the method they proposed but also because of their physical and intellectual accessibility. Lisbet Koerner notes that "his botanical handbooks were brief enough to be read with ease, and small enough to carry into the field. He wrote them in a straightforward, unornamented Latin, and encouraged vernacular translations."[13] The Linnaean system was quickly adopted by scientists as well as the expanding field of amateur botanists, who found it a ready point of entry into the direct, empirical study of the natural world. In fact, Linnaeus's taxonomy would remain central to popular botany long after it had been eclipsed in scientific circles by other classification systems. Linnaean ideas intersected with an already-intense interest in horticulture and new plant species, feeding a surge of botanical curiosity in the later eighteenth century.[14] This culture of "botanophilia" included participants from across the social spectrum, from the aristocracy to philosophes, from intrepid world travelers to humble explorers who documented the flora of local country fields.

Botany in the early modern era was already a profoundly visual discipline, dependent on observation (increasingly assisted by the microscope) to identify and classify specimens. Linnaeus simply refocused the observer's visual scrutiny by determining that all the information necessary to classify plants was contained in their flowers and associated sexual organs. The Linnaean revolution greatly reduced the scope of observation essential for classification and, thus, for illustration. Two centuries earlier, Fuchs had boasted about the illustrations in his herbal, pointing out that "each plant is painted with its roots, its stalks, leaves, flowers, seeds and fruits," precisely because each of these structures was essential in classifying every plant.[15] By the middle of the eighteenth century, though, the flower became the true focus of botanical illustrations (fig. 4). For instance, in the sophisticated work of Georg Dionysius Ehret, who collaborated with Linnaeus in the 1730s, the plant's nonfloral structures were often depicted abruptly severed, and the

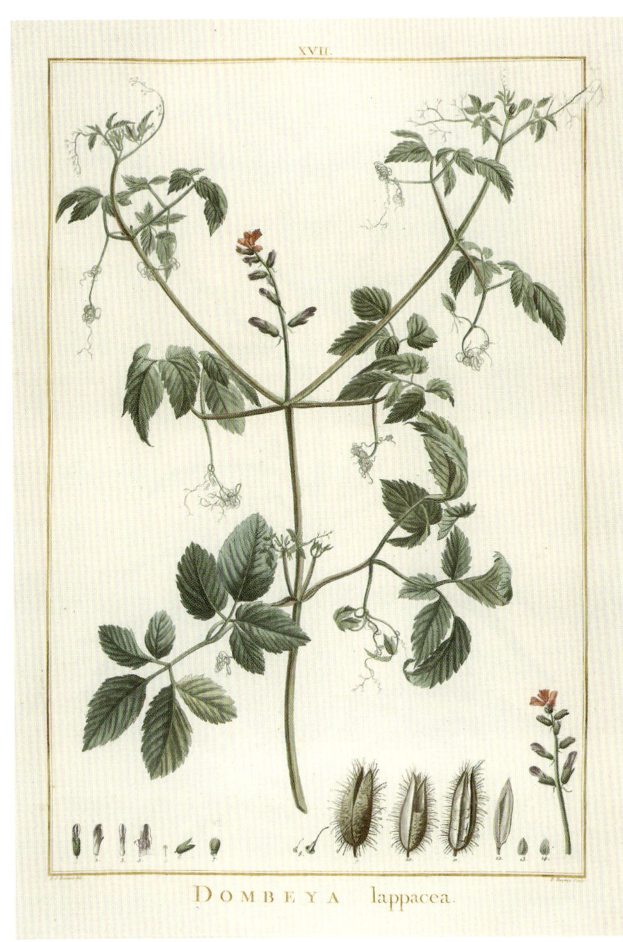

FIG. 5 Pierre-Joseph Redouté, *Dombeya lappacea*, 1784–85, from Charles Louis L'Héritier de Brutelle, *Stirpes novae: aut minus cognitae, quas descriptionibus et iconibus* (1785–91), colored copper engraving. Courtesy Missouri Botanical Garden, St. Louis

blossoms were usually positioned with stamens and pistils clearly visible from several perspectives. Floral dissections revealed in still-greater detail the plant's sexual organs.

The narrowing of attention from the plant as a whole to its flower inevitably brought scientific botanical illustration closer to floral still life or the hybrid, quasi-scientific genre of the florilegium. The fullest expression of this transformation was the work of Pierre-Joseph Redouté, the most important botanical illustrator of the late eighteenth and early nineteenth centuries. Like so many "French" flower painters, Redouté was actually of Flemish origin, born to a family of modest decorative and religious painters. Shortly after his arrival in Paris in 1782 or 1783, Redouté made several flower drawings that were engraved and published, and this early work may have led to his acquaintance with van Spaendonck, who became his mentor and teacher. Around the same time, Redouté met the wealthy magistrate and important amateur botanist Charles-Louis L'Héritier de Brutelle, who likewise took the young artist under his wing. L'Héritier instructed Redouté in the principles of Linnaean botany, enabling him to turn his talent for flower painting into serious scientific illustration.

L'Héritier commissioned Redouté to produce more than half of the illustrations for his book *Stirpes novae* (1785–91), the first of several landmark publications on which they collaborated. Among the fifty or so plants that Redouté depicted for this project was the *Dombeya lappacea*, an African species described and represented for the first time (fig. 5). In these early efforts, Redouté adopted a conventional approach, close to that of the *Vélins du roi* (which he was soon to take over from van Spaendonck). He centers the plant—or rather its crown, since little is shown of its stalk or roots—on the page. Its diminutive red flowers are clearly visible at the top of the image, framed by symmetrical stems against the bare white page. The flowers appear again at the bottom of the sheet, alongside dissections of the other reproductive organs of the plant. Here, as in nearly all botanical illustration, no context is provided in terms of a natural habitat or environment. Somewhat paradoxically, the suppression of any such contextual information serves to secure the objective realism of the representation, which seems to be almost a "real" botanical specimen, freshly cut from the plant and presented to us on a clean, white sheet of paper. This illusion of the plant's physical presence is reinforced at the upper right, where Redouté adopts an old trick of the botanical illustrator's trade, allowing the small tendrils of the plant to overlap the gilded border.[16]

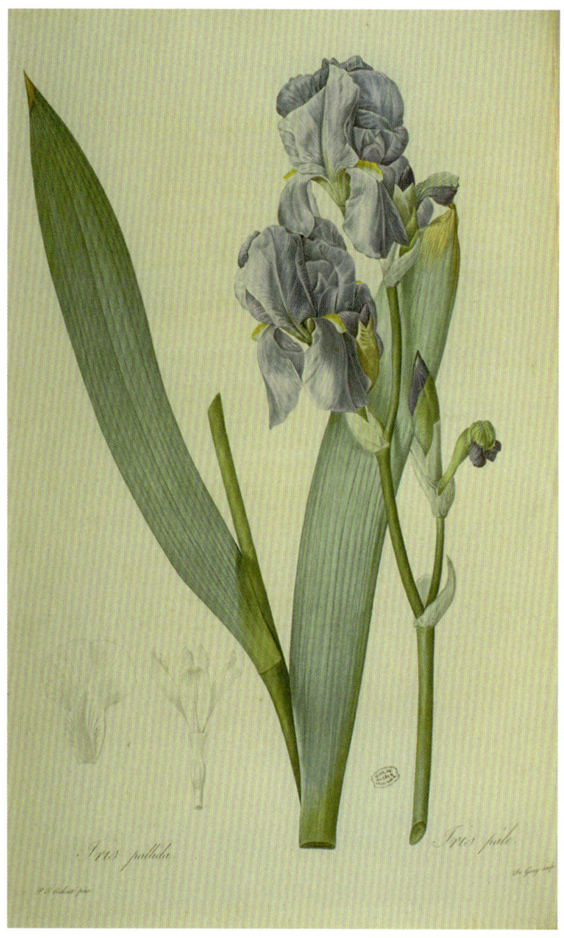

FIG. 6 Pierre-Joseph Redouté, *Pale Iris*, 1813, from *Les Liliacées* (1802–16), stipple engraving printed in color with hand coloring. Muséum national d'Histoire naturelle, Paris

By the end of the 1790s, Redouté was the premier botanical illustrator in France and had attracted the devoted patronage of Napoleon's botanophile wife, Joséphine. She had a profound interest in horticulture, and her extensive gardens and greenhouses at Château de Malmaison were filled with unusual and exotic plants, providing the material for a number of major botanical publications illustrated by Redouté. In the first decades of the nineteenth century, Redouté created two landmark publications, *Les Liliacées* (1802–16) and *Les Roses* (1817–24), the first herbals published under the name of the illustrator rather than the author. The botanists who wrote the accompanying scientific descriptions were commissioned by the artist, reversing past precedent.[17] Redouté's books featured hundreds of painstakingly prepared plates using the technique of color stipple engraving, which the artist had learned in England and then brought to a high level of technical sophistication (fig. 6). For this type of print, the engraver translated an image into thousands of dots, or stipples, that were then embossed into the printing plate, allowing for more subtle effects of shading than the linear marks and cross-hatching of traditional engraving. Colored inks were then applied to the copperplate before printing, with all of the colors printed together and the plate re-inked for each impression, a labor-intensive process. Though technically demanding, it allowed Redouté to translate for publication the translucent color and illusionistic dimension that characterized his *Vélins* and his watercolor illustrations, which were prized by collectors.[18]

The popular appeal of Redouté's publications at the turn of the nineteenth century owed much to their meticulous illusionism and the artist's virtuosic command of new reproductive technologies. They also served to translate the fashionable horticultural interests and botanophilia of the era's cultural elite into an immediately collectible format. His illustrations, though, were also products of an Enlightenment culture that privileged visual observation of the natural world as the catalyst for analysis, classification, and, ultimately, knowledge. These preoccupations emerged from the empirical sciences, but their effects were also powerfully felt in the artistic sphere, particularly among artists obliged by genre convention and subject matter to study nature.

Visual Ways of Knowing

The introduction of Linnaeus's taxonomy had a surprisingly broad cultural impact. On the one hand, it created a shared language for European botanists during a period when scientific inquiry was taking place on an increasingly global scale. On the other, Linnaean botany also provided a methodology for study that was broadly accessible to nonscientists, less

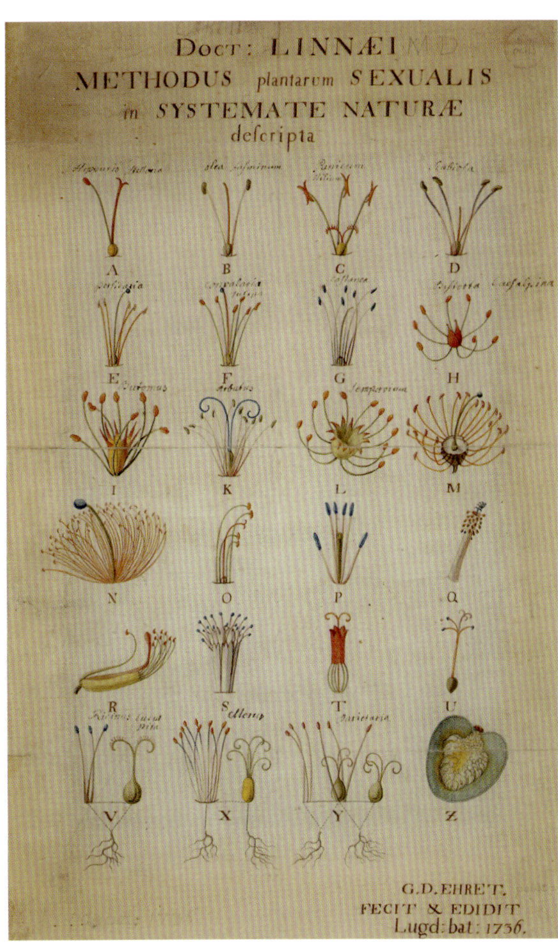

FIG. 7 Georg Dionysius Ehret, Illustration of the Linnaean plant sexual system, 1736, drawing. Natural History Museum, London

reliant on extensive book learning and more dependent on acute visual skills honed by experience in the field. The rise of a botany centered on the visible structures of floral anatomy did not, however, immediately dismantle the bias against images that had persisted in science since antiquity. Linnaeus himself argued vehemently against the use of images in botanical classification. "I absolutely reject them," he declared, "although I confess that they are more pleasing to children and to those who have more of a head than a brain. I admit that they offer something to the illiterate. Before people became accustomed to the use of letters, it was necessary for everything to be expressed by pictures."[19]

The surprising force of Linnaeus's dismissal is also a judgment of the role of vision and visual labor in the scientific process. The system of natural history that Linnaeus proposed moved from visual examination of the botanical specimen, in the field or in the herbarium (a collection of dried plant specimens), to a rigorously textual description and classification. Linnaeus's taxonomy was famously characterized by Michel Foucault as a paradigm of how Western Europeans represented and structured knowledge of the natural world before the modern era: "As Linnaeus says, the naturalist . . . 'distinguishes the parts of natural bodies with his eyes, describes them appropriately according to their number, form, position, and proportion, and he names them.' The naturalist is the man concerned with the structure of the visible world and its denomination according to characters."[20] More specifically, this structuring process of classification (both describing and naming) is understood to be post-visual, taking place within the realm of language.

In Foucault's account of Linnaean botany, it was the visual accessibility of plants (relative to the more visually resistant bodies of animals) that gave them their "epistemological precedence" in the eighteenth century.[21] Vision was the precondition of natural history, bringing empirical information to the scientist, a specialized and highly trained observer, who then turned to the systematizing force of language to classify the visible world. The text was thus the ultimate product of scientific work, allowing that which was seen or collected to be truly known: "The plant is thus engraved in the material of the language into which it was been transposed, and recomposes its pure form before the reader's very eyes. The book becomes the herbarium of living structures."[22]

Linnaeus's first edition of *Systema naturae* unsurprisingly dispensed with illustrations and included only a text table of the organization of new plant classes according to his system. He soon replaced this table, though, with a pictorial chart (created by Ehret) that illustrated the key taxonomic structures, or sexual organs, of the twenty-four classes (fig. 7). This chart, which was quickly copied and adapted for other publications, allowed analysis and ultimately classification through a process of visual comparison with specimens or even other images. Daniela Bleichmar, in her account of botanical representation in the Spanish Empire, has argued that this simple change reveals much about the fundamental character of botanical knowledge during the eighteenth century. At its heart (and despite the protestations of its founder), "the Linnaean system provided an immediate taxonomy based exclusively on sight."[23]

Linnaean botany was, in practice, immersed in a field of visual and material culture. "Eighteenth-century naturalists," Bleichmar writes, "thought visually, worked visually, and posed visual questions to which they offered visual answers."[24] The visual work of the botanist did not end with the empirical gathering of information but was extended indefinitely through a continual process of collating data between specimens, texts, *and* images.[25] Images, she argues, "provided an entry point to the exploration of nature, functioned as a key instrument for producing knowledge, and constituted the foremost result of natural investigations."[26] The image was a privileged source, method, and product of botanical inquiry.

In order to understand just how thoroughly scientific perceptions of images changed in the course of the eighteenth century, we could compare Linnaeus's abrupt dismissal of their utility with the words of his foremost disciple, Sir Joseph Banks. Writing in 1796 about a new botanical publication by the artist Franz Bauer, Banks acknowledged that:

> *it will appear singular, at first sight, that engravings of plants should be published without the addition of botanical descriptions of their generic and specific characters; but it is hoped, that every Botanist will agree, when he has examined the plates with attention, that it would have been a useless task. . . . Each figure is intended to answer itself every question a Botanist can wish to ask, respecting the structure of the plant it represents.*[27]

It is worth taking a moment to recognize just how authoritative a role is claimed for images in this statement. The engravings do not simply stand in for the specimens visually by virtue of their precision or the persuasive naturalism of the illustrator's art. Rather, Banks imagines the image as an active participant in future scientific dialogue, answering the botanist's questions and generally serving as an authoritative informant to the scientific process. The image is invested for the imagined viewer with "the unadorned presence of a real specimen," to borrow Martin Kemp's phrase, not only because of its pictorial language but also as a function of its scientific orientation.[28] The confidence that botanist Leonhard Fuchs expressed in the information value of his illustrations in the mid-sixteenth century found its true footing only at the turn of the nineteenth century, when scientific and aesthetic ideas coalesced around a new faith in the epistemological force of vision.

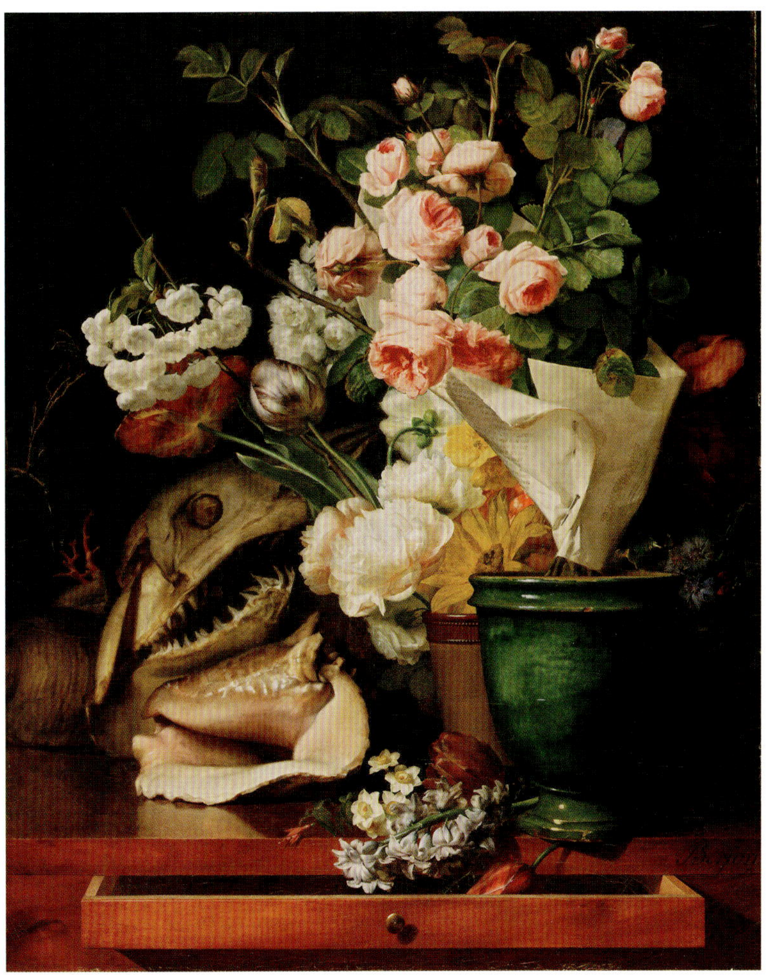

FIG. 8 Antoine Berjon, *Still Life with Flowers, Shells, a Shark's Head, and Petrifications*, 1819, oil on canvas. Philadelphia Museum of Art, Purchased with the Edith H. Bell Fund, 1981, 1981-62-1

Acts of Persuasion

In her searching history of French still life in the nineteenth century, Jeannene Przyblyski describes the "visual authority and persuasiveness" produced by the botanical precision of flower painters such as van Spaendonck, Redouté, or their contemporary Antoine Berjon. Such images, she argues, "speak simultaneously to both the dispassionate objectivity and the lingering love of looking . . . that bind the empirical sciences to aesthetic delectation. Both exhibit the same confidence in the eye, the same trust in the naked power of observation."[29] Whether working in support of botanical analysis or producing still lifes for elite patrons, these painters were adept in manipulating the visual codes that signaled to their viewers the process of close observation and objective representation. They worked within the physical and institutional loci of scientific authority and produced images that circulated alongside plant specimens and texts, the other fundamental tools of botanical knowledge. Their still-life paintings operated at but one remove from the scientific enterprise.

The eerily beautiful still life that Berjon exhibited at the Salon of 1819 (fig. 8) elevates precision from simply a stylistic hallmark of the flower painter to a visual spectacle in its own right.[30] In this, Berjon follows in the tradition of van Spaendonck, translating the flower painter's talent for minute illusionism to the more complex performance of visual persuasion required of still life in an exhibition context. He invites us to delight in the skill with which he imitates not only the satiny structures of floral anatomy but also the dull sheen of polished mahogany or the glossy surface of glazed pottery, scattered with firing flaws. The incongruous grouping of floral and marine specimens—particularly the bizarre, grimacing shark's skull—draws our attention to their haptic contrast, while an equally powerful physical invitation is offered by the straight pins that secure the paper sleeve curled around the roses at right or by the brass pull of the open drawer at the bottom of the painting. Berjon's virtuoso naturalism strains against the limitations of sight by appealing to our instinct to touch, to confirm with our hands the illusion offered to our eyes.

The success with which Berjon acquits himself in this mimetic task, though, is a reminder that the visual authority of flower painting emerged from a synthesis of highly specific representational techniques and pictorial strategies. It could rest equally well on the image's indexical relationship to a given specimen or on the illustrator's skill in conjuring a wholly imaginary plant to represent a species with artificial, impossible completeness. Flower painters crafted the illusion of the objective gaze through a codified, collective style that was passed along through scientific institutions and networks. In their still-life paintings, these artists sought to strike a balance between the immediate pleasures of illusionism and the expectation that painting, which operated in the public sphere, was called to address the cultural priorities of an educated viewer. To find that balance, they drew on the strategies of both botanical illustration, which aimed to endow the image with the scientific self-sufficiency of a natural specimen, and still life, which sought to invest the disparate objects of nature with a pictorial logic of their own, a belonging together, and even a kind of narrative coherence. In the first half of the nineteenth century, flower painters continued to work comfortably, and often quite skillfully, in the field of practice between these two vital and popular genres.

NOTES

1. This source was kindly identified by Guillaume Faroult. Clodion's marble bas-relief, *Sacrifice à l'amour*, is now in the collection of the Musée des Art Décoratifs, Paris (GR 162).
2. See Kemp 1990, 127–28.
3. For information on the history of botanical illustrations, see Blunt 1994, Saunders 1995, and Rix 1981.
4. Pliny 1980, book 25, 8.
5. Fuchs reported that the illustrators who provided images for his herbal "have paid careful attention that the shading, and other less crucial things, with which painters sometimes strive for artistic glory, should not obliterate the basic form of the plants; and we have not allowed the artists thus to indulge their whims, in such a way as to make the pictures correspond less to the truth." Quoted in Freedberg 1994, 249.
6. Smith and Findlen 2002, 8.
7. Saunders 1995, 20.
8. For information on the illustrators who worked for Fuchs, see Blunt 1994, 49.
9. On the emergence of floral still life in Holland and Flanders, see Wheelock 1999, esp. 32–36. For further information on the florilegium, see Saunders 1995, 41–64, and Wheelock 1999, 25–30.
10. Saunders 1995, 54–55.
11. See Wheelock 1999, 76n 23.
12. See ibid., 76n 28.
13. Koerner 1996, 147.
14. See Williams 2001. Among the many intellectuals who participated in the culture of botanophilia, Jean-Jacques Rousseau was the most influential. The popularity of his Linnaean botanical texts, such as *Lettres Elementaires sur la botanique* (1781), helped to ensure the longevity of Linnaeus's ideas in the realm of popular botany.
15. Quoted in Freedberg 1994, 249.
16. The use of a gilded border is a standard feature of the *Vélins du roi*.
17. See van Druten 2013, 18.
18. Redouté had learned the technique of watercolor on vellum from van Spaendonck, who used it in some of his *Vélins*. The technique came to replace the use of opaque gouache in the *Vélins du roi* series and in botanical illustration more generally.
19. Quoted in Freedberg 1994, 256.
20. Foucault 1994, 161.
21. Ibid., 137.
22. Ibid., 135.
23. Bleichmar 2008, 6.
24. Bleichmar 2012, 8.
25. Ibid., 53.
26. Bleichmar 2008, 4.
27. The unsigned preface to Franz Bauer, *Delineations of Exotick Plantes Cultivated in the Royal Garden at Kew* (London: 1796), is quoted in Bleichmar 2012, 61.
28. See Kemp 1996, 199. Kemp is here describing the illustrations for Banks's own publications.
29. Przyblyski 1995, 137.
30. For a more detailed discussion of Berjon's career and the history of this painting, see Rishel 1982, 16–24.

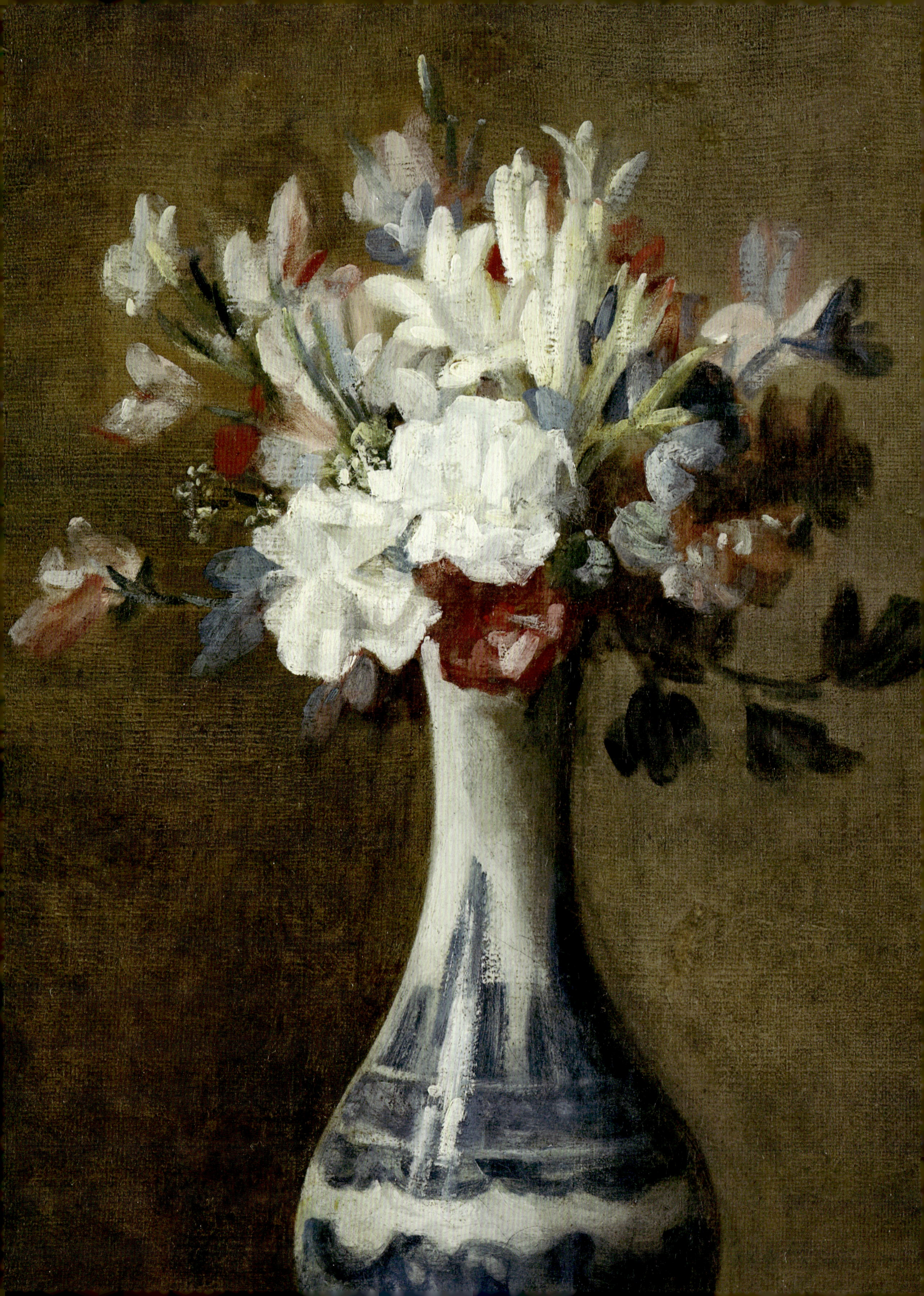

The Path to the Modern Floral Still Life: Academy to Avant-Garde

Mitchell Merling

The eye must be taught to look at nature.
—Jean-Siméon Chardin, lecture to the Academy, 1765[1]

[The floral still life] is, I think, an excellent subject to paint.
—Claude Monet to Frédéric Bazille, 1864

OVER THE COURSE OF THE NINETEENTH CENTURY, FRENCH ART experienced a radical transformation as still lifes and landscapes supplanted historical, mythological, and biblical scenes as major subjects. The still life played an important part in that epochal transition, helping to pave the way for an emerging "New Painting," known later as Impressionism. A true understanding of that role is owed to an ongoing effort that began with John McCoubrey's 1958 thesis on the French still life in the mid-nineteenth century and extends through Henri Loyrette's seminal essay in the 1994 exhibition catalogue *The Origins of Impressionism* and the subsequent fundamental exhibition *Impressionist Still Life*, curated by George Shackelford and Eliza Rathbone in 2001.[2]

This catalogue and accompanying exhibition continue that line of inquiry, further exploring the significance of the still life—specifically the floral still life—in the evolution of French art. In addition, the project proposes that flower painting in France not only had its own art historical trajectory but also occupied a singular position within the genre of still-life painting generally. Moving away from the careful imitation of natural appearances practiced during the late eighteenth and early nineteenth centuries, later painters used the floral still life to assert such themes as the liberty of the artist's imagination and, more broadly, art's power and mission to transform experience.

Traditionally, still-life painting (initially considered in France to be limited to floral and other natural subjects) was held in low esteem. In the seventeenth century, the erudite André Félibien summarized the official position of the French Academy emphasizing still life's inferior status among all other genres of painting:

> *He who perfectly paints landscapes is above the other who makes only fruits, flowers, or shells. He who paints living animals is more estimable than they who only represent things which are dead and without movement . . . [thus]*

FIG. 9 Jean-Siméon Chardin, *A Vase of Flowers* (detail), mid 1750s, cat. no. 2

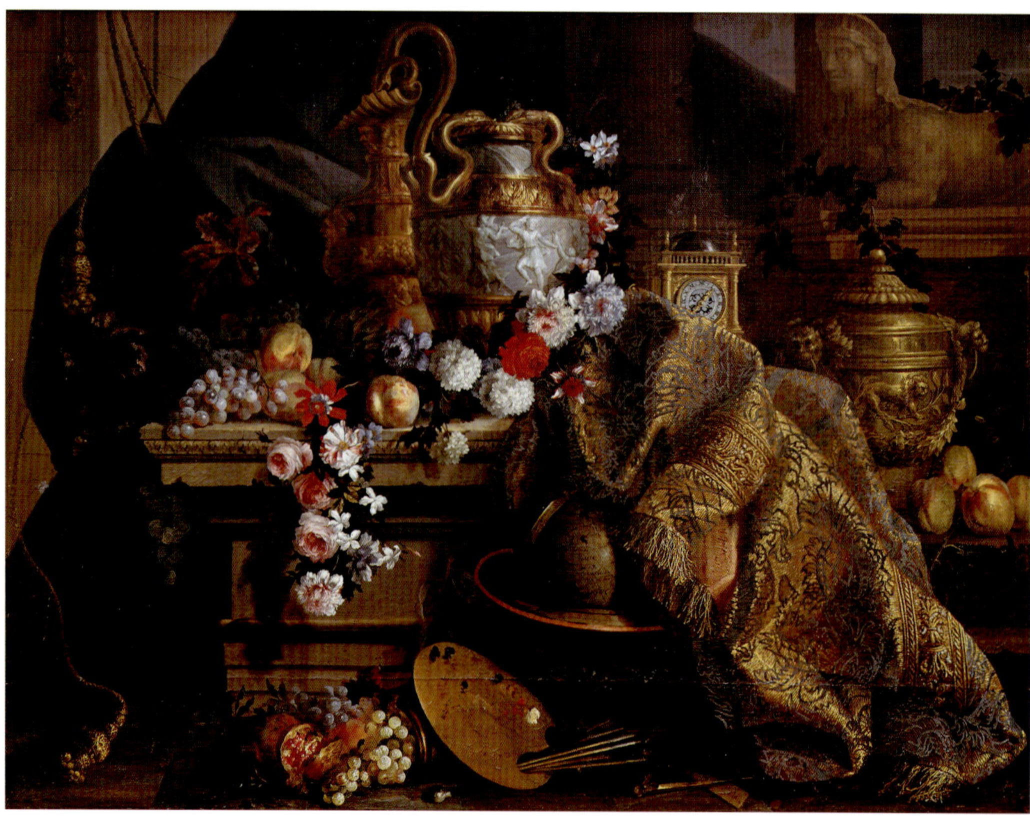

FIG. 10 Jean-Baptiste Monnoyer, *Still Life of Flowers, Fruit, and Objects of Art*, 1665, oil on canvas. Musée Fabre, Montpellier, Dépôt de l'État 1803, D803.1.13

> *one must represent grand actions as recounted by historians or agreeable actions as recounted by poets; and even higher . . . the most subtle mysteries.*[3]

It is important to stress here that for the critic, painting still life meant recording the exalted creations of nature (fruit, flowers, and such other *mirabilia* as shells) rather than the mundane products of human industry, let alone humble everyday objects that were then considered beneath the painter's consideration. In practice, however, the Academy deigned to accept still-life painters into its ranks, perhaps because of the role these artists necessarily played in supplying works for decoration, particularly in minor spaces, such as over doors and staircases in aristocratic and royal residences, where more lofty subjects may have been considered out of place.[4]

The greatest French flower painter of Félibien's time was Jean-Baptiste Monnoyer. His *Still Life of Flowers, Fruit, and Objects of Art* (fig. 10), which gained him acceptance into the Academy, may be considered indicative of his own painterly ambition to supersede the proscribed limitations of his chosen genre. In this remarkable work, Monnoyer, who also created designs for the royal Gobelins manufactory, took pains to proclaim his aspirations by representing highly wrought products of human artifice (for example, an elaborate clock, a historically resonant sphinx, historiated vases, and a globe) as well as fruit and flowers. A significant gesture in this complex accumulation of objects is the prominent placement of the artist's means of representation: brushes and a palette in the central foreground, indicating that the painter's practice itself constituted an elevation of the subject represented.

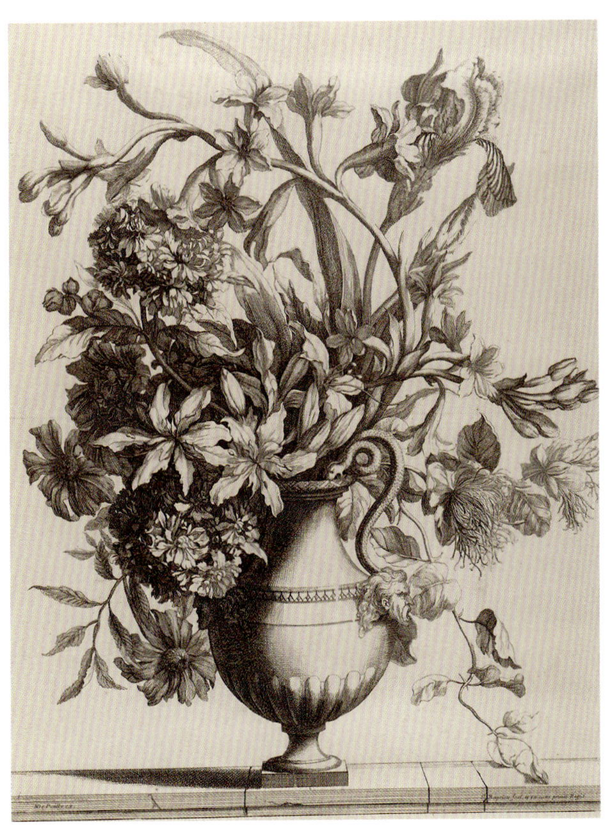

FIG. 11 Jean-Baptiste Monnoyer, *Flowers in a Vase*, seventeenth century, etching and engraving. Metropolitan Museum of Art, New York, Rogers Fund, 1920, 20.16.2(39)

Monnoyer literally provided a pattern for French flower painting, both in decorative applications and as independent easel works, through the widespread diffusion of his vision in prints. In an engraving of Monnoyer's *Flowers in a Vase* (fig. 11), a varied bouquet is placed artfully in an elaborate container set on a stone ledge—but while this model may reflect the contribution of his Dutch and Flemish contemporaries, Monnoyer condensed and restated it in a way that became the standard not only among French artists but also for Northern artists themselves.[5]

Monnoyer's reputation as master of the genre is indicated by a discourse delivered by the still-life and animal painter Jean-Baptiste Oudry in 1752. This fascinating but little-known piece of criticism prescribes various manners of paint handling appropriate for different genres. It concludes that Monnoyer was an important model for all students of art because he varied his touch according to the object portrayed: "In his works, each object is handled by especially appropriate brushwork: his roses are thin, but his lilies are full-bodied."[6] Oudry in particular condemned the Dutch and Flemish painters—usually held up as exemplars—for their uniform handling and lack of variety, thereby anticipating the later critical position developed by Eugène Delacroix, discussed below.[7]

The critical fortune of Jean-Siméon Chardin, Oudry's rival in still-life painting, is pivotal to this discussion. It is fair to say that Chardin, who won praise by respected artists and critics during his own lifetime as well as during his rediscovery in the mid-nineteenth century, transformed the "lower" arts of genre and still-life painting. He accomplished this feat by not only treating common subjects with unusual dignity but also insisting on the importance of his personal visual experience, explored through such technical means as open, rather than highly finished, brushwork. This painterly process, known as *la manière heurtée* (literally, "brusque"), is most evident in *A Vase of Flowers* of the mid-1750s (fig. 9; cat. no. 2).

Chardin (born in 1699, the year of Monnoyer's death) was an articulate, professed advocate for a more considered manner of painting: "In order to paint only the truth, I must forget everything I have seen, and even the way the subjects have been treated by others."[8] The resulting purposefully loose handling, according to critic Denis Diderot, caused a prevarication on the part of the viewer, who could only apprehend the wholeness of the subject when standing back from the painting.[9] Chardin's particular manner of undermining the substantiality of the objects he depicted by insisting on his painterly technique was considered by Diderot a product

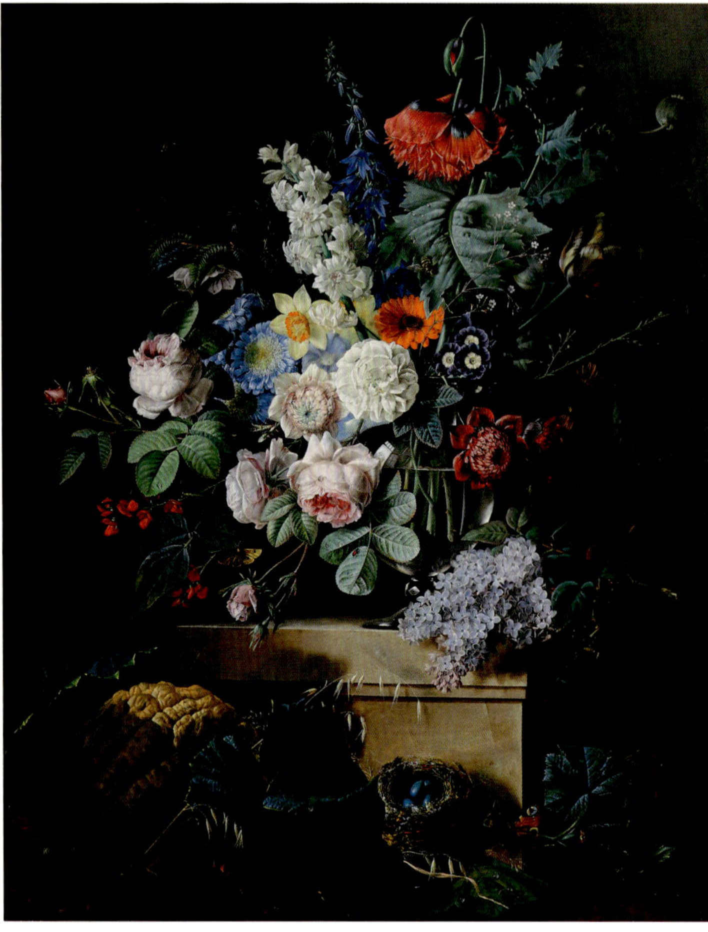

FIG. 12 Pierre-Joseph Redouté, *Flowers in a Crystal Vase*, 1796, oil on canvas. Private Collection

of "unfathomable wizardry" that defied understanding.[10]

Chardin's relationship to Anne Vallayer-Coster was highly complex, in part because, as a woman artist, she was officially considered a different order of painter by both the Academy and contemporary critics. Nevertheless, she was often compared to him.[11] Indeed, her work was sometimes so close to his that Diderot chose the same term, "magic," to describe it, though her use of *la manière heurtée* is more evident in her fruit and game still lifes than in her floral paintings, a type that seems to have carried with it the expectation of more precision.[12] While she pursued a variety of subjects, including portraits, she gained most praise for her "truth"[13] in still lifes and became known above all as a painter of flowers:[14] "that genre in which she has principally practiced till today. Those are so fresh, alive and brilliant that she may be deemed a worthy follower of van Huysum and Monnoyer."[15]

The renewed taste for precision, as opposed to the *manière heurtée* practiced by Chardin and occasionally by Vallayer-Coster, was brought to France by an influx of Northern practitioners including the Dutch-born brothers Gerard and Cornelis van Spaendonck, their contemporary Jan Frans van Dael, and the Belgian-born Pierre-Joseph Redouté. Even Diderot was forced to admit in 1781 that Vallayer-Coster had in Gerard van Spaendonck a serious rival for the title of master of floral subjects.[16]

When Gerard van Spaendonck made his Paris Salon debut in 1775,[17] the unsigned review published in the *Correspondance littéraire* accorded him fulsome phrase: "I don't think art can go any farther. It's nature itself, but nature in all her freshness and brilliance; and there is as much grace, harmony and taste in the manner in which the flowers are gathered here as there is exactitude and truth, even in the smallest details that successfully describe every form and nuance, even those that seem too fugitive for the brush."[18] Like Monnoyer, van Spaendonck established his reputation through series of engravings after his work,[19] as well as through his influence on such painters as Redouté, whose *Flowers in a Crystal Vase* (fig. 12) must be considered a masterpiece in his mentor's manner of minutely and illusionistically replicating a plethora of detail.

Redouté earned acclaim through his watercolor studies on vellum (called *vélins*), innovations in color printing, successful teaching career at the Jardin des plantes, and extensive patronage received from Empress Joséphine.

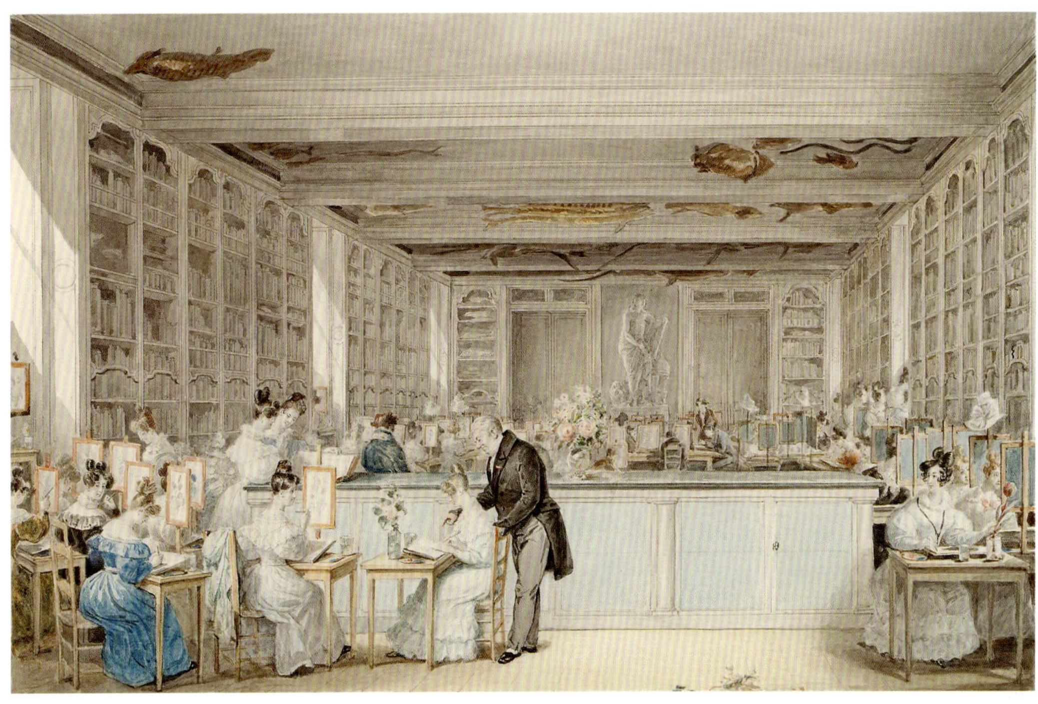

FIG. 13 Julie Ribault, *Redouté's School of Drawing in the Salle Buffon at the Jardin des Plantes*, 1830, pencil and watercolor. Fitzwilliam Museum, Cambridge, United Kingdom

In the genre of floral painting, Redouté was most important for his insistence on studying the structure of the individual flower such as a lilac or a rose, which he pictured not in bouquets but as isolated dissected specimens presented on the printed page. Redouté's pedagogy is illustrated by a recently rediscovered watercolor by Julie Ribault that depicts his class in the Salle Buffon at the Jardin des plantes (fig. 13). This work not only confirms the number of Redouté's students, most of whom were female, but it also supplements written descriptions of his teaching method.[20] Once they mastered drawing individual flowers, Redouté's pupils progressed to copying prints and applying colors and shading.[21] Though a few students in Ribault's watercolor are shown depicting vases of mixed flowers, Marianne Roland-Michel has surmised that Redouté likely differentiated between such bouquets—meant to be aesthetically pleasing to a broader public—and botanical illustrations, which became influential as scientifically significant representations.[22]

Redouté's influence spread beyond his immediate circle in Paris and its suburbs to the industrial city of Lyon, made famous as the most important silk manufactory in France,[23] through the return of native son Antoine Berjon after the Revolution. Berjon, who was appointed professor at the municipal École des Beaux-Arts in 1810, encouraged students to copy engravings, especially those by Redouté and the Spaendoncks, and to practice drawing continually.[24] Berjon's instruction was supplemented by a gallery at the Lyon museum officially dedicated to the permanent exhibition of flower paintings. Known as the Salle des fleurs, the gallery was formally inaugurated in 1814 (though it had effectively been opened earlier) and, at least during its earliest years, displayed primarily works by Northern artists, such as Jan Davidsz. de Heem and Jan van Huysum. Students were expected to copy these examples.[25]

In the early nineteenth century, the Lyon school, and flower painting generally, enjoyed both an incredible vogue and critical acceptance. In a review of the 1817 Salon (where Berjon was exhibiting), a Monsieur "M. M." exclaimed: "Happy the mortal who can spend his life among flowers! . . . Even if the painter of flowers need not make the same studies to make or conquer the same difficulties as the history painter, does that mean that flower painting is a lower or more limited genre?"[26] The sentiment was a keen contrast to the earlier disdain of Félibien.

Berjon was succeeded by the more sympathetic (personally and politically) Augustin-Alexandre Thierriat as instructor of floral design at the Lyon École des Beaux-Arts in 1823. Among his most successful pupils was Simon Saint-Jean, who exhibited extensively at the Paris Salons in the 1830s and 1840s, where he gained notable success with such elaborately conceived paintings as the *Flowers in a Hat* (cat. no. 14; Salon of 1835, where it won a third-class medal), *The Gardener* (*La Jardinière*) (cat. no. 15; Salon of 1838), and *An Offering to the Virgin* (see fig. 56; Salon of 1842).

Saint-Jean was generally very well regarded, with two great and consequential exceptions. The latest works and writings of Eugène Delacroix and his champion, the poet and critic Charles Baudelaire, inspired other, new questions about the artistic merit of flower painting—a merit that had itself been generated in large part by the success of the Lyon school. Indeed, as early as 1833, Delacroix had already begun formulating important pictorial and critical challenges to the precision and finish that had by then become synonymous with successful practice in this genre.

Delacroix's shift away from this formulaic understanding is clearly evident in both the style of the two flower paintings he created at this time (cat. nos. 18 and 19) as well as his critical statements about the subject. First, according to the artist, "one must follow one's impressions, and work freely, being neither too demanding nor too severe. The excess of severity is as much a fault as excessive self-satisfaction."[27] And, continuing, he implicitly downgraded mechanical copying and handling, advising that "only the wrist and not the hand must guide the brush, the hand serves only as the tool that draws, writes and paints."[28]

The most pointed criticism of the high finish employed by Lyonnais artists appeared in Baudelaire's review of the Salon of 1845, which included a particularly acid condemnation: "Saint-Jean . . . is of the Lyonnais school—the penitentiary of painting—that part of the known world where they manage the infinitely small details best."[29] It is likely that Saint-Jean's academic process, which involved preparatory drawings squared for transfer (fig. 14), contributed to the stilted effects noted by Baudelaire.[30]

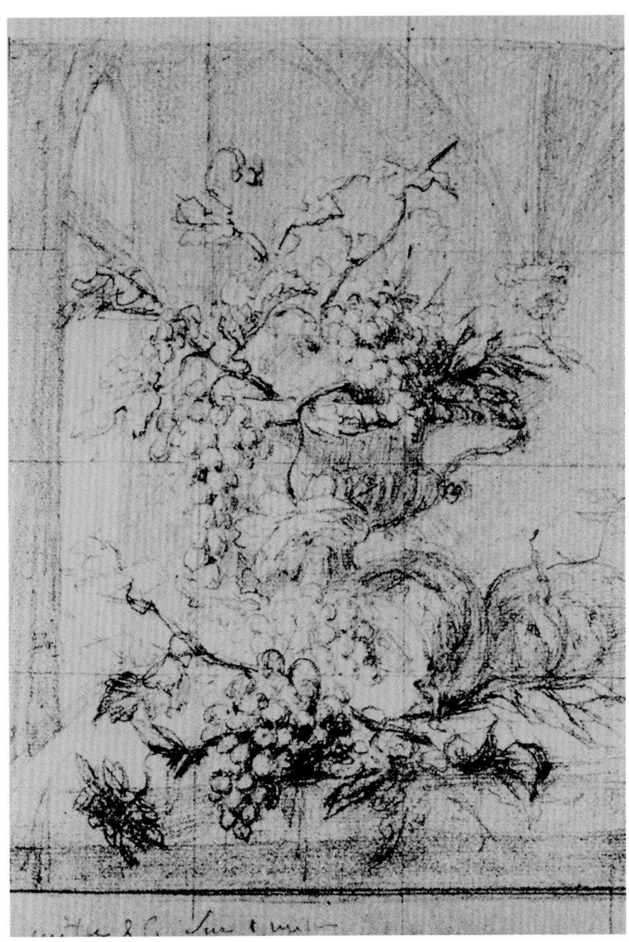

FIG. 14 Simon Saint-Jean, Sketch for *Flowers and Fruits in a Gothic Room*, 1844, pencil on paper. By kind permission of the Trustees of the Wallace Collection, London

Nonetheless, the pull of the Lyonnais example was so strong that Delacroix probably framed some of his most ambitious works of the late 1840s in response to the school's ever grander productions spearheaded by Saint-Jean, and paintings such as Delacroix's *Basket of Flowers* of 1848–49 (fig. 15) must be considered as a programmatic response to Saint-Jean's *Flowers in a Hat*. In fact, the two artists' approaches were specifically contrasted by contemporary Salon reviewer Léon Cailleux and other critics.[31]

Part of Delacroix's second campaign in the floral genre during the 1840s was accompanied by sustained critical reflection, most famously in a letter to his friend, the painter Constant Dutilleux, which bears quotation at length:

> *As soon as I received your letter I went to see the two flower paintings [by old masters]; and I entirely agree with what you say of them. They show great talent; the brushwork is particularly remarkable; their only fault seems to be that which is common to almost all works of this sort, painted by specialists; the study of details, highly elaborated, somewhat detracts from the effect of the whole. Since the artist, in carrying out his work, proceeded not so much by broad local divisions of lines and colors as by an extremely careful rendering of the various parts, those objects which in the picture serve, as it were, as background to each of these too lovingly emphasized details, eventually fade out, and the consequent dispersal of interest rather spoils the general effect. All this does not really detract from the value of these pictures, whose masterly execution precludes comparison with most other productions in this genre. You kindly enquire after the flower paintings which I am at present finishing. As it happens, I have been working in exactly the opposite way to the two works in question, and I have subordinated details to the whole as far as possible. I tried to get away from the convention which seems to condemn anyone who paints flowers to reproduce the same vase with the same columns of fantastic draperies to serve as background or provide contrast. I have tried to paint bits of nature as we see them in gardens, only assembling within the same frame and in a fairly probable manner the greatest possible variety of flowers. I am worried now as to whether I shall have time to finish, for I have not been able to get back to them and there is a great deal to be done. If they are finished in time, and to my liking, I shall probably send them to the Salon. There are five of them, neither more nor less.*[32]

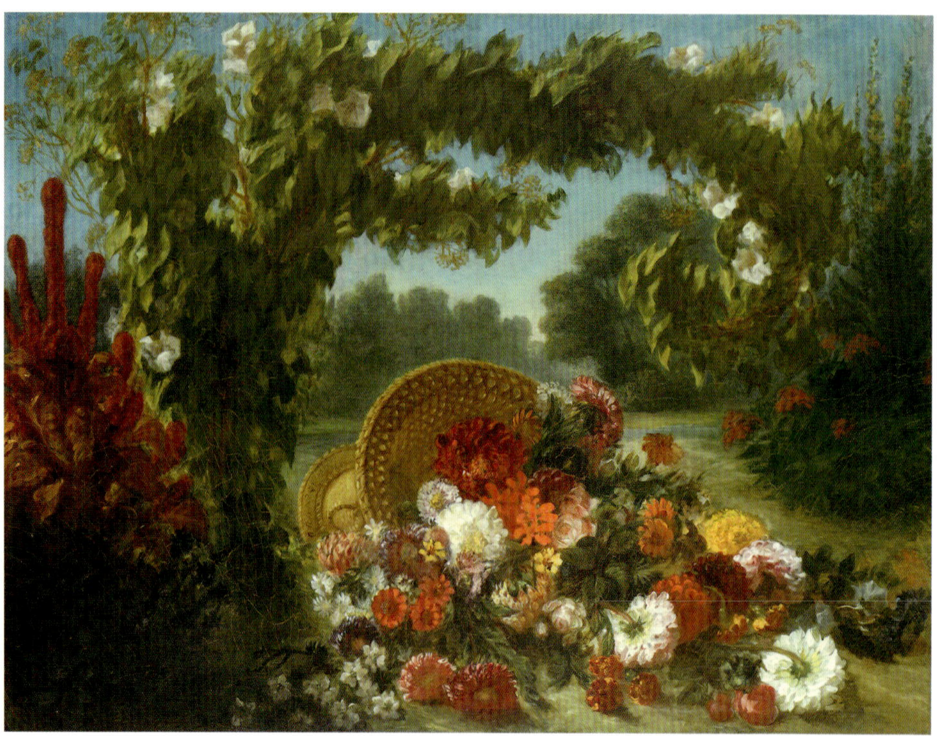

FIG. 15 Eugène Delacroix, *Basket of Flowers*, 1848–49, oil on canvas. Metropolitan Museum of Art, New York, bequest of Miss Adelaide Milton de Groot (1876–1967), 1967, 67.187.60

As it happened, only two (figs. 15 and 16) of the set of five projected paintings made their way to the Salon of 1849, where they were acclaimed as avatars of a new kind of art and seen as devastating pictorial critiques of the more meticulous floral art practiced by Saint-Jean and others. According to the modernist poet and critic Théophile Gautier:

> *This year, as an easily understood whim of a colorist, Delacroix sent two large paintings of flowers to the exhibition. These flowers, as you can imagine, do not resemble the flowers of Van Spaendonck, much less those of Redouté, nor even those of Saint-Jean; to find comparisons one should go back to [Jean-] Baptiste [Oudry], Monnoyer, or rather even the tables of fruit and flowers of Juan de Avellaneda and Velasquez.*[33]

Further, the critic for the *Constitutionnel*, Louis Peisse, confidently and excitedly proclaimed:

> *Both [paintings] are brilliant in color, gracefully composed and arranged, broadly and vigorously painted. I've heard talk about the identity of these beautiful products of art and the artist, and also blame for the infidelity of his painting. First, we assuredly recognize melons, peaches, grapes, dahlias and creepers, the rest is more doubtful, but who cares? I am little worried about what sort are those fruits and flowers, that is the business of the botanist and horticulturist; I can just see that they are flowers and fruits, and the finest fruits and flowers in the world. It is a complete error to focus on this. . . . Aesthetic truth does not consist in exactitude. Painters specializing in flowers are of this prejudice, they copy, they imitate what they have before their eyes, and make portraits. But to imitate and copy flowers is not the same as making flowers and fruits; the essence of art is to make, to create, as is the way of nature . . . but without repeating slavishly. If so, a mirror would be the greatest painter. . . . Anyway, I maintain these two points: first, that the fruits and flowers of M. Delacroix are truly fruits and flowers and not something else,*

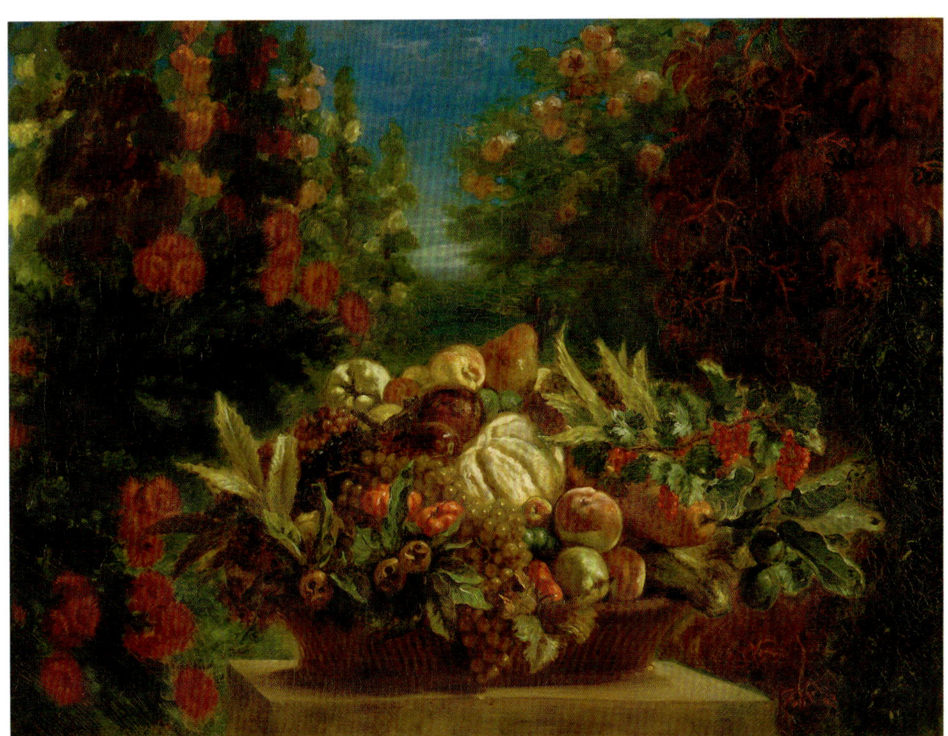

FIG. 16 Eugène Delacroix, *Still Life with Flowers and Fruit*, 1848, oil on canvas. Philadelphia Museum of Art, John G. Johnson Collection, 1917, 974

> *and, moreover, that they serve perfectly—not for being picked nor eaten—but truly observed.*[34]

On a later occasion, when Delacroix exhibited his ambitious floral pendants of 1848–49 in the Exposition Universelle of 1855, Gautier concluded,

> *It is a consoling thought to see how the day of reckoning arrives for those gallant, proud talents who in their love of art have not begged the crowd's approval. . . . Such has been the life of M. Eugène Delacroix: for a quarter of a century his name has been surrounded by a deafening tumult of abuse, diatribes, ridicule, and extremely violent controversy; now the dust of battle has settled, and the master, long treated like a zealot and a lunatic, appears radiant in the brilliance of a serene and henceforth inarguable glory.*[35]

Ideas such as these, which promoted not only free handling but also the floral subject, symbolized the effort to regenerate the practice of painting, preparing the way for a revelatory exhibition of privately owned works organized in 1860 by the critic Philippe Burty as a rebuttal to the official museum presentation of French art history.

Though Chardin's *A Vase of Flowers* (fig. 9; cat. no. 2) was not included in the 1860 exhibition, its then-owner Camille Marcille made it known to critics Edmond and Jules de Goncourt. The brothers published an account of it in the *Gazette des Beaux-Arts* in 1863[36] that was then developed into a chapter on Chardin in their *L'art du dix-huitième siècle* of 1874:

> *Consider also these rare bouquets composed, so to speak, from the flowers of his palette, and in which his genius shines out with a light that obscures, extinguishes, the talents of all other flower-painters. These two carnations, for example: they are nothing but a fragmentation of blue and white, a kind of silvered enamellings in relief. But when we stand away from the picture, the flowers seem to rise up from the shadow, its crinkled, laciniate substance coalesces and blossoms. Such effects are the miracle of Chardin's art.*[37]

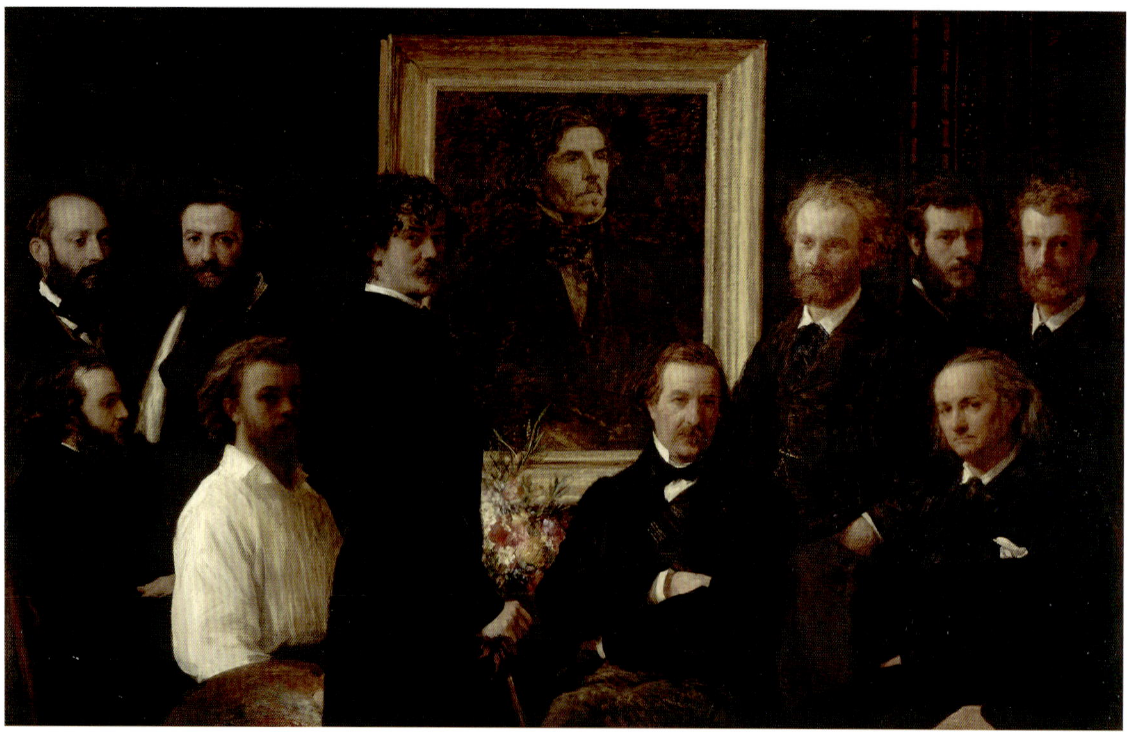

FIG. 17 Henri Fantin-Latour, *Homage to Delacroix*, 1863–64, oil on canvas. Musée d'Orsay, Paris, RF 1664

The year 1863 saw both the recognition (by the Goncourt brothers) of Chardin as an original and uncommon painter and the passing of Delacroix, who was credited with revitalizing the modern French school. This confluence of events may be a coincidence, but the date is important. From then on, Delacroix and Chardin continued to appear as explicit referents in the art of the painters later called the Impressionists. Indeed, this younger generation's productions in the genre, such as those included in this catalogue, were experimental and tactical—not merely works that were less expensive to make than those requiring a model. Though he never joined the Impressionist group, Henri Fantin-Latour was an early friend of some of the most radical members. As he was the most dedicated practitioner of the genre in the second half of the nineteenth century, leaving the final word to him, appropriately expressed in eloquent pictorial rather than literary form, seems fitting. Indeed, Fantin's pithy contribution to the dialogue in which freely painted floral still lifes came to connote "modern" artistic tendencies and concerns, consisted of a simple act: placing a modest bouquet of mixed flowers before the commemorative portrait of the deceased Romantic painter in the final version of his *Homage to Delacroix* of 1863–64 (fig. 17). In this work, intended as a manifesto of radical painting though framed in the form of a tribute to the past, Delacroix is shown surrounded by many champions of modern art, including admiring writers and artists such as Fantin himself (in shirt-sleeves), Édouard Manet (standing immediately to the right of the portrait), and Baudelaire (seated second from right).

Though many preparatory studies exist for this great painting (the genesis of which has been meticulously documented in two exemplary exhibitions), none contain the vase of flowers, which provides the only note of color to this purposeful revolutionary gathering.[38] Instead, Fantin's earliest sketches show Delacroix's advocates gathered around a statue (an incongruous

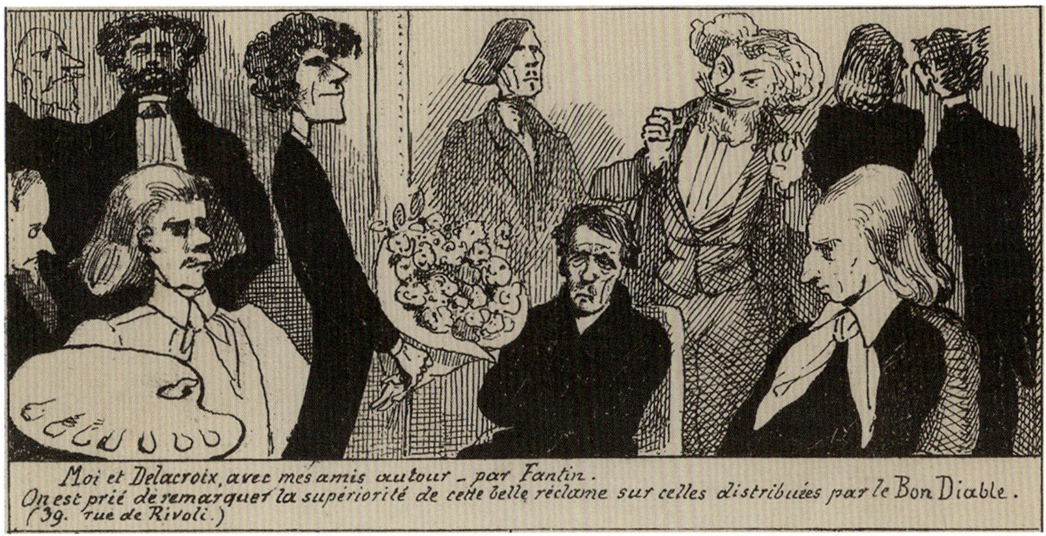

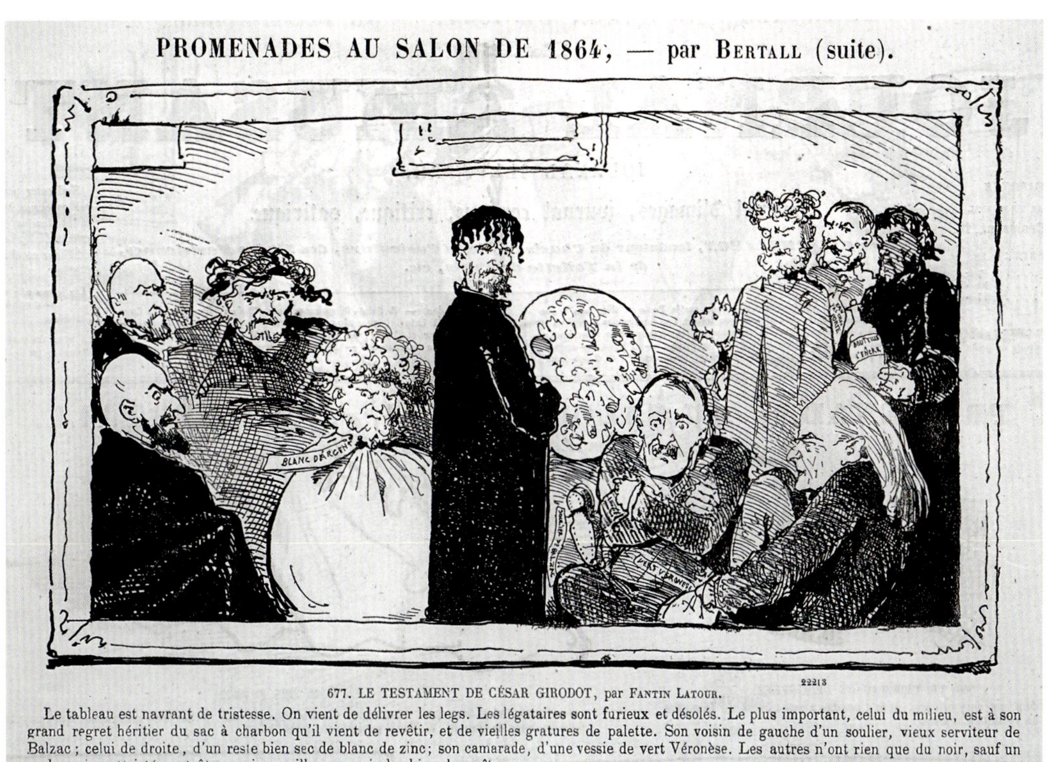

FIG. 18 André Gill, "Moi et Delcroix avec mes amis autour—par Fantin," from *Le Salon pour rire*, 1864

FIG. 19 Bertall, "Le Testament du César Girodot, par Fantin-Latour," from *Journal amusant*, June 4, 1864. Bibliothèque national de France, Départment des estampes et de la photographie, Paris, FOL-LC2-1681

choice to represent the champion of color). Fantin did indicate a floral tribute in the form of garlands midway in his project, but the final appearance of the bouquet is not similarly documented.

Perhaps Fantin's inspiration is connected to a comment by Baudelaire, who described Delacroix's palette as a "bouquet of skillfully arranged flowers."[39] Indeed, Fantin is purposefully shown holding his own palette slightly to the left of the centrally placed bouquet. Significantly, the visual import of this suggestion is borne out in the visual reception of the painting. Period caricatures by André Gill and Bertall (figs. 18 and 19) present the palette and bouquet in the foreground, as if they—more than anything—conveyed the high import of this work as a declaration of an artistic war. This war, as this exhibition and catalogue hope to demonstrate, was waged not only with brushes but also with bouquets and only ended with the death of representational art itself.

NOTES

1. This excerpt is from Chardin's 1765 speech about artistic education (as reported by Denis Diderot), quoted in Démoris 2000, 107. For the full passage, see Kahng 2002, 53.
2. See McCoubrey 1958; Loyrette 1994, 149–82; Rathbone and Shackelford, 2001.
3. The full passage reads: "Celui qui fait parfaitement des paysages est au-dessus d'un autre qui ne fait que des fruits, des fleurs ou des coquilles. Celui qui peint des animaux vivants est plus estimable que ceux qui ne représentent que des choses mortes et sans mouvement; et comme la figure de l'homme est le plus parfait ouvrage de Dieu sur la Terre, il est certain aussi que celui qui se rend l'imitateur de Dieu en peignant des figures humaines, est beaucoup plus excellent que tous les autres . . . un Peintre qui ne fait que des portraits, n'a pas encore cette haute perfection de l'Art, et ne peut prétendre à l'honneur que reçoivent les plus savants. Il faut pour cela passer d'une seule figure à la représentation de plusieurs ensemble; il faut traiter l'histoire et la fable; il faut représenter de grandes actions comme les historiens, ou des sujets agréables comme les Poètes; et montant encore plus haut, il faut par des compositions allégoriques, savoir couvrir sous le voile de la fable les vertus des grands hommes, et les mystères les plus relevés." Félibien 1667, preface. All translations in this essay are by the author.
4. McCoubrey 1964, 40.
5. Kahng 2002, 24–30.
6. "Chez lui, chaque objet est caractérisé par un travail qui lui est spécialement propre; ses roses son minces, ses lis ont du corps." Oudry (1752) 1861, 115.
7. Ibid., 115–17.
8. Charles-Nicolas Cochin (1715–1790) recalling the words of his friend Chardin, quoted in Kahng 2002, 42.
9. Diderot (1759–81) 1975–1983, 1:222–23.
10. Ibid.
11. Kahng 2002, 39–58.
12. Ibid., 17, 48–49.
13. "elle a de la verité." Diderot (1763) 1975, 4:287–88.
14. Reviewer Maurice Tourneux wrote that in Vallayer-Coster's still lifes "on reconnaît le vrai talent de cette estimable artiste." Tourneux 1877–82, 16:270.
15. "fleurs, genre dans lequel elle s'est principalement excercée jusq'aujourd'hui. Elles sont si fraîches, si vives, si brillantes. . . . Digne Emule des van Huysum et des Monnoyer." *Lettres pittoresques* 1777, 36.
16. "dans le genre où elle n'a qu'un rival, Van Spaendonck." Diderot (1781) 1975, 4:324.
17. Faré 1962, 191.
18. "Je ne pense pas que l'art puisse aller jamais plus loin. C'est la nature même, mais la nature dans toute sa fraîcheur, dans tous son éclat; et il y a autant de grâce, d'harmonie et de goût dans la manière dont ces fleurs se trouvent rassemblées qu'il y a d'exactitude et de verité jusque dans les moindres détails qui en caractérisent si heuresusement toutes les formes, toutes les nuances, celles même qui semblent trop fugitives pour ne pas échapper au pinceau." Tourneux 1877–82, 16:271.
19. van Spaendonck ca. 1800.
20. Hardouin-Fugier 1981.
21. Ibid., 15–16.
22. Michel et al. 2002, 20. See also MacDonald in the present volume.
23. Barker 1969, 185–213, esp. 193–95.
24. "Il faut dessiner beaucoup, sans trêve." *Dessins* 1984, 105.
25. Grafe 2007, 37–47.
26. "Heureux le mortel qui peut passer sa vie avec les fleurs ! . . . Si le peintre de fleurs n'a ni les mêmes études à faire, ni les mêmes difficultés à vaincre que le peintre de l'histoire, s'ensuit-il que la peinture des fleurs soit un genre subalterne et circonscrit?" Miel 1817, 566–67.
27. "Il faut se laisser aller à ses impressions, travailler librement, n'être trop exigeant, ni trop sévère. Le trop de sévérité est un défaut aussi nuisible que le trop grand contentement de soi-même." Robaut and Chesneau, 1885, 266 [as quoted originally in Louis de Planet, *Souvenirs de travaux de peinture avec M. Eugène Delacroix* (1843–44).

28. "Le poignet seul et non la main imprime le mouvement au pinceau. . . . La main ne sert qu'à tenir l'outil qui écrit, dessine, ou peint." Ibid. 267.
29. From Baudelaire's review of the 1845 Salon, quoted in Hardouin-Fugier 1978, 3. ["Saint-Jean qui est de l'école de Lyon, le bagne de la peinture –l'endroit du monde connu où l'on travaille le mieux les infiniment petits."] See also Grafe 2007, 6–7.
30. See Hardouin-Fugier 1978, esp. 7 and for a reproduction of the drawing, 4.
31. Cailleux 1849, article III.
32. Delacroix to Constant Dutilleux, February 6, 1849, cited in Delacroix 1970, 286–87. See also Pomarède 1998, 117–39, and Willsdon 2004, 37–39.
33. "Cette année, par un caprice bien compréhensible chez un coloriste, il a envoyé à l'exposition deux grands tableaux de fleurs. Ces fleurs, vous l'imaginez bien, ne ressemblent pas aux fleurs de Van Spandonck [*sic*], encore moins à celles de Redouté, pas meme à celles de Saint-Jean; pour leur trouver des analogues il faudrait remonter à Baptiste, à Monnoyer, ou plutôt encore aux tableaux des fruits et de fleurs de Juan de Avellaneda et de Velasquez." Gautier 1849.
34. "Tous deux éclatans de couleur, gracieusement composés et agencés, largement et vigoureusement peints. J'ai entendu discuter sur le nom de ces beaux produits de l'art, et reprocher à l'artiste l'infidélité de sa peinture. D'abord on reconnait positivement des melons, des pêches, des raisins, des dahlias et des liserons; le reste est plus douteux; mais qu'importe? Je m'inquiète peu de savoir quels sont ces fruits et ces fleurs; c'est l'affaire du botaniste et de l'horticulteur; il me suffit de voir que ce sont des fleurs et des fruits, et les plus beaux fruits et fleurs du monde. C'est errer *toto caelo* que s'attacher en ceci à la pure imitation de ce qu'on appelle la nature. La vérité esthétique n'est pas l'exactitude. Les peintres de fleurs spéciaux sont dans ce préjugé; ils copient, ils imitent ce qu'ils ont devant les yeux; ils font des portraits. Mais imiter, copier des fleurs et des fruits, ce n'est pas *faire* des fleurs et des fruits; l'essence de l'art est de *faire*, de créer, à la manière de la nature, sans doute, mais sans la répéter servilement. S'il en était ainsi, un miroir serait le plus grand des peintres. Raphael a formulé en quelques mots les vrais principes. Ecrivant à Balthasard Castiglione au sujet de sa Galatée, de la Farnesine, à laquelle il travaillait, il se plaint de la disette des beaux modèles de femmes; mais, ajoute-t-il, "*je m'en passe et mi servo d'una certa idea che mi viene alla mente*." Pour faire des fruits et des fleurs, il ne faut pas non plus autre chose que cette certaine idée qui vient à l'esprit. Quoi qu'il en soit des principes, je maintiens en fait ces deux points: d'abord, que les fruits et les fleurs de M. Delacroix sont véritablement des fruits et des fleurs et non autre chose, et, de plus, que sont des fleurs et des fruits excellents et parfaits pour leur destination, qui est d'être, non pas cueillis ou mangés, mais simplement regardés." Peisse 1849.
35. See Jobert 1998, 265.
36. Goncourt and Goncourt, 1863, 521–22.
37. Goncourt and Goncourt 1873–74, 117.
38. Druick and Hoog 1983, 167–96. See also Leribault 2011, esp. 43–63, and Meslay 2009, 235.
39. Rubin 1994, 109.

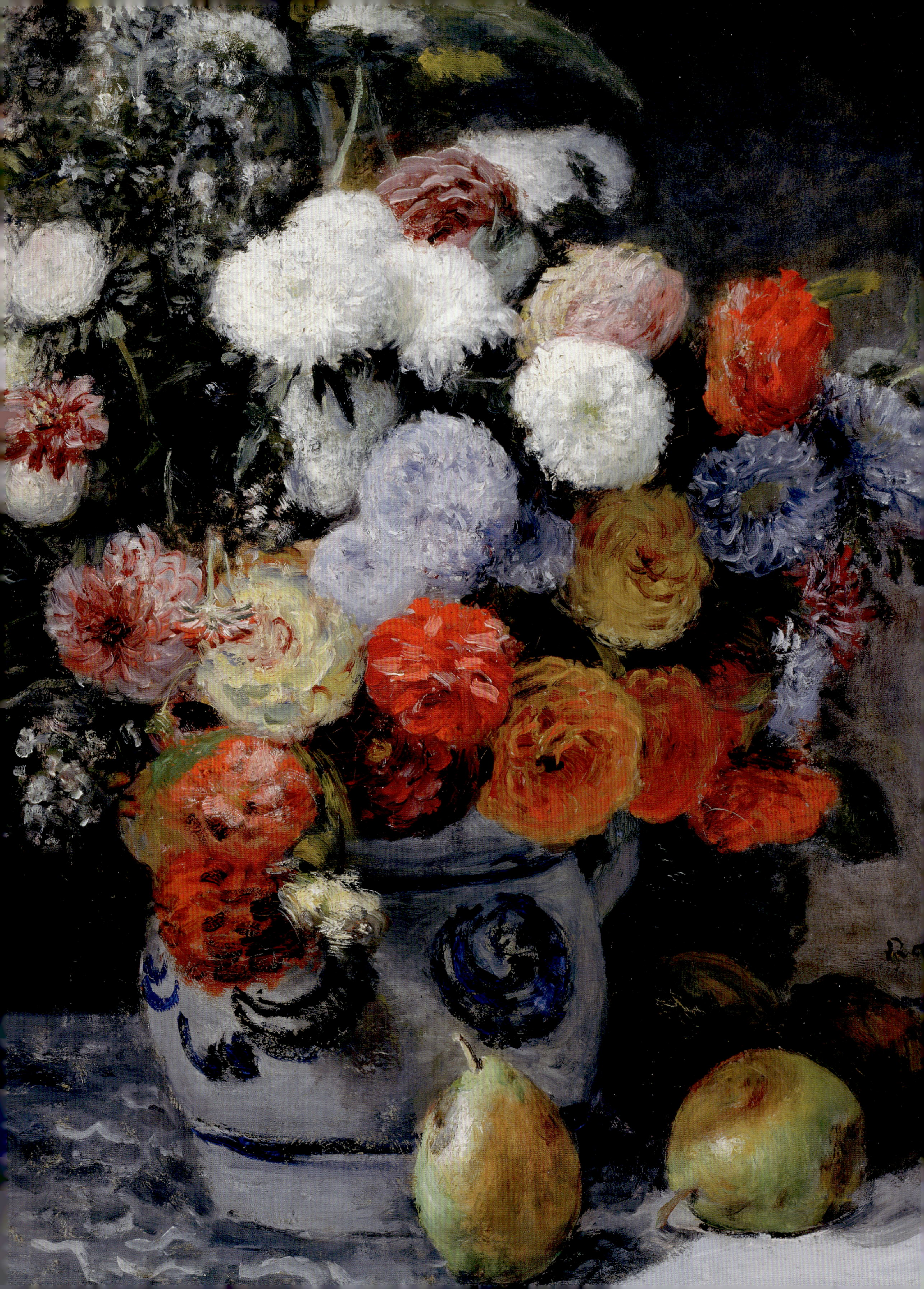

Impressionist Flower Paintings and the Market

Sylvie Patry

MORE THAN TWO HUNDRED MASTERPIECES BY IMPRESSIONIST ARTISTS are counted among the floral still-life paintings often condemned in the second half of the nineteenth century as, at best, overabundant and excessively conventional. At worst, they were deemed "Old vegetation, worn-out themes! / What vegetable mistakes! / Fake flowers from stuffy Salons!"[1] This number represents the works by those Impressionists who were the most prolific painters in the genre: Pierre-Auguste Renoir, Paul Cézanne, Claude Monet, Gustave Caillebotte, Camille Pissarro, and Berthe Morisot. Viewed as a whole, however, these pictures profoundly renewed the maligned genre of flower painting.[2] Other than landscape, what motif could have so perfectly satisfied these self-professed devotees of nature? What better artistic response is there to this essentially ephemeral subject than the Impressionist *far presto*? And thus, the combination of the flower subject with an aesthetic that was presented as the triumph of pure painting could be celebrated in the name of a common liberation from the tyranny of subject. Though this formalist reading is no longer widely accredited, or has at least been complemented by iconographic and historical approaches, attention continues to focus primarily on the spectacular visual components of Impressionist flowers—imitation of nature, daring color, and vibrant presence.

Flower painting, however, is still considered a minor and commercially motivated genre, and these Impressionist examples have long been treated as potboilers better suited than other genres to conquer a market resistant to the "New Painting." They have also been seen as concessions to bourgeois tastes and practices, reflecting the interiors and gardens where they were so perfectly at home. Renoir, after all, encouraged his dealer to exhibit flower paintings because they were "less compromising."[3] Today, these floral works continue to prompt the question often asked of their ilk—as the title of a 2012 Paris gallery installation by Camille Henrot posited—"Is it possible to be a revolutionary and like flowers?"

Without ignoring the undeniable pleasure that these paintings have afforded both artist and spectator—an established principle in a field generally qualified as joyful or charming—I will attempt in this essay to determine whether the Impressionists sought to inscribe their own flower paintings into an already abundantly supplied genre often criticized for its commercial character. The increasing vogue for gardening as well as

FIG. 20 Pierre-Auguste Renoir, *Mixed Flowers in an Earthenware Pot* (detail), ca. 1869, cat. no. 24

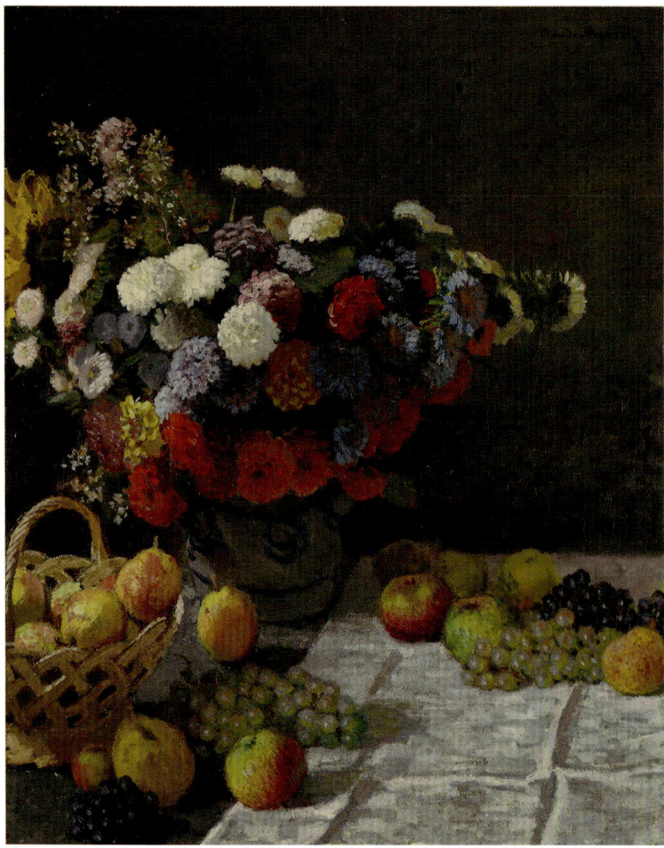

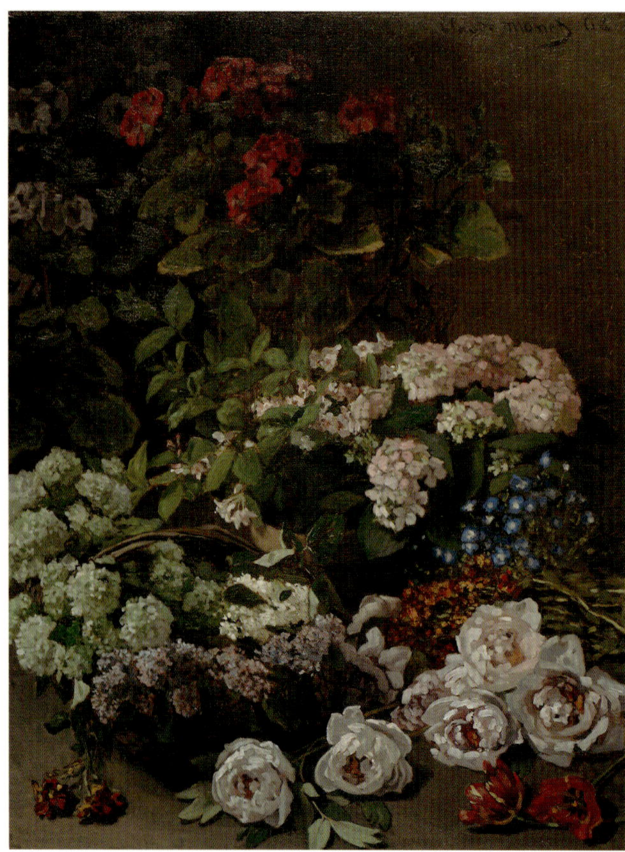

FIG. 21 Claude Monet, *Still Life with Flowers and Fruit*, 1869, oil on canvas. The J. Paul Getty Museum, Los Angeles

FIG. 22 Claude Monet, *Spring Flowers*, 1864, oil on fabric. Cleveland Museum of Art, Gift of the Hanna Fund

floral painting and watercolors drew a further accusation, quite opposite in tendency—that of amateurism. Assimilation into the category of "female works" designed merely to please—such as the watercolor roses that the Goncourt brothers' heroine, Renée Mauperin, felt herself obliged to paint[4]—was an even worse stigma. Flower painting was, in short, characterized by individual and regional specialization, increasing feminization, and proximity to industry and the decorative arts.

It should be said from the outset that flower paintings represent only a small part of the Impressionists' works (between one and five percent) and were produced unevenly over the course of their careers. They were painted essentially in the early 1860s, again around 1875, and finally in the early 1880s. Though a lack of overall historical data makes it difficult to situate the Impressionists precisely within the flower-painting market during the second half of the century, certain key moments and comparison with allied painters—such as Frédéric Bazille, Gustave Courbet, Henri Fantin-Latour, and Édouard Manet—elucidate the "horizons of expectation" that governed their floral production. These artists, after all, inscribed the genre into the history of pictorial modernity.

"Do not condemn me to perpetual still life,"[5] Bazille pleaded to his mother in 1866. The young artist needed money to execute the figure paintings with which he sought—alongside Monet and Renoir—to found a "New Painting." Though Monet had earlier declared flowers an "excellent thing to paint,"[6] they, like other still-life subjects, were considered mere stopgaps. Yet the fifteen or so flower paintings by Bazille, Monet, and especially Renoir dating from the 1860s are striking for their quality and ambition. It is sometimes forgotten that flowers afforded one of the first motifs, along

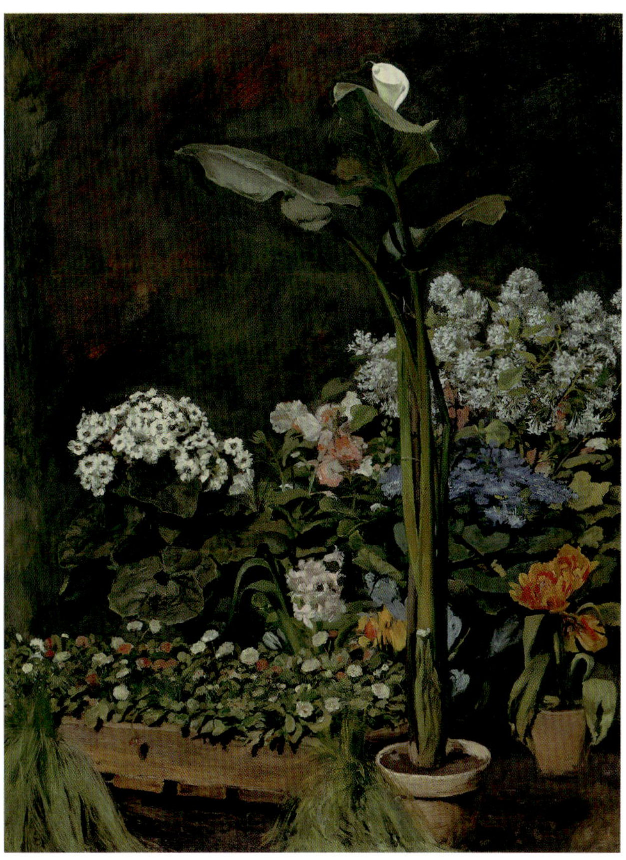

FIG. 23 Pierre-Auguste Renoir, *Lily and Greenhouse Plants*, 1864, oil on canvas. Collection of Oskar Reinhart "Am Römerholz", Winterthur

with the La Grenouillère bathing site, that the young Monet and Renoir shared as they were working out the language of the New Painting together at Bougival in 1869 (fig. 21). Significantly, Renoir chose to include a youthful flower painting in the first Impressionist exhibition of 1874, as did Monet for the second group show in 1876.

Considering that these artists had been reusing their canvases in the 1860s because they could not afford new ones, the ambitious formats of these flower paintings, which suited the genre's traditional decorative role, went well beyond studio exercises and signaled an intention to sell or at least attract attention. In 1864, Monet painted "the best thing [he had] done till now,"[7] *Spring Flowers* (fig. 22), on a canvas measuring approximately 3½ by 3 feet (1.1 × 0.9 m). That same year, Renoir used some of his largest canvases of the period for flower paintings of almost 4¼ by 3¼ feet (1.3 × 1 m); only his figure paintings were larger. One might infer that when Renoir started a second version of his unfinished flower painting (fig. 23), he did so at the request or in the hope of a buyer. At the same time, Bazille executed three flower paintings, all of them monumental. The vigorous, realist brushwork in some of the pictures by these three artists matched a recent tendency in flower painting (for instance, works by François Bonvin and Jean Seignemartin as well as the place of flowers in the teaching of the "Petite École")[8] and attracted buyers at a point when their modern figure paintings mainly remained unsold. In 1866 Bazille received a commission for a still life of flowers and fruit for a dining room—ironically confirming Charles Baudelaire's condemnation of "dining-room pictures" as opposed to "gallery-pictures."[9] The 500-franc commission was later changed from still life to portrait.[10] Despite the strictures on flower painting mentioned above,

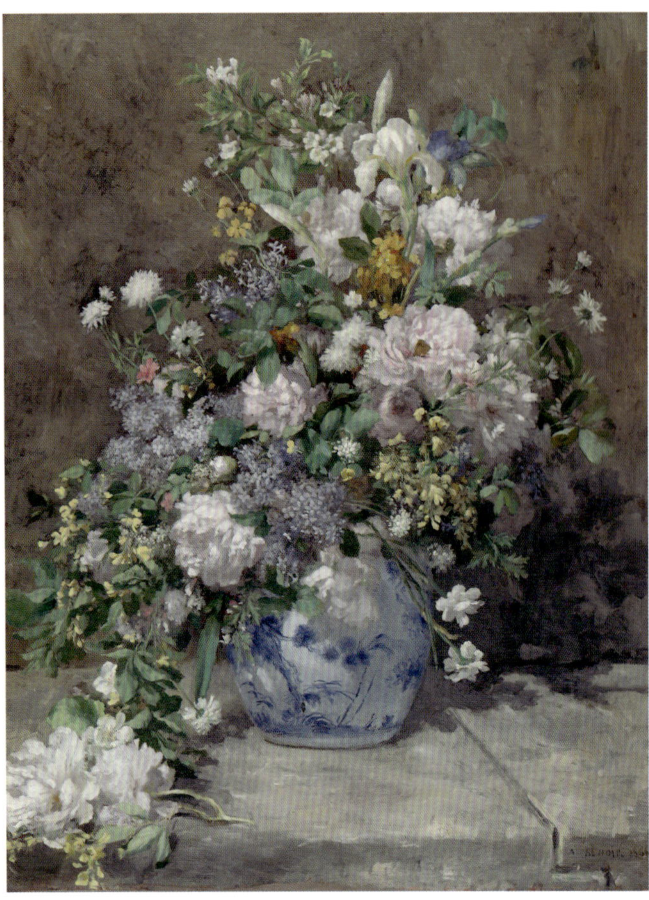

FIG. 24 Pierre-Auguste Renoir, *Spring Bouquet*, 1866, oil on canvas. Harvard Art Museums, Fogg Museum, Cambridge, Massachusetts, Bequest of Grenville L. Winthrop, 1943.277

the two genres often seemed to function in a similar fashion in terms of commissions and client networks. Thus two flower paintings by Renoir were acquired by architect Charles Le Cœur, a friend and one of the first to commission portraits from the artist. Though one of these, *Spring Bouquet* (fig. 24), is slightly bigger, the two seem to work as companion pieces, contrasting the elegance of peonies and lilies with the boisterous rusticity of the poppies, daisies, and other wildflowers. A somewhat later photograph of the Le Cœur family's Paris home shows *Spring Bouquet* set into paneling and framed by porcelain pieces in a decorative composition.

The beauty of these bouquets suggests that the Impressionists also depicted flowers to demonstrate the technical ability they were often accused of lacking, especially important in a domain where brio was a popular requirement. *Vase of Peonies on a Pedestal* (see fig. 37) was the most ambitious of Manet's first series of 1864 flower paintings in regard to the format (almost 3¼ by 2½ feet [1 × 0.7 m]), breadth of composition, and care with which it was executed. It was exhibited in 1865 and again in 1867, and in 1872 it was the only flower painting among the twenty-three works that the dealer Paul Durand-Ruel included in his first purchase from Manet. One of his earliest acquisitions from Renoir was also a bouquet of peonies, underlining the commercial attraction of this flower, so much in vogue during the Second Empire. Monet sent a "flower picture," probably *Spring Flowers*, to the twentieth municipal exhibition at Rouen in 1864, a year before he first participated in the Paris Salon. The choice of Rouen was likely dictated in part by his family connections in the Normandy region—particularly with his brother Léon, the owner of the picture[11]—and the city's reputation for exhibiting "an exceptional quantity of flower paintings."[12] The picture was not a great success in Rouen but was admired in Le Havre[13] and, thanks to Eugène Boudin's intervention, was responsible for Monet being offered the chance to "paint a flower panel for a citizen of Le Havre."[14] That commission was perhaps the decoration for Louis Gaudibert, father of his first Rouen patron.[15] Finally, at the Salon of 1868, Bazille exhibited a large floral composition (fig. 25), a work that he had already given his cousins Lejosne and was no longer for sale.[16] Its presence at the Salon, however, and in the Lejosnes' apartment, which was frequented by artists such as Manet, drew attention to its author's virtuosity.

Like Renoir, Cézanne, and Pissarro, Monet did not exhibit flower paintings at the Paris Salon, a choice that attests to the provincial character of flower painting in nineteenth-century France with regard to both its production and distribution. The floral genre was, at this time, primarily a

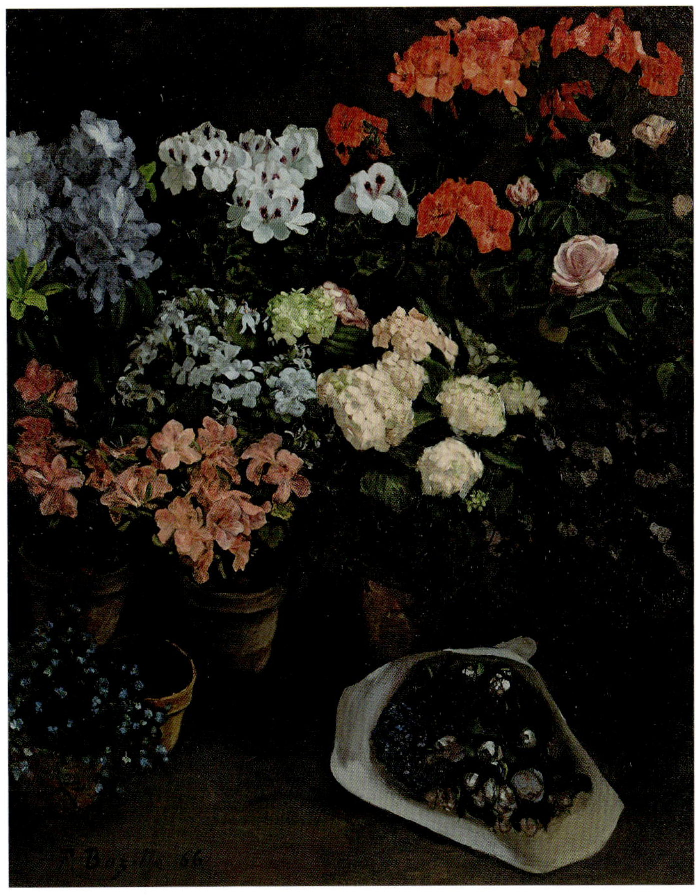

FIG. 25 Frédéric Bazille, *Flowerpots (Study of Flowers)*, 1866, oil on canvas. Formerly property of the Greentree Foundation from the collection of Mrs. John Hay Whitney, New York

specialty of regional centers directly connected to the textile and wallpaper industries—for example, Alexis Kreyder at Mulhouse; Simon Saint-Jean (a former silk designer) and André Perrachon in Lyon; and Castex-Dégrange in Paris and Lyon. In provincial exhibitions, which were increasing in popularity throughout France during the second half of the nineteenth century, flower paintings were particularly well represented. This reversal of status[17] may be attributed to the demand for smaller artworks that were financially accessible and easy to integrate into a bourgeois interior. The result was an "annual tour of France by the *fleuristes*,"[18] a ritual observed, for instance, by Victoria Dubourg, Fantin's wife and a specialist in flower painting. (Records show that Dubourg exhibited work in Lyon in 1869 and 1870. In 1872, she was represented in Lyon, Nevers, and Nantes; she exhibited again in Lyon in 1875, in Dijon in 1892, and in Strasbourg in 1907.)

Certain examples from the elder Impressionists Boudin and Courbet illustrate the link between flowers and provincial clients around 1860: Boudin's two pairs of bouquets, which are exceptional in his oeuvre and probably the result of encouragement from Le Havre and Fécamp,[19] and the flowers painted by Courbet at Saintes. During a single visit to this southwestern French town in 1862–63, Courbet painted no less than fifteen flower paintings. His infatuation with a genre that he had scarcely explored until then was probably inspired by the beauty of the garden at Rochemont Castle, home to collector Étienne Baudry.[20] The possibility of commercial success was also a motivating factor. Courbet wrote Léon Isabey to say, "I am coining it with flowers."[21] Local republican eminences such as Frédéric Mestreau and Phoedora Gaudin were collecting his floral works. In January 1863, Courbet exhibited five of his flower paintings at Saintes, and the unanimous praise created a marked contrast to the reception generally accorded his work in that town.[22] The same year, he sent two of these paintings to Bordeaux for exhibition, *Vase with Marigolds* (1862, private collection; marked on the back "Cares Wither the Roses of Life")[23] and *Still Life with Poppies and Skull* (1862, private collection), a pair of symbolic compositions painted for Gaudin. Furthermore, the first of Manet's pictures to be sold by Durand-Ruel (perhaps with *Music in the Tuileries Gardens* [1862, National Gallery, London]) was *Vase of Peonies on a Pedestal*, for which the dealer had paid 400 francs.[24] On April 29, 1872, John Saulnier, a major collector from Bordeaux, acquired it for 1,100 francs, by no means a negligible sum.[25] Having perhaps admired Manet's *Vase of Peonies* at the Société des

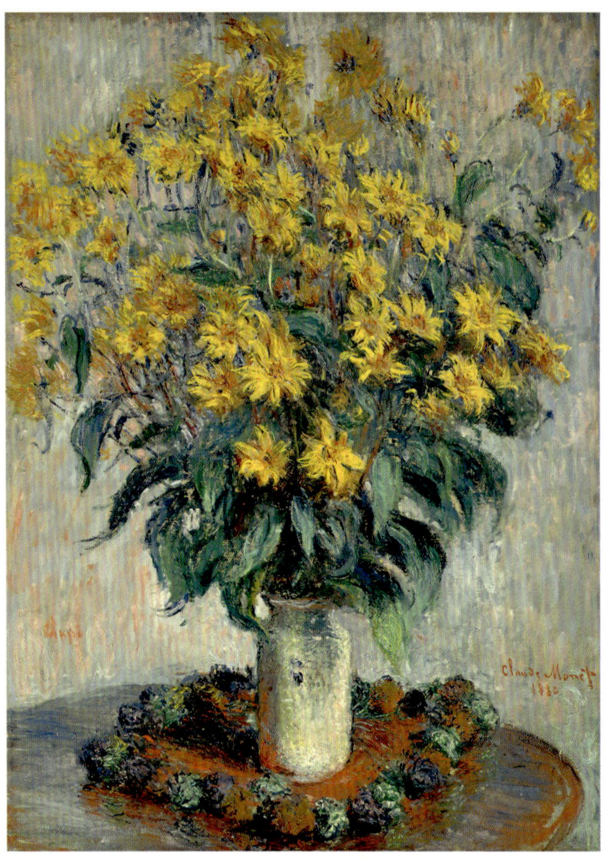

FIG. 26 Claude Monet, *Jerusalem Artichoke Flowers*, 1880, oil on canvas. National Gallery of Art, Washington, D.C., Chester Dale Collection

amis des arts de Bordeaux three years earlier, in 1869 (no. 411), Saulnier decided to add Manet's flowers to a collection dominated by Jean-Baptiste-Camille Corot, Constant Troyon, Eugène Delacroix, Narcisse Diaz de la Peña, and Théodore Rousseau.[26]

The episodic nature of these floral campaigns, however, should be noted. Their limited success did not mark the advent of a strategy. Monet complained that his Rouen picture was "abominably placed in bad light" and "impossible to make anything of," but he also conceded that the "exhibition had no importance in [his] eyes from the sales point of view" since the work already belonged to his brother.[27] Furthermore, he showed no flower paintings at Bordeaux in 1867 or 1868 or at Le Havre in 1868, preferring seascapes and figures (*Camille*, 1866, Kunsthalle Bremen) as he did in Paris. Finally, of the seventeen flower paintings completed in Saintonge, Courbet sold or gave away only four, so his boast about "coining it" was hardly justified.

Was the genre considered commercial by the Impressionists? The eight collective exhibitions held between 1874 and 1886 and the two public sales organized at the painters' initiative suggest that flowers had only a marginal role. Considering these sales and exhibitions as efforts by the artists to control the promotion and diffusion of their work, it is noteworthy that only fifteen flower paintings appeared in the catalogues of the eight exhibitions and only one in the sales of 1875 and 1877. (This was Renoir's *Vase of Flowers*, which sold for a mere 180 francs in the calamitous sale of 1875 to Ernest Balensi, a collector and banker close to Durand-Ruel.)[28] Some Impressionist flower paintings did find an audience—as shown by the fact that five of the pictures in the Impressionist exhibitions were loans from owners. In a tactic also used by other Impressionists to demonstrate that these works were not pariahs and in fact enjoyed the favor of collectors, the catalogues carried the names Georges Charpentier, Caillebotte, Cahuzac, and perhaps Henri Rouart[29] alongside works by Monet. It should be said that Monet was the principal exponent of the genre in these exhibitions; he painted ten of the fifteen pictures cited above, and in 1882 he showed five. At a time when he sought "the most complete exhibition possible,"[30] he had to include flower paintings if he was to demonstrate the full extent of his savoir faire. Of those five exhibited in 1882, *Jerusalem Artichoke Flowers* (fig. 26) belonged to Cahuzac and *Chrysanthemums* (whereabouts unknown) to Caillebotte, but the three others (*Bouquet of Sunflowers* [1881, private collection] and a pair of gladioli pictures [Pola Museum of Art, Sengokuhara]) had been bought by Durand-Ruel in 1880 and 1881 respectively and were for sale.

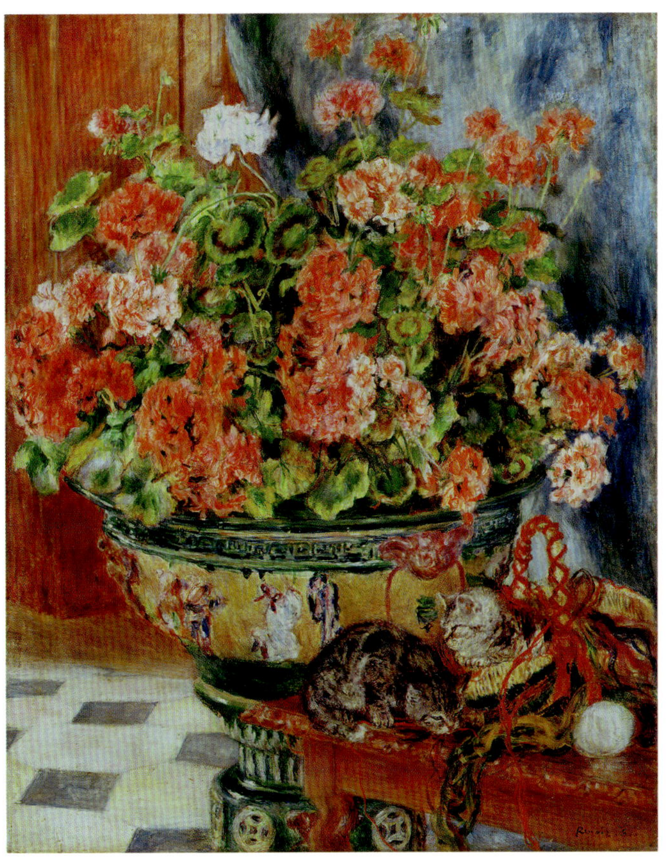

FIG. 27 Pierre-Auguste Renoir, *Geraniums and Cats*, 1881, oil on canvas. Private Collection

This period was marked by Monet's return to the genre he had abandoned in the early 1870s. Between 1878 and 1885, he painted twenty-two floral compositions.[31] His productivity was sometimes driven by bad weather that forced him into the studio[32] but was primarily inspired by the challenge of the subject and his love for a motif without which, he later confided, he would never have become a painter. More than half of these pictures were immediately purchased, including six by Durand-Ruel between 1881 and 1890. The dealer exhibited five of these repeatedly between 1883 and 1886 until all of them were sold in the United States. Durand-Ruel further commissioned floral decorations for the doors of his Paris apartment at the same time (see fig. 66). Monet's flowers were deemed particularly successful. A. W. Kingman bought his flower pictures by Monet—along with some by Renoir, including *Geraniums and Cats* (fig. 27)—at the 1886 Impressionist exhibition organized by Durand-Ruel in New York. Others later figured in the significant collection assembled by the American banker and industrialist Catholina Lambert. In 1897, Frank Thomson of Philadelphia bought the pair of Monet gladioli paintings shown in 1882 and 1883 by Durand-Ruel. At the end of his life, Monet wrote of his own flower paintings: "the only ones that I had have long since left."[33] His interest in them, and the attention they elicited in turn, reflected a general renewal of the genre in the late 1870s. New specialists were emerging, such as Ernest Quost, whom van Gogh much admired, and society painters Georges Jeannin, Pierre Bourgogne, and Alexandre Couder (the flower painter most purchased by French museums) as well as Madeleine Lemaire, the "empress of roses" in the words of her friend Marcel Proust.[34] These artists attained real success, earning both prizes and the official consecration constituted by purchase for the Musée du Luxembourg. Thus Jeannin's *Embarkation of Flowers* was purchased by the state at the Salon of 1884 for 2,000 francs. Closer to Monet was Renoir, who in 1879 decorated the Norman country home of Paul Berard, one of the most important Impressionist collectors of the time, with delightful bouquets painted in vibrant colors (fig. 28).

The Impressionist flower paintings of the 1880s thus enjoyed a more favorable attitude from *fleuristes* in general. Did this positive reception ensure that the genre had become more lucrative? True, Manet was able to sell *Flowers in a Crystal Vase* (fig. 29) to Dr. Thomas W. Evans for the substantial price of 1,000 francs, despite the intimate and valedictory dimensions of the bouquets that he painted in 1882–83. But prices for flower pictures remained relatively modest compared to figure paintings and landscapes. Thus in the 1870s, even for successful artists such as Fantin,

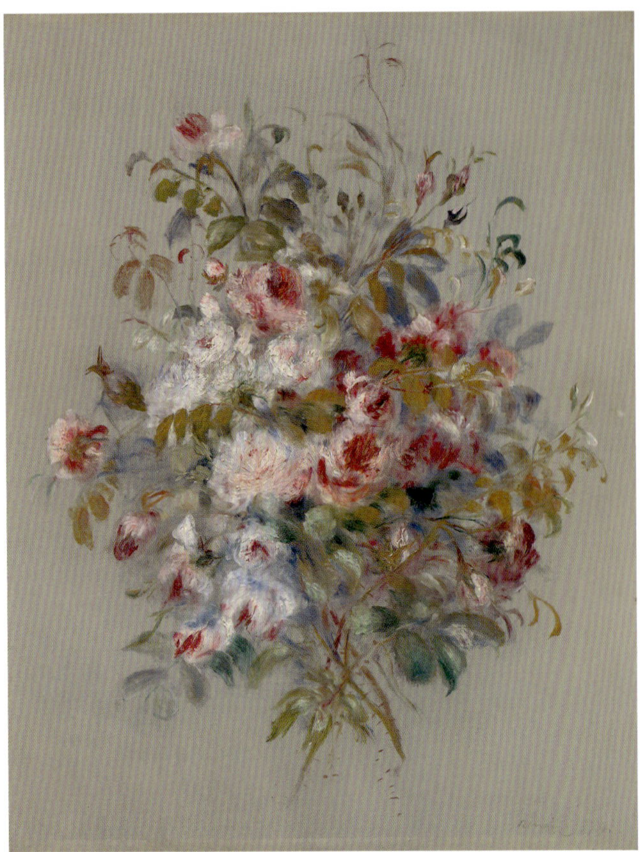

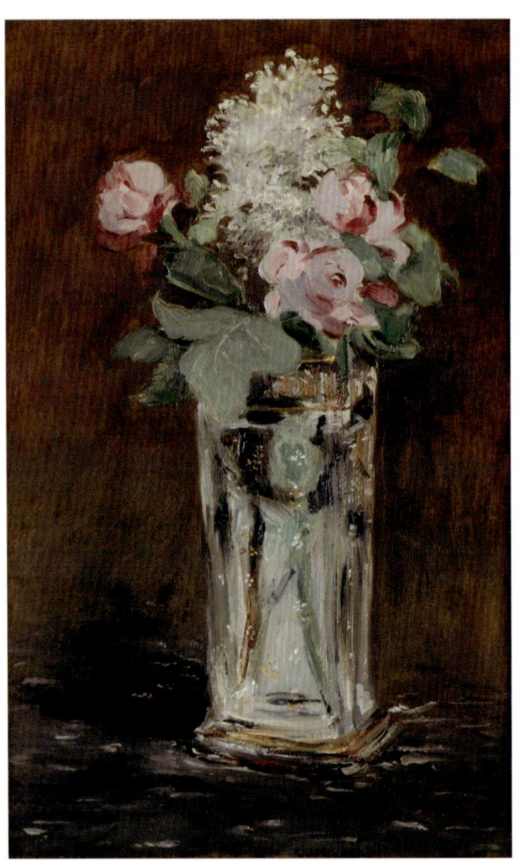

FIG. 28 Pierre-Auguste Renoir, *Bouquet of Roses*, 1879, oil on panel. The Sterling and Francine Clark Institute, Williamstown, Massachusetts, 1955.592

FIG. 29 Édouard Manet, *Flowers in a Crystal Vase*, 1882, oil on canvas. Private Collection

prices were in the range of 200 to 400 francs. In 1864, James McNeill Whistler advised Fantin to set up a pricing system based on the format of the painting: "Do not spoil your fortunes which are rising, as you see, by a lower price for the large flowers—The point to start from is easy—200 frs for the little ones . . . so for the large pictures the price is proportional. There must be a price for each size—I suppose that the large bunches we are talking about should be around 300 to 350 frs each."[35] In 1871, Fantin sold his studies to Edwin Edwards for forty francs each.[36] By October 1872, similar studies cost Edwards between 275 and 800 francs when he bought them from Durand-Ruel. By comparison, *By the Table* (see fig. 50) was sold by Durand-Ruel to an English collector for 5,000 francs.[37] The high prices in public sales confirmed this tendency: around 1890 an Impressionist flower painting might cost between 1,000 and 2,000 francs—and even so, the genre remained the least expensive. In 1895, at the sale of the American Art Association in New York, *Chrysanthemums* by Monet obtained the handsome sum of 3,375 francs, but at the same sale, an 1888 Antibes landscape reached 12,500 francs and the 1872 *View of Rouen* fetched 13,000.[38]

The fact remains that Impressionist flower paintings did reap a degree of financial reward. For example, those by Cézanne sold for 2,000 francs at the Chocquet sale in 1897, provoking the wrath of one of the most popular flower painters of his time, Ernest Quost, whose own works were available for a few hundred francs during the 1890s.[39] Vollard is a witness here. Quost, standing in front of a flower painting by Cézanne in the window of Vollard's gallery, burst out: "But has your painter so much as looked at a flower? I who stand before you now, I have spent years in the intimacy of flowers! . . . More than 3,000 detailed studies, I tell you, before ever daring to attack even the smallest wildflower! And I can't sell a thing!"[40]

These examples also demonstrate the success flower paintings enjoyed on the British market. Indeed, they came to be considered an export genre, as illustrated by Émile Zola's emblematic hero Claude Lantier, who created "little paintings of flowers for England, the proceeds of which sufficed for their daily bread."[41] Surely this remark was inspired by the success of Fantin, who found such a demand in England for his "flower studies" that it seemed to him "a business," writing, "I'm becoming a picture dealer."[42] Whistler and subsequently Edwin Edwards and Charles W. Deschamps, who was connected to Durand-Ruel, served as intermediaries. There were ups and downs, but his success caused Fantin to lead a parallel career, reserving almost all of his flowers for England, where a rise in interest in the early 1880s contrasted with the relative indifference of the Parisian market. Throughout his life, he swung between jubilation and weariness, between acceptance of his commercial success and perplexity: "I'm astonished that these painted studies of flowers find any takers, it is such a painterly feeling I'm always astounded that anyone but painters has a taste for them. I'm delighted to have you there to show them to collectors, I wouldn't dare show that kind of thing here. I feel so strongly that anyone who hasn't done any painting is bound to find them somehow lacking, even painters must be of a certain quality to appreciate them."[43]

This unpublished letter articulates precisely the contradiction inherent in the genre: a facile and seductive kind of painting that is, in the end, demanding precisely because of its insignificance and the emphasis placed on formal research. This uneasy appreciation also explains why the Impressionists perpetuated the tradition of the flower painting as a gift and token of gratitude, friendship, homage, or respect; such floral gifts by Renoir, Monet, and Manet are in the collections of Caillebotte, Monet, and Berthe Morisot. In the last analysis, the Impressionists seem to have placed no particular emphasis on the commercial potential of flower paintings as a genre likely to attract or widen their audience. These works followed more or less the same commercial circuits as their landscapes (for example) and do not appear to have been any more easily accepted. Because of their moderate prices and decorative value, flower paintings did attract occasional buyers, such as the little-known Ratisbonne or Cahuzac, who purchased Monets in the early 1880s, but this was also true of his landscapes and portraits. However, buyers of flower paintings also included some of the most fervent collectors of Impressionism, such as Georges de Bellio, Victor Chocquet, and Ernest Hoschedé. Thus, the variety of buyers and, more broadly, the "circuits of consumption"[44] seem to indicate that Impressionists found a balance between painting for the market and "pure painting"; it appears that they contrived to be both revolutionaries in painting and bourgeois in their love of flowers.

Translated from the French by Chris Miller

NOTES

I would like to thank Léa Saint-Raymond, Coline Zélal, and Simon Kelly.

1. Rimbaud 2008, 125. This quote is from "Remarks to the Poet on the Subject of Flowers" by Arthur Rimbaud (1854–1891). (The last line in Paul Schmidt's fine translation reads "stuffy living rooms," but the capital letter for *Salon* in the French text indicates that the annual exhibition rather than a living room is meant and I have changed it accordingly.)
2. The number of oil paintings of flowers between 1855 and 1903 was established on the basis of the catalogues raisonnés of the artists: Berhaut and Pietri 1994, Clairet et al. 1997, Dauberville and Dauberville 2007, Daulte 1959, Fernier 1978, Pissarro et al. 2005, Rewald et al. 1996, Rouart and Wildenstein 1975, Schulman 1995, and Wildenstein 1996. The resulting inventory is: Pierre-Auguste Renoir, 42; Paul Cézanne, 36; Édouard Manet, 31; Claude Monet, 25; Gustave Caillebotte, 23; Gustave Courbet, 23; Camille Pissarro, 18; and Berthe Morisot, 18. Further, this group includes all those pictures representing cut flowers in sheaves and bouquets (but not those of flowers in the ground) inventoried before 1903, the date of the latest flower paintings by Cézanne. (The list excludes Mary Cassatt, Alfred Sisley, and Edgar Degas, whose oeuvres contain only two, one, and no independent floral still lifes, respectively.) As of 1900, it seems inappropriate to identify as independent flower paintings the many studies of flowers by Renoir, some of which are on canvas cuttings; none of them are more than a few centimeters in size. In the case of Monet, the panels painted for Durand-Ruel's doors and studies related to the *Nymphéas* cycle have not been taken into account. For Caillebotte, similarly, the doors of the Petit Gennevilliers salons and the panels made in preparation for them have not been included.
3. Renoir, December 2–15, 1866, in Schulman 1995, letter 151.
4. Goncourt and Goncourt 1902, 5. The authors quote Mauperin: "Then too with the accomplishments we're allowed to learn, we must not go beyond a certain average. . . . I ought only to paint roses and only in watercolors." I would like to thank Dominique Péty for this suggestion.
5. Bazille to his parents, June–July 1886, in Schulmann 1995, letter 144.
6. Monet to Bazille, Honfleur, August 26, 1864, quoted in Wildenstein 1974–85, letter 9.
7. Monet to Bazille, Honfleur, July 13, 1864, quoted in Wildenstein 1974–85, letter 8.
8. The "Petite École" was a forerunner of the École supérieure des arts décoratifs. Its teaching was intended for workers in the decorative-arts industries, but it quickly began to accept future artists alongside the École des Beaux-Arts. The teaching of the "Petite École" was founded above all on the observation of nature and particular of flora. Its students included Carpeaux, Rodin, and Dalou but also Fantin-Latour, who took the famous courses by Horace Lecoq de Boisbaudran.
9. Baudelaire, 1965, 27. (The expression is used of a painting, *Fruit and Flowers*, by a member of the Lyon School, Simon Saint-Jean.)
10. Bazille to his parents, June–July 1866, in Schulmann 1995, letter 144.
11. Léon Monet was certainly in Rouen in 1870 and may have been there or had connections there before that. In 1872, Monet, Pissarro and Sisley took part in the twenty-third municipal exhibition at his initiative.
12. Hardouin-Fugier and Grafe 1992, 260.
13. Monet to Bazille, Honfleur, July 15, 1864, in Wildenstein 1974–85, letter 8.
14. Ibid.
15. See Monet to Boudin, Honfleur, late October–early November 1864, in Wildenstein 1974–85, letter 13. Gautier is said to have painted four or five, Boudin was to paint one or two, and Monet two.
16. See Schulmann 1995, 142.
17. This phenomenon has been described in Dussol 1997, 214–17, and Buchaniec 2010, 207–9.
18. Hardouin-Fugier and Grafe 1992, 265.
19. One pair (Schmit 210 and 211) was given to the Legris family of Fécamp; the other

(Schmit 223 and 224) was bought from Boudin on October 20, 1865, for 70 francs by Lebas of Le Havre.

20. Baudry's cousin was Théodore Duret, the critic, art lover, and future historian of Impressionism.

21. Courbet to Léon Isabey, Saintes, April 1863, in Courbet 1996, 199.

22. *Explication des ouvrages*, 1863. On Courbet's critical reception, see Bonniot 1986 and Soubiran 2007, 91–112. Fantin also exhibited five flower paintings according to Druick and Hoog 1983, 112, but I have found no trace of this in the 1863 catalogue or the studies of the exhibition cited above.

23. The French for marigold is *souci*, which also means "cares."

24. Guégan 2011. See Paul-Louis and Flavie Durand-Ruel, "Les premiers achats de Paul Durand-Ruel à Edouard Manet," 284–85: "N° 968 Manet, Fleurs, 400 francs."

25. "Sold (cash) to Saulnier, 29 April 1872 for 1100 francs." Durand-Ruel, stock book of 1868–73, Paris Archives. I would like to thank Paul-Louis and Flavie Durand-Ruel for this information. On Saulnier, see le Bihan et al. 2007, 35, 73nn 46–51.

26. It is not absolutely certain that the painting acquired by Saulnier is identical with the one exhibited in Bordeaux in 1869.

27. Monet to Bazille, Honfleur, July 15, 1864, in Wildenstein 1974–85, letter 8.

28. Spelled "Bolensi" in Bodelsen 1968, 335. It seems possible that this was *Corbeille de fleurs / Basket of Flowers*, no. 181, in the posthumous sale of Ernest Balensi (1828–1885), for which the expert advisor was Durand-Ruel; the sale was held February 21, 1885. (I would like to thank Monique Nonne for this information.) On the other hand, we have not found any flower paintings of equivalent dimensions in the Renoir catalogue raisonné or the Musée d'Orsay's documentation.

29. The initials *M. R.* are usually taken to refer to the collector Henri Rouart.

30. Monet to Durand-Ruel, Pourville, February 23, 1882, quoted in Wildenstein 1974–85, letter 249.

31. The total figure is higher, since Monet destroyed at least "one large flower picture," which he restarted before again destroying it. See Monet to Durand-Ruel, Pourville, September 18, 19, and 26, 1882, in ibid., letters 288, 289, and 290. In 1883, he noted the destruction of six. See Monet to Durand-Ruel, Giverny, October 18, 1883, in ibid., letter 377).

32. Monet to Durand-Ruel, Giverny, September 6, 1883, quoted in ibid., letter 373.

33. Monet to Geffroy, Giverny, December 19, 1920, quoted in ibid., letter 2395. In fact, his son Michel inherited some unsold floral compositions.

34. Proust 1903.

35. Whistler to Fantin, January 4–February 3, 1864, quoted in www.whistler.arts.gla.ac.uk/correspondence.

36. Fantin to Edwards, July 19, 1871, Fondation Custodia, Paris, inv. 1997-A-540.

37. Fantin to Otto Scholderer, Paris, January 23, 1873, quoted in Arnoux et al. 2011, 188.

38. See Mireur 1911–12, 5: 247. For the Antibes landscape, see Wildenstein 1974–85, 1171 and for *View of Rouen*, 217.

39. See Mireur 1911–12, 2: 130–31; 6: 97. Of seven Quost flower paintings inventoried, the prices varied between 100 and 250 francs in 1890, with an average of 160 per picture.

40. Vollard 1938, 40.

41. Zola (1886) 1902, 292. See archive.org.

42. Fantin to Edwards, May 15, 1862, cited in Druick and Hoog 1983, 111.

43. Fantin to Edwards, July 19, 1871, unpublished letter, Fondation Custodia, Paris, inv. 1997-A-540.

44. Green 1999, 29–34.

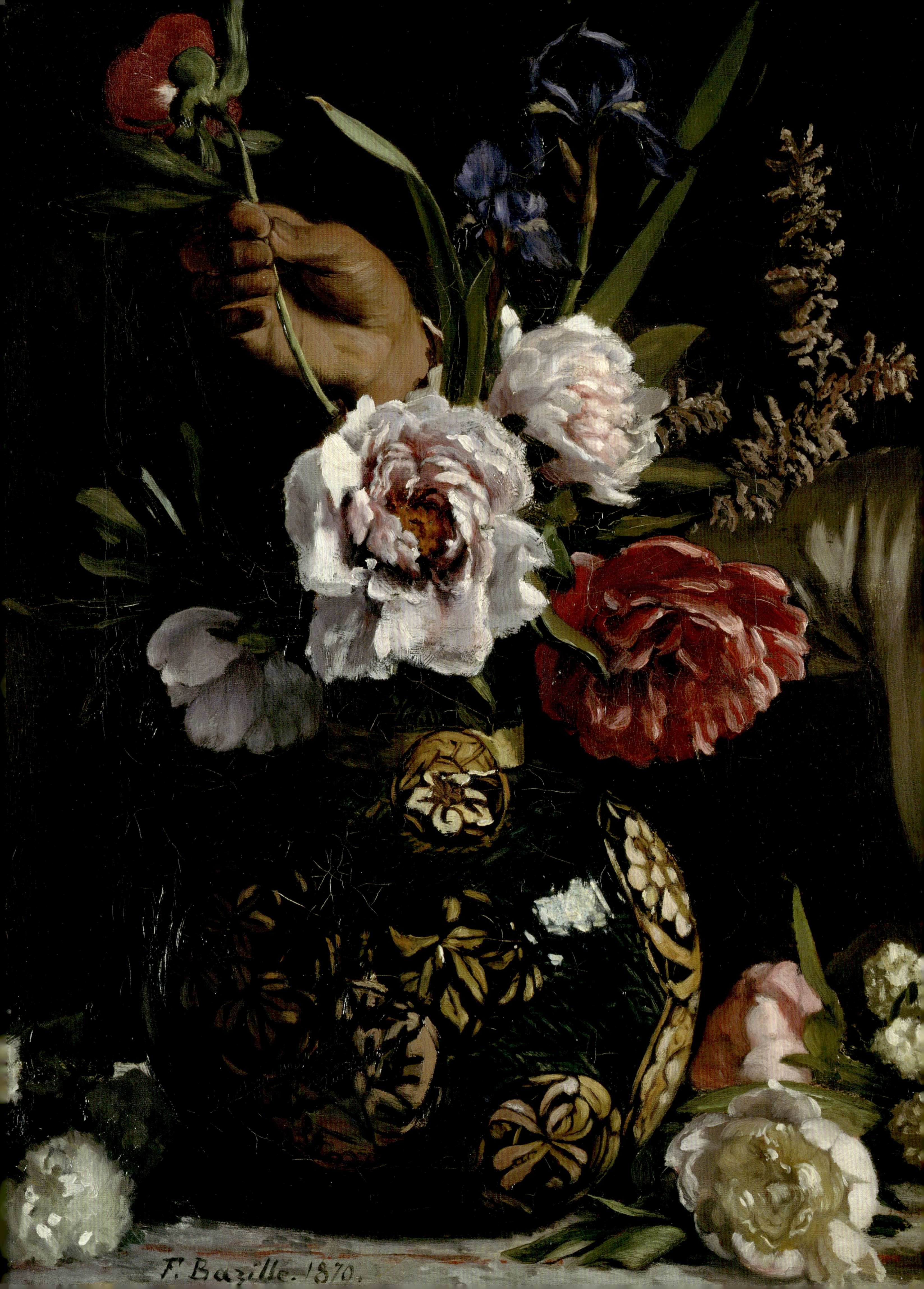
F. Bazille. 1870.

Ceramic Containers in French Nineteenth-Century Flower Painting

Audrey Gay-Mazuel

IN HIS *ESSAY ON PAINTING*, WRITTEN IMMEDIATELY FOLLOWING HIS *Salon of 1765*, Denis Diderot recommended that painters of flowers give particular attention to the vases they chose to hold their bouquets. The critic exhorted these artists to enliven their compositions through the various forms and styles of such receptacles:

> *Will these flowers be more brilliant in a pot from the Nevers manufacture than in a vase of more elegant form? If this vase has handles, why should they not take the shape of two interwoven snakes, and why should the tails of these snakes not then wind themselves around the bottom of the vase? And why should their heads, leaning towards the opening, not seem to be seeking the water to quench their thirst? To do this, you would first have to know how to animate dead things; and the number of those who know how to conserve life in things that have received it can be counted on the fingers of one hand.*[1]

As Diderot realized, the vase in a flower painting is no mere decorative accessory; its material, color, form, and size influence not only the arrangement of its contents but also the composition in general by dictating the work's chromatic range, luminous effects, and texture. The choice of vases is therefore influenced by the aesthetic effect desired, but it also pertains to fashion, the history of the collection of art objects, and taste in general.

Despite their significance, the ceramic containers in French floral still lifes of the nineteenth century have never been studied. Historians of paintings sometimes venture into botanical digressions but for the most part remain silent on the subject of receptacles.[2] The ascribed titles of such paintings reflect this lack of interest; ceramics of all types are invariably designated simply as "vases" whether they are jugs, apothecary pots, ewers, beer carafes, grease pots, or oil pitchers.[3] At best, the title of the work specifies the color or material; only in very rare cases, it suggests a specific ceramic type.

This discussion will consider only paintings of flowers in ceramic containers; flowers painted in the open air or freshly cut and scattered over a table or a floor, floral garlands or handfuls of flowers escaping from baskets, bouquets in bronze, brass, or copper basins or in vases made of marble, alabaster, stone, or glass are not included in this study. This defined focus should help determine the object's precise attribution and the nature of its specific character in the pictorial composition. Unlike paintings of previous

FIG. 30 Frédéric Bazille, *African Woman with Peonies* (detail), 1870, cat. no. 23

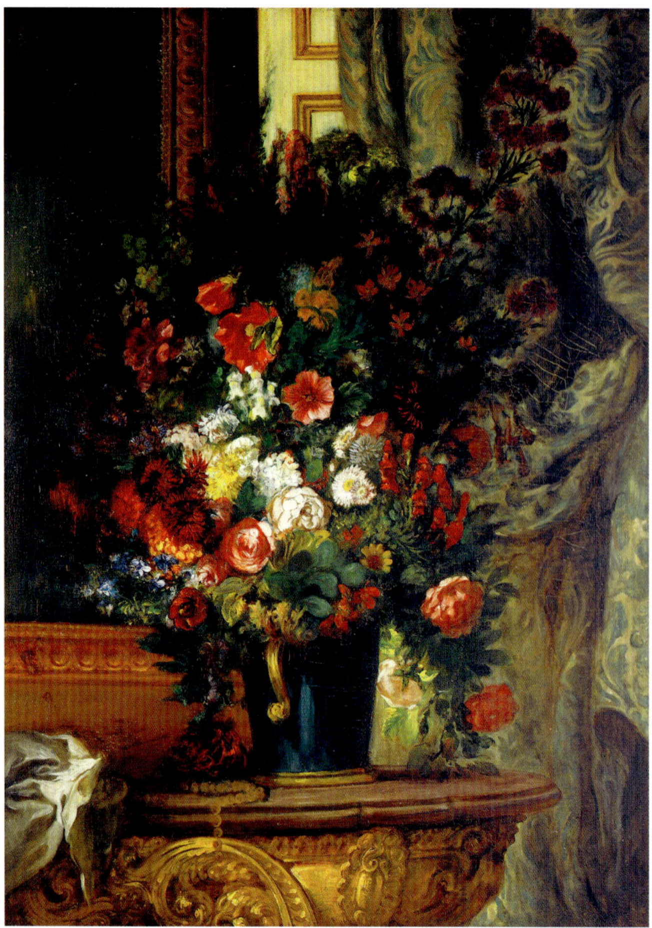

FIG. 31 Eugène Delacroix, *Vase of Flowers on a Console*, 1849–50, oil on canvas. Musée Ingres, Montauban

centuries, which often featured imagined objects, nineteenth-century compositions represented actual, recognizable items. These painters, though they sometimes exaggerated the forms and decoration of ceramic vases, based their pictures on real pieces.

While maintaining the Dutch tradition of the still life as it was practiced in France in the seventeenth and eighteenth centuries, French painters of the early nineteenth century began to break with precedent by choosing less valuable floral containers for still lifes. Sumptuous vases of gold and silver ceased to appear in paintings; instead, the works of the first half of the nineteenth century depicted receptacles of alabaster, marble, or carved stone.[4] Flowers also appeared in baskets and garlands, or without any sort of container or structure. Chantilly porcelain—a delicate and often-fanciful ceramic represented in paintings of the 1760s by Jean-Siméon Chardin and Louis Tessier[5]—had fallen out of fashion by the turn of the century, giving way to mounted porcelain. Inspired by pieces from the studio of her father, who was goldsmith to the king, Anne Vallayer-Coster specialized around 1775–80 in floral still lifes in elaborate porcelain containers—Chinese or Sèvres—set in ormolu mounts. The vases are often turquoise, as in her 1776 *Bouquet of Flowers in a Blue Porcelain Vase* (cat. no. 3),[6] and probably contemporary Chinese pieces of the Qianlong period (1736–95) mounted in France by the finest bronzesmiths for royal and aristocratic collections. Vallayer-Coster persisted with this repertoire under the empire and, a year before her death, exhibited flowers in a Chinese porcelain vase enriched with ormolu at the Salon of 1817.[7]

Mounted porcelain containers remained much appreciated for flower pictures at the middle of the nineteenth century. Produced by the Parisian porcelain manufacturers, these pieces featured less ornate mountings than those of the late eighteenth century and were favored in the *haut bourgeois* salons of the Second Empire.[8] When Eugène Delacroix painted a *Vase of Flowers on a Console* (fig. 31) in 1849–50, he was extending the still-life tradition of earlier centuries and therefore chose a large vase in dark blue porcelain with scroll handles mounted on a bronze base. Similarly, Théodore Chassériau's 1852 *Bouquet of Flowers in a Vase* (private collection), painted to decorate a salon, included a porcelain vase with a green background on a rococo ormolu mount.[9]

In the first half of the century, artists also favored eighteenth-century Delft faience (tin-glazed earthenware) vases with chinoiserie decoration in blue and white (or in the Imari style with its traditional colors of red, blue, and gold) for their flower paintings.[10] Contemporary ceramics made their first appearance around 1840 in French flower paintings, such as Jean-Baptiste Gallet's *Strawberry Flowers and Cherries* (1840, Musée de Brou, Bourg-en-Bresse) and Simon Saint-Jean's *Bouquet of Roses on a Marble Table* (1843, private collection). These pieces were very similar in style to the stoneware created by Jules-Claude Ziegler and imitated by many manufacturers. Between 1839 and 1843, Ziegler had rediscovered the sixteenth-century process of salt glazing stoneware. In his studio at Voisinlieu, near Beauvais, he employed the technique to make vases decorated with incised and relief motifs, influenced by the traditional ceramics of central Europe and the Near East.

The 1840s marked a turning point in French flower painting. Seeking to escape "the kind of cliché that seem[ed] to doom flower painters to paint the same vase with the same columns and the same fantastical draperies," Eugène Delacroix, and subsequently Gustave Courbet, painted "corners of nature such as we find in gardens."[11] The liberation of touch and color went hand in hand with open-air studies in which rustic pots, jardinieres in glazed earthenware, or stoneware vases were sometimes used.[12]

From Henri Fantin-Latour in the 1860s to Odilon Redon at the beginning of the twentieth century, artists were increasingly influenced by a burgeoning renaissance of flower painting. The rediscovery of Jean-Siméon Chardin (whose works entered the Louvre between 1850 and 1860), the new appreciation of Dutch painting, and the gradual collapse of the hierarchy of genres all favored a reevaluation of the floral still life. The genre moreover reflected the invasion of Second Empire interiors by bouquets and potted plants. The flower picture was not only a reliable source of income for painters but a valuable format for the study of colors and luminous effects—the preferred domains of the Impressionist painters. In their revival of flower painting, the Impressionists made new and different choices for the vases containing their bouquets. Beginning in the 1860s, the representation of commonplace ceramics, with a particular emphasis on simple faience and the rustic textures of stoneware and glazed earthenware, indicated the advent of modernity. Valuable ceramics such as Chinese porcelain or mounted Sèvres disappeared. The only porcelain receptacle for flowers I have been able to identify in an Impressionist painting is a white vase of rococo lines depicted in *Bouquet of Roses* by Camille Pissarro (cat. no. 33) around 1873. Such vases were often used in churches to decorate altars and were popular in bourgeois interiors until the mid-twentieth century; they were produced in large numbers between 1840 and 1850 by the porcelain manufacturers in Paris and Limoges. Impressionist painters were not collectors of ceramics. They depicted the ordinary containers that belonged in their rooms, thereby paving the way for the characteristic twentieth-century still lifes in which everyday pieces of little or no value came to predominate. Thus Pierre-Auguste Renoir

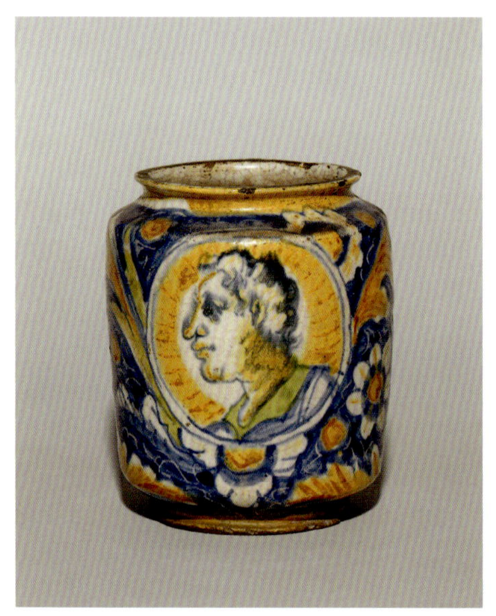

FIG. 32 Albarello, Sicily, early seventeenth century, faience, 6½ × 5½ in. (16.5 × 14 cm). Musée d'Orsay, Paris, OD 25

painted "two penny vases that [Aline, his wife] had bought in the market."[13] The ceramics preserved today at Claude Monet's house at Giverny exemplify the eclecticism of the objects that found a place in many painters' lives: Delft faience plates, Chinese export porcelain plates of the eighteenth century decorated in blue and white, many commonplace French faience pieces (mostly from Rouen), green-glazed earthenware jugs of the nineteenth century, three Chinese vases from the eighteenth and nineteenth centuries, and two inexpensive contemporary Japanese pieces.

Direct observation of nature combined with the development of gardening—most of the Impressionists were passionate gardeners—contributed to a notable rise in pictures of flowers in pots set in hothouses or gardens. Earthenware flowerpots, produced on an industrial scale from the middle of the nineteenth century by the major French ceramics centers, had by this period taken on the form that is recognizable today. Shaped like a truncated cone, they featured a projecting rim at the open end. The regularity of their lines distinguishes them from the pots represented in the still lifes of the eighteenth century. Around 1862 and 1863, Gustave Courbet made several paintings of flowers in terracotta pots half buried in the ground.[14] In 1864, Monet sent the Rouen Salon his new *Spring Flowers* (see fig. 22), a painting in which potted plants are combined with freshly cut flowers. That same year, in *Lily and Greenhouse Plants* (see fig. 23), Renoir depicted a greenhouse or florist's floor studded with wooden pot stands and earthenware pots. In the summer of 1866, in the greenhouse of the family estate at Méric, Frédéric Bazille executed *Study of Flowers*, also known as *Flowerpots* (see fig. 25), representing hydrangeas, azaleas, and several varieties of geraniums in pots. The lack of artifice in this piece, painted "without unpotting or any arrangement whatever,"[15] was severely criticized in the *Journal de Montpellier* of June 9, 1868, when the picture was exhibited at the Paris Salon. In the 1880s, Paul Cézanne painted several series of pots of flowers in the greenhouse at the Jas de Bouffan estate.[16] Gustave Caillebotte did the same in the 1890s in the greenhouse that he had built at Petit Gennevilliers.[17]

Italian majolica is the traditional ceramic found in the painter's studio and appears in several pictures from the second half of the century. Around 1870, Camille Pissarro painted a bouquet of chrysanthemums in a rather stubby *albarello*, or apothecary jar, decorated with yellow acanthus leaves on a blue background; the piece is typical of the production of Sicilian workshops of the seventeenth century. These watertight jars, cylindrical in body with narrower necks, were glazed inside and out. Made in great quantities by Italian faience producers from the sixteenth to the eighteenth century, they were later much appreciated by collectors. Pissarro's *albarello* is recycled as a flower vase (alas, this example has been identified as a "Chinese vase" in the artist's catalogue raisonné).[18] Another Sicilian *albarello* (fig. 32) that can be dated to the seventeenth century is

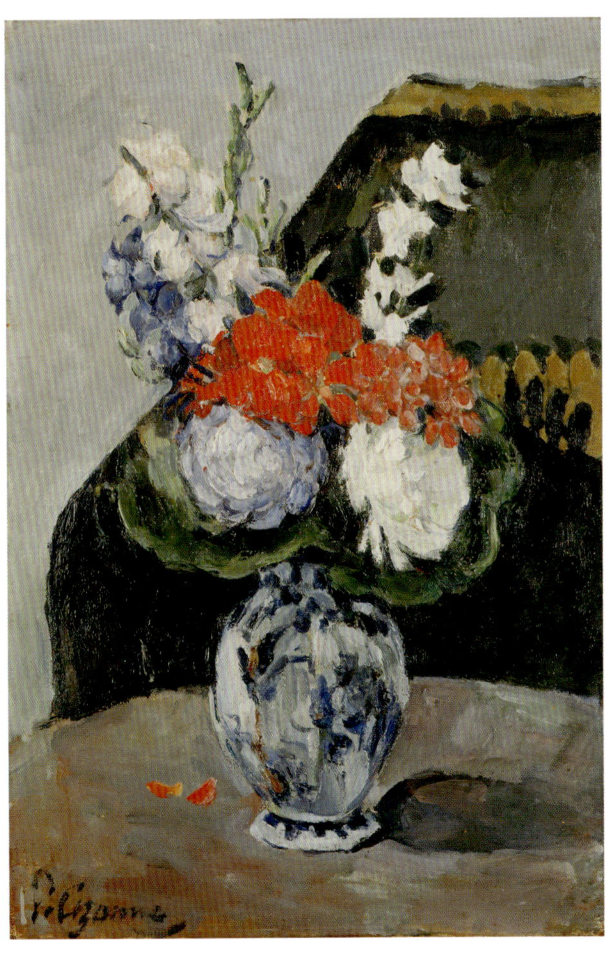

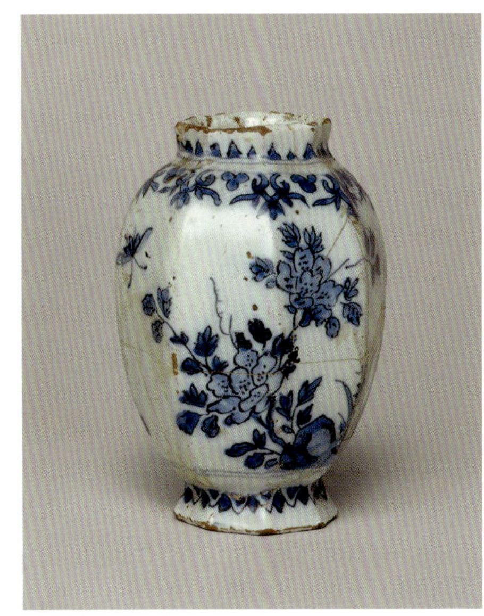

FIG. 33 Paul Cézanne, *Small Delft Vase with Flowers*, 1873, oil on canvas. Musée d'Orsay, Paris, RF 1951 33

FIG. 34 Vase, Delft, 1670–80, Samuel van Eenhoorn, manufacture *Grieksche A* (Greek A), faience, 4 5/16 × 3 1/8 in. (11 × 8 cm). Musée d'Orsay, Paris, OD 24

represented in a still life incorrectly titled *Urbino Vase* (private collection) that Cézanne painted between 1872 and 1873 in the Auvers-sur-Oise studio of arts advocate Dr. Paul-Ferdinand Gachet.[19] Renoir several times painted a bouquet of flowers in a contemporary Italian vase probably made in Sicily at Caltagirone, a faience center that in the nineteenth century returned to the forms of decoration that had first earned it renown.[20] The floral motifs in blue, green, and yellow and the medallion portrait that decorates its globular belly are inspired by seventeenth-century majolica. The same vase, which must have been part of the furnishings of the Renoir home, appears again in the 1892 *Two Young Women at the Piano* (Musée d'Orsay, Paris).

The faience vases produced in the many manufactories at Delft, southwest of Amsterdam, between the mid-seventeenth century and the end of the eighteenth century were also popular models for painters. Their decoration, inspired by Chinese porcelain and painted in blue *camaïeu* on white glaze, attracted artists no less than their dazzling surfaces, which were covered before firing with a lead glaze known as *kwaart*. In 1873, Cézanne painted two famous flowers pictures with Delft vases, *Small Delft Vase with Flowers* (fig. 33) and *Dahlias in a Large Delft Vase* (fig. 36). We know that they belonged to Gachet, as the doctor's son donated the two vases in 1951 to the Musée du Louvre. The little faceted vase is monogrammed with the initials *SVE* for the faience maker Samuel van Eenhoorn, who worked in the 1670s and 1680s in the famous Delft manufactory Greek A (De Grieksche A) (fig. 34).[21] A modest piece, just over four inches tall, it is irregular in form and reveals a number of firing accidents. Cézanne clearly appreciated the imperfect appearance of this small vase, detailing a long strip of rough

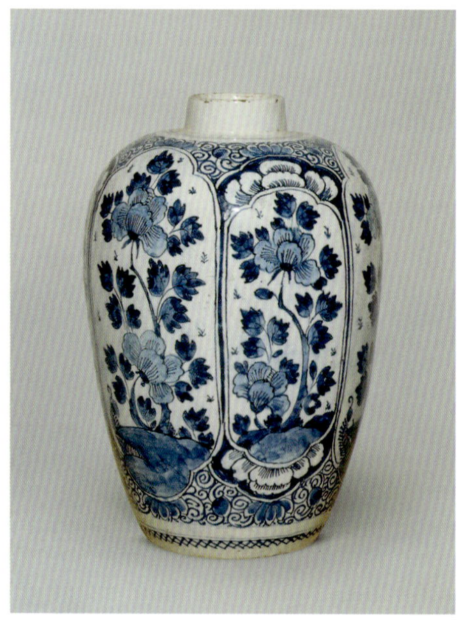

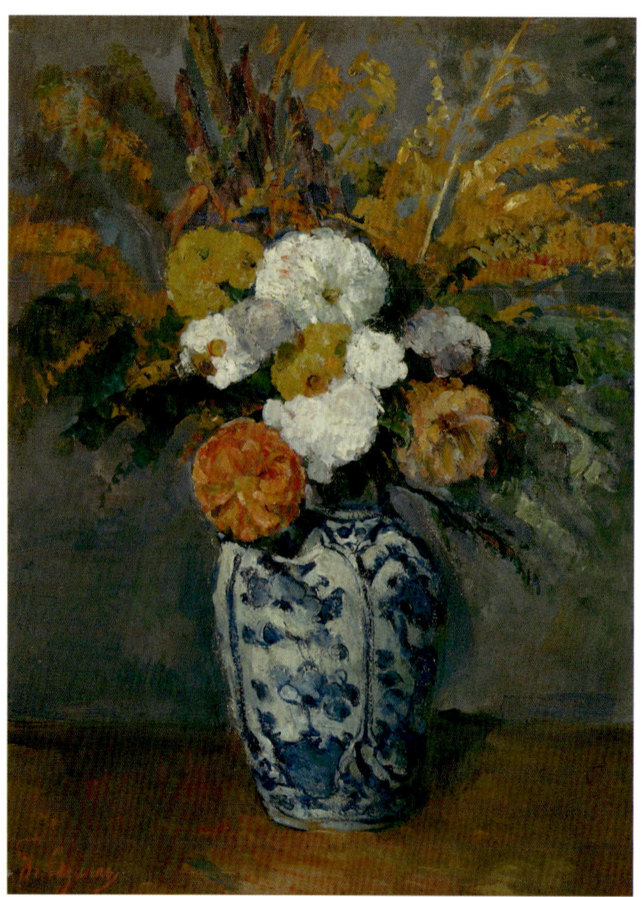

FIG. 35 Vase, Delft, early eighteenth century, faience, 9⅞ × 6½ in. (25 × 17 cm). Musée d'Orsay, Paris, OD 23

FIG. 36 Paul Cézanne, *Dahlias in a Large Delft Vase*, ca. 1873, oil on canvas. Musée d'Orsay, Paris, RF 1971

terracotta that was exposed from shrinking of the glaze. The second vase can be dated to the early eighteenth century (fig. 35).[22] Its swelling forms show a compartmented decoration of flowering shrubs painted in cobalt blue on the dazzling white of the stanniferous (tin-rich) glaze, which Cézanne reproduces faithfully. The bouquet has evidently been depicted larger than life; the narrow opening of the actual vase would not have been able to contain the foliage in the background. During the eighteenth century, Delft also produced many pieces with a polychrome decoration—in blue, red, purple-brown, green, and yellow—inspired by Chinese and Japanese porcelains. Renoir thus placed a polychrome Delft vase, datable to the middle of the eighteenth century and embellished with a Chinese scene in a cartouche, in his 1871 *Still Life with Bouquet* (Museum of Fine Arts, Houston) painted in homage to Édouard Manet. Around 1878, Camille Pissarro twice represented a baluster Delft vase with Imari decoration.[23] Eva Gonzalès's 1884 *Bouquet of Violets* (private collection) also features a Delft cornet vase with a green and red floral motif, combined with a Delft figure in "oriental" costume and a fan.

Many flower paintings of the second half of the nineteenth century picture vases and jugs made in the major French faience centers. The painters' interest in even the most commonplace of these pieces coincided with the French rediscovery of regional faience styles in the late 1850s. The number of collectors increased rapidly during the period, with some specializing in sets of faience from Nevers, Rouen, Lille, Marseilles, Moustiers, or Strasbourg. The large garden vases made in Nevers throughout the eighteenth century made it possible to paint great handfuls of flowers. These vases of standard Medici shape stood on heavy pedestals and were decorated

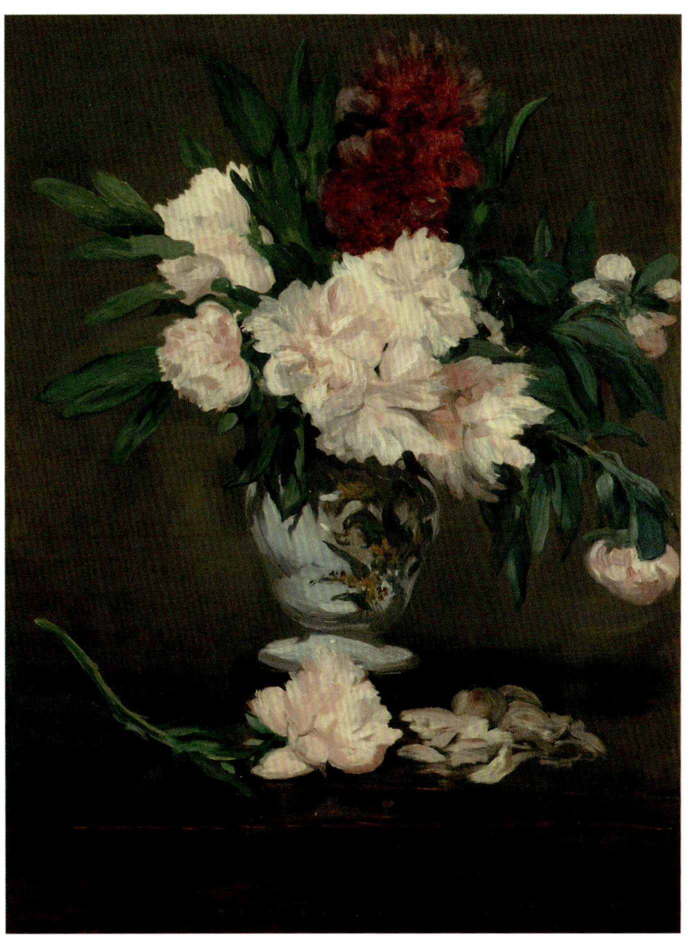

FIG. 37 Édouard Manet, *Vase of Peonies on a Pedestal*, 1864, oil on canvas. Musée d'Orsay, Paris, RF 1669

with *camaïeu* blues. It is likely one of these pieces, probably from the family estate in Méric and dating to the mid-eighteenth century, that Bazille represented in his *Flowers* of 1868 (frontispiece; cat. no. 22).[24] The ornamentation in foliated scrolls complements the carved rococo console on which it rests. The combination constitutes an ensemble of art objects typical of Second Empire bourgeois taste. A mid-to-late eighteenth-century water pot in Rouen faience decorated in high-fired polychrome can be identified in Berthe Morisot's *Flowers* (1880, private collection) and Pissarro's *Still Life with Apples and Pitcher* (1872, Metropolitan Museum of Art, New York). The refined interiors of the residence Morisot shared with her husband, Eugène Manet (brother of Édouard), were furnished with handsome Louis XV, Louis XVI, and Empire pieces, supplying her ("la demoiselle de Passy") with many examples of eighteenth-century French faience pieces.[25] Thus in 1876 she painted *Dahlias* (private collection) in an elegant low-fired faience bottle cooler that can be dated to 1760–80 and was probably made in Sceaux or some other eastern French studio.[26] The floral decoration of this piece—and the bright pink, green, and blue obtained by the new low-firing technique—fit beautifully with Morisot's palette of predominantly silvery white, blues, and pinks. Among his many flower paintings, Édouard Manet included only a single ceramic vase, a faience piece that appears in two 1864 paintings: *Peonies* (Metropolitan Museum of Art, New York) and *Vase of Peonies on a Pedestal* (fig. 37). The form of this baluster vase on a pedestal with its pronounced shoulder is very like that of the *pots pourris* with lids produced in Marseilles between 1754 and 1770 by the manufactory of Gaspard Robert.[27] Covered with a thick, milky-white glaze, clearly visible in Manet's paintings, this vase is decorated with yellow flowers and long green leaves. Its undulating line, particularly noticeable around the belly of the vessel, matches the movement of the peonies. In these pictures, the vase does not sit directly on the table but is rather artfully displayed on a wooden pedestal or a red lacquer tray, a clear indication that Manet valued this centennial faience object.[28] While in Pont-Aven in 1886, Paul Gauguin made a series of flower pictures incorporating a Quimper faience piece, a vase on a footed base with a handle and a spout made in the first half of the nineteenth century as a feeding bottle for babies.[29]

The rugged texture of stoneware containers and their glazes came to be appreciated by painters during the second half of the century when they were seeking new accessories. Unlike their predecessors, who painted sixteenth- and seventeenth-century German stoneware produced in the Rhine Valley, they turned to contemporary French stoneware, which held a familiar place in their domestic interiors.[30] Stoneware has been made in Europe since the Middle Ages. It is composed of clay with a high silica content, which forms a very dense texture that becomes wholly impermeable after firing at temperatures of around 1,250° C (2,282° F). Popular and utilitarian pieces, often found in the kitchen and used for storing food, became objects of interest for the Impressionist painters, who recycled them as flower vases. In 1866, for example, Renoir painted a bouquet of wildflowers in a stocky, brown stoneware jug, probably made in the central French region of Berry during the same period.[31] This new appreciation of stoneware was linked to the reevaluation of the material by French ceramicists who, inspired by Japanese craftsmen, seized upon this "wild earth" to renew their own production. Beginning in the first third of the eighteenth century, Betschdorf in Alsace was renowned for its salt-glaze stoneware; the gray, shiny body of the stoneware was incised before firing with stylized floral and animal motifs and painted with cobalt blue. It reached a peak of popularity in the mid-nineteenth century and was distributed throughout France. While they were working together in 1869 at Bougival, Monet and Renoir painted the same Betschdorf storage pot in grayish clay, summarily decorated with two slender stripes of cobalt blue and a row of roses sketched out in large circles: *Still Life with Flowers and Fruit* (see fig. 21) and *Mixed Flowers in an Earthenware Pot* (cat. no. 24), respectively.[32] These heavy, waterproof pots with handles were primarily used to store cooking fat, rillettes, pâtés, and eggs. Renoir seems to have particularly liked the salt-glaze texture; he pictured a Betschdorf vase in his *Gladioli* (ca. 1874, private collection, deposited with the National Gallery, London) and a pitcher in *Flowers in a Vase* (1881, Philadelphia Museum of Art). The same tubby gray stoneware pitcher (fig. 38), also from Betschdorf, appears several times in the paintings of Pissarro and Cézanne made around 1873: Pissarro's *Bouquet of Pink Peonies* (fig. 39) and Cézanne's *Two Vases of Flowers* (private collection) and *Bouquet of Yellow Dahlias* (Musée d'Orsay, Paris). The jug, decorated with

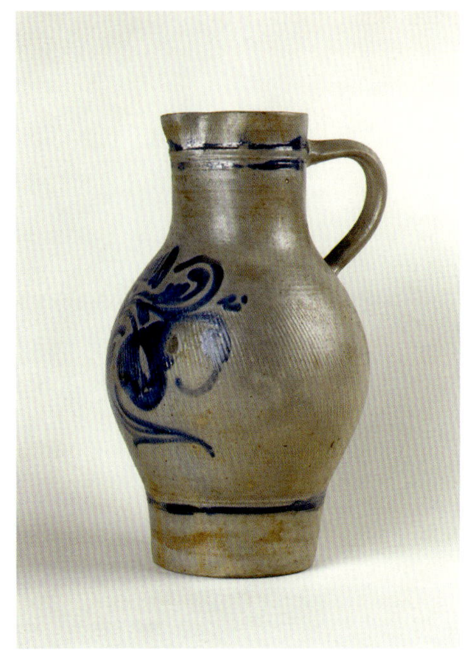

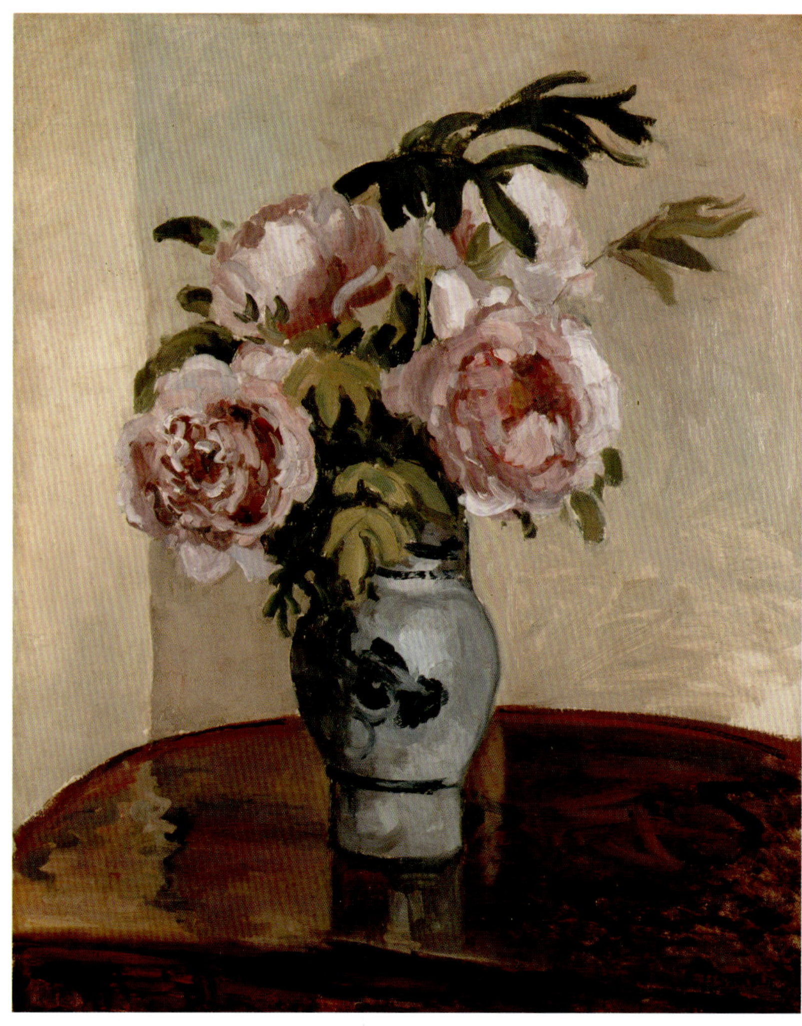

FIG. 38 Pitcher, Alsace, nineteenth century, attributed to Betschdorf, stoneware, 8½ × 5¾ in. (21.5 × 14.5 cm). Musée d'Orsay, Paris, OD 27

FIG. 39 Camille Pissarro, *Bouquet of Pink Peonies*, 1873, oil on canvas. Ashmolean Museum, University of Oxford

slender blue bands and a floral branch on its curved body, now forms part of the collection of the Musée d'Orsay.[33] Finally, Redon painted numerous little stoneware pitchers whose attributions are difficult and around 1900 made a series of works with an oil jug in brown stoneware, probably from Berry or southeastern France.

Though glazed earthenware can be found in the still lifes of previous centuries, the Impressionists were the first to introduce the pieces into their paintings in any significant number and to recycle these rustic and domestic containers as vases. Glazed earthenware has been made in France since the Gallo-Roman era and is the simplest expression of worked clay. These terracotta forms, covered with a lead compound–based glaze that gives a brilliant surface, offer a limited range of colors: faded browns, ochers, blues, and greens, obtained respectively by oxides of manganese, iron, cobalt, and copper. Transcribing both the metallic reflections of light on the glaze and the texture of the unglazed earthenware underlying it was an exercise that painters appreciated. Many fat-bellied pitchers in green-glazed earthenware were recycled as vases and contain large bouquets of flowers in the canvases of Renoir and Pissarro, such as the latter's *Bouquet of Flowers* (cat. no. 56).[34] Though made throughout France at one time, glazed earthenware was a specialty of ceramics centers in the Ardèche, Drôme, Languedoc, and southeastern France by the nineteenth century;[35] they produced kitchen utensils and food-storage containers in large numbers. Both Paul Cézanne and Vincent van Gogh lived for periods in

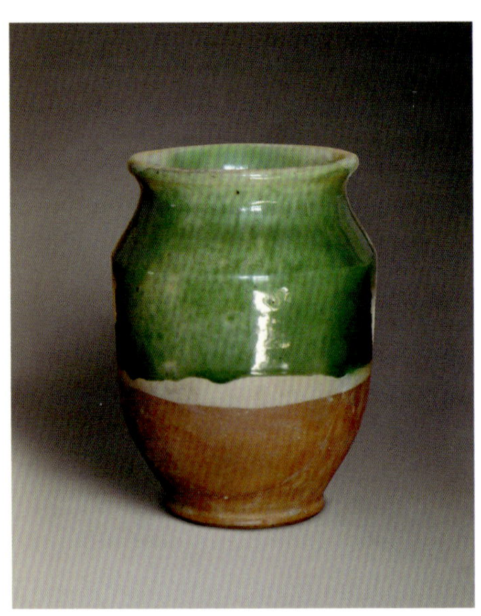

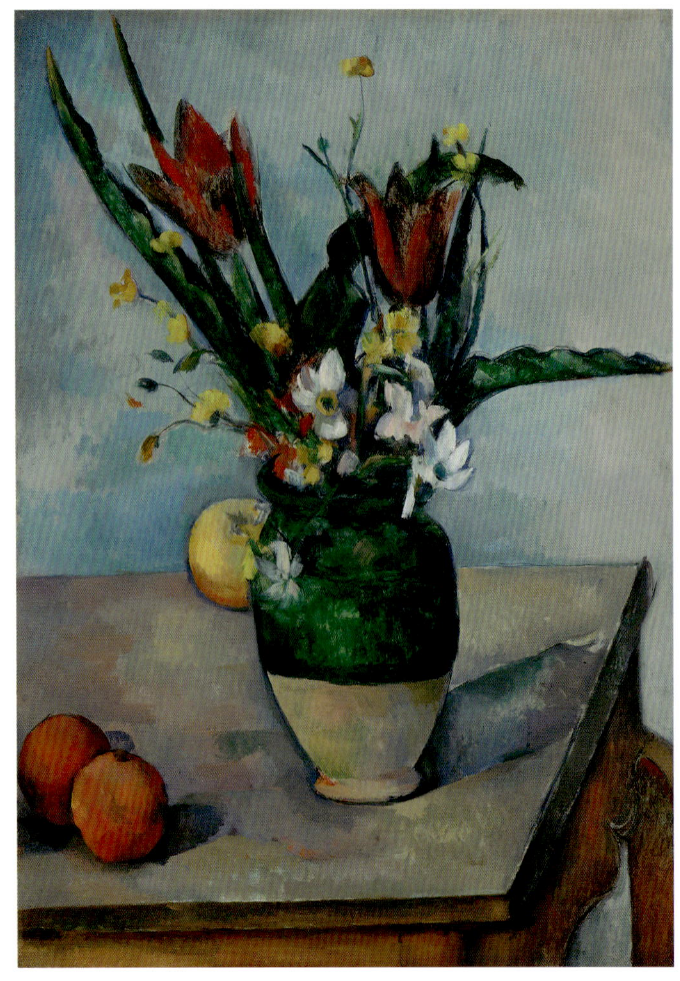

FIG. 40 Olive Pot, southeastern France, nineteenth century, glazed earthenware, 6 5/16 × 4 3/16 in. (16 × 10.5 cm). Atelier des Lauves, Aix-en-Provence

FIG. 41 Paul Cézanne, *The Vase of Tulips*, ca. 1890, oil on canvas. Mr. and Mrs. Lewis Larned Coburn Memorial Collection, Art Institute of Chicago, 1933.423

southeastern France, and glazed earthenware pots therefore feature particularly frequently in their flower paintings. Beginning in the early 1880s, Cézanne represented bouquets of wildflowers in rustic olive pots (fig. 40) and in *The Vase of Tulips* (fig. 41) did the same with garden flowers.[36] Entirely glazed on the inside to retain the juice or oil of the olives, these wide-neck, ovoid jars have only partly glazed exteriors for reasons of economy. The color of the earthenware varies from pinkish beige to red-brown, and the varying runs of glaze combined with a rugged surface supplied much-appreciated textural motifs for the painters. These utilitarian vessels, bought at local markets, are still found in the Lauves studio in Aix-en-Provence, where Cézanne lived from 1901 until his death in 1906.[37] In 1886, van Gogh painted several bouquets arranged in a broad green-glazed earthenware pot, undoubtedly a fat-storage vessel reused as a vase, including *Bowl with Zinnias and Other Flowers* (cat. no. 49).[38] His compositions were inspired by Monet's *Bouquet of Mallows* (1880, Courtauld Gallery, London) and *Chrysanthemums* (1882, Metropolitan Museum of Art, New York), depicting pots of the same proportions. The emblematic series *Sunflowers*, painted in 1888, also features standard olive pots with exteriors half-glazed in yellow or green, surfaces and colors that reinforce the rusticity and tortuous aspect of the sunflower. Fat-bellied Provençal pots with two handles, glazed exclusively on the inside, also provide broad, solid containers for great handfuls of roses (*Roses*, 1890, National Gallery of Art, Washington, D.C.) or irises (*Irises*, 1890, Van Gogh Museum, Amsterdam) painted by van Gogh.

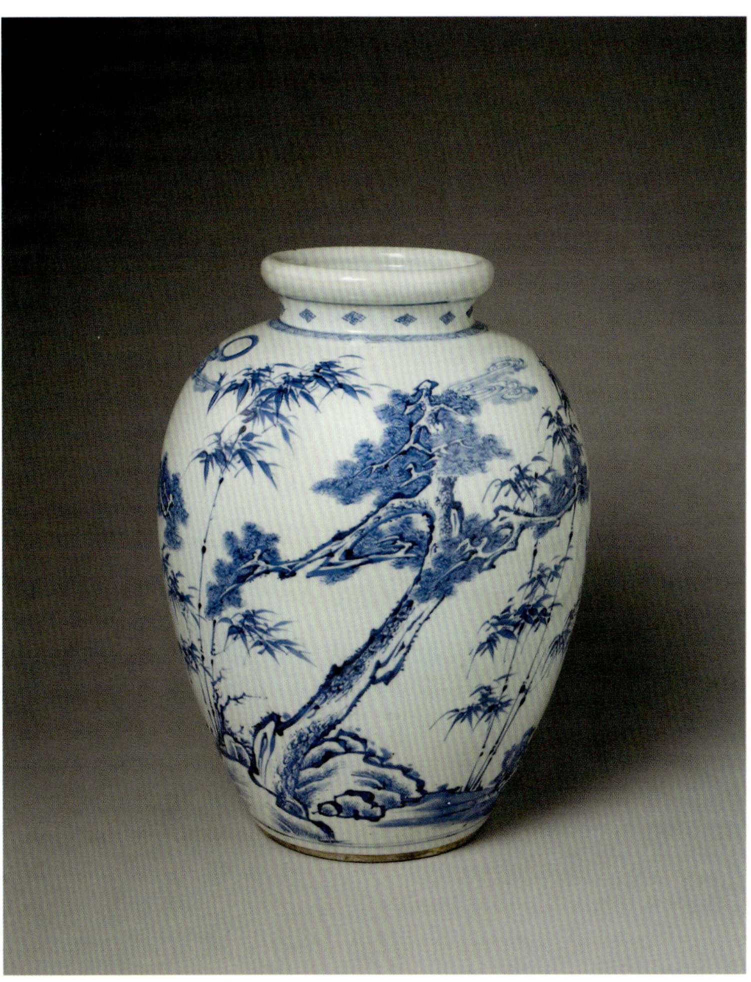

FIG. 42 Vase, China, late eighteenth century, porcelain, 13¼ × 10³⁄₁₆ in. (33.6 × 25.8 cm). Cité de la Céramique, Sèvres, MNC 5923

Despite the French discovery of the art and aesthetics of Japan, which began in the 1860s, Japanese vessels rarely appear in flower paintings. Chinese vases remained more common, though the painters were perhaps unable to identify them as such. The traditional Chinese porcelain of the eighteenth century, decorated in blue and white and widely distributed throughout Europe, was still greatly appreciated. Thus Henri Fantin-Latour placed a little Chinese cornet vase decorated with rocks and flowering shrubs in the center of his *The Engagement Still Life* in 1869 (cat. no. 25). A large egg-shaped vase of Chinese porcelain from the eighteenth century, decorated with knotty shrubs and bamboos painted in blue on a white glaze (fig. 42), contains the large *Spring Bouquet* (see fig. 24) painted by Renoir in 1866. Polychrome Chinese porcelain in the most fantastical forms, produced during the nineteenth century for export to the West, provided new models. In 1878, Monet placed his *Gladioli, Lilies and Daisies* (private collection) in a tall rouleau ("roll") vase mounted on three lions and adorned with elephant-head handles; it is decorated with the traditional Chinese motif of "children at play" painted in the five high-fired colors.[39] Flambé Chinese porcelain with marbled decoration also inspired painters of the era. Renoir's *Bouquet in a Vase* of 1878 (cat. no. 38) is one example. Here, the porcelain vase with a red background is studded with yellow medallions and decorated with a relief dragon. A large porcelain bottle vase made in China in the nineteenth century, its turquoise background sprayed with cobalt blue, still stands enthroned on the mantelpiece of the Monet house at Giverny. It appears in the 1882 *Vase of Chrysanthemums* (private collection) and contains sunflowers in *Portrait of Suzanne with Sunflowers* (1899, private collection). Caillebotte in his turn painted the vessel for *Chrysanthemums in a Vase* (1893, private collection) of a baluster shape decorated in blue and white. This vase incorporates two brown bands of biscuit incised with a Greek key pattern in imitation of bronze. Redon at least twice represented a Chinese vase of similar form and decoration with a cream glaze and bands of brown biscuit.[40]

Although the exposure to Japanese wares, particularly the numerous examples at the Exposition Universelle of 1867, constituted a veritable aesthetic shock for painters,[41] references to Japanese ceramics were rare. French painters collected Japanese prints, which they purchased at large department stores such as Printemps or in the many smaller shops selling Chinese and Japanese objects that proliferated in Paris during the 1860s, but they did not collect ceramics.[42] In Monet's house at Giverny, the fascination with Japan found its only ceramic expression in two pieces of limited value—a little square stoneware vase and a fan-shaped flower holder—alongside the *Japon* dinner service made in 1876 of fine blue-and-white faience by the French Creil and Montereau manufactory. Japanese ceramics appeared rather late in flower paintings. In 1888, the Nabi painter Pierre Bonnard, known as the *nabi japonard*, took as his model for *Pot of Flowers* (private collection) a rouleau vase with celadon background and polychrome *pâte-sur-pâte* (paste-on-paste) decoration. The little faceted vase of contemporary Japanese stoneware[43] (fig. 43) in van Gogh's 1890 *Roses and Anemones* (fig. 44) forms part of the collection of the Musée d'Orsay, as does the painting. On a green-tinted cream background, the vase displays a polychrome overglaze decoration representing plum flowers and a bird. Van Gogh showed limited interest in the motif and the texture of its thick glaze, focusing instead on the stylization of its volume and playing with the perspective of its facets. From about 1905 to 1908, Redon several times represented a contemporary piece, a stoneware *Vase with Japanese Warrior* illustrating the combat of a samurai and a demon;[44] the inspiration for this decoration was the Noh play by Kanze Nobumitsu, written around 1420.[45]

In the second half of the nineteenth century, a gradual erosion of the boundaries between fine arts and decorative arts led many painters to attempt making or decorating ceramics at the Sèvres manufactory or in independent studios like those of Théodore Deck, Édouard Dammouse, or Ernest Chaplet. Though painters frequented the ceramicists, and artists no longer limited themselves to a single material, the territories remained unchanged in terms of motifs, and these new ceramic works by painters are very rarely represented in their pictures. Thus the vase with gilt rosettes on a black background by Laurent Bouvier is almost unique as an example of French contemporary ceramics appearing in the "New Painting."[46]
It served as a model for two paintings in 1870: Fantin's *A Studio at Les Batignolles*[47] (Musée d'Orsay, Paris) and Bazille's *African Woman with Peonies*

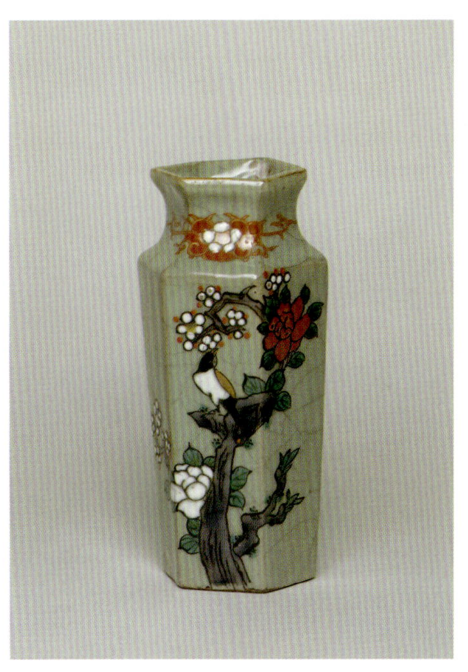

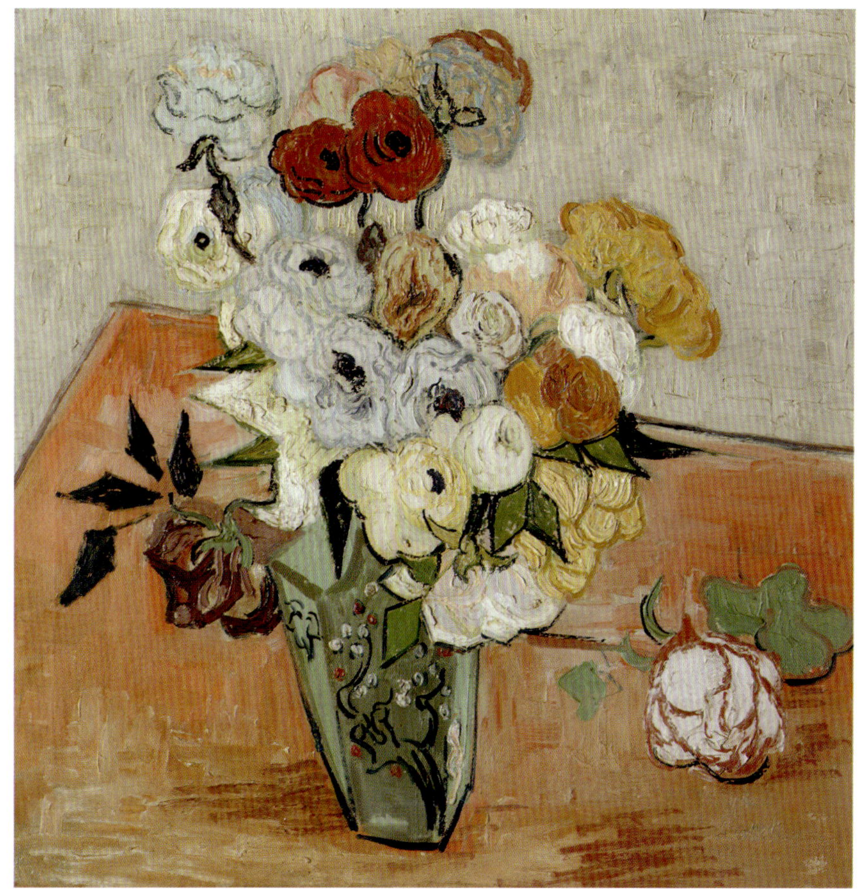

FIG. 43 Vase, Japan, 1850–1900, stoneware, 10¼ × 3½ in. (28.5 × 9 cm). Musée d'Orsay, Paris, OD 37

FIG. 44 Vincent van Gogh, *Roses and Anemones*, 1890, oil on canvas. Musée d'Orsay, Paris, RF 1954 12

(fig. 30; cat. no. 23). Bouvier was a friend of Fantin, Edgar Degas, Félix Bracquemond, and Manet and decorated his first ceramics in the summer of 1869 when living in Saint-Marcellin near two potters, Célestin Méary and Régis Ginet, who fired his pieces. His works were inspired by Persian and Japanese ceramics and enjoyed great success in Paris in the autumn of 1869 during the exhibition of the Union centrale des Beaux-Arts appliqués à l'Industrie (Central Union of Fine Arts Applied to Industry). In *African Woman with Peonies*, Bouvier's boule vase of glazed earthenware, ornamented with passages of layered slips incised with lozenges, is placed in the foreground.[48] The large balls of gilt flowers that decorate it echo both the peonies that it contains and those scattered on the wooden table. The ceramics that are today called Impressionist—avant-garde *barbotines* produced under the direction of Félix Bracquemond in the Haviland pottery at Auteuil between 1876 and 1881—do not appear in pictures, though some were exhibited in Impressionist shows and were therefore known to the painters.[49] Porcelain from the Sèvres manufactory, which experienced a renaissance under the artistic direction of Albert Carrier-Belleuse between 1875 and 1887, is similarly absent. It is very difficult to find a painting featuring a piece by one of the independent potters, such as Ernest Chaplet, Albert-Louis Dammouse, Adrien-Pierre Dalpayrat, and Auguste Delaherche, who were working to renew forms and techniques in the last third of the century.[50] One such canvas is Cézanne's *Portrait of Gustave Geffroy* (Musée d'Orsay, Paris), painted in his Belleville studio between 1895 and 1896. It introduces not only a Rodin plaster but a plump little vase in flambé porcelain that is closely akin to the pieces made by Chaplet between 1888 and 1895 in his Choisy-le-Roi studio. On a number of occasions, Gauguin placed his own ceramics in his paintings. In his 1889 *Still Life with Japanese Print* (Museum of Contemporary Art, Teheran), a stoneware self-portrait in the form of a beer mug is transformed into a vase of flowers.[51] An admirer of Gauguin's ceramics and the flambé stoneware by Delaherche, Redon depicted vases decorated by his Russian friend Marie Botkin in many of his flower pictures and pastels.[52] Botkin's work has not yet been much studied; the abstract decoration is formed by glaze runs in bright colors of blue, green, and ocher and is not unlike the experimental pieces by the contemporary Dutch potter T. C. A. Colenbrander. This attracted Redon, who harmonized Botkin's colors with the pyrotechnics of his own bouquets, as in the 1912 pastel *Bouquet of Wildflowers in a Long-Necked Vase* (Musée d'Orsay, Paris).

The ceramic vases represented in floral still lifes thus evolved over the course of the nineteenth century alongside the history of taste and the containers collected by painters. The break with precedent was quite clear beginning in the first third of the century, as these artists began to show a preference for domestic, rustic containers over precious porcelain vases. These common vessels were appreciated by artists especially for the surface texture of their clay and glazes. Contrary to expectation, the fascination with Japan did not translate into an invasion of Japanese ceramics in paintings, and even though avant-garde painters and ceramicists worked together, contemporary ceramics remained a marginal subject in painting. Still-life artists instead chose their ceramic models from examples close at hand, often in their own homes: terracotta pots, common glazed earthenware, popular modern stoneware, and inexpensive Dutch and French regional faience, all of which were characteristic of mid-nineteenth-century bourgeois interiors. Around 1910 to 1930 Pierre Bonnard, for instance, frequently represented the same pitcher, probably in faience, with a cream ground decorated with cherries (cat. nos. 63 and 64). This pitcher was an ordinary ceramic and certainly came from his own home. Redon and Matisse also expanded the field of inspiration. On several occasions Redon depicted an "Etruscan" vase (cat. no. 61), actually a modern ceramic imitating antique Greek red-figure vase and sold to tourists, while Matisse introduced into his paintings vases brought back from his travels in North Africa, simple wares from the bazaar rather than precious ceramics.[53] For the floral still-life painter, modernity brought with it an interest in rustic household containers—whether Betschdorf oil pots reused as vases, olive pots in glazed terracotta, or simple domestic objects from trips afield.

Translated from the French by Chris Miller

NOTES

I should particularly like to thank Eric Moinet, Director of the Département du Patrimoine et des Collections de Sèvres-Cité de la Céramique, for his invaluable aid in identifying the many pieces cited. I should also like to thank Stéphanie Brouillet, Céline Paul, Virginie Desrante, Laurence Tilliard, Florence Slitine, Cécile Dupont-Logié, Sylvie Patry, Sylvie Patin, Claudette Lindsey, Geneviève Lacambre, Véronique Kientzy, Elsa Badie-Modiri, Louis van Tilborgh, Juliet Bareau, Asher Miller, Emilie Vanhaesebroucke, Olivier Omnès, Véronique Ayroles, Régine de Plinval de Guillebon, Sébastien Quéquet, Virginie Perdrisot, and Pierre Bonnaure.

1. Diderot 1798, 13:464.
2. I should nevertheless cite van Tilborgh 2008, in relation to the nineteenth century, and Rochebrune, an invaluable study, in relation to the eighteenth century. To my knowledge, no treatise of painting published in the nineteenth century gives any recommendations concerning the vases to be used in flower pictures.
3. Wildenstein, A. 1996. Volume 3 of this Redon catalogue raisonné is organized according to vague typologies of vase forms and colors: "pitchers and little vases of flowers," "stoneware vase," "vase with handles," "decorated vases," etc.
4. Antoine Berjon, *Flowers in an Alabaster Vase* (1813, Musée des Beaux-Arts, Lyon) and *Bouquet of Lilies and Roses in a Basket on a Chiffonier* (cat. no. 13); Simon Saint-Jean, *Flowers in a Hat* (cat. no. 14); Pierre-Adrien Chabal-Dussergey, *Concordia* (cat. no. 17).
5. Louis Tessier, *Flowers in a Chantilly Vase* (cat. no. 1).
6. It could be a Chinese jardiniere transformed into a vase and mounted.
7. Faré and Faré 1976, 239.
8. See, for example, Edouard Dubufe, *Portrait of Madame F . . .* (1850–51, Musée d'Orsay, Paris).
9. Oil on panel, Château de Paray-le-Fresil, Allier.
10. Augustin-Alexandre Thierriat, *Flowers in a Vase from Japan* [*sic*] (1854, Musée des Beaux-Arts de Lyon); Henriette de Vesvres, *Flowers and Grapes on a Marble Table*, 1837 (reproduced in Hardouin-Fugier and Grafe 1992, 99); and Andrée-Emma-Félicité Desportes de la Fosse, *Flowers in a Faience Vase*, 1838 (reproduced in Hardouin-Fugier 1992, 83).
11. Delacroix 1936, 2:372. See letter to Constant Dutilleux, February 6, 1849.
12. Eugène Delacroix, *Flower Still Life* (1843, Belvedere, Vienna); *Two Vases of Flowers* (ca. 1848–49, Kunsthalle, Bremen); Gustave Courbet, *Bouquet of Asters* (1859, Kunstmuseum, Basel) with a glazed earthenware pitcher. Only one stoneware vase is known in Delacroix's painted oeuvre, in *Bouquet of Flowers in a Stoneware Vase* (1848–49, Guezireh Museum, Cairo).
13. Renoir, quoted in Patry 2009, 45.
14. Fernier 1978, 178, 206 and nos. 301, 303, 360, 363.
15. J. Ixe, quoted in Le Foll 1997, 177.
16. For example, *Begonias* (ca. 1879–80, private collection) and *Pots of Flowers* (ca. 1885, Musée d'Orsay, Paris), a crayon, gouache, and watercolor on paper.
17. See, in particular, *Orchids in the Petit Gennevilliers Hothouse* (1893, private collection).
18. Pissarro and Snollaerts 2005, 2:153.
19. The jar was donated by Dr. Gachet's son to the Musée du Louvre in 1951 and is now in the collection of the Musée d'Orsay (OD 25). This *albarello* also appears in *Italian Faience* (1872–73, private collection).
20. *Flowers in a Vase* (1878, former Durand-Ruel Collecton, sale brochure, Paris, Drouot-Montaigne, "Importants dessins et tableaux impressionnistes et modernes," November 27, 1997, lot no. 36); *Vase of Flowers* (1881, sale brochure, Christie's, London, "Impressionist and Modern Art Evening Sale," June 24, 2008, lot no. 52); *Still Life, Flowers and Fruit* (1889, sale brochure, Sotheby's, London, "Impressionist and Modern Art Evening Sale," June 24, 2009, lot no. 13), *Flowers and Fruit* (ca. 1889, London, Richard Green Galleries).

21. Musée d'Orsay, Paris (OD 24). This vase is also represented in *Geraniums and Larkspur in a Little Delft Vase* (1873, private collection) and *Geraniums and Coreopsis* (former Bernheim de Villers Collection).

22. Musée d'Orsay, Paris (OD 23).

23. *Bouquet of Chrysanthemums* (ca. 1878, sale brochure, Christie's, New York, November 4, 2003, lot no. 11); and *Bouquet of Flowers: Peonies and Syringas* (ca. 1877–78, formerly Sara Lee Corporation Collection, Chicago).

24. It has also been suggested that the vase might be a Montpellier product because of the painted foliage decoration on the base. However, this kind of garden vase does not feature in the corpus of Montpellier productions.

25. Blanche 1921, 83.

26. The form of this cooler is also very close to those produced at the Sèvres manufacture between 1750 and 1760, and this remains a possible attribution. See also Rathbone and Shakelford 2001, 110; despite the statement here, it is certainly not a Chinese vase.

27. This characterful form seems to derive from a long Marseilles tradition inherited from apothecary pots produced by the studio in Saint-Jean-du-Désert in the last third of the eighteenth century.

28. This vase was still in the home of Suzanne Manet around 1902. It is mentioned in a late addition to the inventory of the studio made in 1883 by Léon Leenhoff (held in the Bibliothèque nationale de France). My thanks go to Juliet Bareau for this information.

29. This faience piece reappears in *White Tablecloth (Pension Gloanec)* (1886, private collection); *Vase of Nasturtiums* (1886, Ottawa, National Gallery of Canada); *Summer Bouquet and Clogs* (1886, whereabouts unknown); *Pots and Bouquets* (1886, private collection). See Wildenstein 2002, W217–19, W239.

30. The only instances of seventeenth-century Rhenish (Westerwald, Siegburg, or Raeren) stoneware that I have been able to identify appear in Cézanne's *Still Life with Stoneware Pot* (1873, Musée Angladon-Dubrujeaud, Avignon) and Redon's *Bouquet of Flowers in a Blue Vase* (n.d., private collection, Japan) in Wildenstein 1996, W1512. The beer pitcher depicted in Cézanne's painting was donated to the Musée du Louvre in 1951 by Dr. Gachet's son and is held today in the Musée d'Orsay.

31. *Flowers in a Vase* (1866, National Gallery of Art, Washington, D.C.).

32. Another version with the same pot is cited in Dauberville and Dauberville 2007, vol. 1, under the title *Large Bouquet of Wildflowers* (ca. 1870, private collection).

33. Donated by Dr. Gachet's son to the Louvre in 1951. Musée d'Orsay, Paris (OD 27).

34. For example, Renoir, *Bouquet of Chrysanthemums* (ca. 1881, Musée des Beaux-Arts de Rouen), and in particular, Monet, *Bouquet of Flowers* (ca. 1898, Fine Arts Museums of San Francisco).

35. Villages specializing in pottery are too numerous to list. Among the most famous are Meynes, Tarnac, Anduze, and Castelnaudary in Languedoc, and Marseilles, Vallauris, Aubagne, and Fréjus in Provence.

36. See also *Still Life with Flowers in an Olive Jar* (ca. 1880, Philadelphia Museum of Art).

37. It is difficult to know whether the glazed earthenware pots in the Lauves studio are original, were bought by Marcel Provence (who reorganized it after Cézanne's death), or placed there during the restoration of 1951. They are, in any case, very similar to those painted by Cézanne.

38. See also: *Roses and Peonies* (Kröller-Müller Museum, Otterlo); and *Vase with Roses and Other Flowers* (Städtische Kunsthalle, Mannheim).

39. Only five colors—blue, yellow, green, red, and brown-purple—can be used in high-fired faience, as the other colors would not resist the high temperature of the kiln.

40. Two pastels: *Bouquet with Anemones and Lilac* (n.d., Albright-Knox Art Gallery, Buffalo, W1491); *Vase of Flowers* (n.d., whereabouts unknown, W1492). See Wildenstein 1996.

41. "Suddenly I discovered some marvellous pots hidden away in a corner, their forms so simple as to be very touching; they had broad strokes of copper-oxide on them, the green that reminds you of waves—in short

porcelain treated with respect, like faience: thick porcelain that you can mess about with and not have to worry about breaking." Renoir, quoted in Patry 2012, 63.

42. Whistler, however, did collect; see Patry 2011, 203. Maison Desoye et la Porte chinoise were pioneers among the shops. See Réunion des musées 1988, 72–82; and Patry 2011, 198.

43. This picture was given to Dr. Gachet by Theo Van Gogh on Vincent's death. The vase was donated to the Musée du Louvre by Dr. Gachet's son, Paul-Louis Gachet, in 1951 and is held at the Musée d'Orsay (OD 37).

44. Oil on canvas (n.d., Pola Collection, Japan) and two pastels of *Vase with Japanese Warrior* (ca. 1905–8, private collections). See Wildenstein 1996, W1525, 1523–24.

45. The title of the piece appears in Japanese on the belly. I should like to thank Shigeru Nakano for translating the inscription and identifying the play.

46. The whereabouts of this vase are, alas, unknown. On Laurent Bouvier, see Moreau-Nélaton 1901, 10:166–72.

47. Fantin-Latour to Edwards, quoted in Jullien 1909, 75, mentions the presence in his painting of a "glazed pot by Bouvier, a painter who makes these objects with excellent taste." On the vase in this painting, see, in particular, Druick and Hoog 1982, 206–7, and Weisberg 1977, 206–15.

48. Its decoration is inspired less by Japanese ceramics and more by the hard-paste porcelain with black overglaze ornamented with golden flowers produced under the reign of Kangxi (1662–1723), some examples of which are in the Sèvres collection (MNC401.2 and 8655).

49. Thus Marie Bracquemond exhibited a "Faience plate (matt-painted)" at the fourth Impressionist exhibition (1879); it was no. 1 in the catalogue.

50. A vase by Delaherche in the collection of the Musée des Arts décoratifs (inv. 14077) has been identified in a flower painting by Albert Aublet (1851–1938), *Bouquet of Peonies* (sale, April 21, 1999, étude Néret-Minet Tessier et Sarrou). My thanks to Véronique Ayroles for this information.

51. In the collection of the Kunstindustrimuseet, Copenhagen.

52. Rapetti et al. 2011, 356. Wildenstein suggests that they may have met through the Moscovite collector, Sergeĭ Ivanovich Shchukin. See also the pastel *Portrait of Marie Botkin* (ca. 1906–7, Musée d'Orsay, Paris). Two vases attributed to Marie Botkin appear in Redon's work: a large vase and a long-neck one. See Wildenstein 1996, W1526–36, W1537–42.

53. *Still Life with Daffodils* (1907, Folkwang Museum, Essen); and *Still Life with "The Dance"* (1909, Hermitage Museum, St. Petersburg).

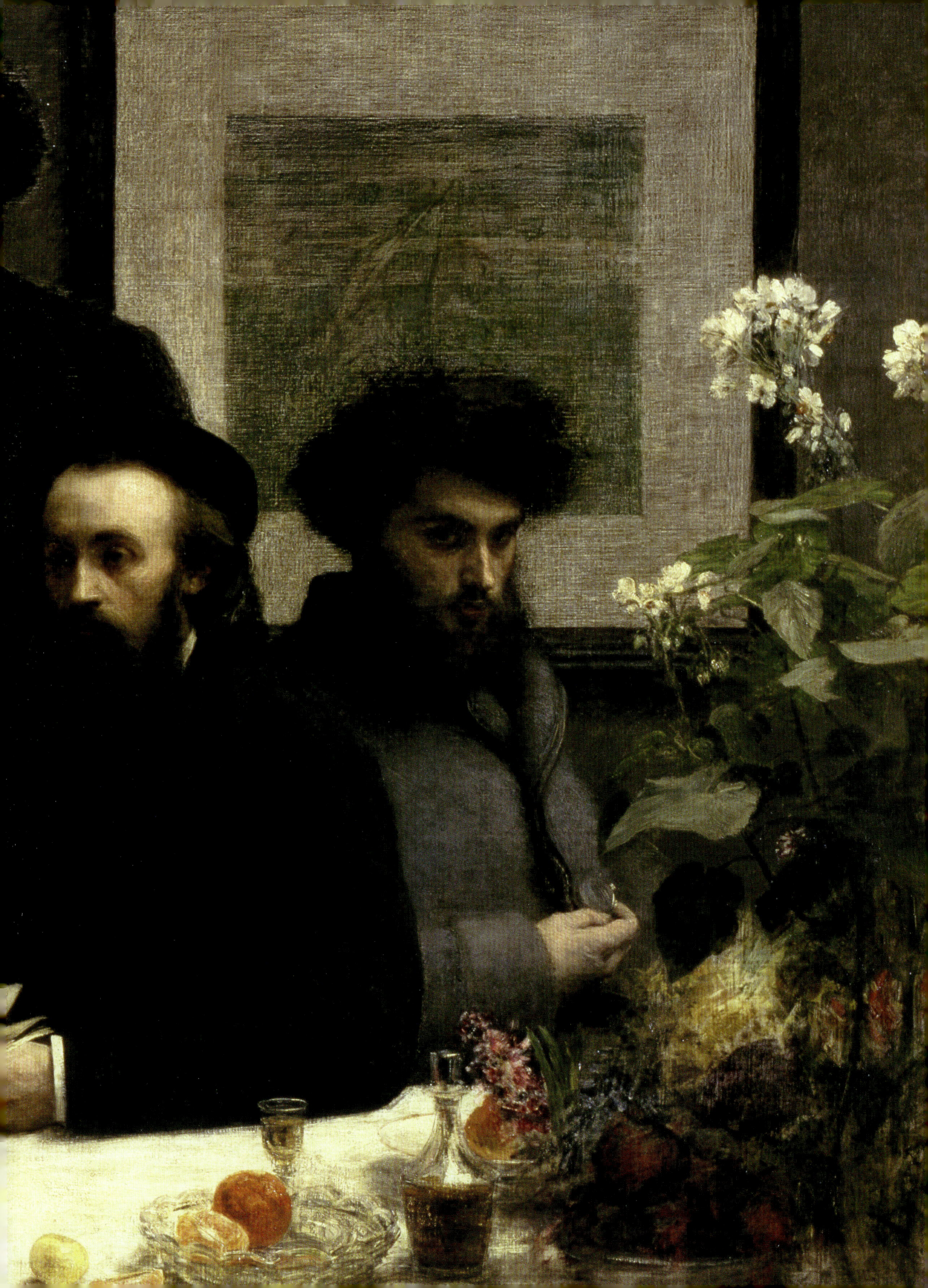

Flowers in Nineteenth-Century French Poetry: A Time to Bloom, a Time to Die

Olivier Meslay

> *Strange evenings when flowers have a soul*
> —Albert Samain

WHEN CONSIDERING THE SIGNIFICANCE OF FLOWERS AND BOUQUETS IN nineteenth-century French painting, it seems strange, if not remiss, to view the floral still life as an independent form of artistic expression having nothing to do with the use of flowers in daily life, or with other aspects of art and culture. The essays in this catalogue examine the transformation of floral painting as it relates to other changes going on in science, French life, culture, and industry during the same period. Looking at flowers in artistic contexts other than painting provides depth of field to this overview.

There is one form of artistic expression whose context and evolution have strong parallels to those of painting, and that is poetry. Both art forms exhibit the same gratuitousness, detachment from the material world, sense of beauty, and emotional appeal, and both share the tradition of being offered as gifts. Despite these strong similarities, however, the use of flowers and bouquets in early nineteenth-century French poetry followed a course completely different than that in the pictorial world. By the early twentieth century, the result of this transformation was as revolutionary as any event in painting and turned out to be so radical that it forever changed the way flowers were used in poetry.

For more than four centuries before that, French poetry offered readers innumerable bouquets of flowers. Beginning with Pierre de Ronsard (1524–1585), floral poetry often combined the ideas of votive offering and beauty with variations on the profane or sacred symbolism of flowers. This sometimes amounted to amorous, if not sexual, blackmail. While the celebrated "Mignonne, allons voir si la rose" (My Love, Let Us Go and See Whether the Rose) remains the most memorable example, many other poems by Ronsard evoke a similar rhetoric, that of the lover seeking to bend to his will the recalcitrant object of his desire by reminding her of that familiar refrain about old age:

> *I send you here a wreath of blossoms blown,*
> *And woven flowers at sunset gathered,*
> *Another dawn had seen them ruined, and shed*
> *Loose upon the grass at random strown.*

Henri Fantin-Latour, *By the Table* (detail), 1872. See fig. 50.

By this, their sure example, be it known
That all your beauties, now in perfect flower,
Shall fade as these, and wither in an hour,
Flowerlike, and brief of days, as the flower sown.

. . . .

Be therefore kind, my love, whilst thou art fair.[1]

Though flowers are often used to symbolize the relationship between the sexes, there are marvelous examples that pay homage to male friendship, as in the charming verses Paul Scarron (1610–1660) wrote about the gift of a bouquet:

Morin, you have filled my chamber
With scents as sweet as amber,
And I may say of them in truth
In this bouquet of flowers smooth
And new as they are lovely
You have contrived to bring me
The Spring and all its gaiety
Gardens, meadow scenery,
Enamel, gold and jewelry
In short your present is to me
Scented, rich and comely.[2]

From the Renaissance to the end of the eighteenth century, poets rarely stepped outside convention, and flowers remained—in poetry as in painting—symbols of beauty, of the brevity of life, and, sometimes, tokens of the simple joy of giving.

Throughout Europe, the nineteenth century was *the* century of poetry, as much for the sheer number of works published as for the quality of the poems and the talent of their authors. The proliferation of magazines, collections, and publishing houses; the significance of literary circles; and the rise in literacy—and therefore readers—brought the production of poetry to new heights. As poetry became more widespread and occupied a more elevated social status, floral poetry also proliferated. The tradition of offering a poem as one might a bouquet became more commonplace in French society, with even military men, lawyers, and civil servants presenting poems of their own making. Descriptions of these transactions—sometimes touching, sometimes moving, and sometimes ridiculous—abound in literature. The number of poems related to flowers also increased because such poetry had strong, popular associations with different domains that were experiencing a birth or renaissance, from politics to religion.

The use of flowers as religious symbols, for example, is a longstanding tradition in both painting and sacred poetry. There are numerous titles

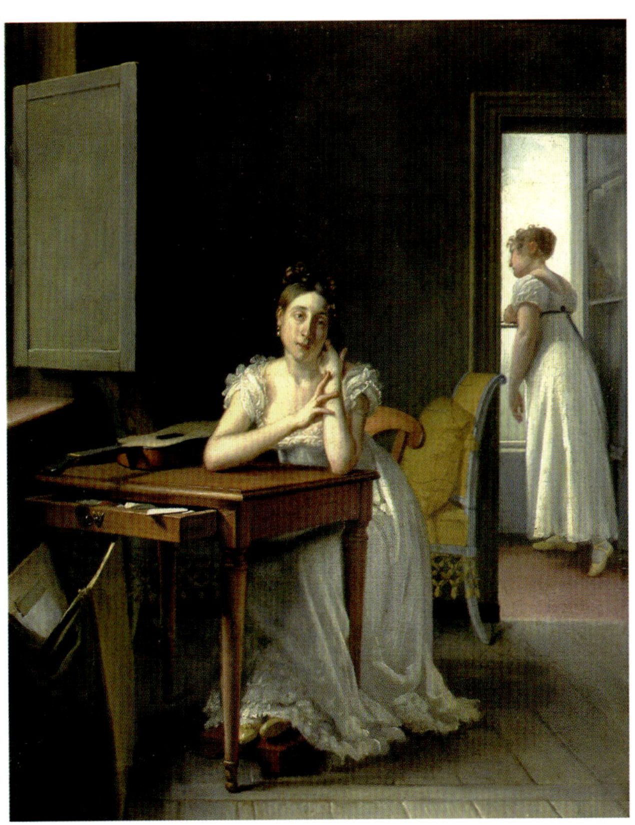

FIG. 45 Martin Drolling, *Portrait of Marceline Desbordes-Valmore*, early nineteenth century, oil on canvas. Musée de la Chartreuse, Douai, 1985.8

in which flowers are associated with divinity and in particular with the Virgin Mary. These poems and collections of poetry associate the Virgin with flowers and bouquets, and their titles possess an innocence and simplicity that cannot help but move the reader: *Bouquet to the Virgin Mary Composed of Thirty-One Flowers*[3] and *Mary's Month, Poetic Flowers to the Holy Virgin*[4] are two examples. In the preface to a similarly named collection, *The Month of the Virgin: Poetic Flowers Offered to Mary*, Aglaé de la Pinière argued in favor of such floral poetry:

> *During this beautiful month sacred to Mary [May], when all the pulpits of the Catholic faith echo with praise of the Queen of Heaven, when the inhabitants of the simplest villages and the most opulent capitals hasten to the altars of the Virgin in order to sing her praises and bless her, poetry can hardly be silent. Too often disdained in a positivist and industrial century, poetry protests against the materialism and realism that seek to proscribe it.*[5]

The candor and enthusiasm of religious poetry contributed to its popularity throughout the century. While religion should not be considered the sole focus of this sort of literature, there are undeniable highlights such as Marceline Debordes-Valmore's "Le bouquet sous la croix" (Bouquet beneath the Cross) (fig. 45):

Whence this bouquet that lies upon the ground?
Still wet with dew or tears and shadow-bound,
Did it fall this evening from the hands of prayer?
Or did some village infant lose it there?

Beneath the cross, did some thoughtful soul
To comfort the poor traveler let it fall?
Redeeming a sinful son's behavior
Does it thus tint the flagstone pallor?

A mother's shadow falls where'er we go;
Everywhere friendship must dream of friends;
The pilgrim who suffers on the foreign road
Offers God this symbol and believes in his amends.

Solitary bouquet, the sad charm you assume
Seems to breathe regret out with your scent.
Perhaps you are a votive to some love now spent:
Love is oft the secret of a flower's perfume.

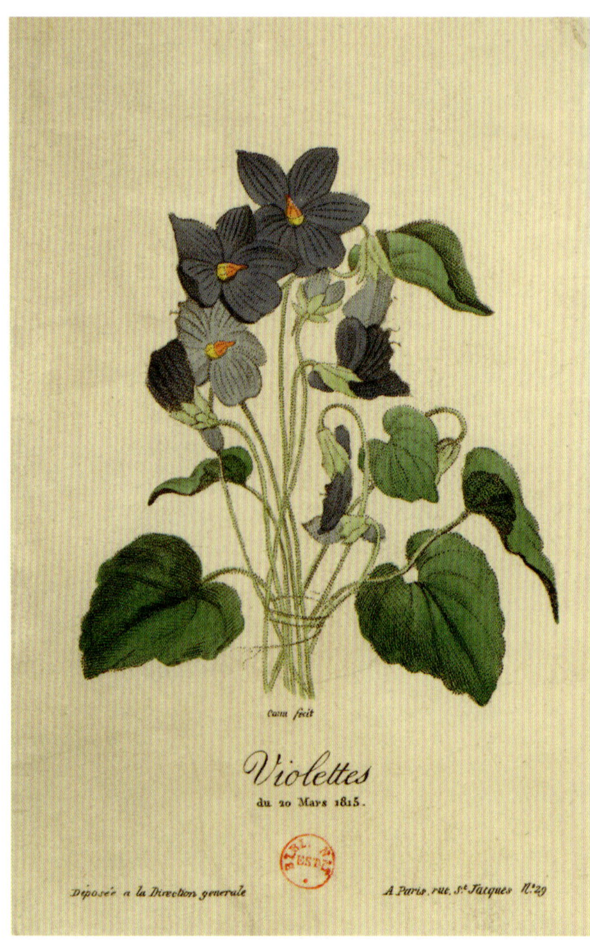

FIG. 46 Jean-Dominique-Étienne Canu, *Violets of March 20, 1815*, 1815, colored stipple engraving, first state. Bibliothèque nationale de France, Départment des estampes et de la photographie, Paris, QB-370 Reserve (72) FT-4

For my part, I have soothed the Virgin's feet
With white lilies suited to my dreaming fate;
If the Virgin knows for whom I dreaming dedicate
These lilies, she sees far into my heart![6]

But religious poetry is not the only poetic field that is sensitive to floral expressiveness. While ancient symbols linked to love or religion belong to that tradition, the expansion of floral poetry is obviously an indication of the success of poetry during the nineteenth century.

In a different domain—one as modern as religion is old—flowers took on a political emphasis. In the late eighteenth century, when political debate entered the public sphere, flowers assumed the unexpected role of representing different parties. This association is not that surprising and can be seen as a natural progression from heraldic emblems such as the French lily and the English rose.

The lily acquired an increasingly important poetic and political role after 1815, when Louis XVIII restored the monarchy, as indicated by the innumerable titles containing the phrase "bouquets of lilies"[7] that belong to collections of monarchist poetry. At that same time, the violet became a symbol of Napoleon. This paradoxical association of this simple flower with the all-conquering emperor seems to have occurred in 1814, when Napoleon, after abdicating for the first time, promised to return with the violets—that is, in the spring (fig. 46).

In a collection dated 1815, a poem by a former soldier named Pradel entitled "The Violet" is notable as an illustration of this political and historical context and demonstrates how floral rhetoric permeated different forms of poetry.

The lily has its purity,
It has no other qualities,
The violet has a sweeter scent
A modest, simple flower it is.
Therefore in Paris, in the name of amity,
While drinking till you're tipsy,
Give Napoleon a soubriquet:
Papa la violette.

The sweetest of all flowers,
Its scent inspires us,
It plays upon the Bourbons' fears,
To exiles' eyes it summons tears.[8]

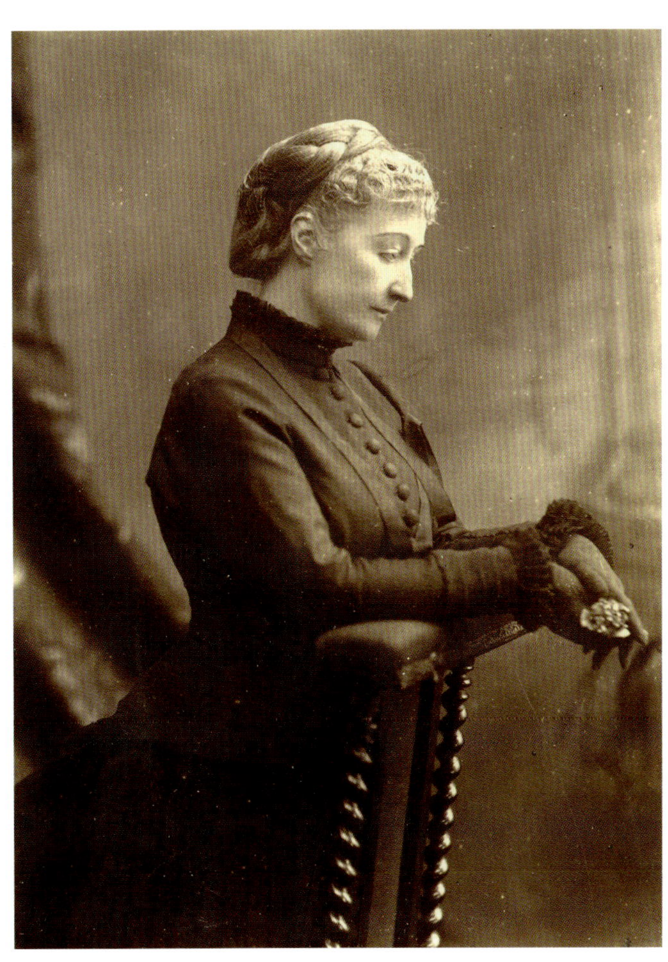

FIG. 47 Empress Eugénie, from *The Cabinet Portrait Gallery*, 1890–94, Woodburytype print after a photograph by W & D Downey

Napoleon's association with the violet continued throughout the 1800s, which explains the presence of this modest flower in images such as the portrait of Napoleon III's widow, Empress Eugénie, kneeling on a prayer stool with a little bouquet of violets in her gloved hands (fig. 47). An earlier poetic tradition associates the violet with chaste, discreet love, and a whole host of titles bear witness to its popularity.

This essay is not the place for an in-depth study of French poetry—even one limited to floral poetry—but it is interesting to note the number of titles that include the violet (in this case devoid of political meaning). The general catalogue of the Bibliothèque nationale de France includes *Bouquets de violettes* by Gaston Barbey; *Les violettes*, poems by Émile le Pelletier; *Les violettes, poésies* by Victorine Rostand; and *Violettes, poésies* by A. Barban. Some collections use the theme of the violet in a number of different ways. In 1850, F. Sténio, in his collection *Bouquet de violettes*, writes successive poems entitled "Viola rosea," "Viola sylvestris," "Viola alba," "Viola parmensis," "Viola oderiferata," "Viola duplex," etc., as if his collection were at once botanical, herbal, and poetical. A list of poems taking the rose as their subject would be even more extensive.

The pervasiveness of flowers in poetry eventually exhausted itself, and in the minds of many readers and authors, flowers and poetry became one and the same: an obsessive leitmotif, an obligatory theme repeated until the reader was satiated if not indeed nauseated. One of the last successful examples of floral poetry in which vases are filled with or emptied of many varieties of flowers is by Albert Samain (fig. 48). His undeniable success in the late nineteenth century demonstrates the complexity of French literary life and its sometimes surprising coincidences. Samain's poetry seems to belong to so ancient a tradition that one forgets he was born in 1858, a year after the appearance of Baudelaire's *Les Fleurs du mal* (*The Flowers of Evil*). Nonetheless, it would be a pity to see his works as nothing more than clichés, since Samain offers the reader magnificent examples of floral poetry, including this poem:

Strange evenings when flowers have a soul,
When the air seems charged with repentance
Or on the slow and heavy wave of sighs
The heart's inmost desires die on the lips.
On such evenings, I wander tender as a woman.

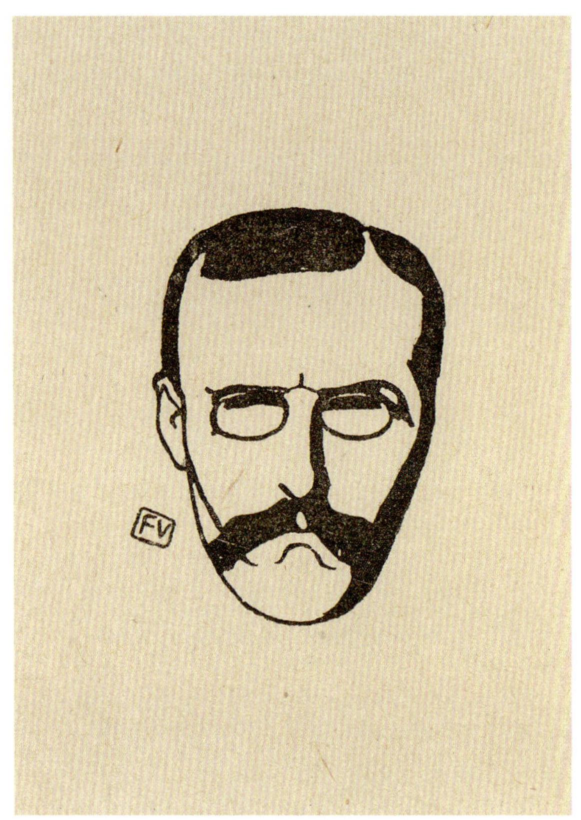

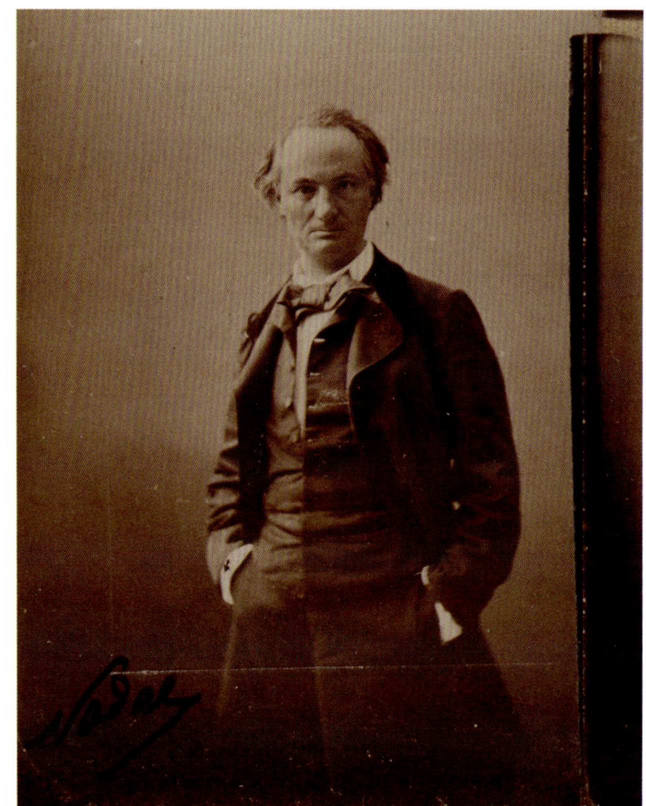

FIG. 48 Félix Vallotton, *Portrait of Albert Samain*, from Remy de Gourmont, *The Book of Masks* (1921), woodblock print. Bibliothèque nationale de France, Paris, DEV 1310 014860

FIG. 49 Charles Baudelaire, albumen print by Félix Nadar. Musée d'Orsay, Paris, PHO 1991-2-53

Bright mornings come, the roses do their hair,
The soul is playful as the mountain stream is wild,
The heart is an Easter sky full of tolling bells,
The flesh is perfect where the perfect spirit dwells.
Bright mornings come, dawn's hair entwined with roses,
On such mornings, I am joyous as a child.

Come nights of doubt, tormented with anguish,
When the soul has spiraled down to its lowest point,
Pale, suspended over an infinite abyss,
Flinching in terror at the wind from Hades' gate.
There are nights of doubt, when anguish holds the whip,
And on those nights I lie in shadow like the dead.[9]

When *Les Fleurs du mal* by Charles Baudelaire (fig. 49) was published in 1857, its very title resounded like a clap of thunder in the French poetic heavens.[10] And though the title includes flowers, they only appear at the end of the third poem, "Elevation":

Fly far above this morbid, vaporous place;
Go cleanse yourself in higher, finer air,
. . . .
Happy the strong-winged man, who makes the great
Leap upward to the bright and peaceful fields!

The man whose thoughts, like larks, take to their wings
Each morning, freely speeding through the air,
—Who soars above this life, interpreter
Of flowers' speech, the voice of silent things.[11]

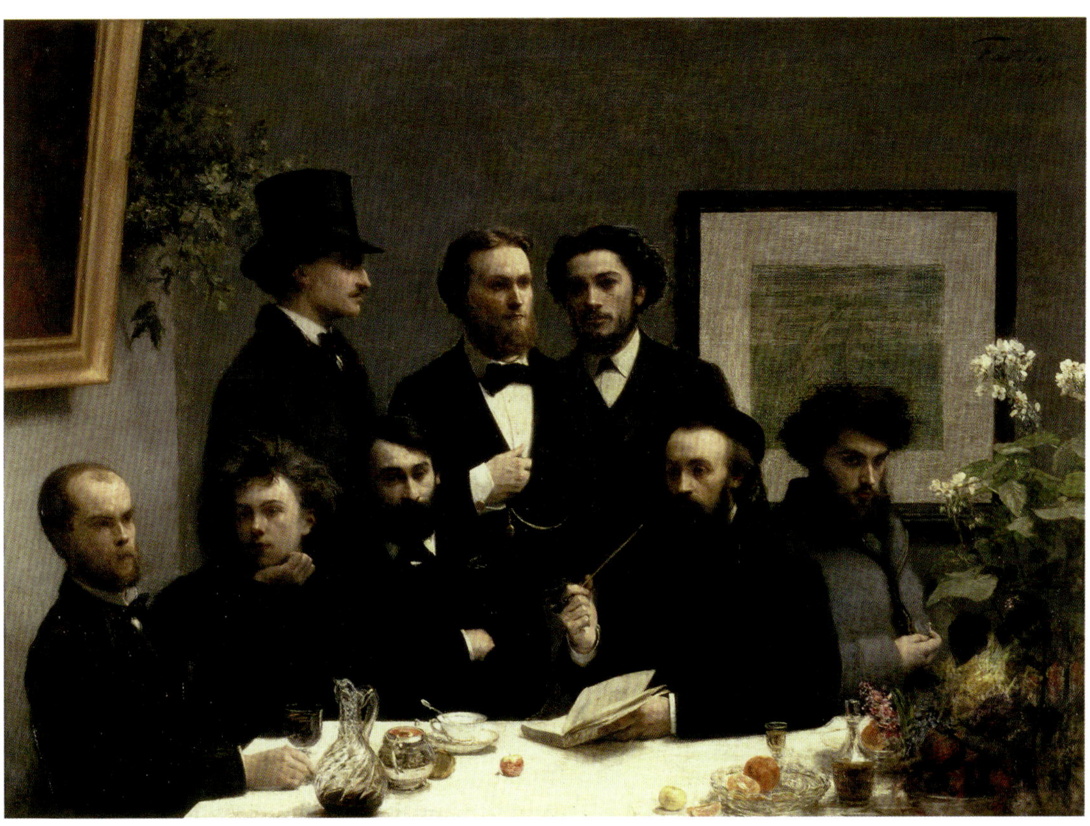

FIG. 50 Henri Fantin-Latour, *By the Table*, 1872, oil on canvas. Museé d'Orsay, Paris, RF 1959

The impact of *Les Fleurs du mal*, and its unchallenged reign over French poetry and literature, revolutionized poetic rhetoric and transformed the way it used symbolism. The themes of flowers and bouquets, of floral offerings and occasional poetry, were routed by Baudelaire's maleficent power. Baudelaire is paradoxical; his title both references the material of so many poems and condemns it at the same time. This process was subsequently used by Marcel Proust when, in a letter to the owners of the château de Guermantes, he stated that he wished "to make free use of the name of Guermantes, which I should like at once to celebrate and to soil."[12]

The slow poison introduced by *Les Fleurs du mal* spread through the whole of French literature and destroyed the component of innocence that flowers once symbolized. While many poets, such as Samain, would continue to poeticize flowers and their scents, the harm had been done and it was irremediable.

The famous painting *By the Table* (fig. 50) by Henri Fantin-Latour, one of the greatest floral artists of the nineteenth century, summarizes many of the poetic debates that followed the publication of *Les Fleurs du mal*. Like Fantin's *Homage to Delacroix* (see fig. 17), it was intended to celebrate a birthday, in this case Baudelaire's fiftieth (although the poet did not live to see that date). In a number of preparatory drawings several people are depicted sitting around a portrait of Baudelaire. But as the painting grew closer to completion, nothing remained of the portrait but the bottom right-hand corner of its gilt frame, which can be seen at the upper left of Fantin's painting next to a bunch of laurel leaves. The picture was finally presented under its current modest title and is now in the collection of the Musée d'Orsay. The men grouped around the end of a table are, from left to right, Paul Verlaine, Arthur Rimbaud, Pierre Elzéar (wearing a hat), Léon Valade, Émile Blémont, Jean Aicard, Ernest d'Hervilly, and Camille

Pelletan (the only one who was not a poet). They were collaborators on the newly founded magazine *La Renaissance littéraire et artistique*, though two members are missing from the picture: Armand Sylvestre and Albert Mérat. The latter refused to pose after quarrelling with Rimbaud and was replaced, without the slightest irony, by a bouquet. The *Renaissance littéraire* may be considered Parnassian in terms of its poetic doctrine (the Parnassians were a group of poets who emphasized metrical form rather than emotion), but while its politics preached national reconciliation and amnesty for the Communards, it was opposed to the major literary figures of the Second Empire: Octave Feuillet, Victorien Sardou, and Alexandre Dumas fils.[13] Many of its members came from provocative literary circles such as the Dîner des Vilains Bonhommes and the Cercle Zutique. The journal also published Stéphane Mallarmé's earliest translations of works by Edgar Allan Poe.

Fantin's picture is a perfect illustration of the transformation of poetry during the last quarter of the nineteenth century and offers a large and contrasting panorama of poets who would soon have very little in common. Most of the subjects can be considered members of the extreme political left, though not of the literary avant-garde. The disparity, indeed the gulf that divides them, is evident in a few verses taken respectively from works by Mérat and Rimbaud, in which flowers and bouquets predominate.

In Mérat's 1872 poem "Paysage" (Landscape), the bouquet of flowers occupies its traditional role:

Sheltered from winter, whose diffuse uproar
Was barely heard in the narrow and tightly closed
Chamber where a bouquet of your favorite flowers died
Amid visions of lassitude and plenty,

With a lover's extreme joy and yet a weary mind
I rubbed against the grain with swooning hand
The static of the silk and the curve of perfumed flesh,
And my blood rose stronger with each beat of my heart.[14]

In 1871, by contrast, Rimbaud dedicated a sulfurous poem to the great Parnassian poet Théodore de Banville. In "Remarks to the Poet on the Subject of Flowers," Rimbaud, the ultimate provocateur, used ferocious irony and blasphemous joy to subject flowers to the ultimate outrage. He violently revolted against a tradition that he despised and that Théodore de Banville partly embodied. These extracts provide a sense of its treacherous tone:

Forever thus, in azure darkness
Beyond the trembling topaz sea,
Your evenings will detail the function
Of Lilies, enema bags of ecstasy!

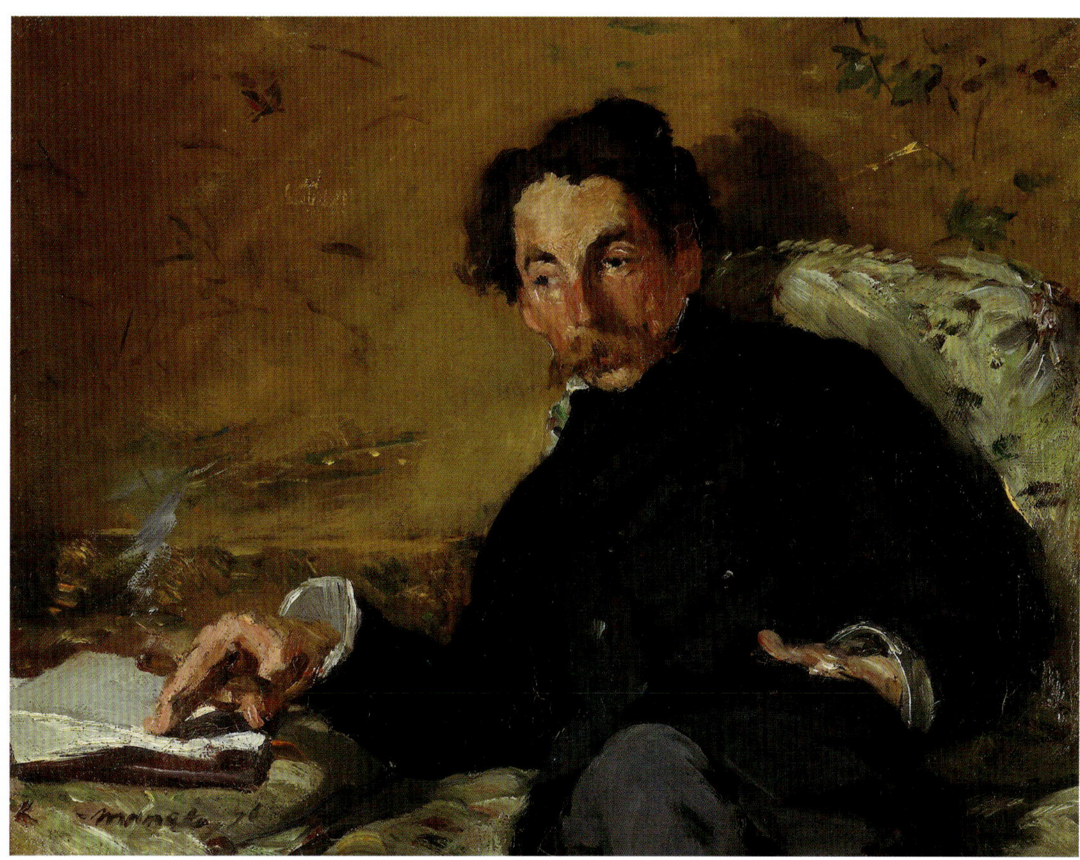

FIG. 51 Édouard Manet, *Portrait of Stéphane Mallarmé*, 1867, oil on canvas. Musée d'Orsay, Paris, RF 2661

. . . .

Yet Lilies still, with blue dismay,
Will droop in your religious Prose!

. . . .

My Dear! Whenever you take a bath
Your shirt with sticky yellow spots
In the armpits swells in the air
Over obscene Forget-Me-Nots!

Love lets through your customs sheds
Only Lilacs—Oh, garden swings!
And sweet wild Violets in the Woods—
Sugar drops of spit on insect wings![15]

After this, flowers will no longer represent mere innocence in poetry. Two poets went on to complete the work begun by Baudelaire and Rimbaud, each in his own style. Mallarmé (fig. 51), playing with words and tradition, continued to write poems such as "Les fleurs," published in 1866 in *Le Parnasse contemporain*:

On the first day you plucked huge calyces
Once from the stars that snow for evermore
And the old azure's golden rock falls for
The still-young earth pure from catastrophes,

Wild gladiolus with the slim-necked swans,
Divine laurel of exiled spirits, red
As the spotless toe of a seraph spread
With scarlet by the shame of rumpled dawns,

Hyacinth, myrtle with its lovely glows
And, like a woman's flesh, the parting bud
Of that garden Herodias, the cruel rose
Who is steeped in a savage radiant blood!

You made the sobbing white of lilies too,
Tumbling lightly across the sea of sighs on
Their dreamy way to weeping moonlight through
The azure incense of the pale horizon!

Hosanna in the censers, on the lute,
Lady, and in our limbo garden bed!
Let echoes through the heavenly dusk fall mute,
Ecstatic glances, haloes brightly shed!

Mother who molded in your strong just womb
Blooms to sway phials waiting in the distance,
Immense flowers offering the fragrant Tomb
For weary poets wilted by existence![16]

Far from being taken in by his subject, Mallarmé's impermeable style (which is particularly difficult to translate as a result of the way he used words for the effect of their sound rather than their meaning) annihilates the traditional weight of words and themes. But twenty years later, in one of those tiny but portentous moments of literature, he wrote one of his most famous aphorisms. It clearly seemed significant to him, since he reverted to this text at least three times in different contexts. Among the most cited of Mallarmé's observations, it relates to flowers. Nothing is more disconcerting than this literary magic; the flowers are executed with all the elegance of his uniquely rich and concise style. In his preface to René Ghil's *Traité du verbe* (The Word's Treaty), written in 1866, Mallarmé wrote: "What good is the marvel of transposing a fact of nature into its almost complete and vibratory disappearance with the play of the word, however, unless there comes forth from it, without the bother of a nearby or concrete reminder, the pure notion." To illustrate his proposition, he takes as his example a flower, the poetic object par excellence: "I say: a flower! and outside the oblivion to which my voice relegates any shape, insofar as it is something other than the chalices, musically rises, the laughing or lofty idea, the one absent from all bouquets."[17] "A flower . . . absent from all bouquets": the death of an idea was "never so well expressed." It announces the movement that will lead to abstraction at the beginning of the twentieth century: the disappearance of the subject and the vanishing importance of representation. The idea of a subject remains even when the representation of it evaporates. This radical transformation became cubism and one of its main heralds was the poet Guillaume Apollinaire.

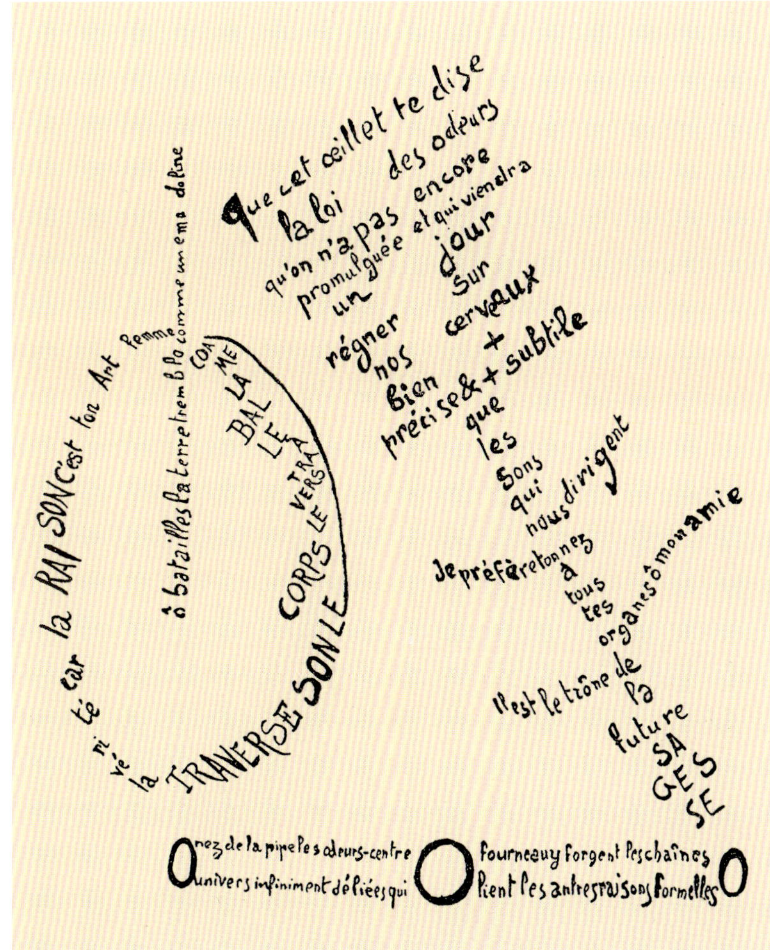

FIG. 52 Guillaume Apollinaire, *Mandolin, Carnation, and Bamboo*, from *Calligrammes*. Courtesy University of Alberta Libraries

There remained, however, one more step that had to be taken in order to cut the last link between poetry, words, and flowers. That link was destroyed by Apollinaire in his *Calligrammes, Poems of War and Peace (1913–1916)*. In this last poetic insurrection, he arranged words in such a way that transformed them into images. The flower in a poem is no longer a word, it is no longer the flower "absent from all bouquets"; it has escaped into the very image of its object as we see in *Mandolin, Carnation, and Bamboo* (fig. 52).[18] With characteristic mastery, Apollinaire contrives to place poetical objects in a cubist still life of the kind that he so ably defended. And here it is as illustration rather than as text that it appears.

The evolution of the bouquet and flowers in painting and poetry seems to lead toward borderless lands. The Mallarméan revolution, with its "hey-presto" magic, "vanishes" the flower from its bouquet. It's not surprising that the revolution in poetry had much in common with the revolution in paintings and drawings of the same period. Remember that many poets were close to the painters. Baudelaire was one of the great art critics of his century, Mallarmé was the friend of Manet, Apollinaire of Picasso, to name only a few. What seem to be two different disciplines were actually created in the same circles, where there were no borders.

Translated from the French by Chris Miller

NOTES

1. *Je vous envoie un bouquet que ma main*
Vient de trier de ces fleurs épanies;
Qui ne les eût à ce vêpre cueillies
Chutes à terre elles fussent demain.

Cela vous soit un exemple certain
Que vos beautés bien qu'elles soient fleuries
En peu de temps cherront toutes flétries
Et comme fleurs périront tout soudain.

. . . .

Pour ce, aimez-moi cependant qu'êtes belle.

Ronsard 1938, 2:814. Translation by Lang 2000, 1:35.

2. *Morin, tu m'as empty ma chambre*
D'une odeur douce comme l'ambre;
Et je puis dire, en vérité,
Qu'en un bouquet de fleurs nouvelles,
Toutes aussi rares que belles,
A la fois tu m'as apporté
Le Printemps et sa gayeté,
Des jardins, des champs, des prairies,
De l'esmail et des pierreries;
Enfin tu m'as faict un present
Musqué, riche, rare et plaisant.

Scarron 1654, 115.

3. Barrera 1856.

4. Boulay 1834.

5. La Pinière 1864, 5.

6. *D'où vient-il ce bouquet oublié sur la pierre?*
Dans l'ombre, humide encor de rosée, ou de pleurs,
Ce soir, est-il tombé des mains de la prière?
Un enfant du village a-t-il perdu ces fleurs?

Ce soir, fut-il laissé par quelque âme pensive
Sous la croix où s'arrête un pauvre voyageur?
Est-ce d'un fils errant la mémoire naïve
Qui d'une pâle rose y cacha la blancheur?

De nos mères partout nous suit l'ombre légère;
Partout l'amitié prie et rêve à l'amitié;
Le pèlerin souffrant sur la route étrangère

Offre à Dieu ce symbole, et croit en sa pitié!
Solitaire bouquet, ta tristesse charmante
Semble avec tes parfums exhaler un regret.
Peut-être es-tu promis au songe d'une amante:

Souvent dans une fleur l'amour a son secret!
Et moi j'ai rafraîchi les pieds de la Madone
De lilas blancs, si chers à mon destin rêveur;
Et la Vierge sait bien pour qui je les lui donne:
Elle entend la pensée au fond de notre coeur!

Desbordes-Valmore 1830, 2:29–30.

7. For one example among many, see Hédouin 1816.

8. . . . .
Le lis a pour lui la blancheur,
Il n'a plus rien du reste
La violette a douce odeur,
Elle est simple et modeste,
Aussi dans Paris, nos braves chéris,
Tout en faisant goguette,
Donne pour surnom
A Napoléon
Papa la Violette.
C'est la plus aimable des fleurs,
Son parfum nous inspire;
Elle met les Bourbons en pleurs,
Et l'émigré à soupirer.

Pradel 1815, 40.

9. *Il est d'étranges soirs où les fleurs ont une âme,*
Où dans l'air énervé flotte du repentir,
Où sur la vague lente et lourde d'un soupir
Le coeur le plus secret aux lèvres vient mourir.
Il est d'étranges soirs, où les fleurs ont une âme,
Et, ces soirs-là, je vais tendre comme une femme.

Il est de clairs matins, de roses se coiffant,
Où l'âme a des gaietés d'eaux vives dans les roches,
Où le coeur est un ciel de Pâques plein de cloches,
Où la chair est sans tache et l'esprit sans reproches.
Il est de clairs matins, de roses se coiffant,
Ces matins-là, je vais joyeux comme un enfant.

. . . .

Il est des nuits de doute, où l'angoisse vous tord,
Où l'âme, au bout de la spirale descendue,
Pâle et sur l'infini terrible suspendue,
Sent le vent de l'abîme, et recule éperdue!
Il est des nuits de doute, où l'angoisse vous tord,
Et, ces nuits-là, je suis dans l'ombre comme un mort.

Samain 1911, 169–70.

10. Baudelaire (1857) 1993, 3. Baudelaire describes his poems thus in the dedication to Théophile Gautier printed at the head of the volume: "To the impeccable poet, to the perfect magician of French letters, to my dearest and most admired master and friend, Théophile Gautier, with feelings of the most profound humility, I dedicate these sickly flowers."

11. *Envole-toi bien loin de ces miasmes morbides;*
Va te purifier dans l'air supérieur,
. . . .
Heureux celui qui peut d'une aile vigoureuse
S'élancer vers les champs lumineux et sereins;

Celui dont les pensers, comme des alouettes,
Vers les cieux le matin prennent un libre essor,
—Qui plane sur la vie, et comprend sans effort
Le langage des fleurs et des choses muettes!

Ibid., 16

12. Pugh 2004, 288.

13. For a detailed study of this work, see Abélès, 1987.

14. *À l'abri de l'hiver qui jetait vaguement*
Sa clameur, dans la chambre étroite et bien fermée
Où mourait un bouquet fait de ta fleur aimée,
Parmi les visions de l'étourdissement;

Pendant qu'avec la joie extrême d'un amant
Je froissais d'un coeur las et d'une main pâmée
L'étoffe frémissante et la chair embaumée,
Mon sang montait plus lourd à chaque battement.

Mérat 1898, 293.

15. *Ainsi toujours, vers l'azur noir*
Où tremble la mer des topazes
Fonctionneront dans ton soir
Les Lys, ces clystères d'extases
. . . .
Le Lys boira les bleus dégoûts
Dans tes proses religieuses
. . . .
Toujours, Cher, quand tu prends un bain
Ta chemise aux aisselles blondes
Se gonfle aux brises du matin
Sur les Myosotis immondes

L'amour ne passe à tes octrois
Que les Lilas,—ô balançoires!
Et les Violettes du Bois
Crachats sucrés des Nymphes noires! . . .

Rimbaud 1954, 95. Translation in Rimbaud 2008, 123–24.

16. *Des avalanches d'or du vieil azur, au jour*
Premier et de la neige éternelle des astres
Jadis tu détachas les grand calices pour
La terre jeune encore et vierge de désastres,

Le glaïeul fauve, avec les cygnes au col fin,
Et ce divin laurier des âmes exilées
Vermeil comme le pur orteil du séraphin
Que rougit la pudeur des aurores foulées,

L'hyacinthe, le myrte à l'adorable éclair
Et, pareille à la chair de la femme, la rose
Cruelle, Hérodiade en fleur du jardin clair,
Celle qu'un sang farouche et radieux arrose!

Et tu fis la blancheur sanglotante des lys
Qui roulant sur des mers de soupirs qu'elle effleure
À travers l'encens bleu des horizons pâlis
Monte rêveusement vers la lune qui pleure!

Hosannah sur le cistre et dans les encensoirs,
Notre Dame, hosannah du jardin de nos limbes!
Et finisse l'écho par les célestes soirs,
Extase des regards, scintillements des nimbes!

O Mère qui créa en ton sein juste et fort,
Calice balançant la future fiole,
De grandes fleurs avec la balsamique
Mort Pour le poëte las que la vie étiole.

Mallarmé 1945, 123–24. Translation in Mallarmé 2006, 15.

17. Preface to *Traité du verbe*, 1945:
A quoi bon la merveille de transposer un fait de nature en sa presque disparition vibratoire selon le jeu de la parole, cependant, si ce n'est pour qu'en émane, sans la gêne d'un proche ou concret rappel, la notion pure?'

Je dis: une fleur! Et hors de l'oubli où ma voix relègue aucune couleur, en tant que quelque chose d'autre que les calices sus musicalement se lève, idée même et suave, l'absente de tout bouquet.

Mallarmé 1982, 75–76.

18. Apollinaire 1956, 209.

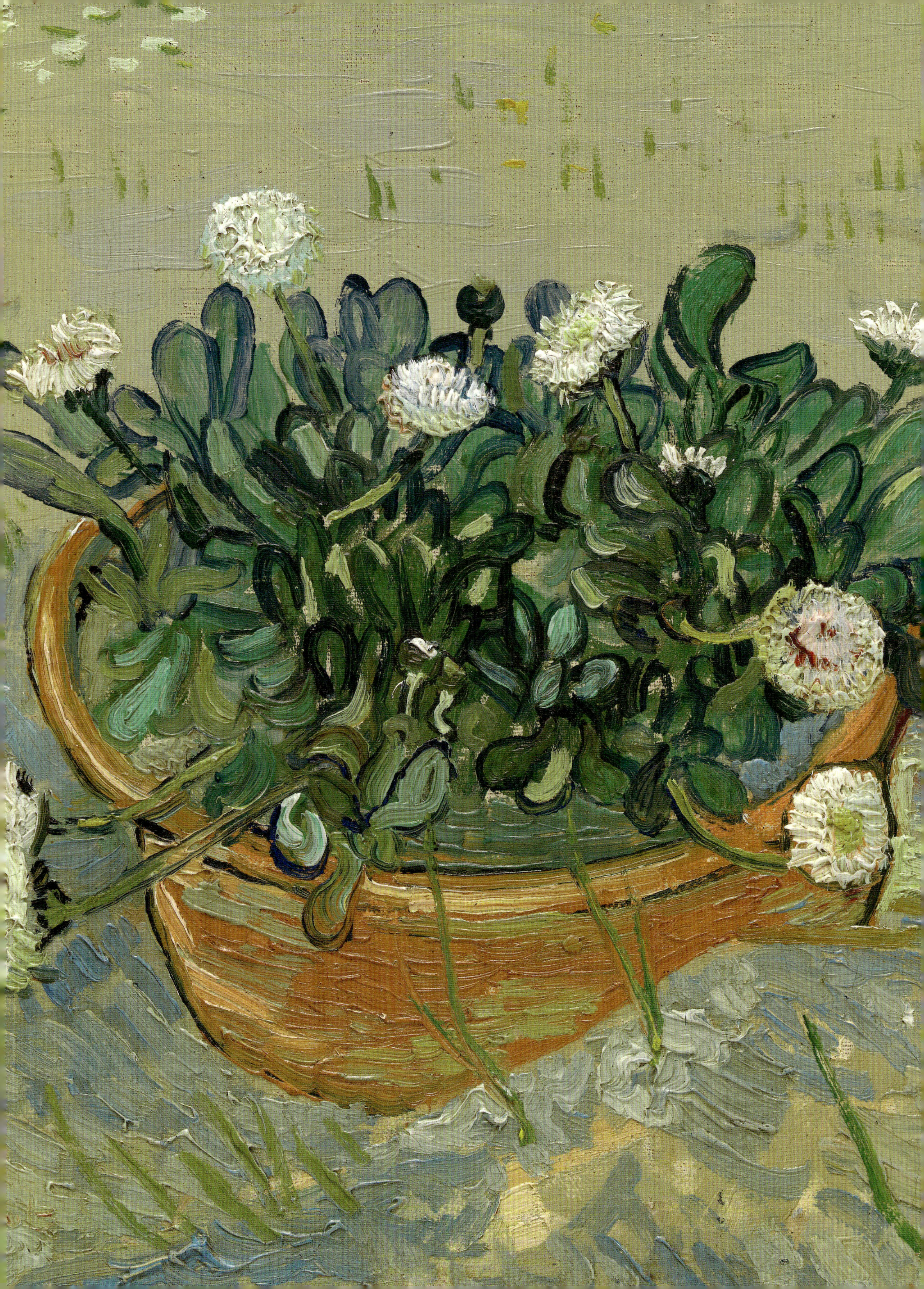

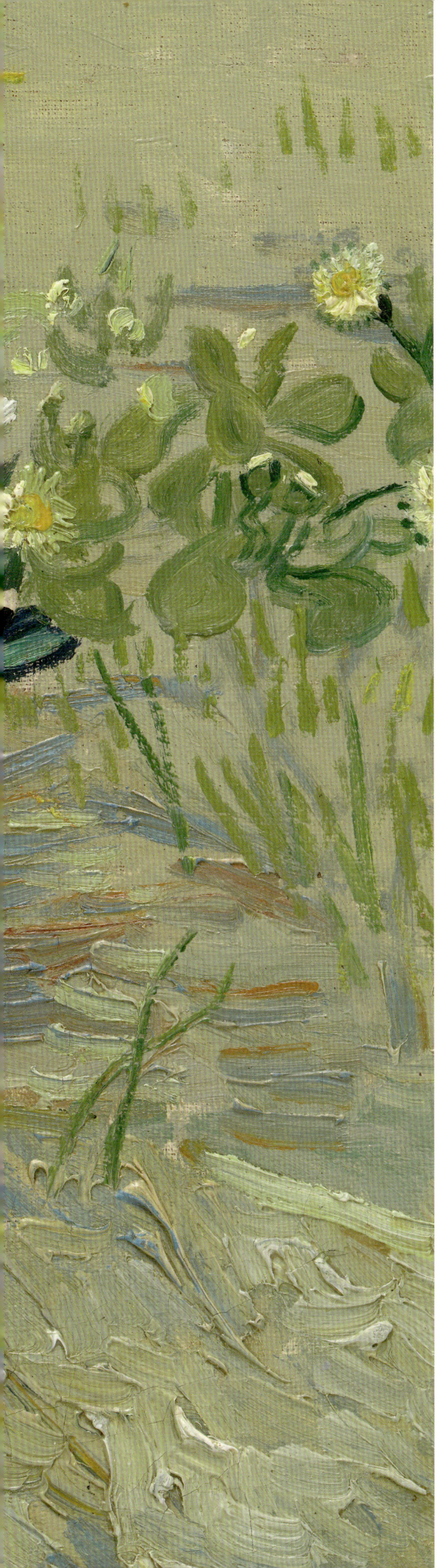

Catalogue

A NEW VOGUE FOR FLOWERS: CHARDIN TO REDOUTÉ AND HIS SCHOOL

DURING THE EARLY SEVENTEENTH CENTURY, FLOWER painting was assiduously practiced in France as an independent genre of two major types. Jacques Linard, Louise Moillon, and Jean-Michel Picart were exponents of one type, creating concise and relatively small, intimate works with a meditative quality, frequently containing *vanitas* elements. The other type, closely allied with large and ornate decorative paintings often made for royal palace interiors, was practiced by Jean-Baptiste Monnoyer and Jean-Baptiste Belin de Fontenay, both of whom were received into the French Academy. Both types were significantly influenced by Netherlandish examples: the first by Jan Brueghel the Elder and Balthasar van der Ast, the second by Jan Davidsz. de Heem and Rachel Ruysch.

Northern artists continued to be the standard point of reference for French painters throughout the eighteenth century. Among those who looked to these examples was Louis Tessier, best known for his work at the Gobelins factory, where he designed floral borders for tapestries. Few of his independent still lifes survive, though *Flowers in a Chantilly Vase* (cat. no. 1), which places him within the context of the decorative arts industry of his day, shows him to be capable of an extremely delicate style that was much appreciated at the time. Tessier's ability to paint flowers both precisely and freely—necessary for floral tapestry borders as well—and his self-conscious use of a fashionable contemporary container of French manufacture (Chantilly wares were known for their imitation of Imari sources) are both notable. However, such canvases by Tessier are rare, and little is known about their patrons. Still-life paintings by French artists Alexandre-François Desportes and Jean-Baptiste Oudry were more steadily exhibited and collected, better documented, and more numerous. Both were Academicians who enjoyed close relationships with the court and worked in a highly prized manner that was extensively influenced by Dutch and Flemish artists. An excellent example of their sophisticated style is Desportes's *Urn of Flowers with Fruits and Hare* of 1715 (fig. 53), a sumptuous painting that unites various subjects of still life (animals, fruits, and flowers) with a contemporary sculptural bronze urn to create a triumphant, copious, and spectacular showpiece of artistic composition and illusionism.

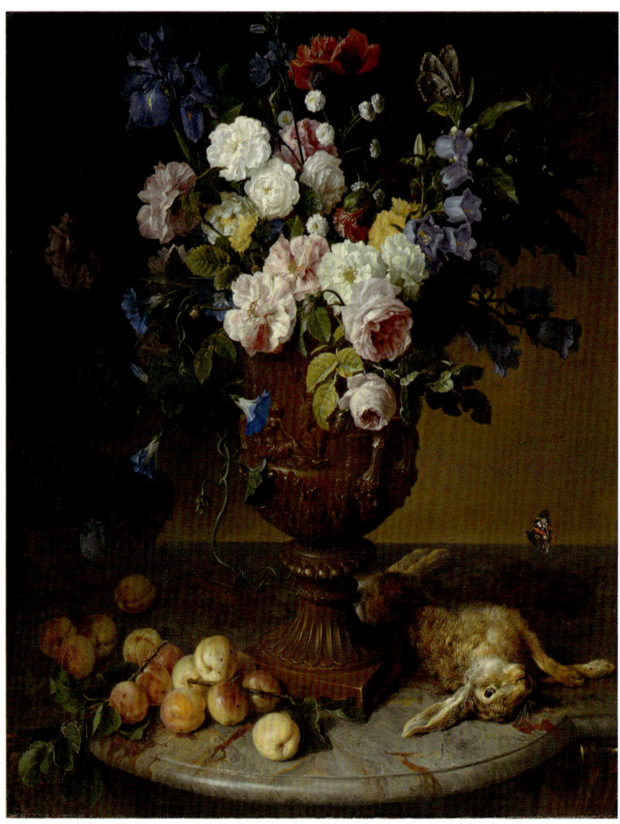

FIG. 53 Alexandre-François Desportes, *Urn of Flowers with Fruits and Hare*, 1715, oil on canvas. North Carolina Museum of Art, Raleigh, purchased with funds from the State of North Carolina

Jean-Siméon Chardin revolutionized French painting of both still lifes and scenes of everyday domestic life. Although it is often claimed that Chardin was forgotten soon after his death, his art—kept alive partly through the writings of contemporary critic Denis Diderot—proved of uncontested value for later still-life painters. Chardin's aims and results were decidedly different from those of his immediate predecessors. His still-life subjects generally depicted ordinary middle-class household goods arranged with seeming casualness, instead of the overtly luxurious items and assured artifice of earlier masters. Though his choice of humble domestic objects was perhaps also influenced by Dutch precedents, such as the breakfast and tobacco pieces of Pieter Claesz., his abandonment of the slick and glossy surfaces then predominant in the works of Desportes, Oudry, and others was revolutionary within the context of the Academy (in fact, Chardin was not only a full Academician, he was also the group's treasurer and the *tapisseur* in charge of arranging the hangings of the annual Salon).

Although Chardin is known to have painted a small number of floral still lifes, only one has survived (cat. no. 2). This example is particularly important, as it made its way from the collection of Chardin's friend, portrait painter Jacques-André-Joseph Aved, to that of Impressionist supporter Camille Marcille. It was seen and rhapsodically described by the nineteenth-century critics Edmond and Jules de Goncourt in seminal essays published in 1863 and 1864, and since then, this single painting has usually been seen as the quintessence of all that is beautiful in Chardin's painting. This beauty has always been considered the product of his unique understanding of the contingency of artistic perception and representation, here underscored by the delicacy of both the flowers and their porcelain container as well as the painter's own transformative touch. (The usual trope of Diderot and other critics for Chardin's handling—assured yet not spontaneous—is "magic.")

Like Chardin, Anne Vallayer-Coster was a member of the Academy, with whom she exhibited regularly as one of the four women admitted at any one time before the Revolution. She enjoyed royal patronage and, as the daughter of a goldsmith at Gobelins, an association with the manufactory. Vallayer-Coster mostly specialized in still lifes and was appreciated for her floral compositions, but she also painted portraits and miniatures. Sometimes wrongly considered a follower of Chardin because a number of her paintings (particularly still lifes of foodstuffs) resemble his, her sophisticated oeuvre actually comprises a variety of styles. Though she commanded the *manière heurtée* similar to the broken brushwork of Chardin, she also chose the *manière fondue*—the slick and perfect finish also widely admired in the period for its truth and illusionism. Indeed, the large-scale *Bouquet of Flowers in a Blue Porcelain Vase* of 1777 (cat. no. 3) might be considered a manifesto for this latter manner as well as the full assimilation of Northern models by the French. The vase of flowers is set on a stone ledge, a traditional arrangement in Northern examples, and is marked by exceptional color harmonies and contrasts, displaying a daring use of the monochrome blue glaze of the gilt bronze-mounted vase as a primary value to play off a range of reds, pinks, whites, and more subtle shades of blue. The engaging optical realism of *Bouquet of Flowers in a Blue Porcelain Vase*, combined with its inclusion of contemporary French decorative arts patronized by royalty and their circle, must have made it exceedingly attractive for the high-ranking court official to whom it belonged with its equally elaborate pendant (fig. 54).

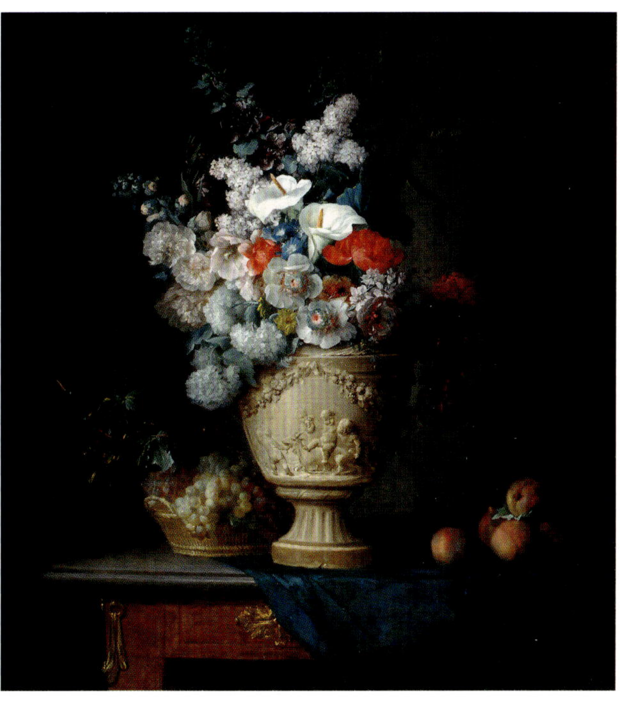

FIG. 54 Anne Vallayer-Coster, *Bouquet of Flowers in a Terracotta Vase with Peaches and Grapes*, 1776, oil on canvas. Dallas Museum of Art, Foundation for the Arts Collection, Mrs. John B. O'Hara Fund and gift of Michael L. Rosenberg, 1998.51.FA

The practice of flower painting in the Northern manner continued during the Revolution and successive regimes among a group of Northern-born artists, including the brothers Gerard and Cornelis van Spaendonck (cat. nos. 4 and 5). These artists' taste for precise brushwork and illusionism, coupled with strong narrative elements and suggestions of memento mori, proved popular both during the ancien régime and after. Gerard van Spaendonck extensively developed the theme of floral subjects juxtaposed with man-made objects such as ancient bas-reliefs, which suited

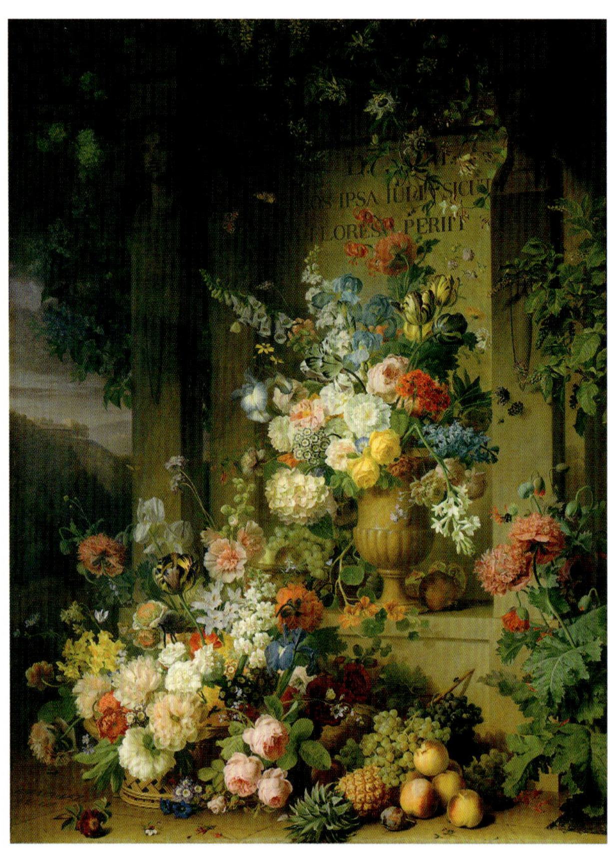

FIG. 55 Jan Frans van Dael, *Julie's Tomb*, 1803–4, oil on canvas. Châteaux de Malmaison et Bois-Préau, Rueil-Malmaison, MMD.16

neoclassical taste (as in his 1785 painting of a basket of flowers next to a bronze vase, cat. no. 4, a royal commission). Both brothers also worked for the Sèvres manufactory and were associated with the Jardin des plantes. Gerard, especially successful as a teacher, is associated with two, among many, illustrious pupils: Jan Frans van Dael (also Dutch-born) and his Belgian-born protégé Pierre-Joseph Redouté. All enjoyed royal patronage. For example, van Dael's immense allegorical and sentimental composition *Julie's Tomb* (fig. 55) was bought by Empress Joséphine, and one of his two works in this exhibition (cat. no. 6) was purchased by Louis XVIII. In the latter, van Dael shows his indebtedness to the widely admired Dutch specialist Jan van Huysum.

Redouté is without a doubt the greatest and best known of France's floral specialists. Primarily an illustrator of great merit and skill, his oil paintings such as *Vase of Flowers* (cat. no. 8) are extremely rare. In this apparently modest example, subtlety is the key to his achievement; he eschews monumentality, allegory, and overt references to Dutch examples, so that the roses seem observed from life rather than based on artistic formulae. The drops of water and the fly emphasize the fragile flowers' carefully observed life cycle rather than their stereotypical use as *vanitas* symbols. The exquisite crystal ormolu-mounted vessel underscores the preciousness and rarity of these specimens.

The van Spaendoncks, van Dael, and Redouté trained numerous female pupils, such as Adèle Riché (student of both van Dael and Gerard van Spaendonck). Riché is represented in the exhibition by a spectacular example (cat. no. 9) that was shown at the Salon of 1832, one year before Eugène Delacroix began to suggest alternatives for the precise manner in which she triumphs. This delicate, minutely observed, and carefully colored painting might be seen as the apogee of the Franco-Dutch tradition to which she was heir.

In this category, finally, Louis-Léopold Boilly, a painter primarily of fashionable genres in a highly finished manner, collected Dutch and Flemish paintings and owned numerous floral works by van Dael. His *Vase of Flowers* (cat. no. 11) synthesizes the many trends of ancien régime and subsequent flower paintings while displaying an extremely personal manner, such as elongation and rhyming of forms. Rather than profusion he presents a few selected blossoms. The almost monochrome palette of dark greens and grays is the very antithesis of celebratory paintings such as those by Riché.

This period's central oppositions between exuberance and reserve, precise or free rendering, and private and public address were significant critical polarities that engaged subsequent painters for the remainder of the nineteenth century.

MM

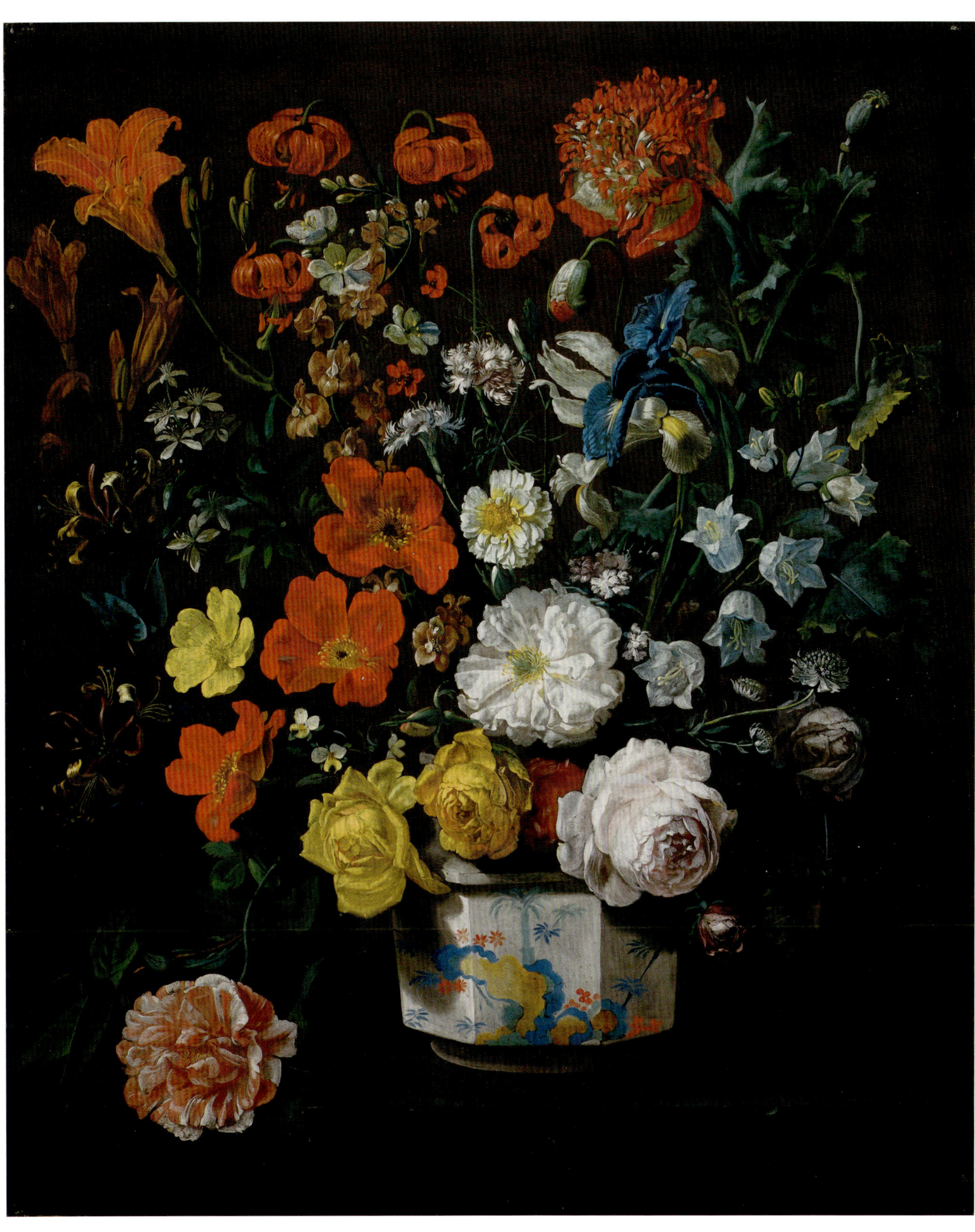

1
LOUIS TESSIER
(FRENCH, 1719–1781)

Flowers in a Chantilly Vase, ca. 1760

Oil on canvas, 25⅝ × 21½ in. (65.1 × 54.6 cm)
Saint Louis Art Museum, Friends Fund, 181:1980

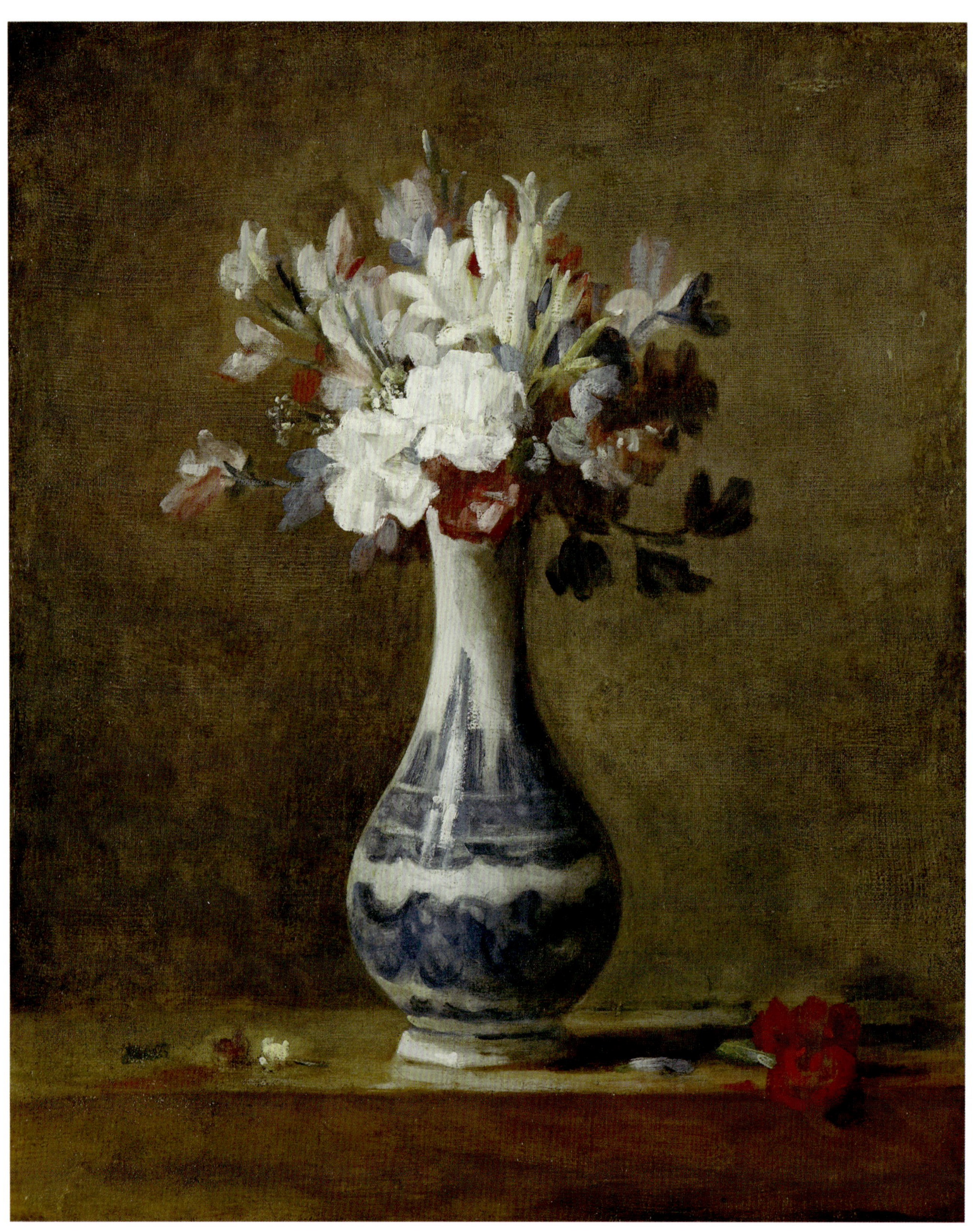

2
JEAN-SIMÉON CHARDIN
(FRENCH, 1699–1779)

A Vase of Flowers, ca. 1750

Oil on canvas, 17 13/16 × 14 5/8 in. (45.2 × 37.1 cm)
Scottish National Gallery, Edinburgh, Purchased with the aid of the Cowan Smith Bequest Fund 1937, NG 1883

Dallas only

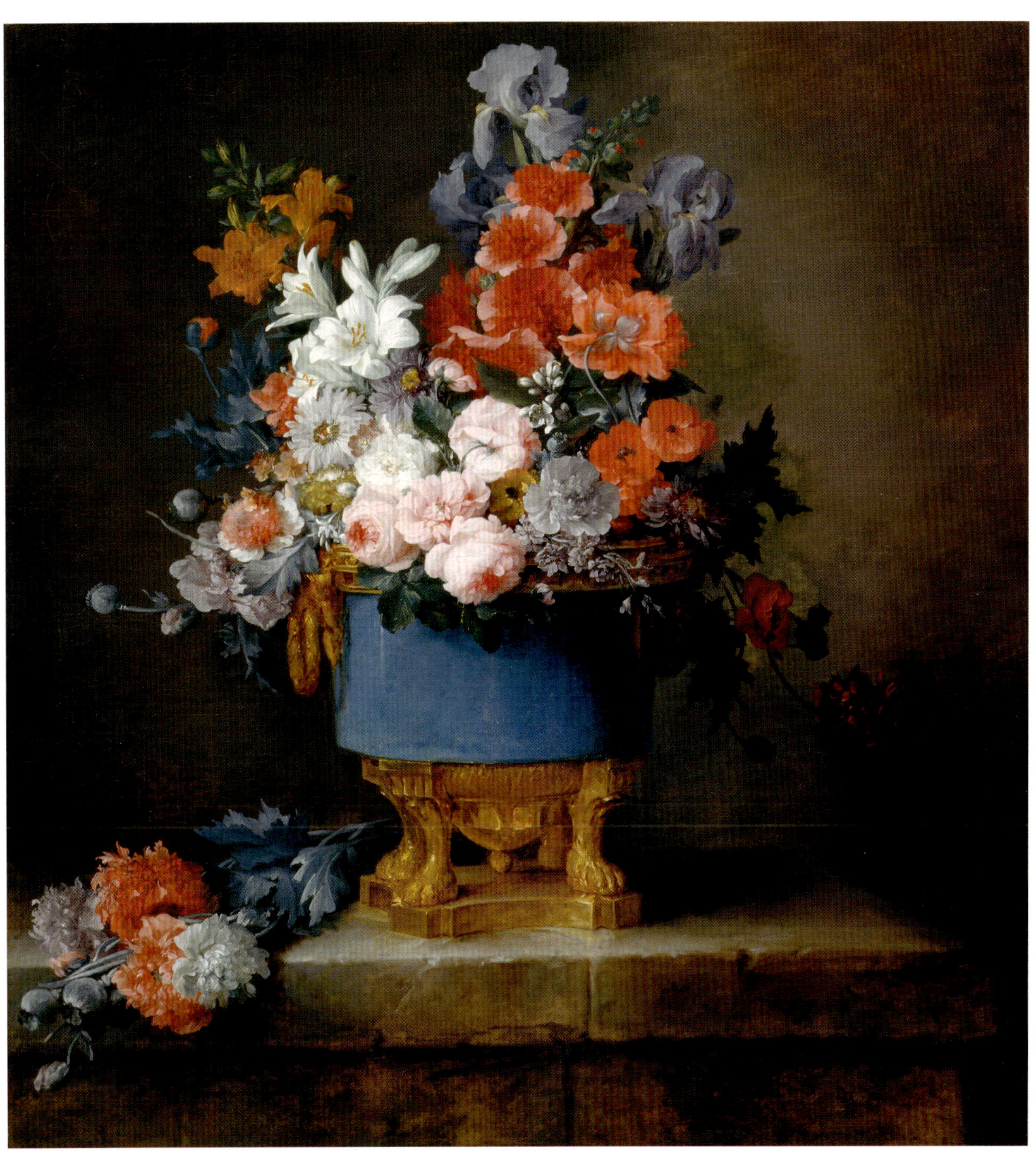

3 ANNE VALLAYER-COSTER
(FRENCH, 1744–1818)

Bouquet of Flowers in a Blue Porcelain Vase, 1776

Oil on canvas, 48¼ × 44½ in. (122.56 × 113.03 cm)
Dallas Museum of Art, Foundation for the Arts Collection,
Mrs. John B. O'Hara Fund and gift of Michael L. Rosenberg, 1998.52.FA

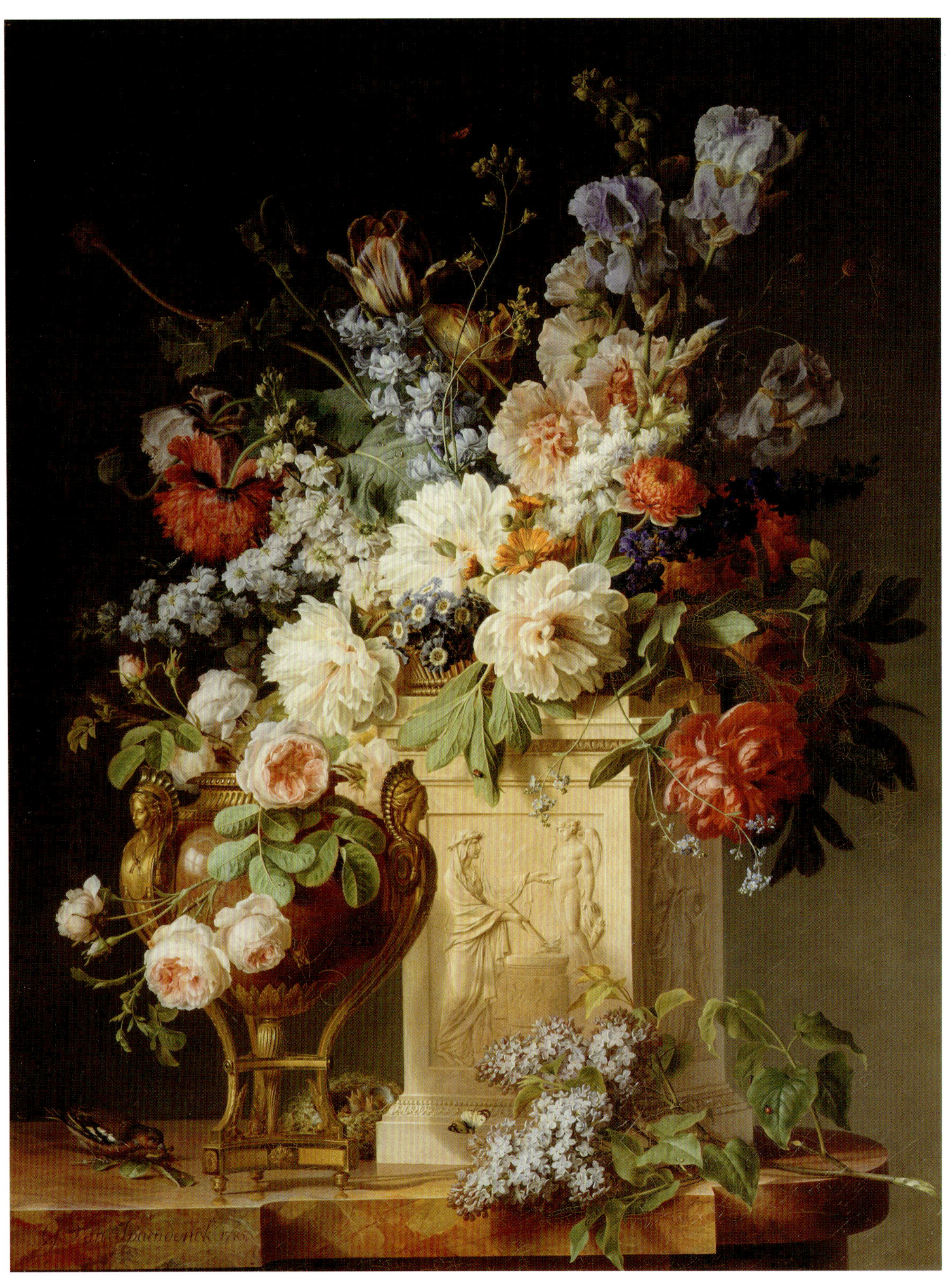

4 GERARD VAN SPAENDONCK
(DUTCH, 1756–1840; ACTIVE IN FRANCE)

Basket of Flowers on an Alabaster Pedestal (Tableau représentant un Piédestal d'albâtre, enrichi de Bas-relief, sur lequel est posée une Corbeille de Fleurs, et à côté un Vase de bronze), 1785

Oil on canvas, 45 11/16 × 35 13/16 in. (116 × 91 cm)
Musée national du château de Fontainebleau, 1854, MR 2596

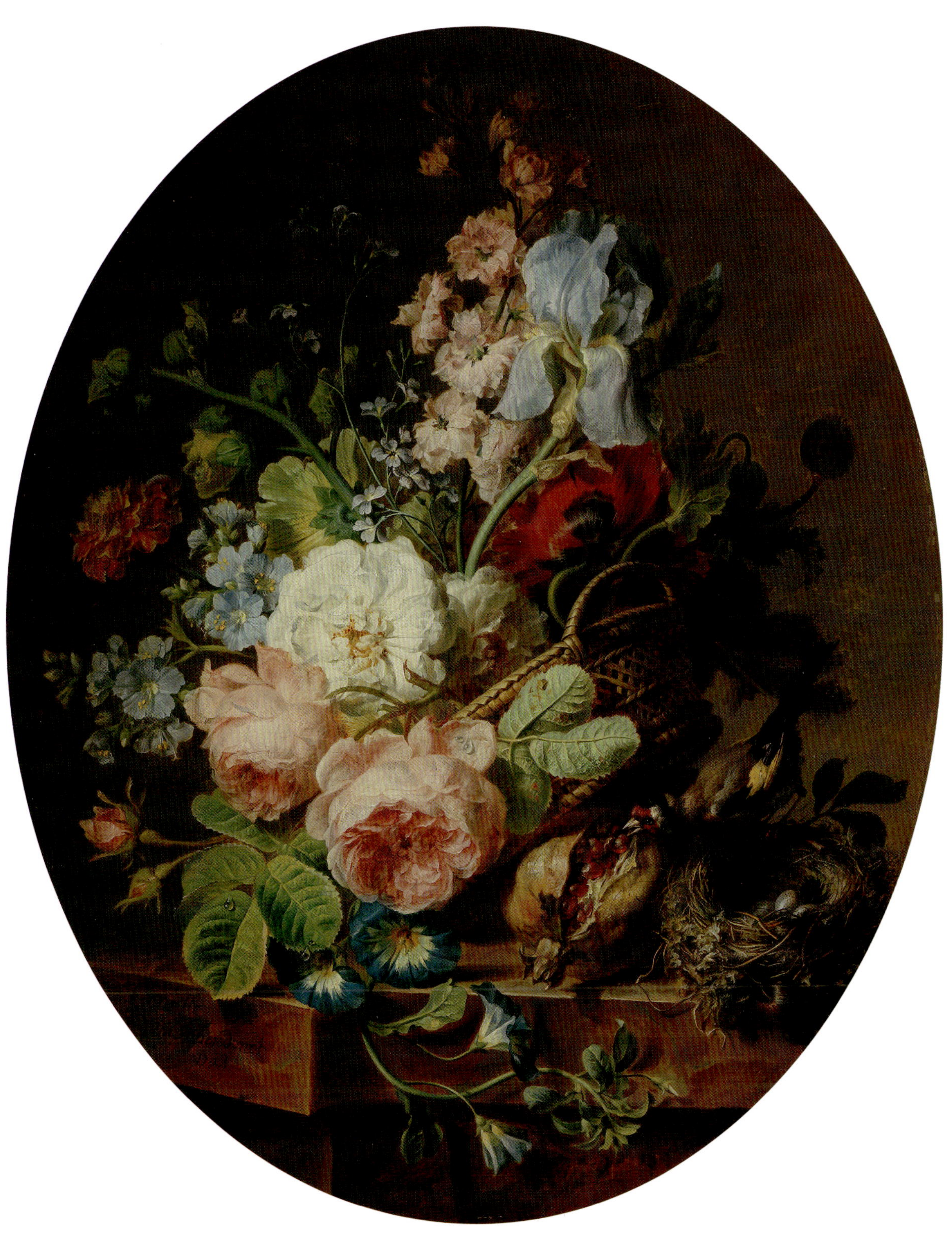

5 CORNELIS VAN SPAENDONCK
(DUTCH, 1746–1822; ACTIVE IN FRANCE)

Open Wicker Basket of Mixed Flowers, 1789

Oil on canvas, 18½ × 15 in. (47 × 38 cm)
The Syndics of the Fitzwilliam Museum, Bequest of Henry Rogers Broughton, Second Baron Fairhaven, PD.90-1973

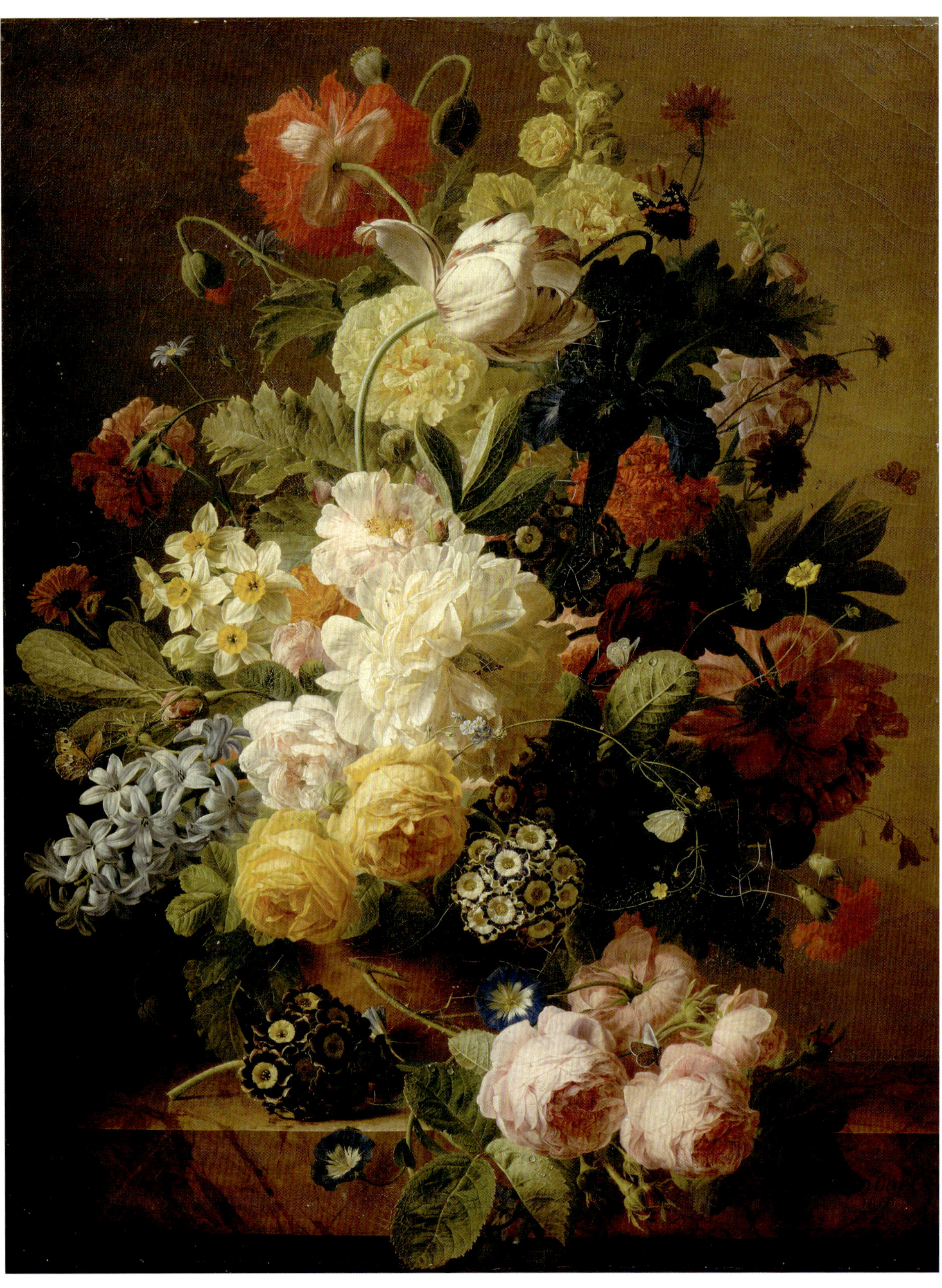

6
JAN FRANS VAN DAEL
(BELGIAN, 1764–1840; ACTIVE IN FRANCE)

Flowers in an Agate Vase on a Marble Table, 1816

Oil on canvas, 33¹⁄₁₆ × 26 in. (84 × 66 cm)
Musée national du château de Fontainebleau, 1197, MR 3578

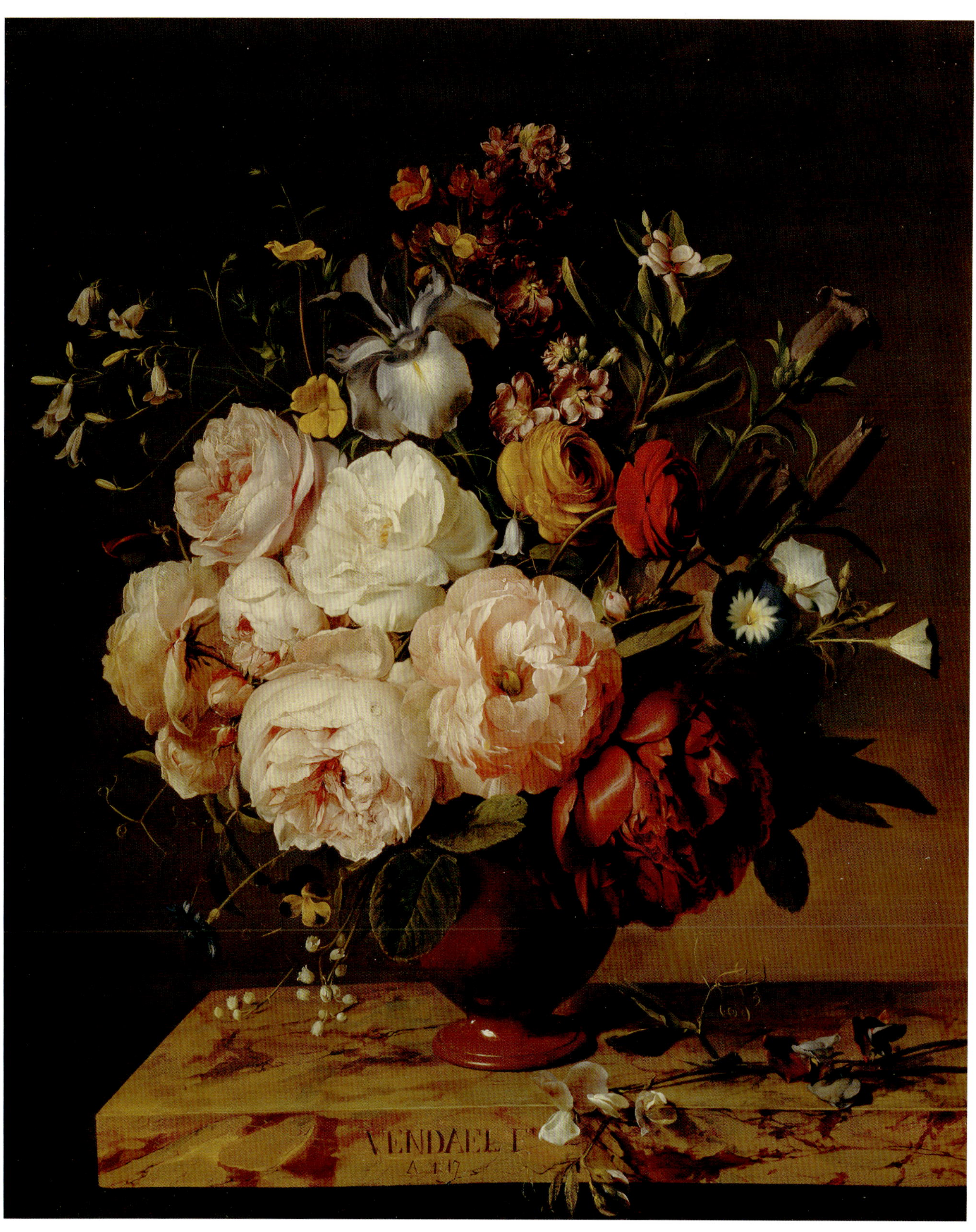

7 **JAN FRANS VAN DAEL**
(BELGIAN, 1764–1840; ACTIVE IN FRANCE)

A Vase of Flowers on a Ledge, 1817

Oil on canvas, 21⅞ × 18¼ in. (55.3 × 46.4 cm)
The Syndics of the Fitzwilliam Museum, Bequest of
Henry Rogers Broughton, Second Baron Fairhaven, PD.19-1987

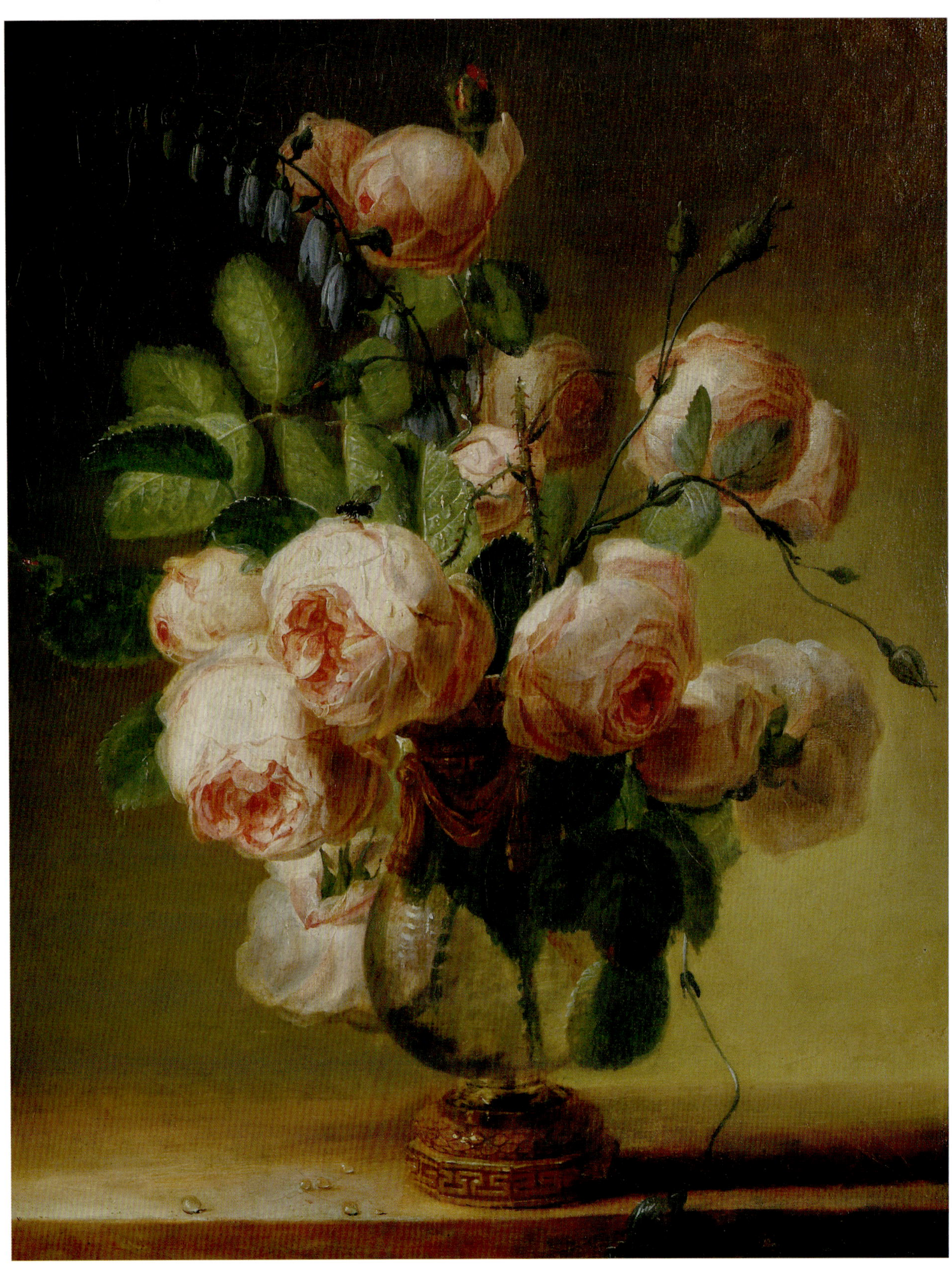

8
PIERRE-JOSEPH REDOUTÉ
(FLEMISH, 1759–1840; ACTIVE IN FRANCE)

Vase of Flowers, 1799

Oil on canvas, 23⅝ × 20⅛ in. (60 × 51 cm)
Musée des Beaux-Arts de Rouen, Bequest of
Mme Vve Eugénie le Maître, 1953.1.4

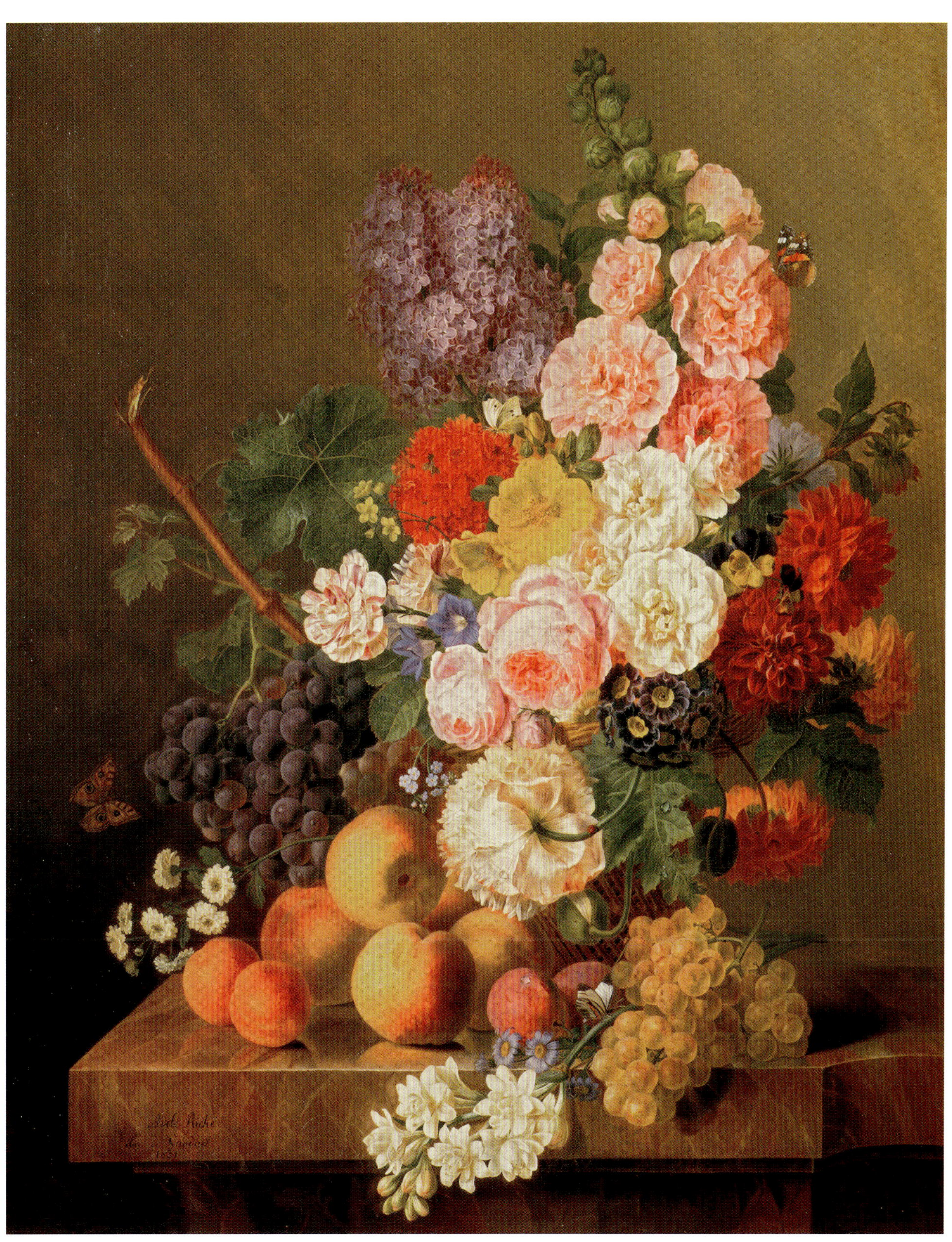

9 ADÈLE RICHÉ
(FRENCH, 1791–1878)

Flowers with Green and Red Grapes, 1831

Oil on canvas, 35 7/16 × 29 9/16 in. (90 × 75 cm)
Musée des Beaux-Arts de Tours, 896-3-1

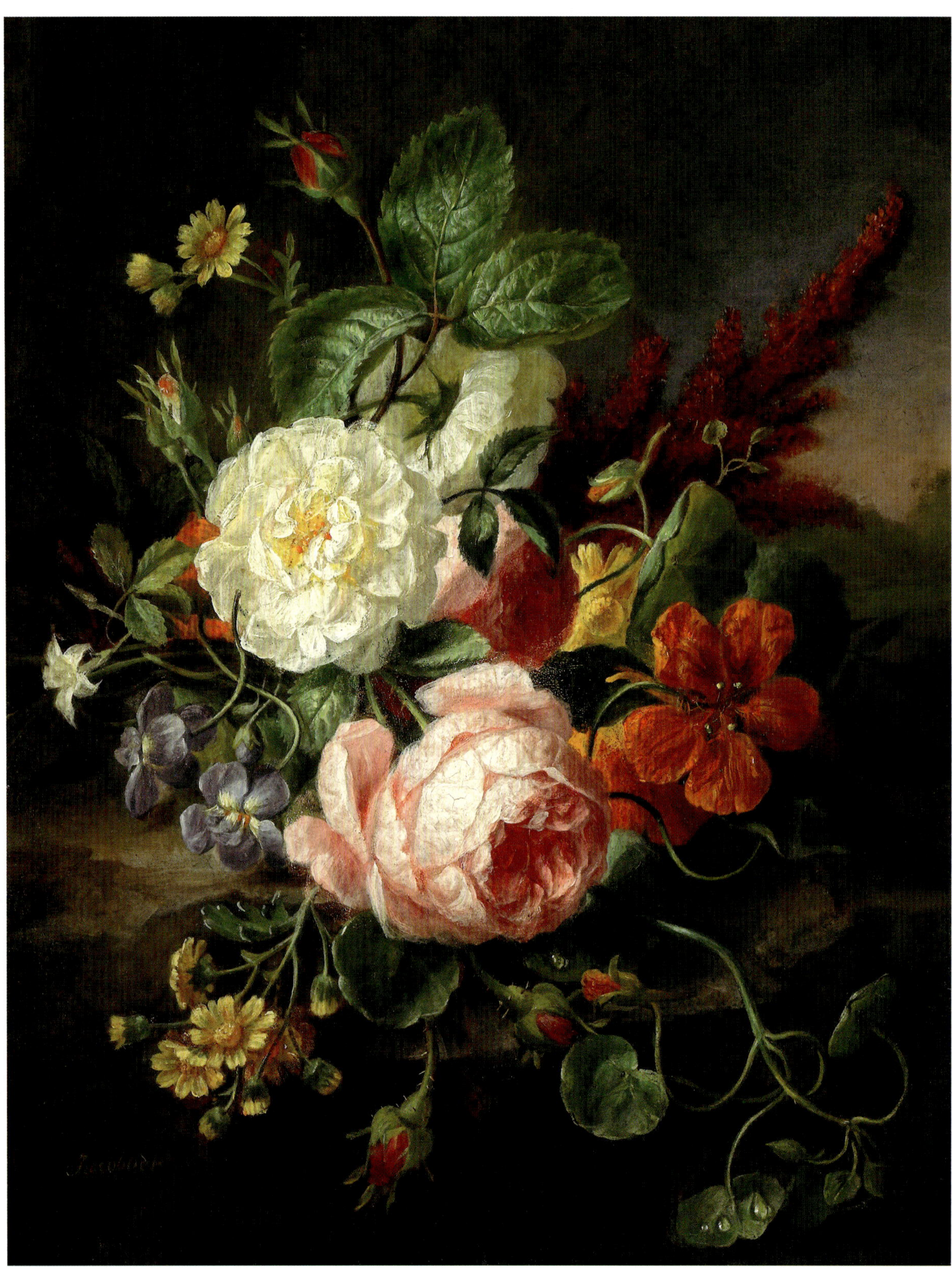

10

MOÏSE JACOBBER

(FRENCH, 1786–1863)

Still Life with Flowers, before 1863

Oil on copper, 13 13⁄16 × 11¼ in. (35 × 28.5 cm)

Musée des Beaux-Arts de Rouen, Association des Amis des Musées de la Ville de Rouen, 2008.8.2

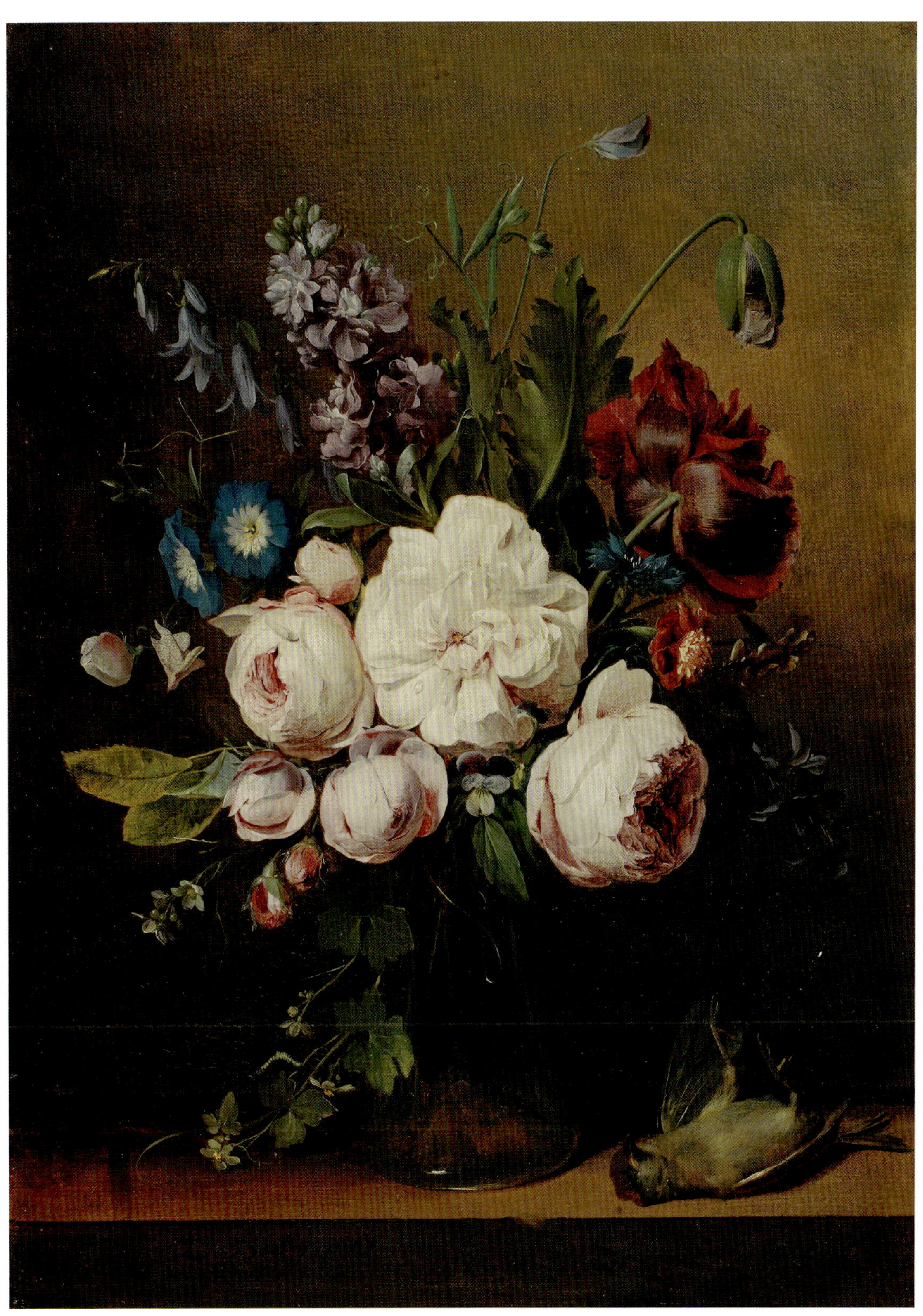

11
LOUIS LÉOPOLD BOILLY
(FRENCH, 1761–1845)

A Vase of Flowers, ca. 1790–95

Oil on paper, mounted on canvas, 18⅛ × 13⁵⁄₁₆ in. (46 × 33.8 cm)
The Syndics of the Fitzwilliam Museum, Bequest of
Henry Rogers Broughton, Second Baron Fairhaven, PD.17-1975

FLOWER PAINTING IN LYON

FROM THE RENAISSANCE TO THE TURN OF THE twentieth century, the French city of Lyon was a world center for commerce and industry that produced many generations of excellent artists. These factors converged in the "Lyon school" of flower painting. The circumstances leading to the formation of this school are complex. First, the city's wealth and international stature were greatly dependent on the silk and other specialty fabrics that had been produced there since the 1500s. Such fine and expensive textiles often featured sophisticated floral motifs. Second, at the beginning of the nineteenth century, Napoleon I undertook administrative reforms that were part of his effort to stabilize and decentralize France after the Revolution. One direct result of this reorganization was the foundation in 1801 of the Musée des Beaux-Arts de Lyon, where some of Europe's greatest artistic masterpieces were subsequently transferred. The museum's small-scale but ongoing effort to gather and exhibit excellent examples of flower painting for the instruction and inspiration of designers working in the silk industry gained formal recognition when it opened the Salle des fleurs, dedicated to that purpose in the early years. The special importance of the art of painting for local industry was also underscored by the institution of a professorship in floral painting at the École des Beaux-Arts (itself founded by imperial decree in 1807 expressly to prepare students for eventual work producing designs for the silk factory). All of the artists represented in this section of the catalogue (and corresponding area of the exhibition) were either professors or students of the École and its Classe des fleurs. Although monolithic myths about the entire Lyon "school" developed within decades of its foundation—epitomized by its abrupt rejection by the critic and poet Charles Baudelaire, who called Lyon the "penitentiary of painting"—historians today must not take such reports at face value. Instead, evaluating the unique but complex contribution of the flower painters from Lyon to the larger history of art in nineteenth-century France calls for more objectivity.[1]

The Lyon-born artist Antoine Berjon is usually, and appropriately, considered the true founder of this school. He was not the École's first appointed professor, but he was arguably the most influential, instructing

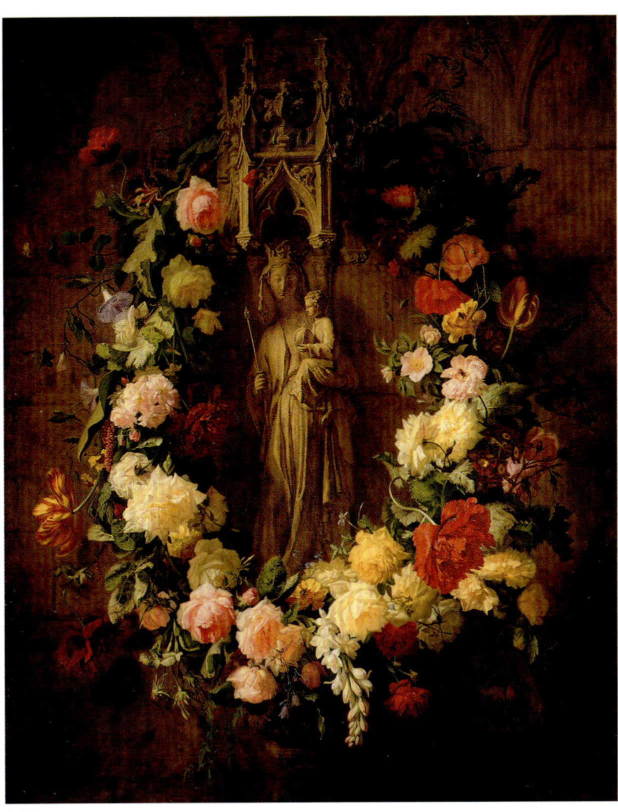

FIG. 56 Simon Saint-Jean, *An Offering to the Virgin*, 1842, oil on canvas. Musée des Beaux-Arts, Lyon, purchased 1844

some six hundred students throughout his tenure. Though he was eventually dismissed from his post for various personal and political reasons, he developed a unique style of painting that differed in several respects from earlier approaches taken by Gerard and Cornelius van Spaendonck, Jan Frans van Dael, and their contemporaries and followers. The earliest painting by Berjon in this exhibition, *Fruits and Flowers in a Wicker Basket* (cat. no. 12), was executed in Paris and shown in the Salon of 1810, after which it was installed in the Salle des fleurs in Lyon. That same year, Berjon was appointed professor at the École. The reception of this painting evidences the esteem accorded to Berjon at the time. In fact, while it might appear similar in some respects to works by artists of the Franco-Dutch tradition, it indicates Berjon's future stylistic direction both in dramatic setting—enhanced by its emphatic vanishing point—and in icily observed details such as the reflection of the wicker basket on the marble ledge. Berjon's tendency to privilege such personal moments of observation rather than traditional artistic formulas is fully developed in the exquisite *Bouquet of Lilies and Roses in a Basket on a Chiffonier* (cat. no. 13), with its playful treatment of space (unfortunately considered incompetent by some contemporary reviewers), its restrained palette, and the evident delight the artist took in transcribing the opposition of various natural and manufactured surfaces.

After Berjon's departure, the leadership of the school (if not the professorship) passed to Simon Saint-Jean. Saint-Jean was the perfect product of the taste for highly finished works that had been fulfilled by his two teachers, each of whom excelled in meticulous painting styles: Pierre-Henri Révoil, the leading Troubadour painter, and Augustin-Alexandre Thierriat, Berjon's long-serving successor at the École. Saint-Jean was very successful and set a standard against which all other practitioners of the genre, including Eugène Delacroix, were compared. He was in great demand by members of the European nobility, such as the fourth marquess of Hertford, founder of the Wallace Collection in London, where Saint-Jean's works are still held. Saint-Jean also took part in the Great Exhibition of 1851 at the Crystal Palace in London. Examples of his earlier successes

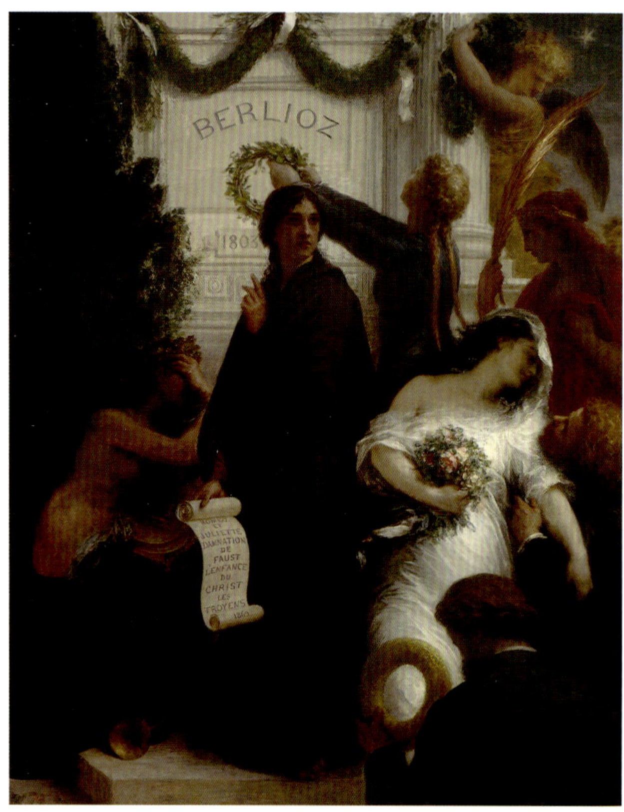

FIG. 57 Henri Fantin-Latour, *The Commemoration*, 1876, oil on canvas. Musée de Grenoble, MG 1219

include *Flowers in a Hat* of 1834 (cat. no. 14), with its charming conceit of flowers presented in a straw bonnet set in a garden, instead of in a vase on a ledge or table, and *The Gardener* (*La Jardinière*) (cat. no. 15), which was bought by the French state for the Lyon museum after it was exhibited in the Paris Salon of 1837. Saint-Jean was also actively involved with the silk factory's industrialization by conceiving complicated designs as challenges to the weaver's art, such as his *An Offering to the Virgin* of 1842 (fig. 56), which was later adapted as a design executed in silk.

Indeed, over the course of Saint-Jean's career, the entire procedure of floral painting in Lyon underwent a profound evolution. The observation of individual flowers and their assembly into bouquets or arrangements gave way to "statement" paintings—whether religious, allegorical, or historical—that could carry the same weight and meaning as figure painting. For example, local prefect Adrien de Gasparin encouraged students thus in 1832: "See the young flower designer looking to the history painter for inspiration, breadth of treatment, artistic feeling and approach, which he will adapt to his own art to imbue it with an ideal he would never find in the mere study of plants."[2]

This idea must have certainly inspired midcentury Lyonnais artists such as Jean Marie Reignier, one of Berjon's most faithful pupils, who sought to imbue flower painting with higher meaning and ever-more ambitious stylistic and technical achievements. For example, his *Homage to Queen Hortense* of 1856 (cat. no. 16) is dedicated to the mother of Emperor Napoleon III and shows her portrait bust surrounded by a multitude of visual compliments, including her namesake flower, *Hortensia*. It was exhibited in the Salon of 1857, from which it was purchased by the city of Lyon. It is perhaps the most highly wrought of Reignier's many such compositions and drew critics' comparisons to poetry. Though the painting's artistry might today be considered contrived and at odds with the simplicity sought by later artists such as Henri Fantin-Latour, it is fruitful to consider the influence of Lyonnais precedents on Fantin's choice to work in the genres of painted tributes as well as flowers (fig. 57).

Pierre-Adrien Chabal-Dussurgey (Chabal) was also a product of the Lyon École des Beaux-Arts. Like Reignier, he was popular, ambitious, and successful and cannot be easily characterized as a latecomer. For example, his *Concordia* of 1878 (cat. no. 17) was understood and savagely condemned by the liberal press as an antirepublican eulogy for the Second Empire (Chabal had been employed by Empress Eugénie). Though his politics may have then seemed rabidly *retardataire* to some critics, he was considered and accepted as an advanced and capable artist and a respected teacher. Indeed, Chabal was not at all doctrinaire according to his pupils, who included such unexpected characters as the critic and amateur Philippe Burty, an avid advocate for the reform of art who had organized the 1860 exhibition at the Galerie Martinet where Chardin was rediscovered.

MM

1. See especially Hardouin-Fugier 1978; Musée des Beaux-Arts, Lyon 1982; Gifu Museum of Arts 1990; Ramond et al. 2007; Béghain 2011.
2. Quoted in Hardouin-Fugier 1978, 16.

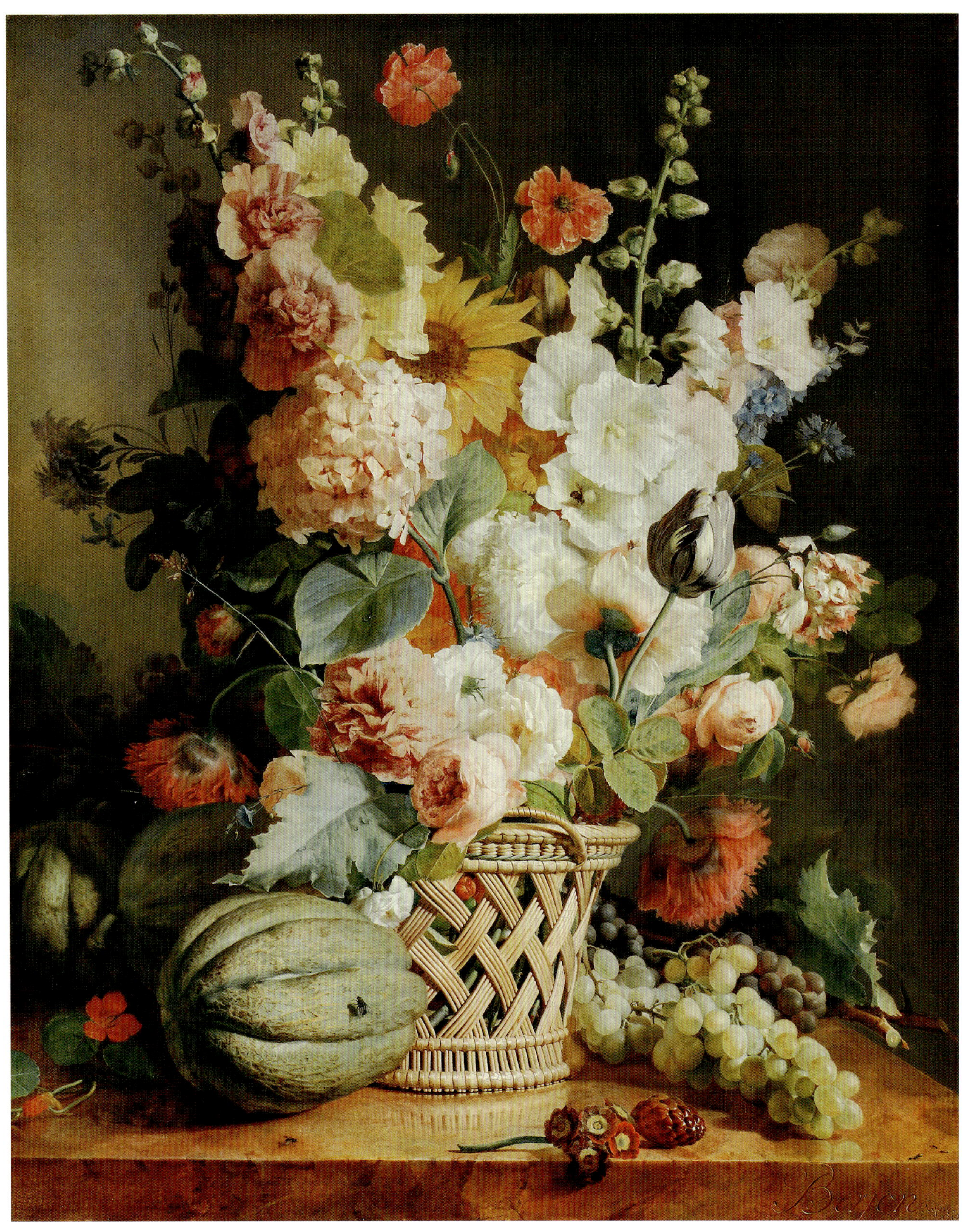

12
ANTOINE BERJON
(FRENCH, 1754–1843)

Fruits and Flowers in a Wicker Basket, 1810

Oil on canvas, 42⅛ × 34¼ in. (107 × 87 cm)
Musée des Beaux-Arts de Lyon, A 181

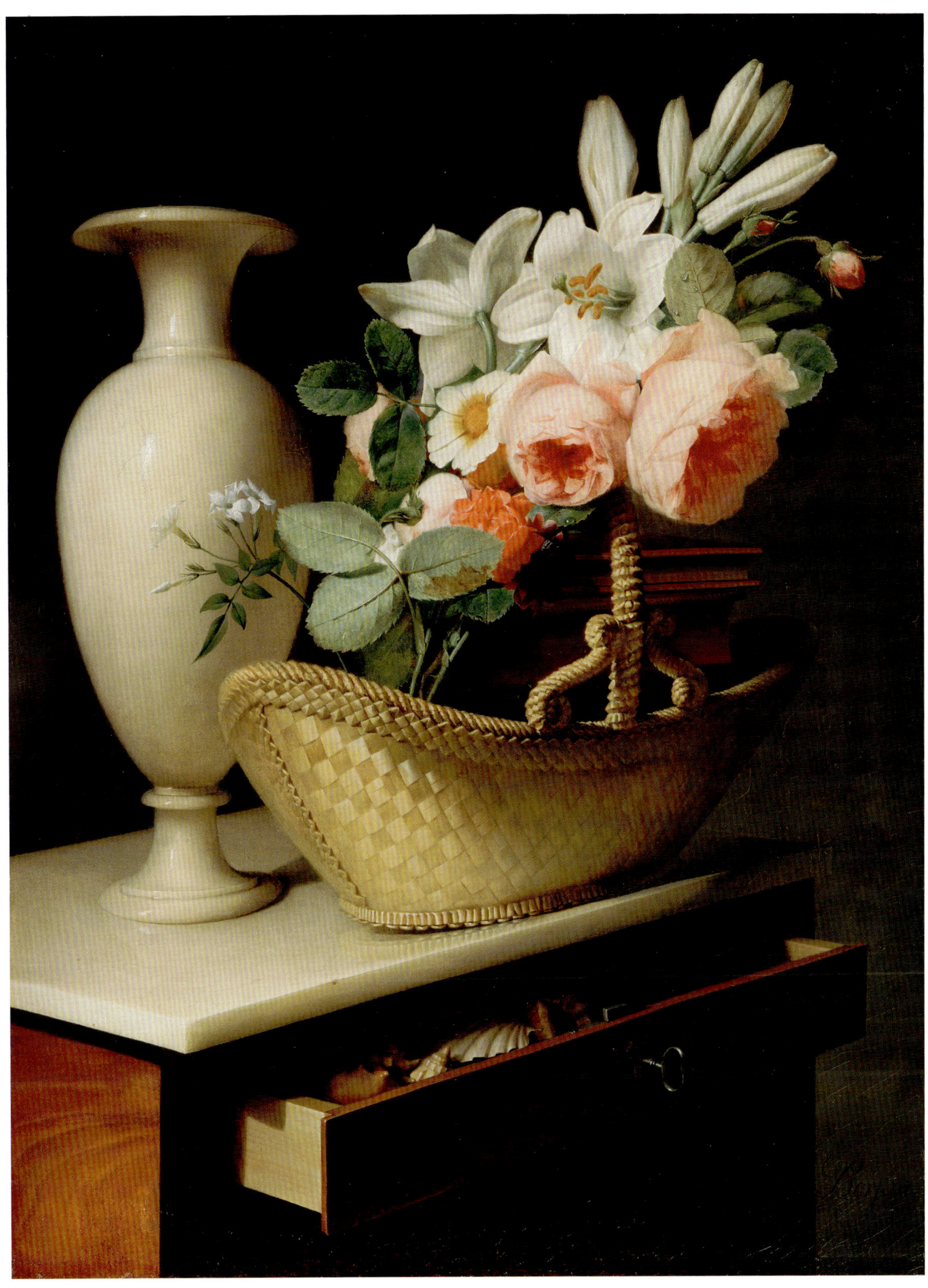

13 ANTOINE BERJON
(FRENCH, 1754–1843)

Bouquet of Lilies and Roses in a Basket on a Chiffonier, 1814

Oil on canvas, 26³⁄₁₆ × 19½ in. (66.5 × 49.5 cm)
Musée du Louvre, Département des Peintures, Paris, RF 1974-10

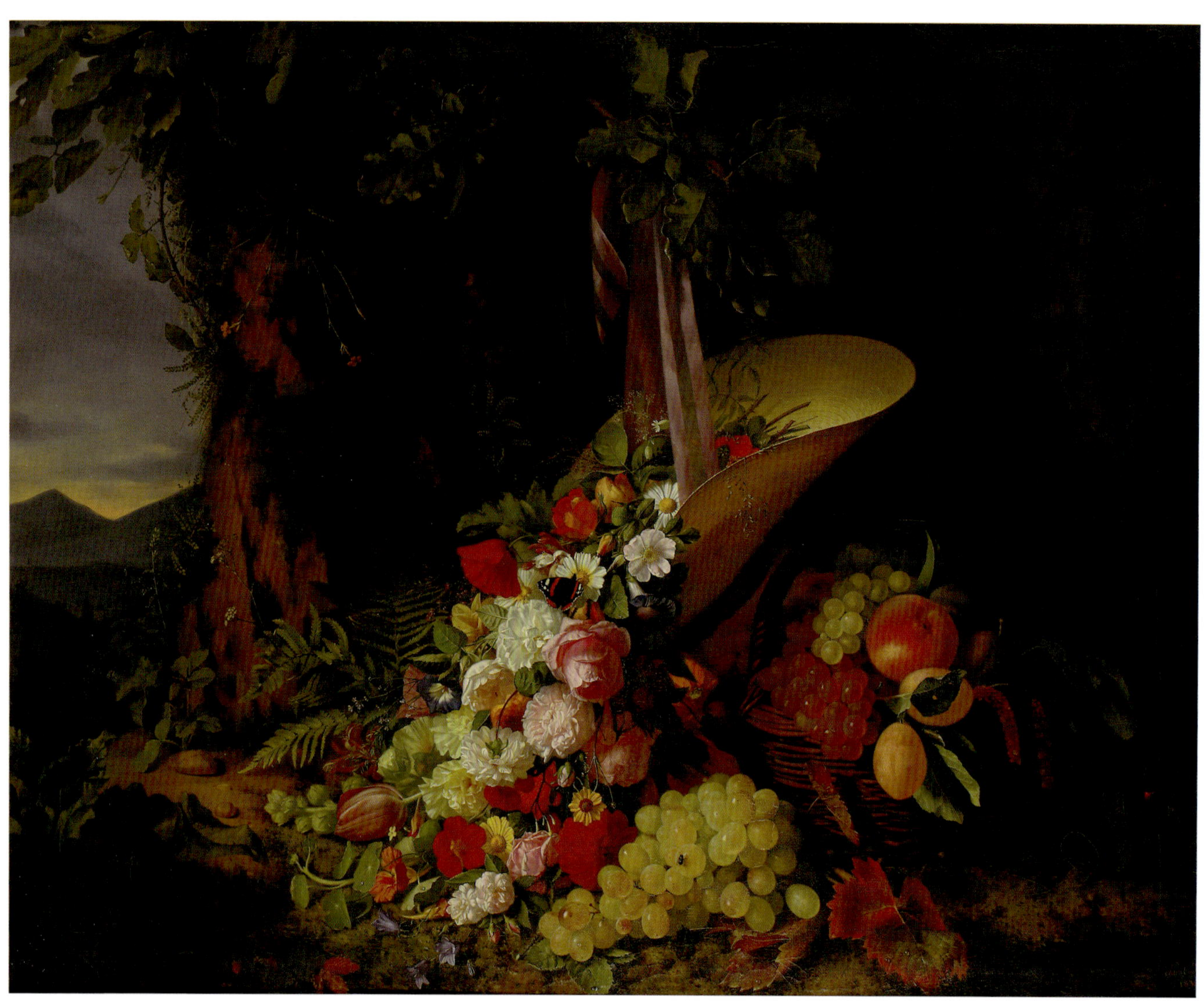

14
SIMON SAINT-JEAN
(FRENCH, 1808–1860)

Flowers in a Hat, 1833

Oil on canvas, 39⅜ × 48⁷⁄₁₆ in. (100 × 123 cm)
Musée des Beaux-Arts de Rouen, Dépot de l'État, 1833, D.834.1

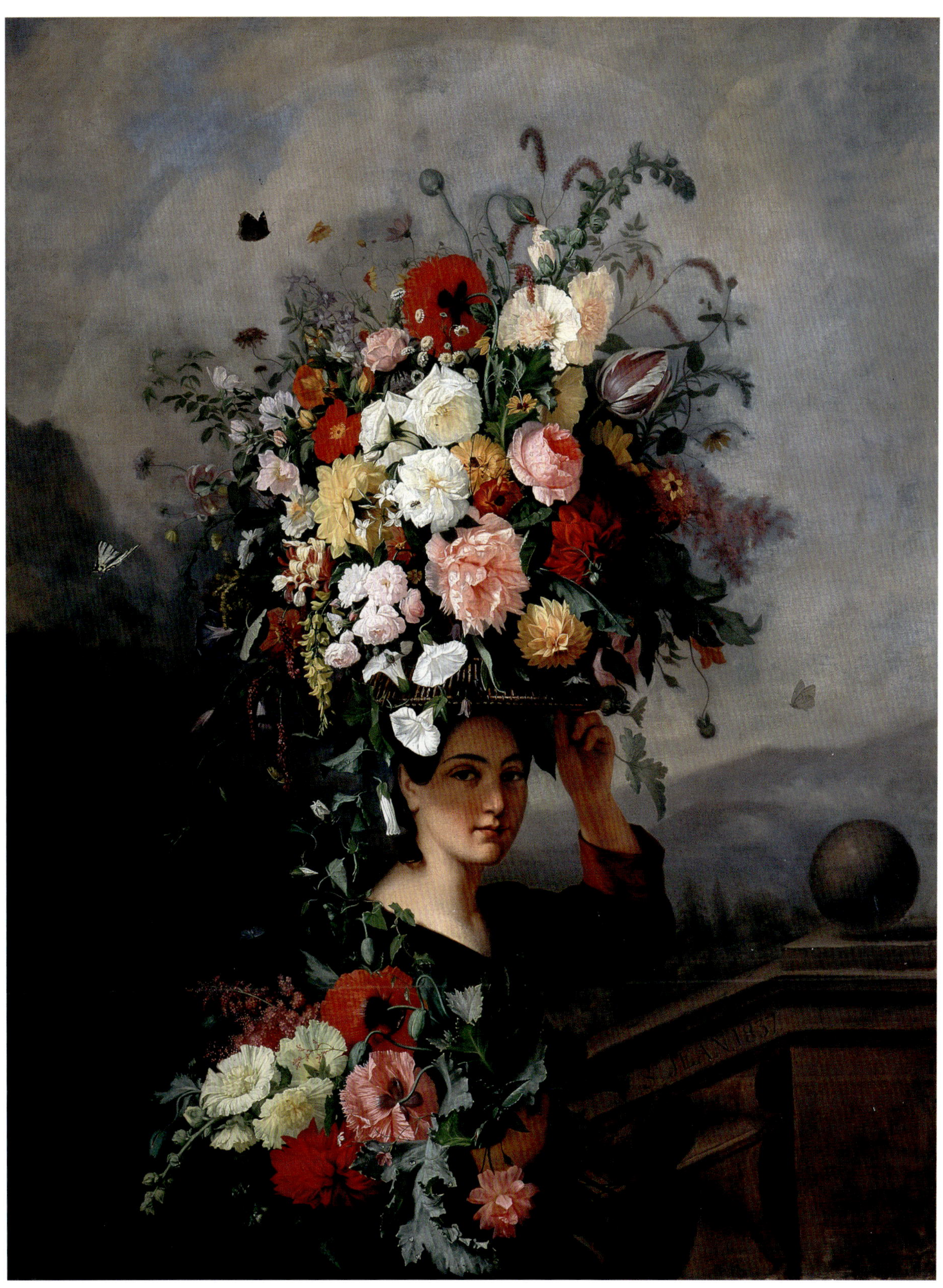

15 SIMON SAINT-JEAN
(FRENCH, 1808–1860)

The Gardener (La Jardinière), 1837

Oil on canvas, 63 × 46½ in. (160 cm × 118 cm)
Musée des Beaux-Arts de Lyon (A 24), deposit of Centre nationale des arts plastiques (France) (FNAC PFH-8116)

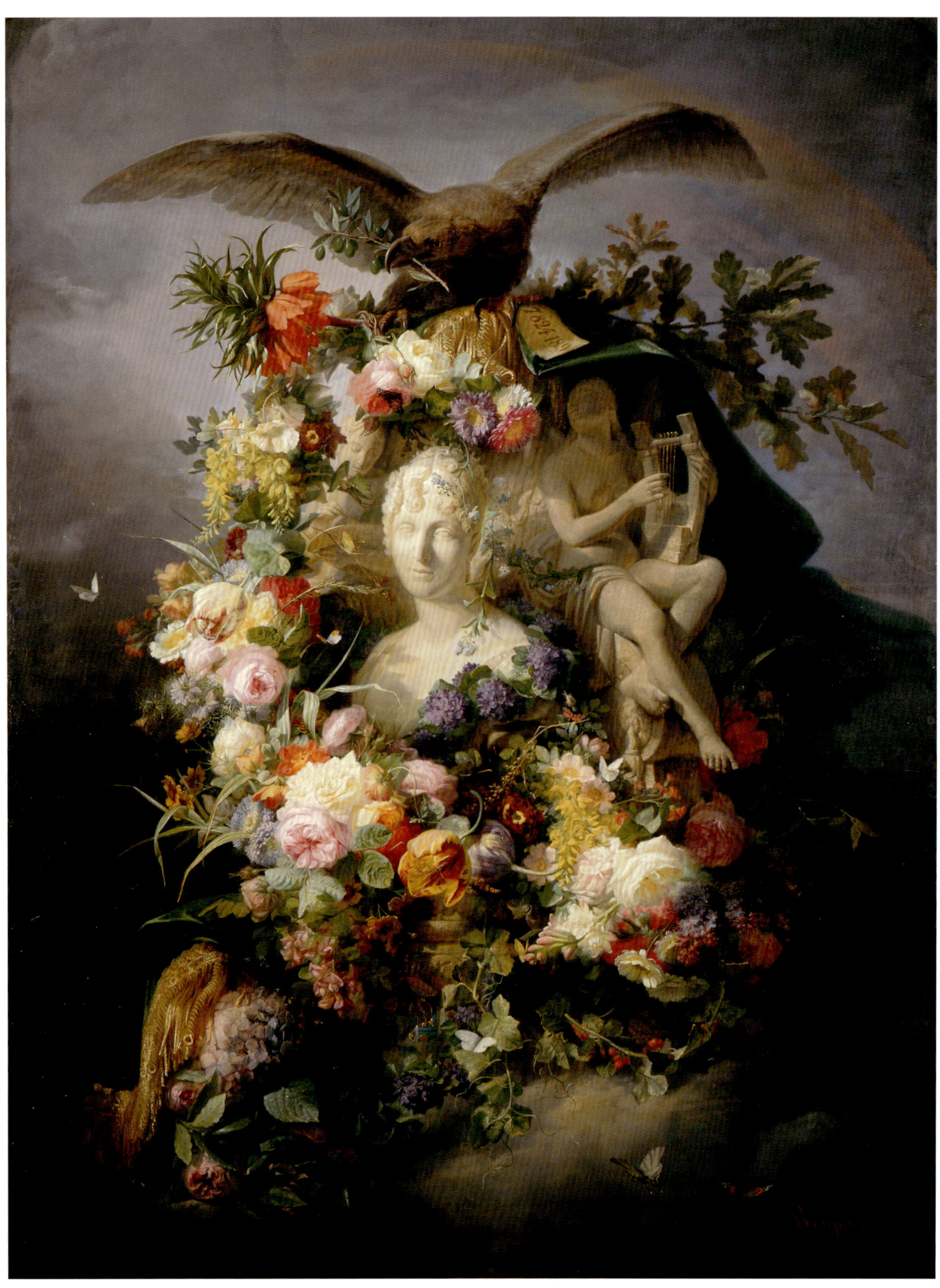

16
JEAN MARIE REIGNIER
(FRENCH, 1815–1886)

Homage to Queen Hortense, 1856

Oil on canvas, 83³⁄₁₆ × 64³⁄₁₆ in. (211 cm × 163 cm)
Musée des Beaux-Arts de Lyon, A 2896

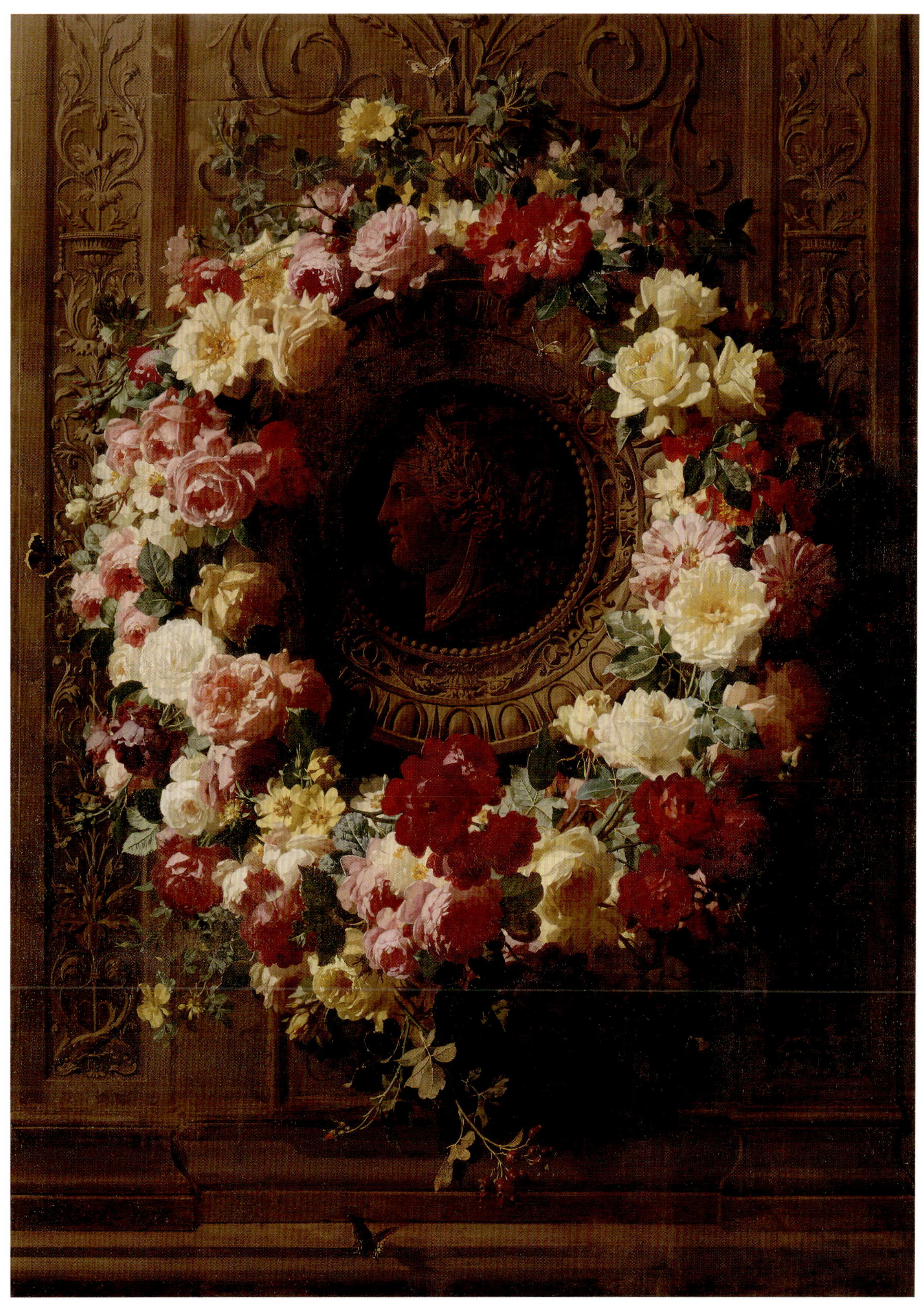

17
PIERRE-ADRIEN CHABAL-DUSSURGEY (CHABAL)
(FRENCH, 1819–1902)

Concordia, 1878

Oil on canvas, 70⅛ × 51$\frac{9}{16}$ in. (178 cm × 131 cm)
Musée des Beaux-Arts de Lyon, B 313

DELACROIX, COURBET, AND THE MODERN EXPERIENCE OF FLOWERS

THREE OF THE PAINTERS CONSIDERED IN THIS section—Eugène Delacroix, Gustave Courbet, and Frédéric Bazille—did not paint floral still lifes continuously or in great quantity during their careers. Nevertheless, each of them made contributions that revolutionized the genre and greatly elevated its status.

Delacroix painted his floral still lifes largely in two separate campaigns. The first, a small output of paintings and sketches, is documented by letters and signatures as early as 1833 (when the two examples included here, cat. nos. 18 and 19, were created) and possibly the years immediately following. The second period was a more sustained effort, culminating in four monumental paintings made around 1848–49 that were exhibited together at the Exposition Universelle of 1855 (the fifth was withdrawn for unknown reasons). These large, ambitious works represented complex arrangements of flowers in various settings: on a simple tabletop (for example, see figs. 16 and 67); in a richly appointed interior (see fig. 31); and casually set in a basket in a garden (see fig. 15). On Delacroix's first presentation of two of these flower paintings at the Salon of 1849, the works met with an immediate and enthusiastic critical response among such admirers as Champfleury and Théophile Gautier but did little to mollify his detractors. Besides these well-known works, only a few other oils are extant, and two garden scenes are known to be lost. In addition to oil paintings, Delacroix left behind an impressive and extremely beautiful group of freely executed watercolor studies that are not still lifes but, significantly, studies of living flowers and gardens.

Delacroix's motivations for turning to this genre in his later years have never been fully explained. Some cite his friendship with Adrien de Jussieu, director of botany at the Jardin des plantes, as evidence of Delacroix's scientific and botanical interests. (Delacroix had already worked extensively there alongside his friend, the animalier sculptor Antoine-Louis Barye.) Others have proclaimed these works as an indication of his desire to be a "universal painter," practiced in every genre (he wrote that "the true painter is one who knows all of nature") and as an outgrowth of the appearance of floral themes as secondary elements in his 1833 Palais Bourbon commission for the Salon du roi. Some have seen his intentions in the context of the "Romantic personality"—as a challenge to the great painters of the past, such as Jan Davidsz. de Heem, or as an attempt to paint an ancien régime–type decorative scheme—while still others interpret them as sentimental souvenirs of friendships, such as with George Sand. And it has been argued, particularly by T. J. Clark, that they demonstrate Delacroix's retreat from the political realities and social complexities of the day, underscored by his withdrawal from Paris to the simplicity of his country villa at Champrosay.

The paintings considered here, dating from the early 1830s, can offer valuable insight into the circumstances of Delacroix's more purely artistic (not to say technical and philosophical) motivations for practicing flower painting, which by this time had become a highly specialized genre in the hands of Franco-Dutch and Lyon school painters. *Still Life with Dahlias* (cat. no. 19) is usually considered an unfinished work. However, the early Delacroix scholar Alfred Robaut implies that it might be an experiment as much as a sketch. He cites an episode when the painter (in the midst of executing the Palais Bourbon murals) suddenly took the opportunity to advise an assistant that art should not follow the model too exactly, using the painting of flowers and foliage as an example. This anecdote anticipates Delacroix's famous letter to Constant Dutilleux about the misguided emphasis on detail and finish in flower painting practiced by more traditional artists (see p. 21). The status of *Dahlias* as a talisman for Delacroix's aesthetic of the free play of the mind in the service of art is perhaps further borne out in the fact that it belonged to the collector Gustave Arosa and was later copied by Gauguin (fig. 58). It is possibly then a mistake to call *Vase of Flowers* (cat. no. 18), firmly dated 1833, as more fully realized, since by the standards of the time, it would have been considered extremely sketchlike. However, this work (made for Delacroix's friend, the artist Frédéric Villot) exactly embodies concepts more fully explored in the 1840s and expressed in the letter to Dutilleux about the importance of subordinating detail to the "general effect."

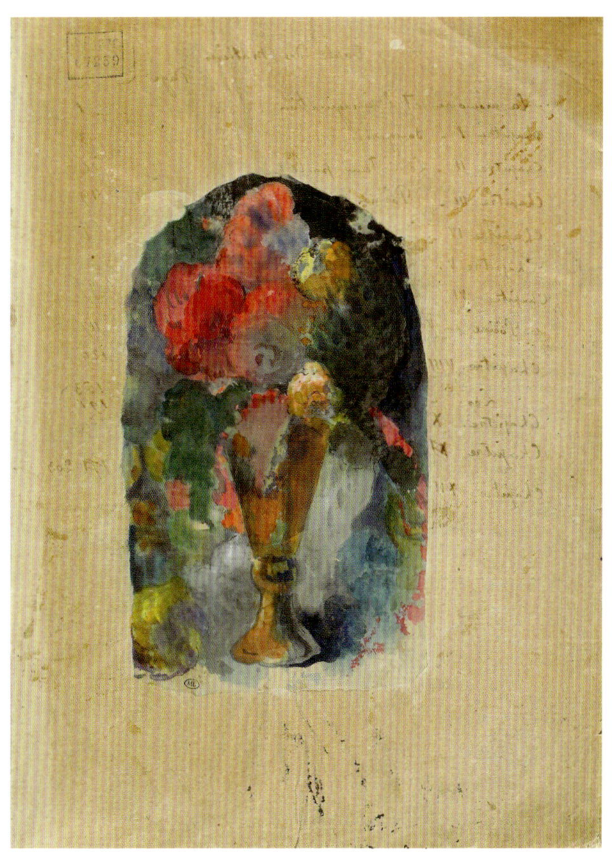

FIG. 58 Paul Gauguin, *Dahlias in a Vase, after Delacroix*, late nineteenth to early twentieth century, watercolor, ink, pencil, and pen on paper. Musée du Louvre, Paris, RF 7259.3

Courbet's personality as well his art were very different from Delacroix's, and though Delacroix was perhaps more eloquent and lucid, neither artist felt inhibited in his verbal self-expression. Unfortunately, Courbet sometimes resorted to brutal quips and barbs and was prone to exaggeration and misstatement. Therefore, his most-quoted comment on his own considerable artistic achievement as a painter of floral subjects—that he was "coining money out of flowers"—should be approached with more than customary caution (but not ignored) by the historian of the genre. Indeed, though it was not Courbet's express intention to become a flower painter, he had an easy way of generously and spontaneously appropriating any pictorial genre when the opportunity presented itself, whether long term as in landscape or more short term as with floral still life. In fact, he did not hesitate when circumstantially or artistically confronted with any kind of subject matter, including the wide extremes of both society portraiture and pornography.

When Courbet was invited for increasingly long visits in 1862 and 1863 to the Saintonge house of his friend Étienne Baudry, he took an interest in his host's avocation in horticulture and botany and began to paint flowers with sustained and serious artistic attention. Many of the resulting paintings, including *Bouquet of Flowers in a Vase* (cat. no. 20), were sent to a charitable group exhibition for the benefit of the poor in the town hall of Saintes in 1863. This was an important event that included both established artists such as Jean-Baptiste-Camille Corot and younger ones such as Henri Fantin-Latour. Not only did Courbet's paintings meet with critical approbation there, but the entire enterprise was understood and set forth in the press as a successful realization of liberal and regional ideals over the traditional segregation of artists from each other and their public reinforced by official exhibitions and institutions in Paris.[1] In this context, it is unfair to Courbet and his convictions to claim these works as rooted in any art historical tradition, whether Dutch, Flemish, Neapolitan, or French. Therefore, even though his bouquets, like Dutch seventeenth-century precedents, are composed of flowers that do not bloom simultaneously in nature, his achievement goes far beyond stating solidarity with that past art for the mere purpose of reinforcing tradition's intrinsic value. Instead, Courbet's flower paintings reference the very tools that artists employed to earn their daily bread, which was their due as laborers in the greater service of the truth of nature itself.[2] Thus, Courbet's success "coining money" out of the flowers that coincidentally crossed his path in the utopian, liberal paradise of Saintonge was a prospect the programmatically opportunistic artist could not pass up without incurring the deepest kind of waste imaginable.

Early paintings by both Frédéric Bazille and Pierre-Auguste Renoir are also discussed here, as they demonstrate the huge impact of Delacroix's and Courbet's example. Though both earlier artists' engagement with the genre was limited, they not only provided direct

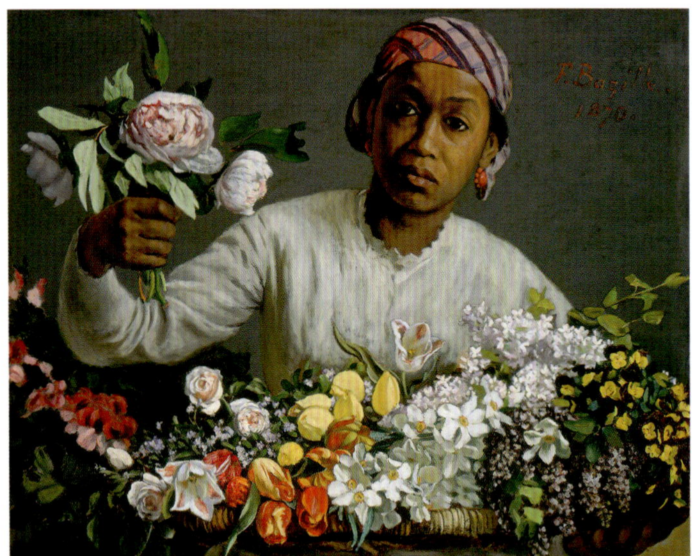

FIG. 59 Frédéric Bazille, *Young Woman with Peonies*, 1870, oil on canvas. National Gallery of Art, Washington, D.C., Collection of Mr. and Mrs. Paul Mellon

influences on the particular works in the exhibition, but they also inspired younger artists to treat this genre experimentally.

Bazille was one of the leaders of the Impressionist group, at that time not a formal association but a circle linked by friendship and common purpose. He died in the Franco-Prussian War in 1870, before reaching his full artistic maturity, depriving him of the title of Impressionist. Of all Bazille's floral subjects, the magnificent *Flowers* of 1868 (cat. no. 22) is most dependent on a precise precedent in Delacroix (see fig. 31). Bazille first saw Delacroix's works in the collection of the forward-thinking Montpellier native Alfred Bruyas, who was also Courbet's patron, and whose collection included one of Delacroix's finest floral watercolors. Bazille also attended Delacroix's posthumous studio sale in 1864, which included other floral subjects. If *Flowers* affectionately summons up the world of splendor the Second Empire created for the *grande bourgeoisie* (to which Bazille and his cousins for whom it was painted belonged), the later *African Woman with Peonies* (cat. no. 23) contrasts that world (now epitomized in the vase) with a human subject, a non-European female sitter. Similar oppositions were also explored, for example, in Manet's *Olympia*, which is often cited as Bazille's inspiration. *African Woman with Peonies* represents Bazille's second attempt at this composition and is thus extremely distilled. The first version (fig. 59) is more explicitly sourced to Courbet's similar treatments such as *Baskets of Flowers* (cat. no. 21).

Renoir dedicated a major part of his large output to this genre, which occupied him continually until his final years. One of his most successful early floral subjects, *Mixed Flowers in an Earthenware Pot* (cat. no. 24), was painted alongside his friend Claude Monet's *Still Life with Flowers and Fruit* (see fig. 21). While working on identical motifs was not an unusual artistic practice at the time, it should not merely be explained away as a cheap solution to the expense of setting up subjects. Rather, their deliberate communal work must be understood as representing true commitment to experimenting in the genre. Both paintings relate to the large scale and format of Courbet's *Bouquet of Flowers in a Vase*; however, Renoir chose a more oblique vantage point and a brighter palette, indicating a more contemporary approach.

The relevance of Delacroix and Courbet to these younger artists has not yet been the focus of much art historical discussion. It is hoped that by bringing them together here, more conversation about the intergenerational dialogue specific to the floral subject and its radical purposes will be encouraged. MM

1. Bonniot 1986, 209–14, and Soubiran 2007, 91–115.
2. Desbuissons 2008, 251–60.

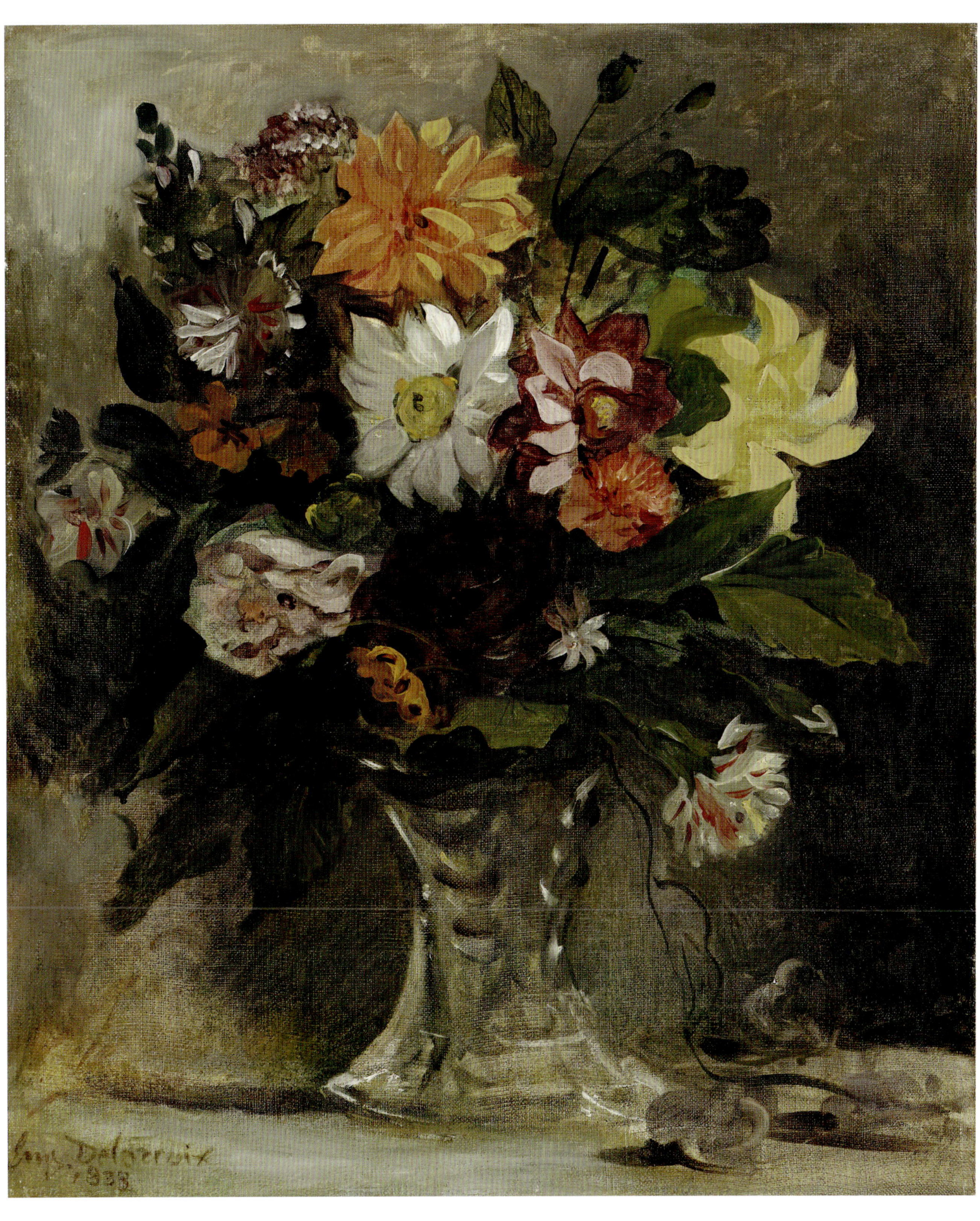

18
EUGÈNE DELACROIX
(FRENCH, 1798–1863)

A Vase of Flowers, 1833

Oil on canvas, 22 11/16 × 19 3/16 in. (57.7 × 48.8 cm)
Scottish National Gallery, Edinburgh, Purchased 1980, NG 2405

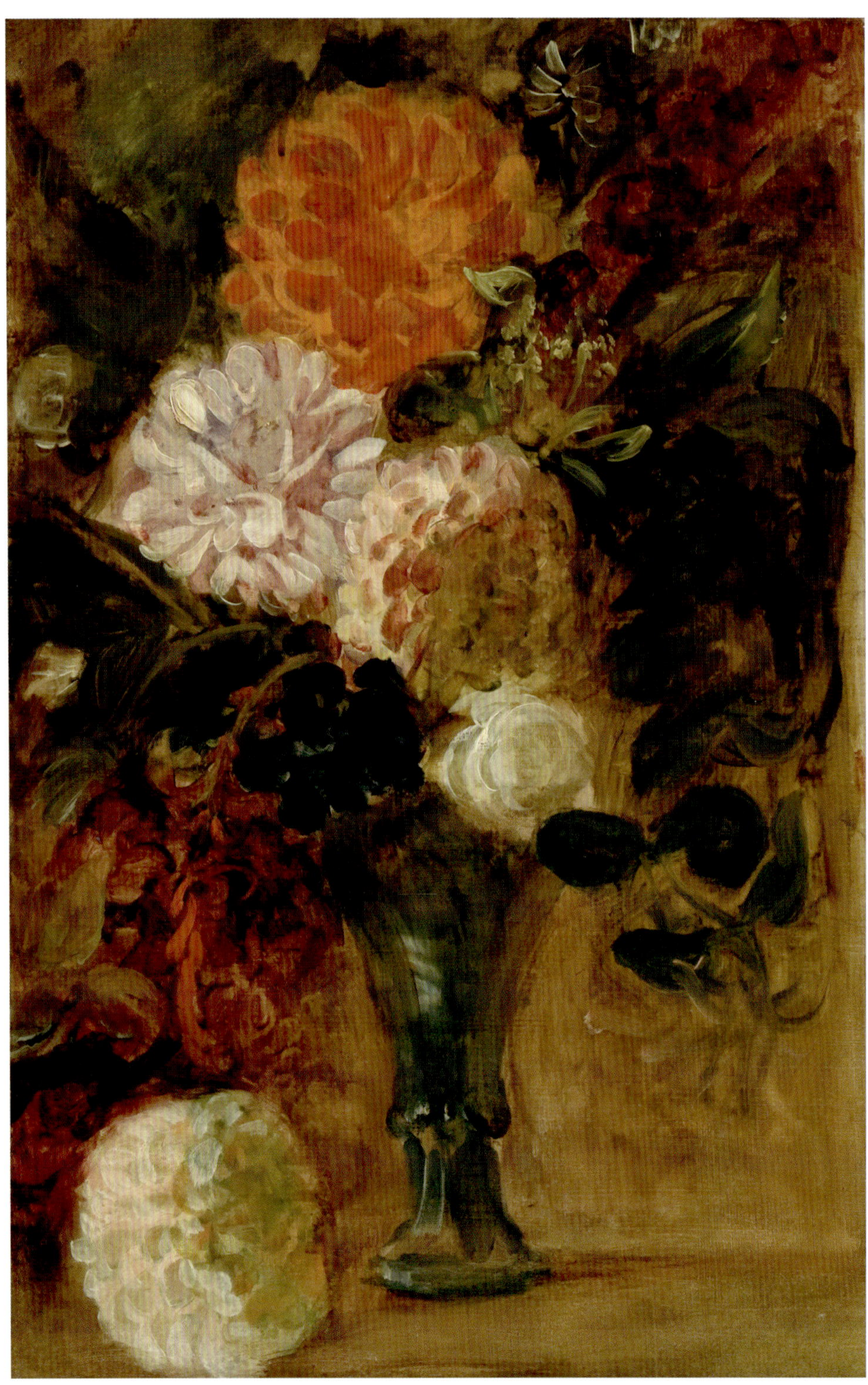

19
EUGÈNE DELACROIX
(FRENCH, 1798–1863)

Still Life with Dahlias, ca. 1833

Oil on canvas, 19 11/16 × 13 in. (50 × 33 cm)
Philadelphia Museum of Art, John G. Johnson Collection, 1917, 976

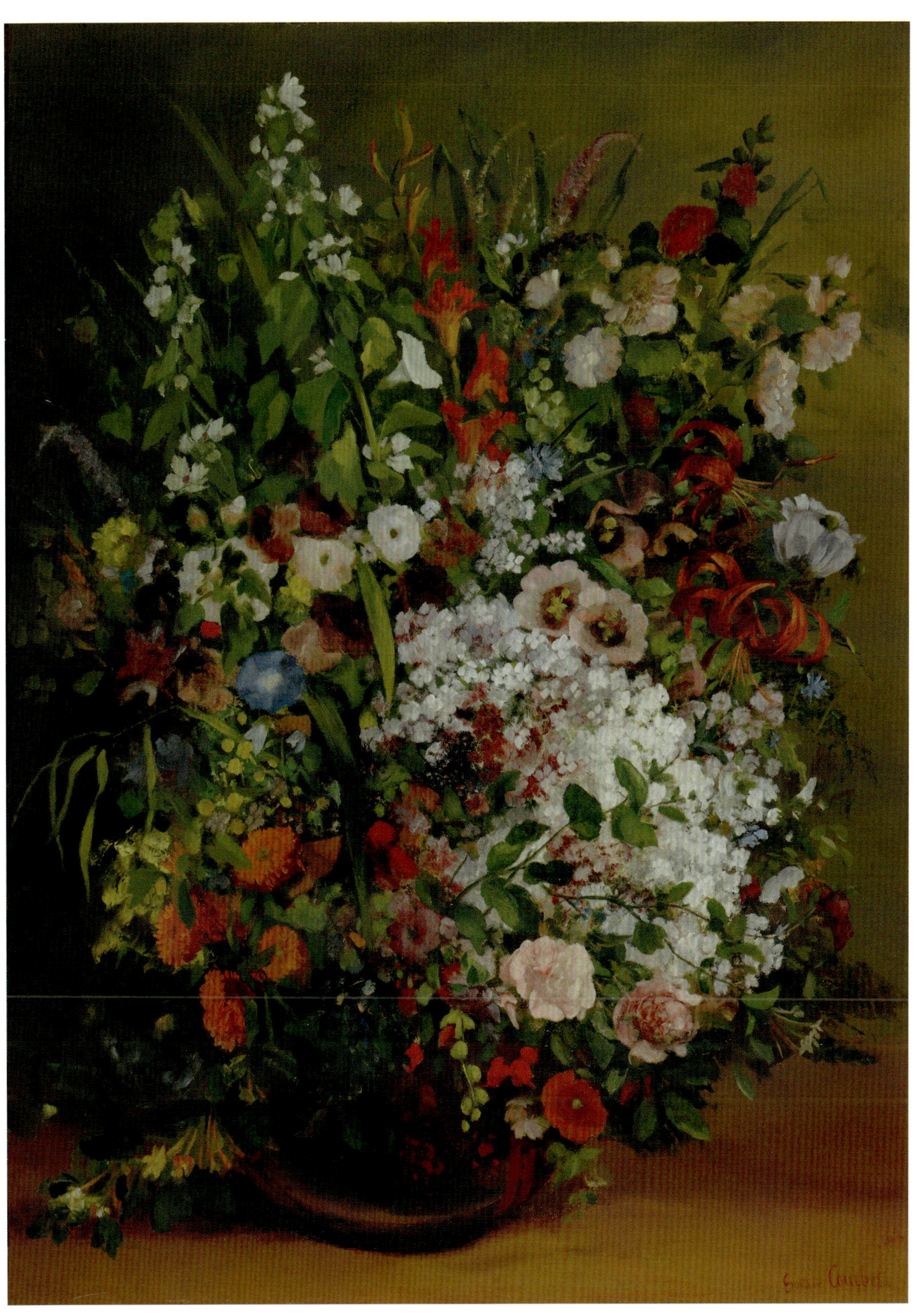

20
GUSTAVE COURBET
(FRENCH, 1819–1877)

Bouquet of Flowers in a Vase, 1862

Oil on canvas, 39½ × 28¾ in. (100.5 × 73 cm)
The J. Paul Getty Museum, Los Angeles, 85.PA.168

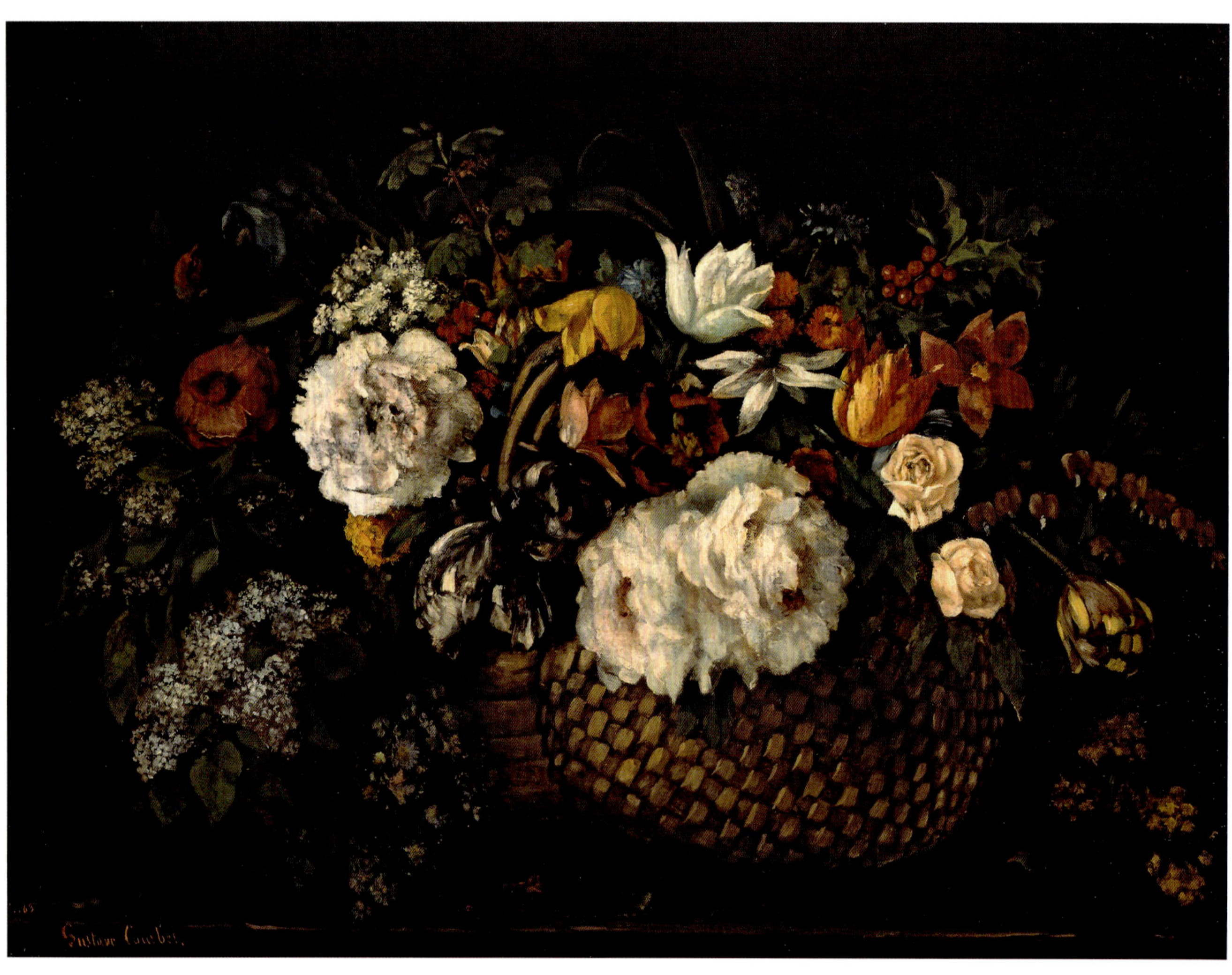

21
GUSTAVE COURBET
(FRENCH, 1819–1877)

Baskets of Flowers, 1863

Oil on canvas, 29⅞ × 39¹¹⁄₁₆ in. (75.9 × 100.8 cm)
Kelvingrove Art Gallery and Museum, Glasgow; Lent by Glasgow Life (Glasgow Museums) on behalf of Glasgow City Council. Presented by the Trustees of D. W. T. Cargill, 1950.

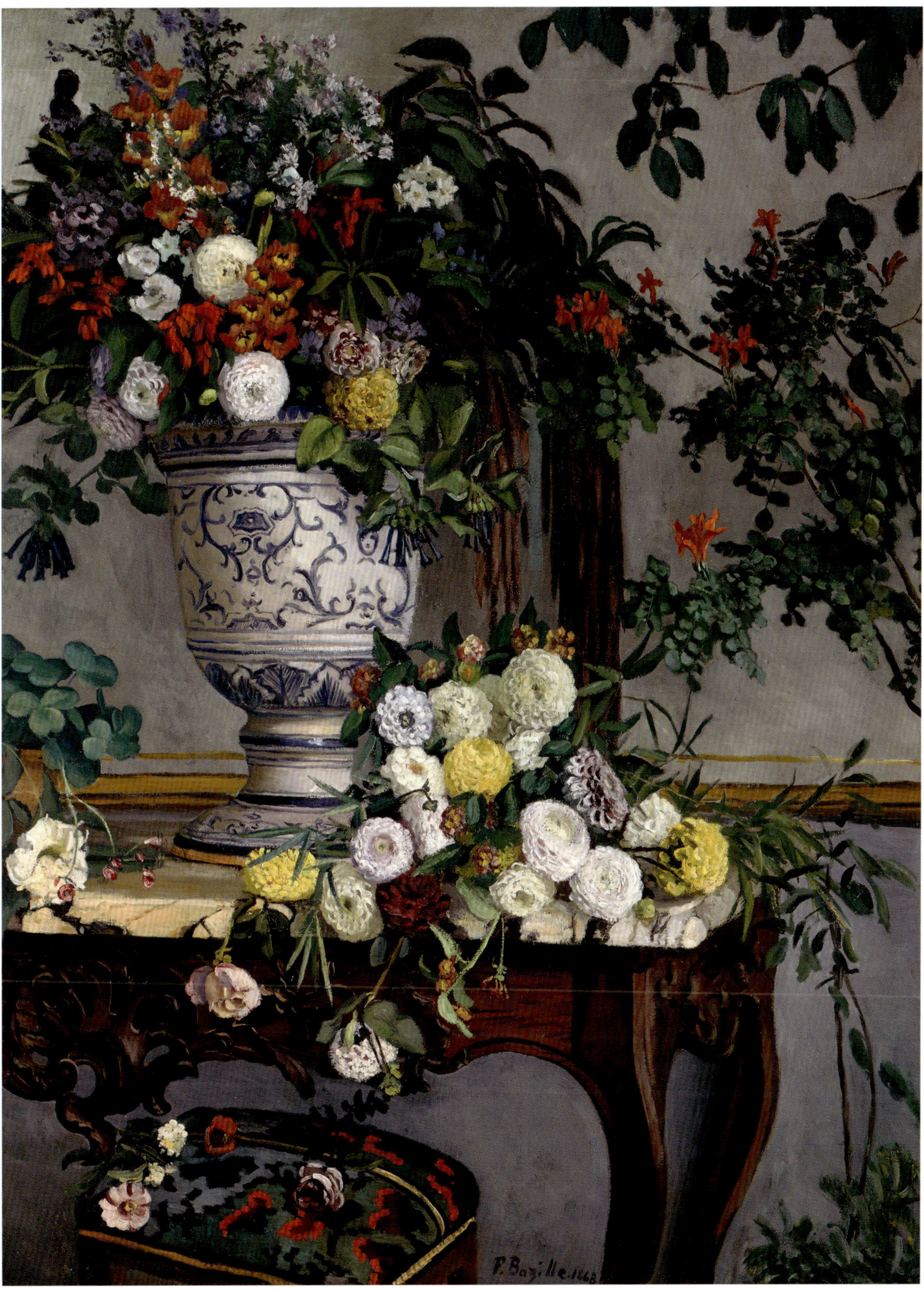

22 FRÉDÉRIC BAZILLE
(FRENCH, 1841–1870)

Flowers, 1868

Oil on canvas, 51³⁄₁₆ × 38³⁄₁₆ in. (130 × 97 cm)
Musée de Grenoble, MG 2911

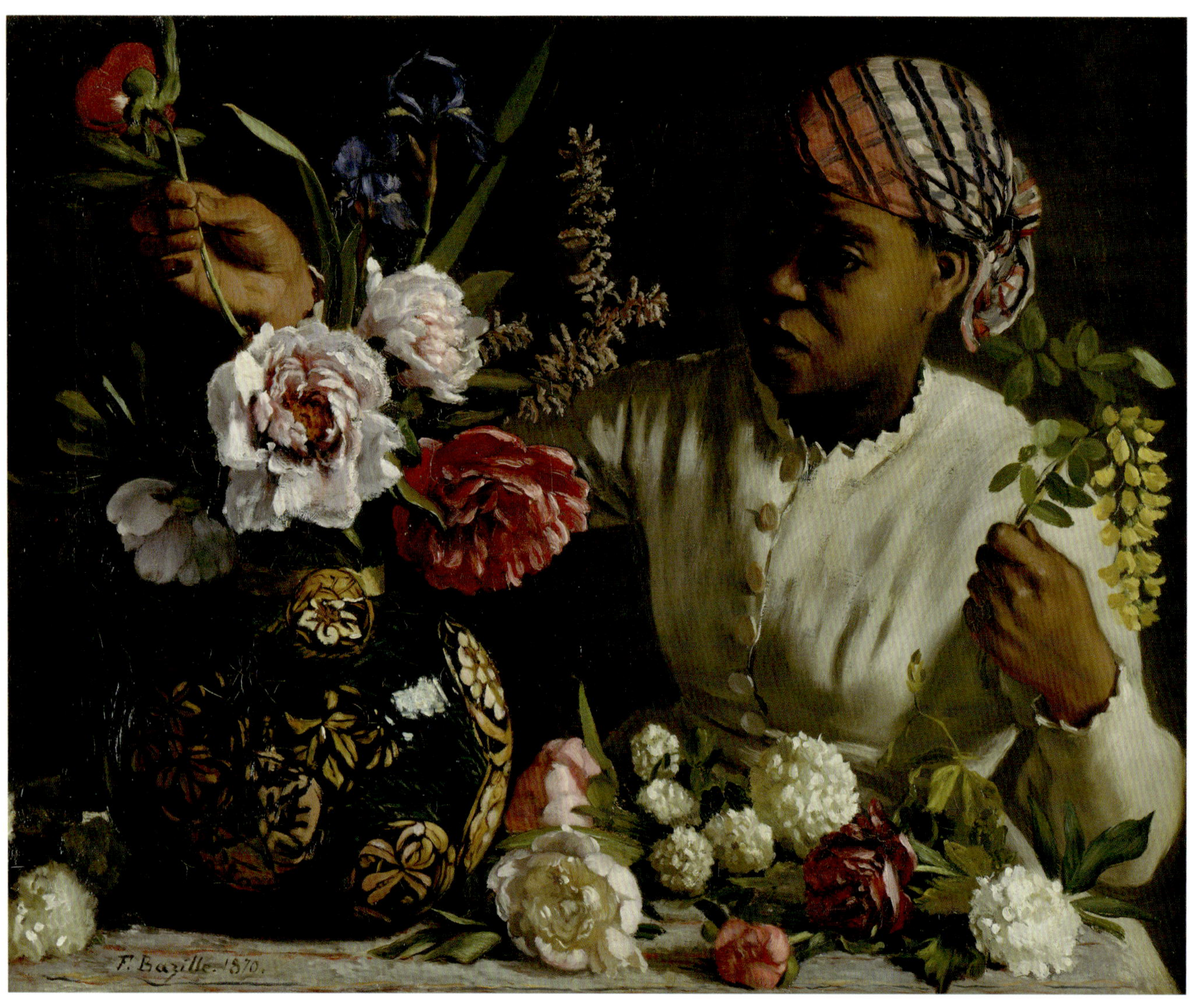

23 FRÉDÉRIC BAZILLE

(FRENCH, 1841–1870)

African Woman with Peonies, 1870

Oil on canvas, 23⅝ × 29½ in. (60 × 75 cm)

Musée Fabre, Montpellier, Gift of Marc Bazille, brother of the artist, 1918, 81-1-3

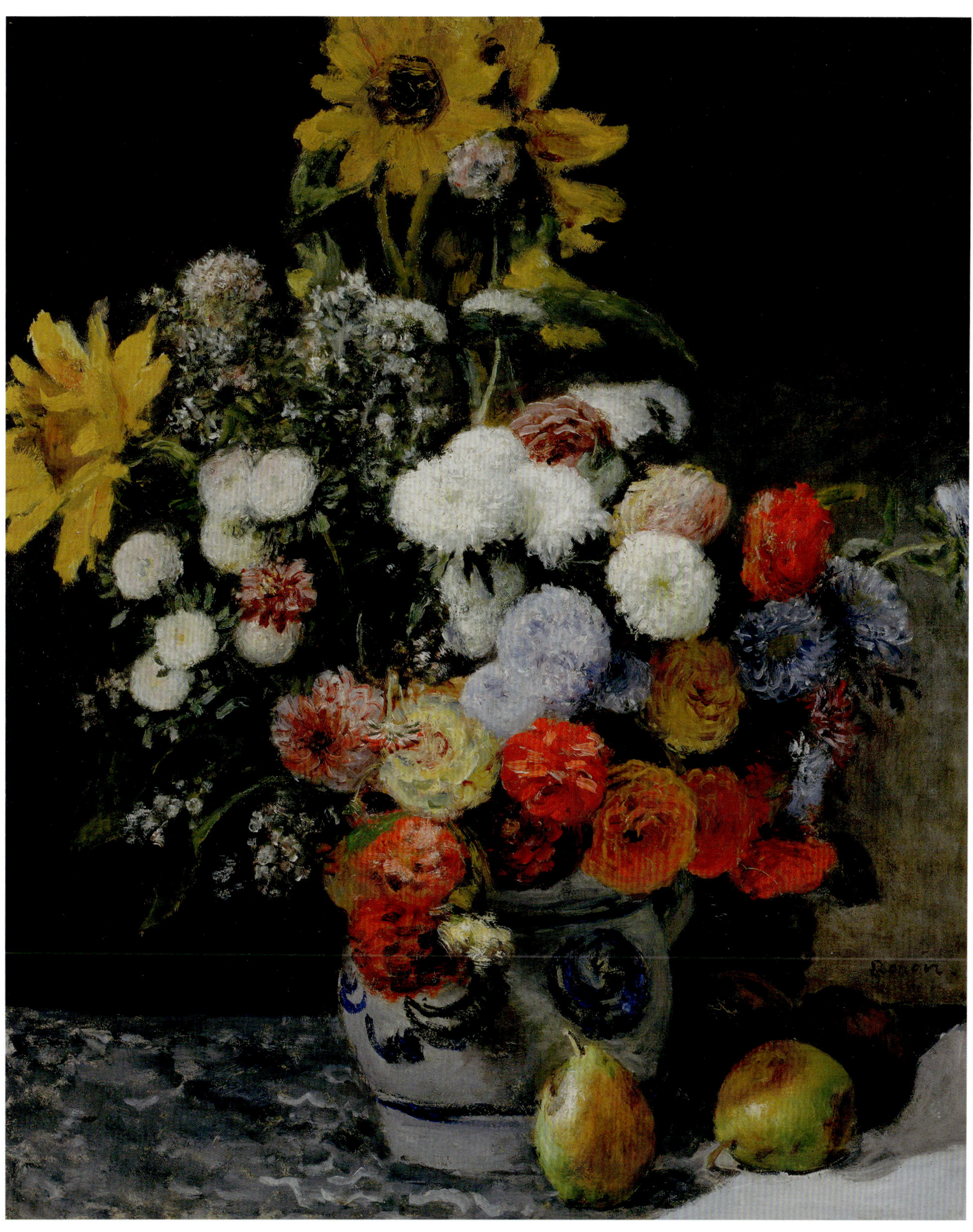

24 PIERRE-AUGUSTE RENOIR
(FRENCH, 1841–1919)

Mixed Flowers in an Earthenware Pot, ca. 1869

Oil on paperboard, mounted on canvas, 25½ × 21⅜ in. (64.8 × 54.3 cm)
Museum of Fine Arts, Boston, Bequest of John T. Spaulding, 48.592

Dallas and Richmond only

FANTIN-LATOUR AND DUBOURG: A SHARED ENTERPRISE

TOGETHER, HENRI FANTIN-LATOUR (FIG. 60) AND Victoria Dubourg (fig. 61) were among the steadiest and most recognized practitioners of flower painting in France in the second half of the nineteenth century. They met in 1866 while copying at the Louvre, which was a regular practice for both. By that time, Fantin had carefully established himself alongside various avant-gardes (English as well as French) but was also committed to exhibiting at the official Salons, as Dubourg did. By then, too, he had fully developed a particular style of painting quietly arranged and somewhat objectively observed still lifes seen against neutral backgrounds, rendered with tenderly applied brushstrokes. Dubourg adopted and pursued this style, certainly a conscious decision not lightly undertaken, for the rest of her life, at least in her known works.[1] They married in 1876 after a long engagement famously marked by his gift to her of *The Engagement Still Life* (cat. no. 25), one of his masterpieces in the genre. The painting definitively recalls the precedent of Jean-Siméon Chardin's sole-surviving floral subject (cat. no. 2). Dubourg's selectivity in her subject matter and approach as well as her market and exhibition strategies mirrored her husband's—together they marked a special terrain for themselves, one that has traditionally defied easy characterization but proved a welcome challenge for open-minded art historians.[2]

Like his friend Frédéric Bazille, Fantin was a crucial figure in the transition toward Impressionism. He was careful, however, to remain apart from the Impressionists and their exhibitions (indeed, he persuaded Manet to do the same, though Manet embraced the style in his later works) and did not adopt their name. Fantin was not averse to participating in artistic movements or to bearing banner-waving labels (he and Alphonse Legros formed the Société des Trois with James McNeill Whistler in 1858). But, as he participated with some future members of the Impressionist circle in the 1863 Salon des Refusés and portrayed others in such works as *Homage to Delacroix* (see fig. 17) and *A Studio at Les Batignolles* (1870, Musée d'Orsay, Paris), his disinterest in identifying himself with the group has troubled some who have tried to set him in this context.[3] Fantin

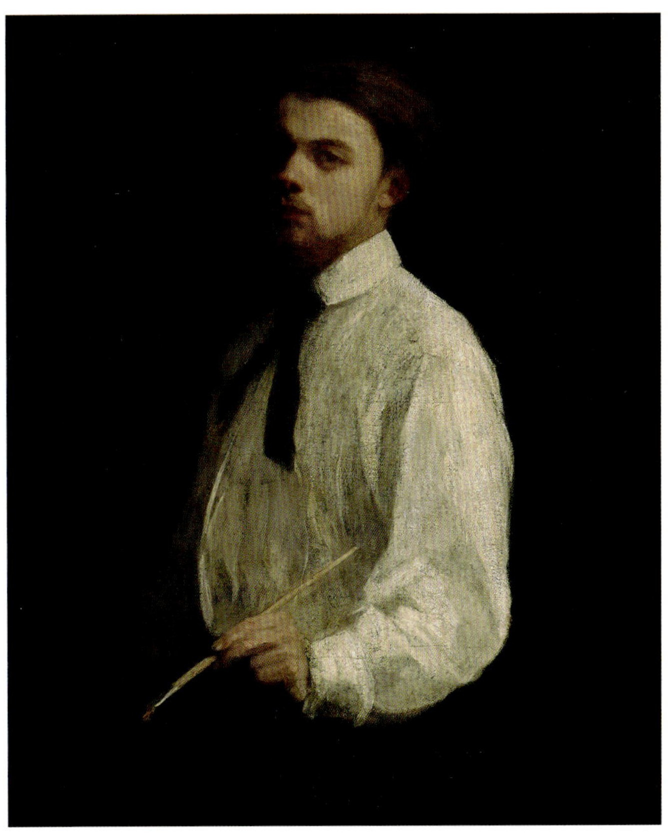

FIG. 60 Henri Fantin-Latour, *Self-Portrait of the Artist at Age Twenty-Three*, 1859, oil on canvas. Musée de Grenoble, MG 1334

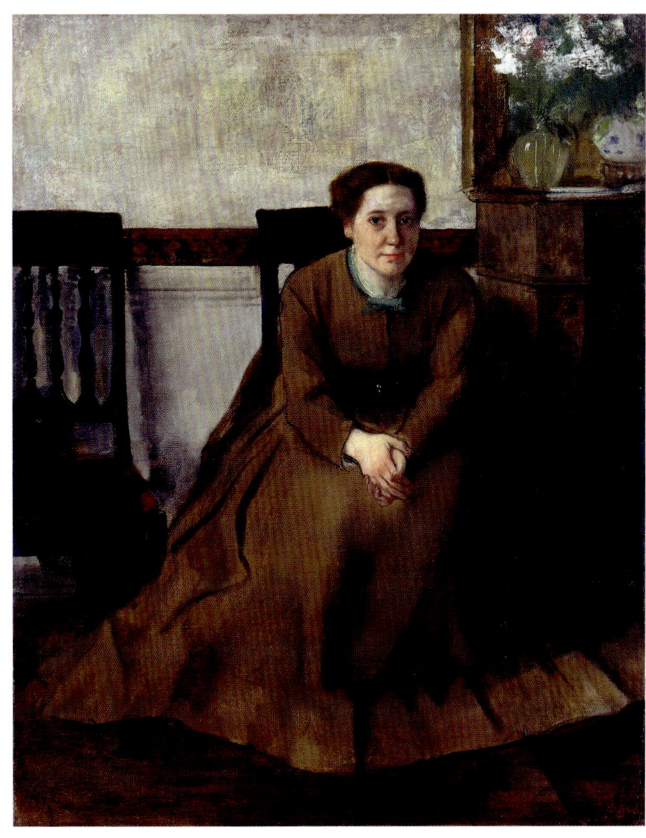

FIG. 61 Edgar Degas, *Victoria Dubourg*, ca. 1868–69, oil on canvas. Toledo Museum of Art, Gift of Mr. and Mrs. William E. Levis, 1963.45

also eschewed such Impressionist stylistic hallmarks as spontaneous brushwork and highly keyed colors and contrasts, such Impressionist practices as painting in the open air, and such quintessentially Impressionist subjects as landscapes and scenes from modern life, whether set in streets, cafés, shops, or suburban gardens and resorts. Of the group, he is best compared with Edgar Degas, who remarked "no art was ever less spontaneous than mine."

Throughout his career Fantin restricted himself to the genres of still life, portraiture, and allegorical and musical subjects, all developed and rendered with equal deliberateness. None of these evolved dramatically over time in terms of style and format, though he was comfortable working in both very large and small scales. This conscious repetitiveness—though not repetition—is often compared to "variations" in music, an art both he and Dubourg loved.

The earliest painting by Fantin in the exhibition is *The Engagement Still Life*. Fantin and Dubourg worked both side by side and in adjacent studios throughout their lives together. The painting is one of his most colorful productions, yet it is still extremely reserved by contemporary avant-garde standards set by artists such as Pierre-Auguste Renoir and Claude Monet. The complexity of this combination of profusion and reserve is underscored by the painting's geometric organization into two horizontal and three vertical zones that, while harmonious and connected (in shape, color, and texture) are yet distinct. But the Chinese blue-and-white vase may also overtly refer to other filiations—not just Chardin but also Whistler, who had a taste for such objects. Indeed, while the idea of domesticity in Fantin's work has received extensive examination, his preference for exquisitely depicting the exquisite in nature and art, less so. Thus, though Fantin was given the vessels for his flower arrangements by his English patrons Mr. and Mrs. Edwin Edwards, he alone selected which one to use for each painting. Often entire paintings were composed through the juxtaposition and rhyming of the few elements at hand such as a container, its floral contents, and their relation to the rectangular format—of which a later and most spectacular example is *Chrysanthemums* (cat. no. 26).

Still Life with a Vase of Hawthorn, Bowl of Cherries, Japanese Bowl, and Cup and Saucer of 1872 (cat. no. 27) and *The Roses* of 1889 (cat. no. 28) continue Fantin's exploration of the domestic interior landscape (or tablescape) marked out as his territory in *The Engagement Still Life*. Indeed, though Fantin claimed despair at the commercial success of these floral subjects and the financial necessity that he said obligated their ongoing production for a hungry market (echoing Gustave Courbet's statement of his own mercenary motivations), he later contradicted himself, remarking that they were a "marvelous thing" to paint.[4]

Fantin successfully sought to convey that marvel through ever-evolving formal means. He was capable of exploiting extremely different types of composition and framing. For example, in *White and Purple Stock* of 1877 (cat. no. 29), he brings the floral subject forward to the picture plane until it fills the entire frame. But he could also step back from his subject, as he did in the nearly contemporary *Asters in a Vase* (cat. no. 30). Here, the potentially banal rhyming of the shape of the extremely plain vase with the overall larger but similar silhouette of the floral arrangement is yet relieved by the conviction with which the artist contrasts their textures and colors. The overall unity of the composition is reinforced by the natural placement within the frame and emphasized by the patient, repetitive nature of the brushwork.

Such formal means are further explored in Dubourg's later and similarly conceived, but more freely rendered, *Still Life with Pink and White Stock* (cat. no. 31). This painting, though reminiscent of precedents in works by Fantin such as *Asters*, achieves—if not originality as defined today—success within the confines set by their shared artistic enterprise. MM

1. Kane 1989, 15, 18. Though she signed her works with her own initials, Dubourg still lacks a dedicated catalogue raisonné despite having carefully prepared one for Fantin after his death.
2. Druick and Hoog 1983; Lourenço et al. 2009; House and Ingram 2011; Patry 2007.
3. See Lourenço et al. 2009, 223–26, for alternative suggestions that go beyond national schools.
4. Druick and Hoog 1983, 113.

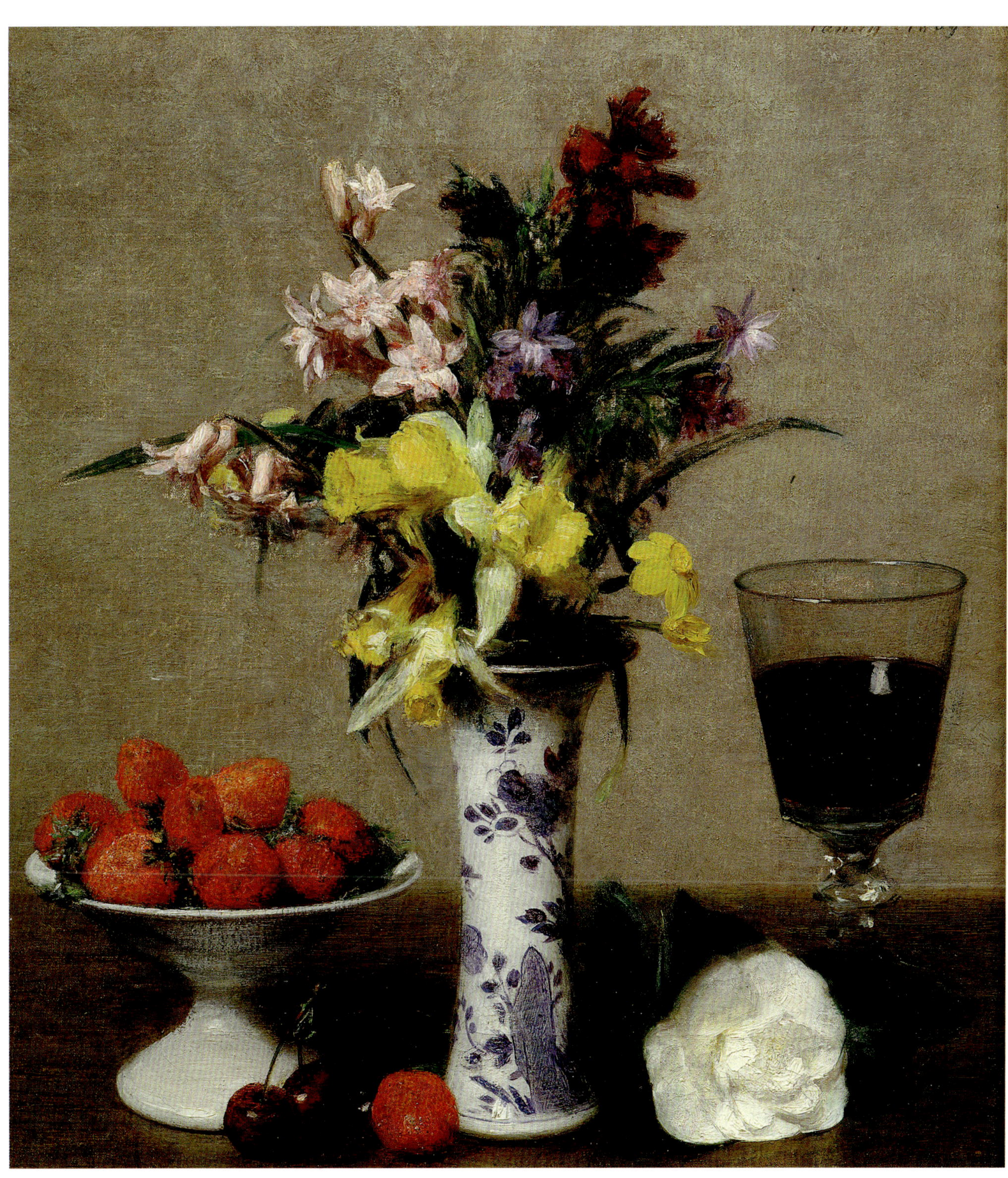

25 HENRI FANTIN-LATOUR
(FRENCH, 1836–1904)

The Engagement Still Life, 1869

Oil on canvas, 12 15⁄16 × 12 in. (32.8 × 30.4 cm)
Musée de Grenoble, MG 2490

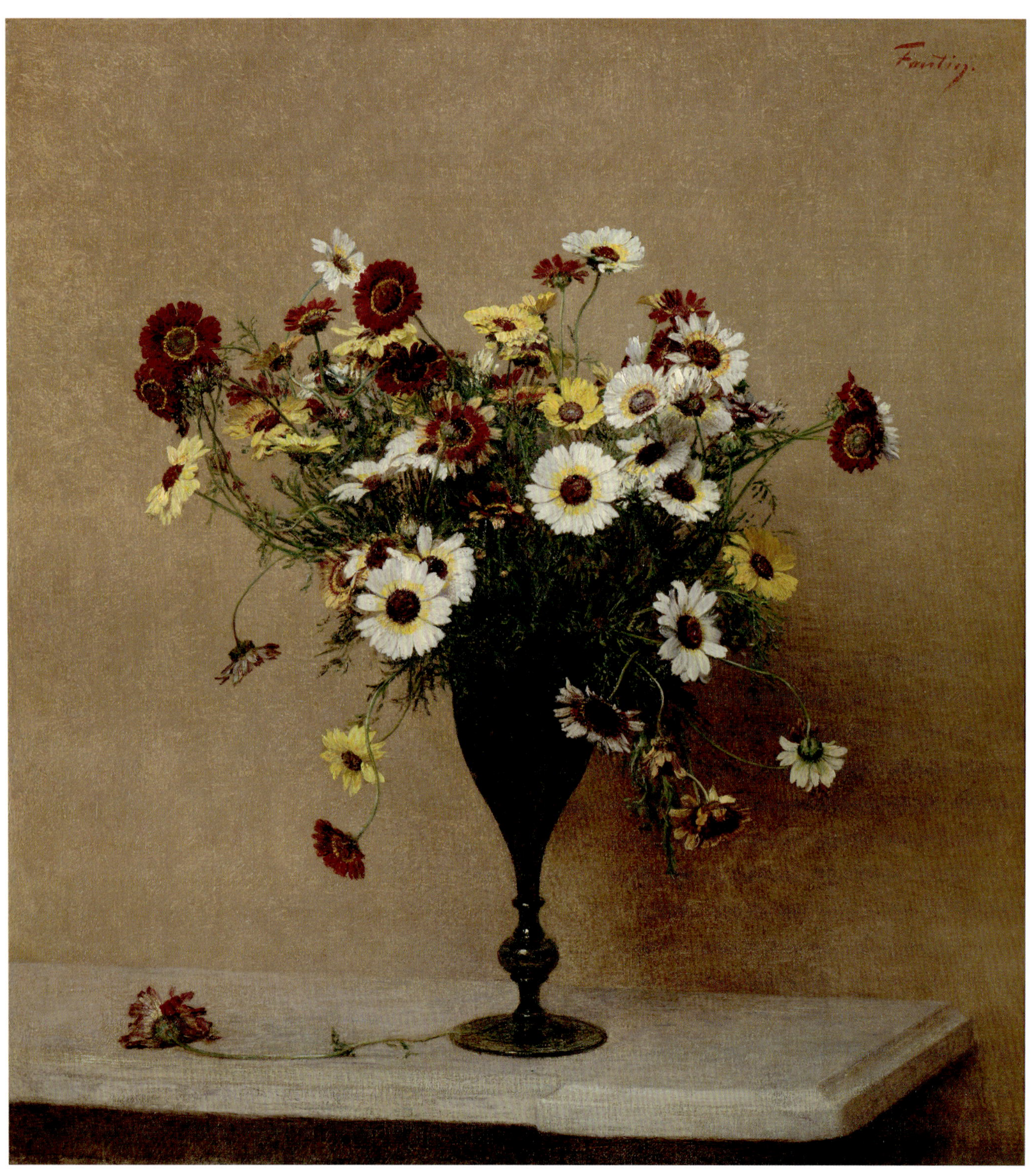

26
HENRI FANTIN-LATOUR
(FRENCH, 1836–1904)

Chrysanthemums, ca. 1889

Oil on canvas, 26¾ × 24¾ in. (68 × 62.9 cm)
Nelson-Atkins Museum of Art, Kansas City, Missouri
(Purchase: William Rockhill Nelson Trust) 33-15/2

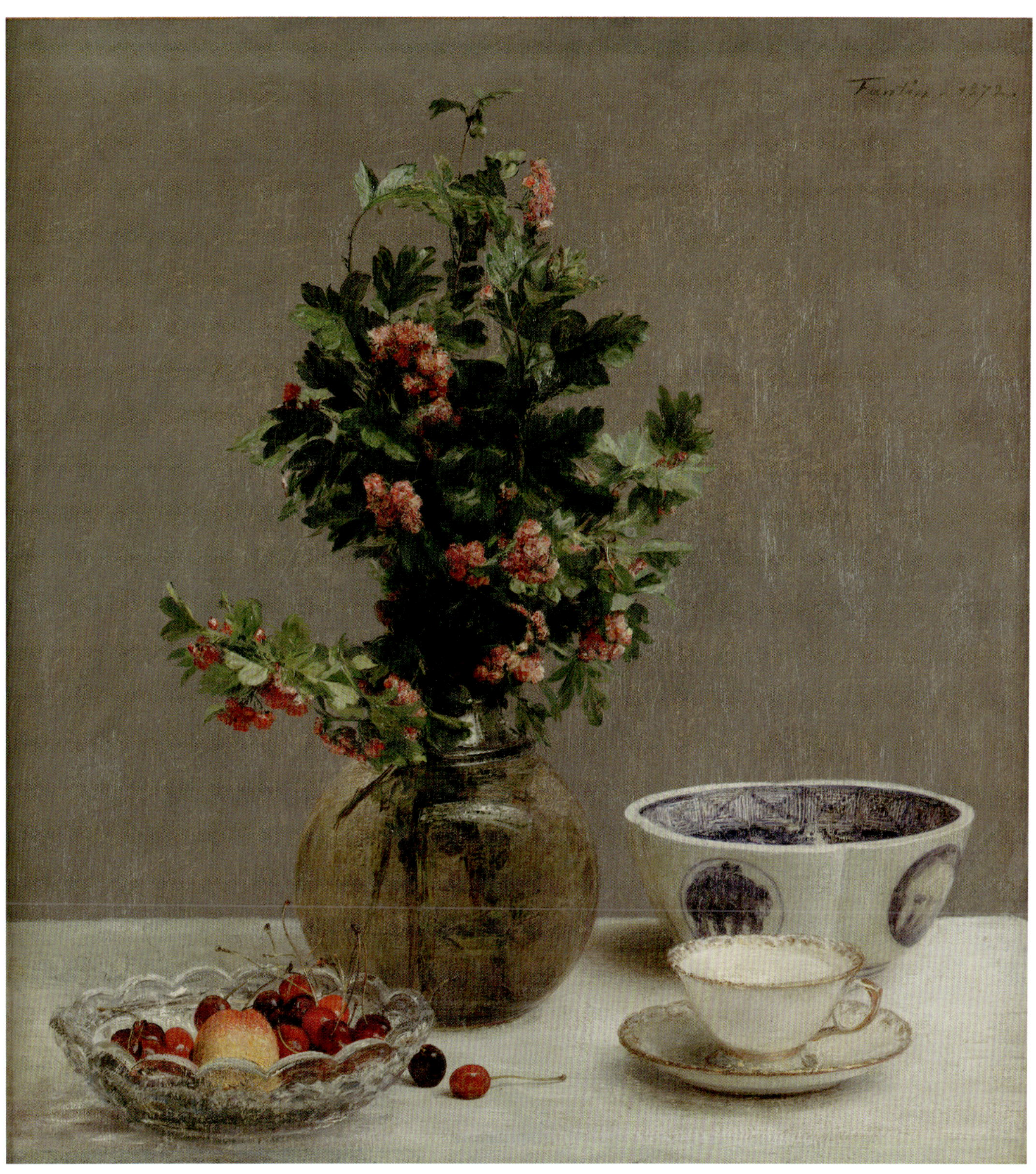

27
HENRI FANTIN-LATOUR
(FRENCH, 1836–1904)

Still Life with a Vase of Hawthorn, Bowl of Cherries, Japanese Bowl, and Cup and Saucer, 1872

Oil on canvas, 23½ × 21¾ in. (59.7 × 55.2 cm)
Dallas Museum of Art, Foundation for the Arts Collection, Mrs. John B. O'Hara Fund and gift of Mrs. Bruno Graf by exchange, 2001.5.FA

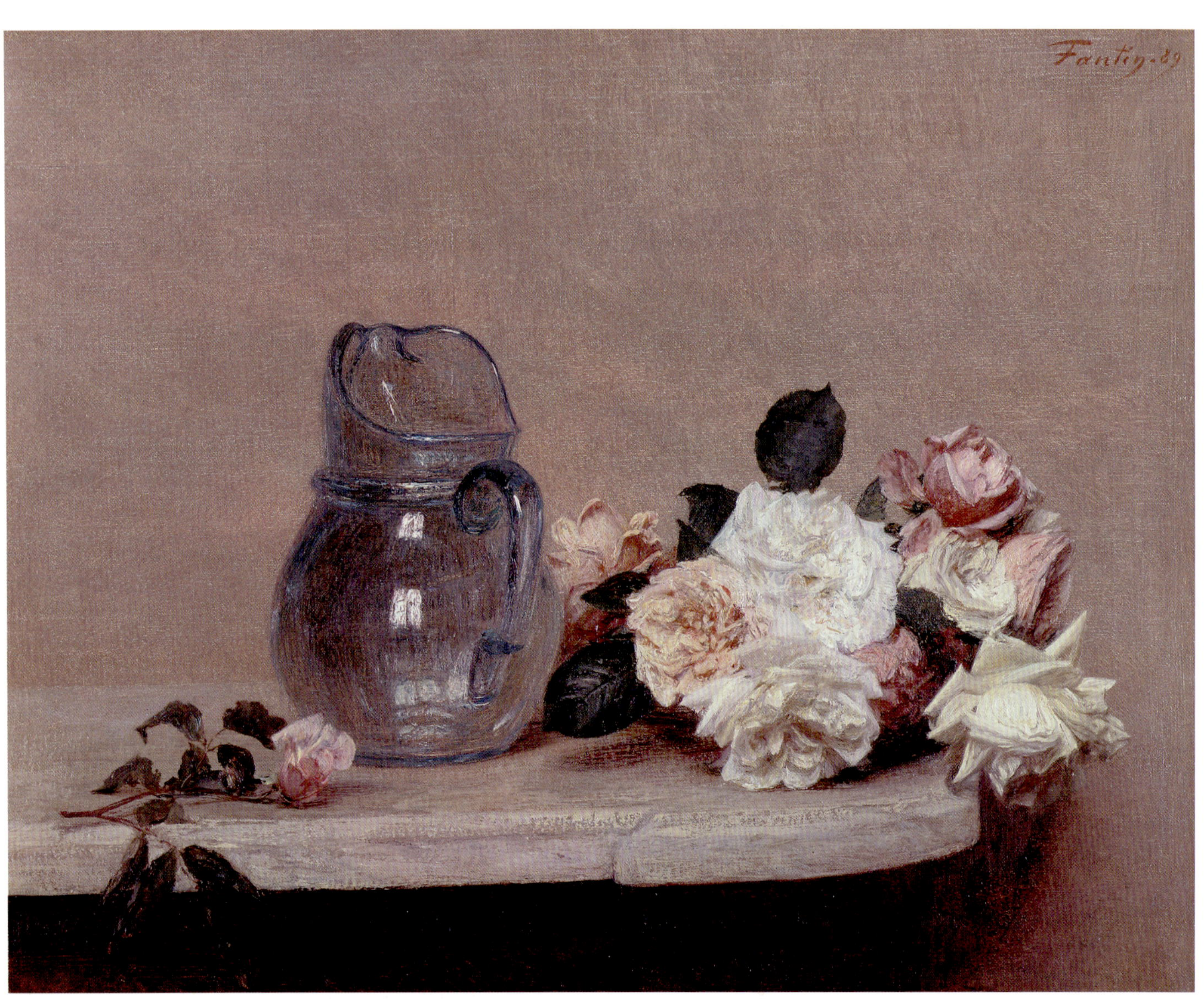

28
HENRI FANTIN-LATOUR
(FRENCH, 1836–1904)

The Roses, 1889

Oil on canvas, 17 5/16 × 22 1/16 in. (44 × 56 cm)
Musée des Beaux-Arts de Lyon, B 804

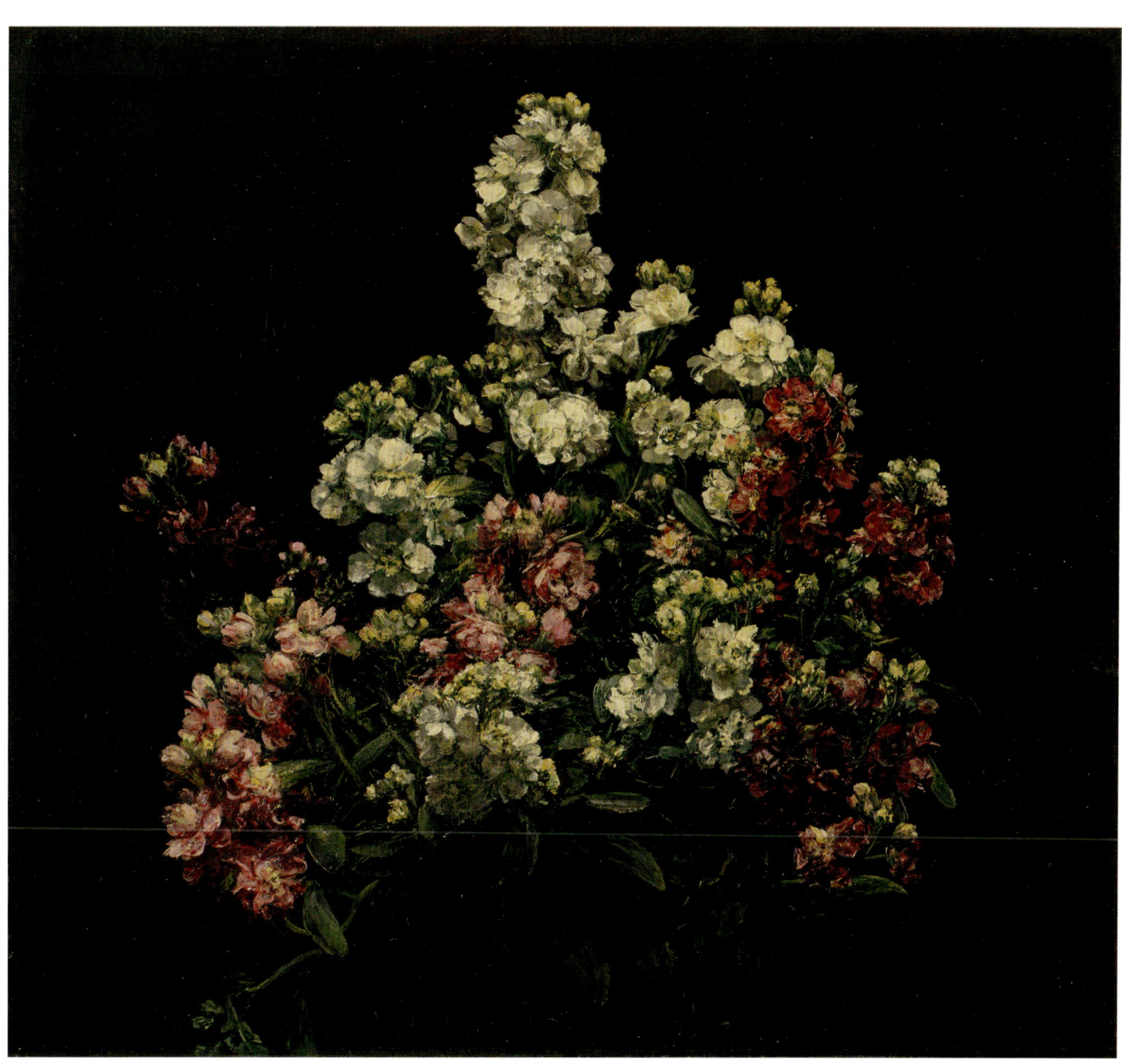

29 HENRI FANTIN-LATOUR
(FRENCH, 1836–1904)

White and Purple Stock, 1877

Oil on canvas, 17 × 19 in. (43.2 × 48.3 cm)
Fine Arts Museums of San Francisco, Bequest of Whitney Warren, Jr., in memory of Mrs. Adolph B. Spreckels, 1988.10.7

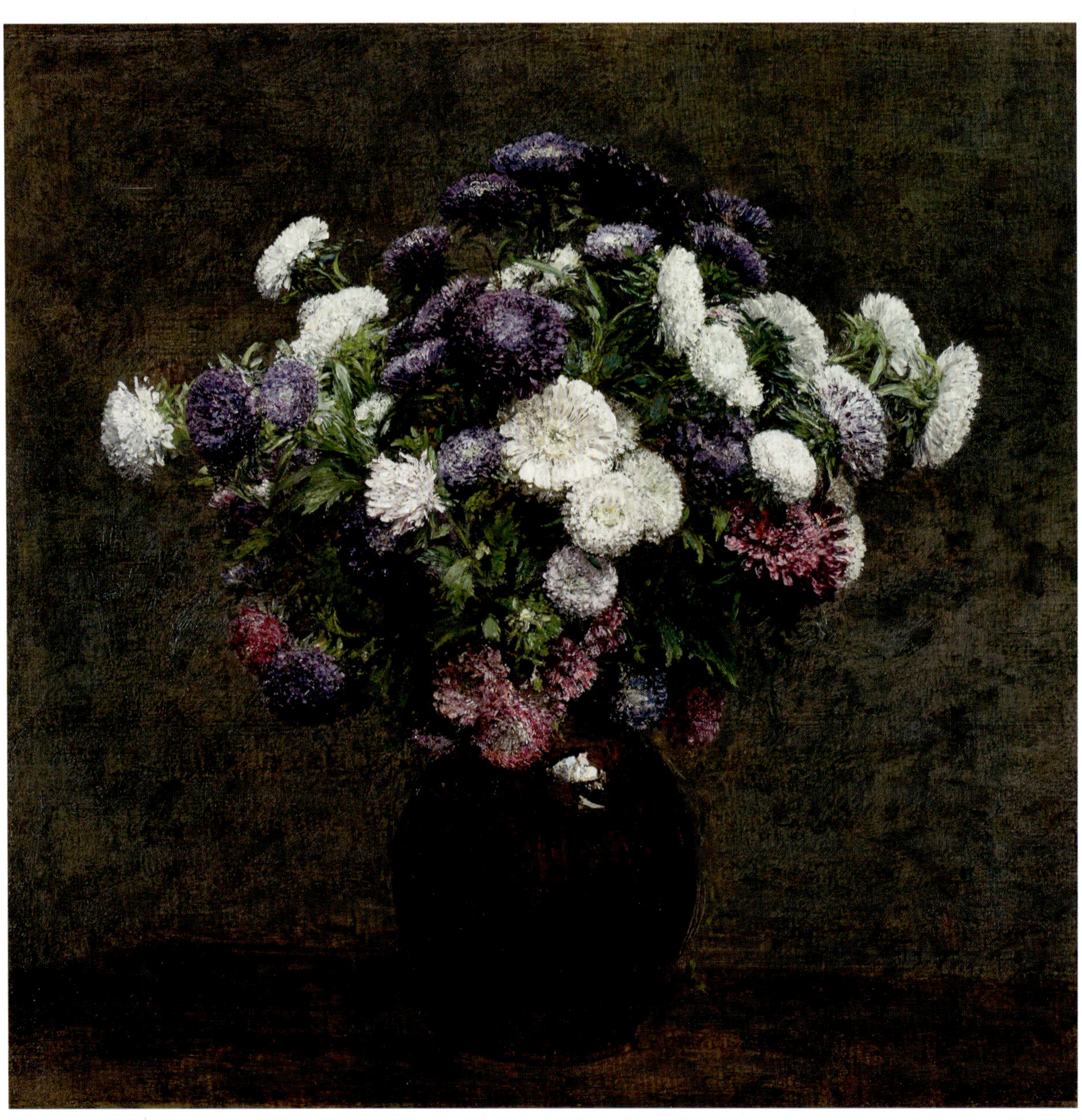

30 HENRI FANTIN-LATOUR
(FRENCH, 1836–1904)

Asters in a Vase, 1875

Oil on canvas, 22⅞ × 23¼ in. (58.1 × 59.1 cm)
Saint Louis Art Museum, Museum Purchase, 4:1944

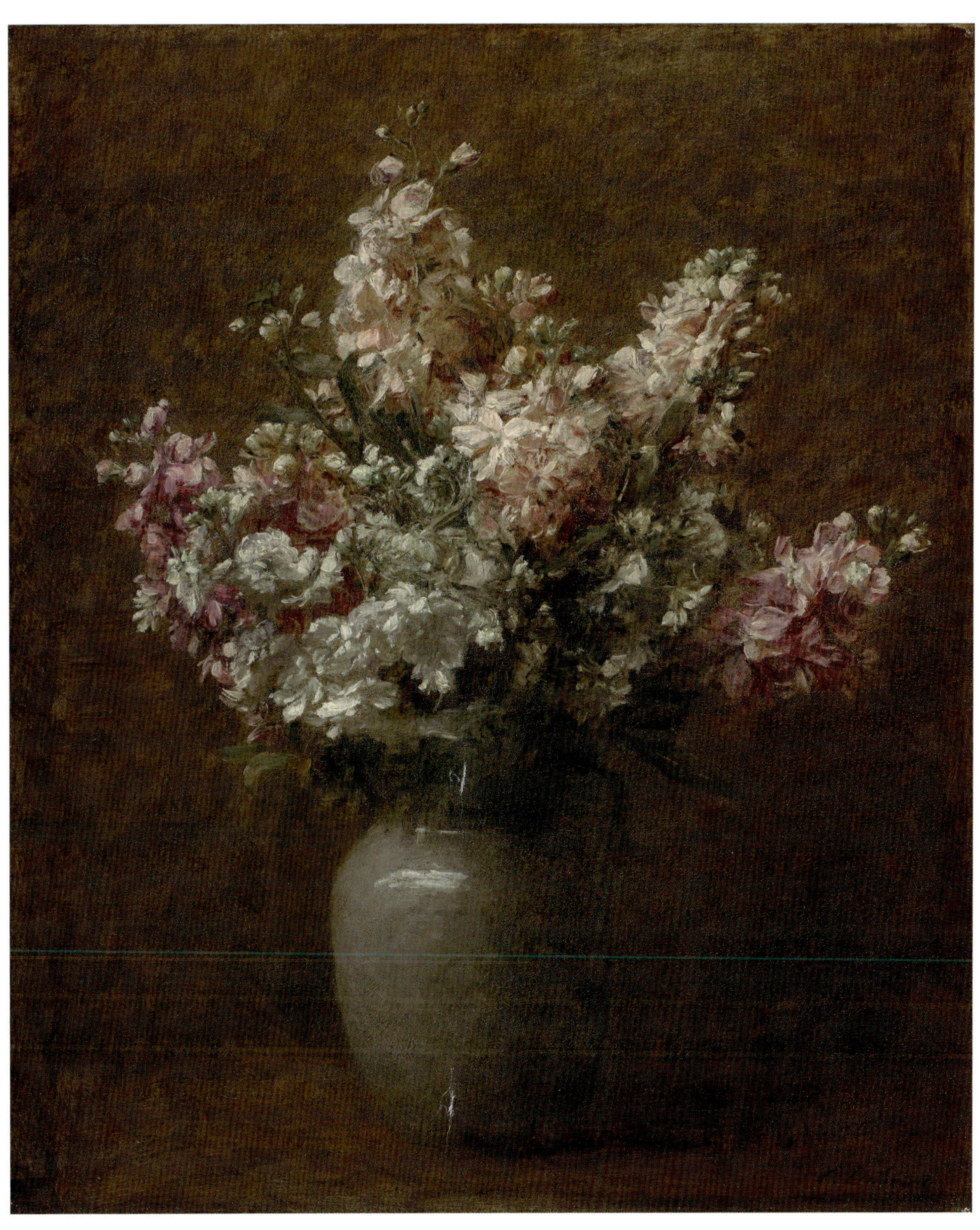

31 VICTORIA DUBOURG FANTIN-LATOUR
(FRENCH, 1840–1926)

Still Life with Pink and White Stock, late 19th–early 20th century

Oil on canvas, 22 × 18½ in. (55.9 × 47 cm)
Fine Arts Museums of San Francisco, Gift of Mrs. Ralph K. Davies, 1975.8

IMPRESSIONISM IS UNDERSTOOD IN THE POPULAR imagination as an art of the outdoors and of sunlight. City streets, suburban landscapes, and country gardens are prominent subjects in the oeuvre of most of the artists of the Impressionist circle. When they turned their gaze indoors, it was often to depict the semipublic spaces of cafés and theaters. Still life, though, is largely an art of private, domestic spaces, and these were also sites of serious, if less fraught, inquiry for modernist artists in the 1870s.

In 1876, at the time of the second Impressionist exhibition, the critic Edmond Duranty published a lengthy review of what he called the "New Painting." Duranty described its concern for "the special characteristics of the modern individual" but recognized that these would not be found in the conventional sites of artistic study, scenes of heroic action, or even portraits.[1] "The language of an empty apartment," he declared, "must be clear enough to enable us to deduce the character and habits of its occupants."[2] Duranty offered an indirect (and provocative) definition of the modern still life as one in which objects, considered independently of the human figure, possess a language of their own and become self-sufficient narrators of their own modernity.

Although Duranty's essay singled out no artists by name, details in the text indicate that he saw Edgar Degas as the foremost practitioner of the New Painting. In 1872, during a brief visit to his extended family in New Orleans, Degas had begun work on a painting of his cousin Estelle Musson Degas (cat. no. 32) that suggests the kind of intimate relationship between modernity and domesticity that was of interest to both Degas and Duranty. This painting, the largest the artist made in Louisiana, stands at the border between portraiture, genre painting (it is a scene of everyday life in his uncle's house in the city's French Quarter), and floral still life. Although Degas made portraits of many family members in New Orleans, he seems to have been particularly close to Estelle, whom he had first met several years earlier when she came to France as a young war widow. By the time they met again in New Orleans, she was remarried to his brother, René Degas, and was pregnant with their third child, a fact that he alludes to discreetly in the painting with a single pink

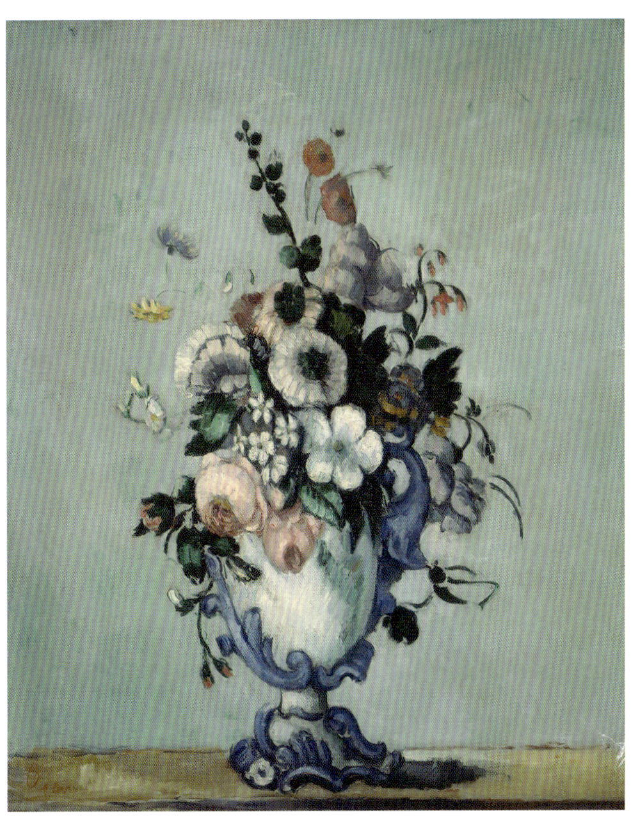

FIG. 62 Paul Cézanne, *Flowers in a Rococo Vase*, ca. 1876, oil on canvas. National Gallery of Art, Washington, D.C., Chester Dale Collection, 1963.10.105

blossom silhouetted against her black dress. Estelle was also by this time nearly blind, having lost her sight over the previous several years. For Degas, who had been struggling with eye problems of his own for two years, Estelle's blindness was a constant reminder of the terror of losing his sight.

The motif of a woman arranging flowers had a recent modernist history (see cat. no. 23), but it also possessed a traditional art historical pedigree. A female figure holding or arranging flowers could stand as a symbol for flora or spring, or for the sense of smell in an allegory of the five senses. In Degas's portrait, Estelle's blindness introduces an unexpected allusion to another sense, that of touch. Her gaze intersects with the bouquet, but uselessly; all information enters by tactile perceptions of the world. Her blindness is expressed in the contact between her lower body and the edge of the table, which grounds her in the otherwise undefined void of the interior setting. It can be read in the way that she caresses the spiky foliage of the gladioli in the vase and fingers the stem of the delicate blossom that has fallen to the table, relying on her tactile memory to guide her aesthetic labors.

Degas returned to Paris from New Orleans in the spring of 1873, and by the next year he took an active role in orchestrating the important group show that is now known as the first Impressionist exhibition. He saw the endeavor as a way out of the recent struggles of modernist painters against the Salon's monopoly of the serious exhibition of contemporary art. As Degas wrote to his friend James Tissot, "The realist movement doesn't need to do battle anymore. It is, it exists, it should appear separately. There needs to be a realist Salon."[3]

Still life played a secondary role in the eight Impressionist exhibitions held between 1874 and 1886, but it figured in the oeuvre of almost all of the principal artists who composed the Impressionist circle, even for those who treated it mostly as a rainy-day exercise. Camille Pissarro, for instance, was not a frequent painter of still life, but he occasionally tackled flower subjects throughout his career. His wife, Julie, was an avid flower gardener and former florist who prepared bouquets for her husband to paint indoors when he was unable to work on landscapes. In *Bouquet of Roses* of 1873 (cat. no. 33), the sprigs of green leaves lying on the table at left and the single fallen blossom imply that this bouquet has just been assembled, and the entire still life suggests something of the provisional and haphazard. The rather informal arrangement is gathered in a porcelain vase with sweeping rococo lines that may have later been a reference point for Paul Cézanne in his highly stylized still life *Flowers in a Rococo Vase* (fig. 62). Cézanne worked closely with Pissarro during these years, but his slow and deliberate approach to painting made capturing the transient freshness of floral subjects difficult. He reportedly turned to the expedient of painting bouquets of paper flowers, which were widely used at the time for decorative purposes such as in millinery. The flatness and seeming artificiality of the flowers in Cézanne's still lifes of the 1870s, and his apparent lack of concern with the details of botanical structure, might be the result of this unusual method. After finding himself unable to resolve the pictorial structure of one complex flower subject, Cézanne cut the unfinished canvas into two separate still-life paintings (cat. nos. 34 and 35).

Like Pissarro, Alfred Sisley was essentially a landscape painter, and he made even fewer forays into the still-life genre than did Pissarro. Of his nine known still lifes, only *Still Life of Wildflowers* (cat. no. 36) focuses on flowers. The bouquet is imposing in scale and vibrating with energy, but it is painted with little botanical specificity. Instead, Sisley's interest seems to have been in the disorienting and flattening pictorial effect of a large bouquet of spiky foliage and feathery sprays of flowers placed close to the picture plane and superimposed over the domestic surroundings. Two landscape paintings, presumably by Sisley himself, form a backdrop to the still life.

Among the core Impressionist group, Pierre-Auguste Renoir was the artist with the strongest and most enduring interest in the floral still life. He made flower paintings alongside Monet in the 1860s (see cat. no. 24 and fig. 21) and continued to explore the expressive and formal possibilities of the genre during the key years of the Impressionist movement. *Roses and Peonies in a Vase* (cat. no. 37) and the closely related *Bouquet in a Vase* (cat. no. 38) reveal the artist's love of including richly decorated porcelain vessels in his still lifes. Renoir, who was born in Limoges, had briefly practiced porcelain painting early in his career, and he remained an exceptionally skillful manipulator of decorative motifs. In *Roses and Peonies in a Vase*, the columnar container is oriented so that the spray of pink flowers seems to be growing from the painted stalk that twines around the vase. Renoir employs a similar visual sleight of hand in the upper right corner, where the bouquet's green foliage merges with the landscape painting hanging above the red chair. In *Bouquet in a Vase*, the elaborate Chinese vase, with a white snake depicted in relief on its richly painted surface, seizes the viewer's attention. Rather than blending with the bouquet in an illusion of organic unity, the vase threatens to upstage the natural beauty of the flowers with an assertion of its status as a man-made artifact of aesthetic pleasure.

The floral still life was frequently, though not exclusively, associated with a domestic context in the art of the Impressionists. In Renoir's *Bouquet in a Loge* (cat. no. 39), however, the setting is a public theater. The bouquet of roses, wrapped in a crisp sleeve of white paper, has been temporarily set aside by a woman attending a performance. Renoir's tight focus on the bouquet renders the red velvet chair on which it sits nearly unrecognizable, a mere chromatic foil for the intensely worked paint that describes the flowers, rather than a comfortable or familiar setting. *Bouquet in a Loge* may have been painted during Renoir's preparations for his modern genre painting *At the Concert* (1880, Sterling and Francine Clark Art Institute, Williamstown), though it also recalls a compositional formula that the artist had used for one of his most ambitious flower paintings, *Still Life with Bouquet* (Museum of Fine Arts, Houston), painted in 1871 as an homage to Manet. HMacD

1. Duranty (1876) 1986, 44.
2. Ibid., 45.
3. "*Le mouvement réaliste n'a plus besoin* de lutter *avec les autres*. Il est, *il* existe, *il doit se* montrer à part. Il doit y avoir un Salon réaliste." Quoted in Boggs 1999, 32.

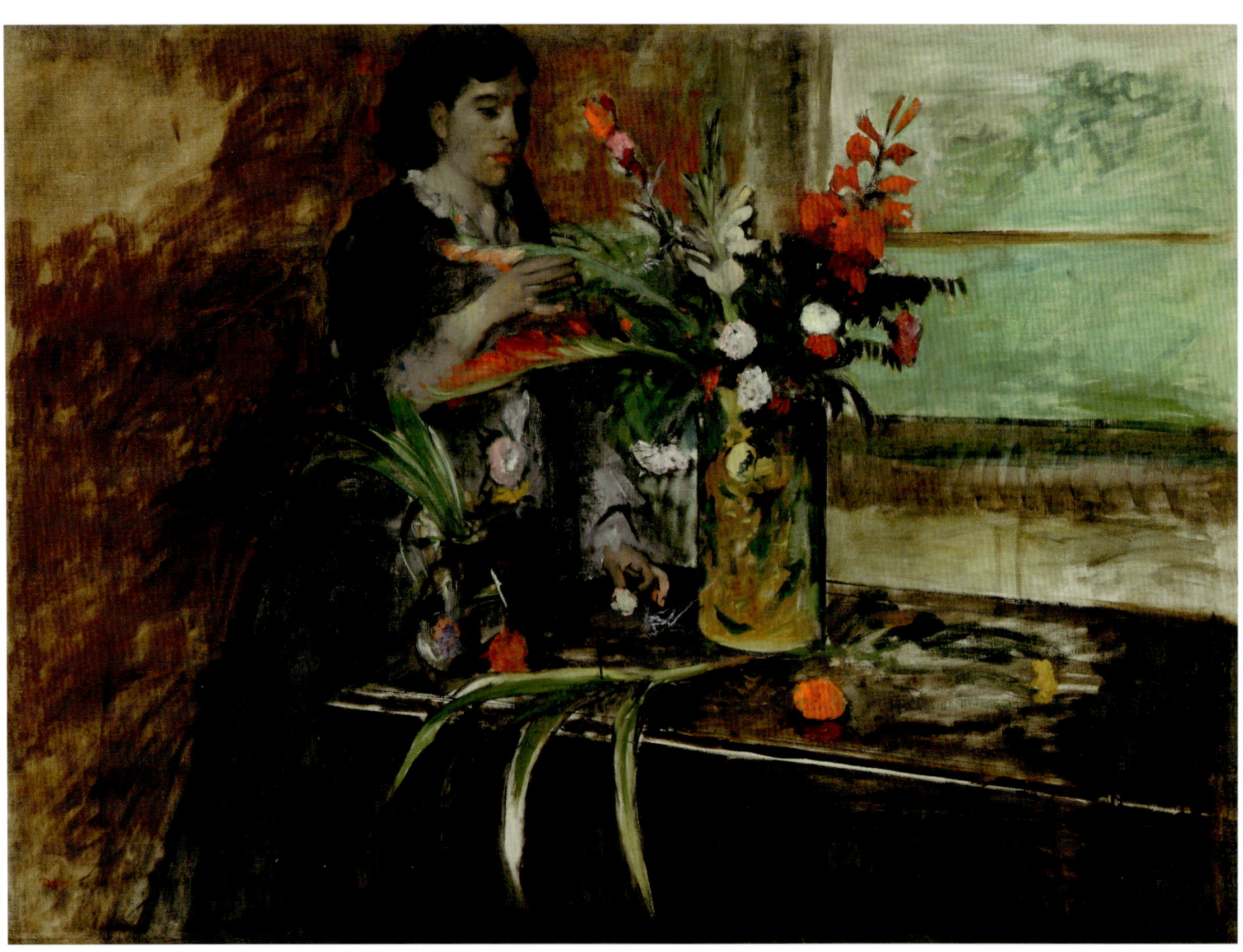

32 EDGAR DEGAS
(FRENCH, 1834–1917)

Portrait of Estelle Musson Degas, 1872

Oil on canvas, 39⅜ × 54 in. (100.01 × 137.16 cm)
New Orleans Museum of Art, Museum Purchase through
Public Subscription, 65.1

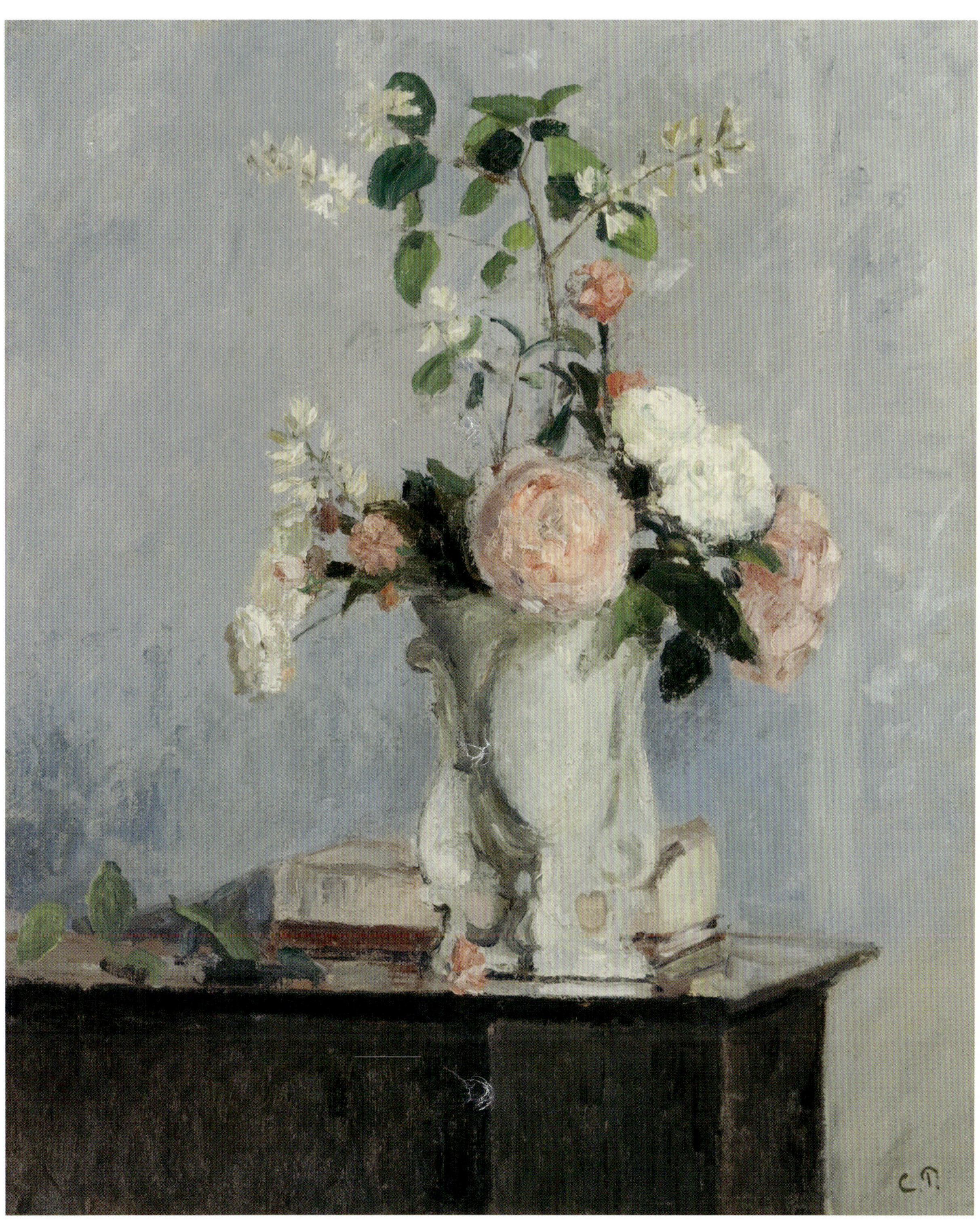

33 CAMILLE PISSARRO
(FRENCH, 1831–1903)

Bouquet of Roses, ca. 1873

Oil on canvas, 21⅝ × 18¼ in. (54.93 × 46.36 cm)
High Museum of Art, Atlanta, Gift of the Forward Arts Foundation in honor of its first president, Mrs. Robert W. Chambers, 74.321

Richmond and Denver only

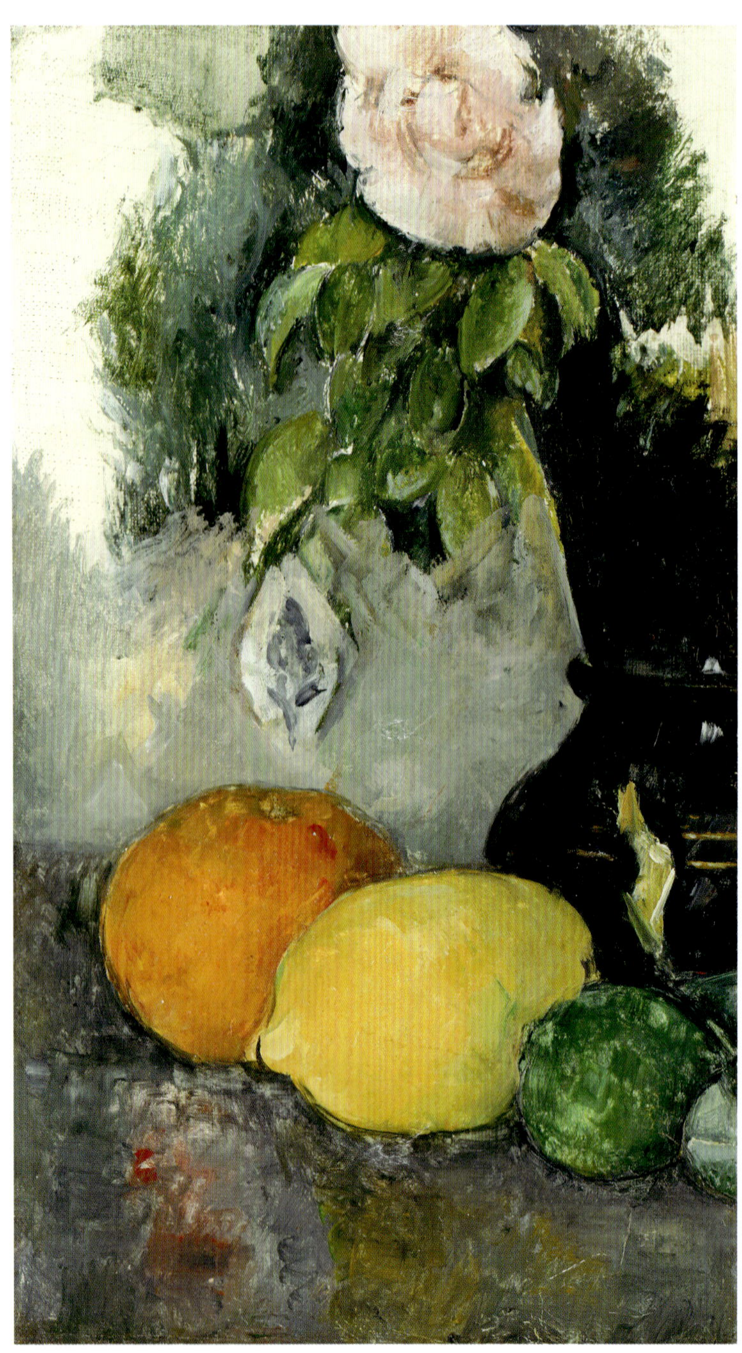

34 **PAUL CÉZANNE**
(FRENCH, 1839–1906)

Flowers and Fruits, ca. 1880

Oil on canvas, 13 × 8¼ in. (33 × 21 cm)
Musée de l'Orangerie, Paris, RF 1963-6

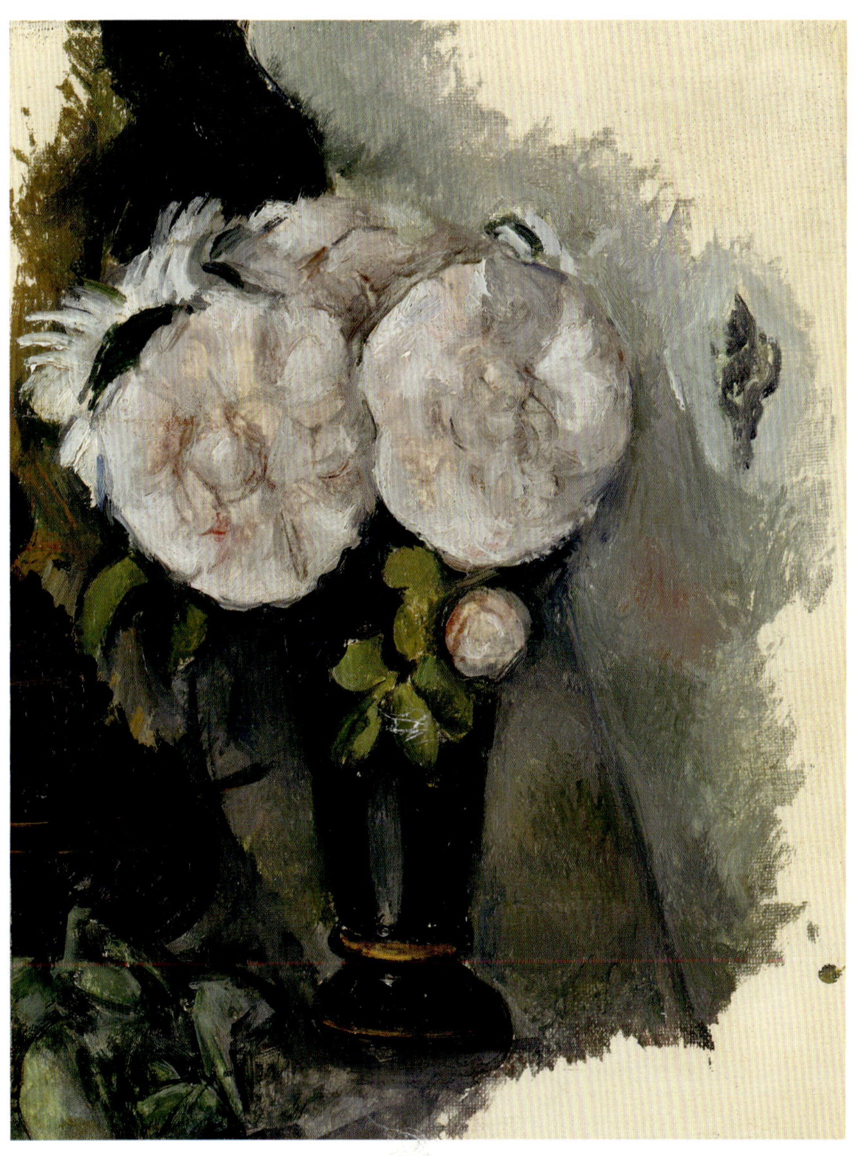

35 PAUL CÉZANNE
(FRENCH, 1839–1906)

Flowers in a Blue Vase, ca. 1880

Oil on canvas, 11 13/16 × 9 1/16 in. (30 × 23 cm)
Musée de l'Orangerie, Paris, RF 1963-12

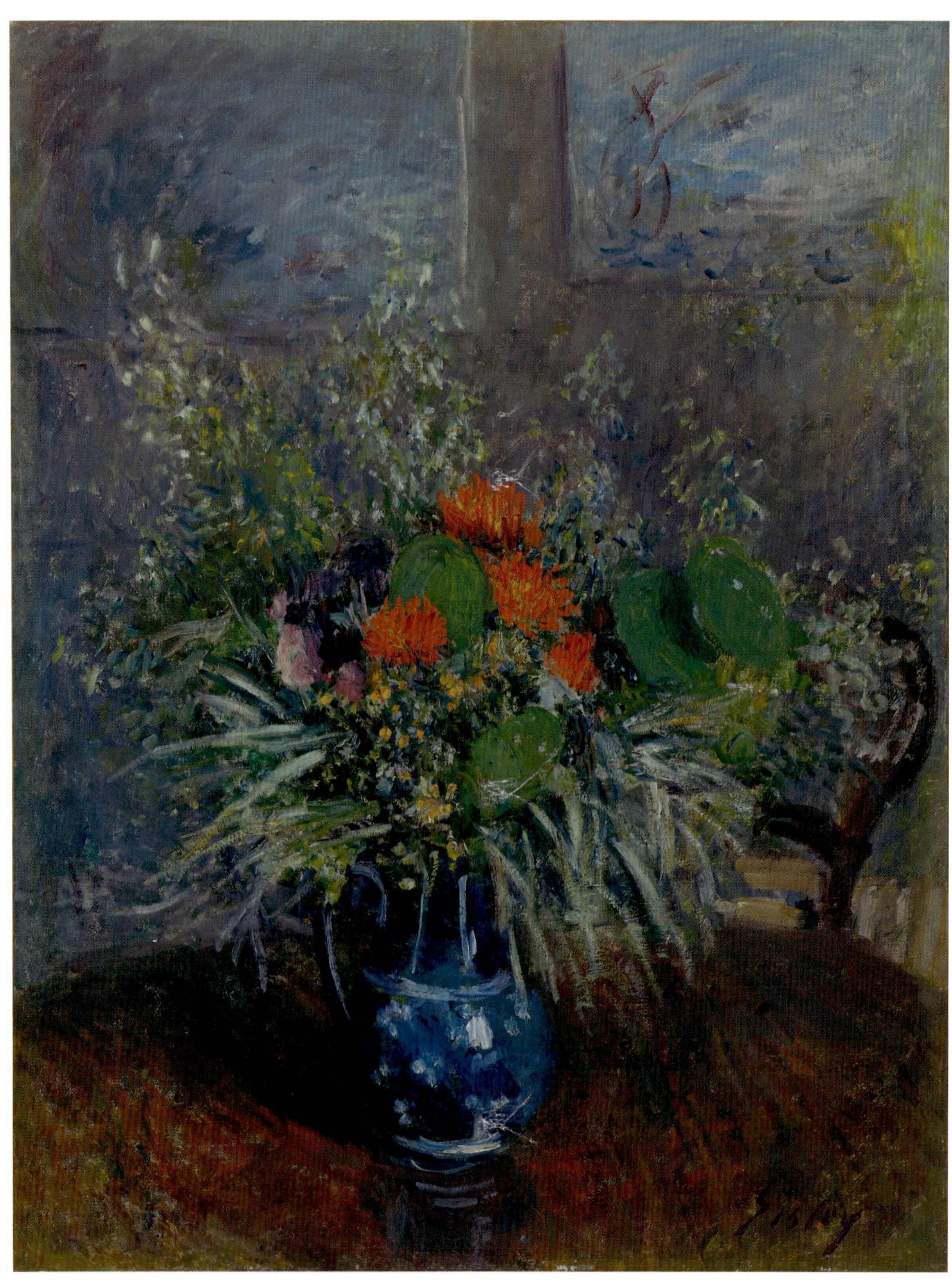

36
ALFRED SISLEY
(FRENCH, 1839–1899)

Still Life of Wildflowers, 1875

Oil on canvas, 25¾ × 19⅞ in. (65 × 50 cm)
Virginia Museum of Fine Arts, Richmond, Collection of Mr. and Mrs. Paul Mellon, 85.500

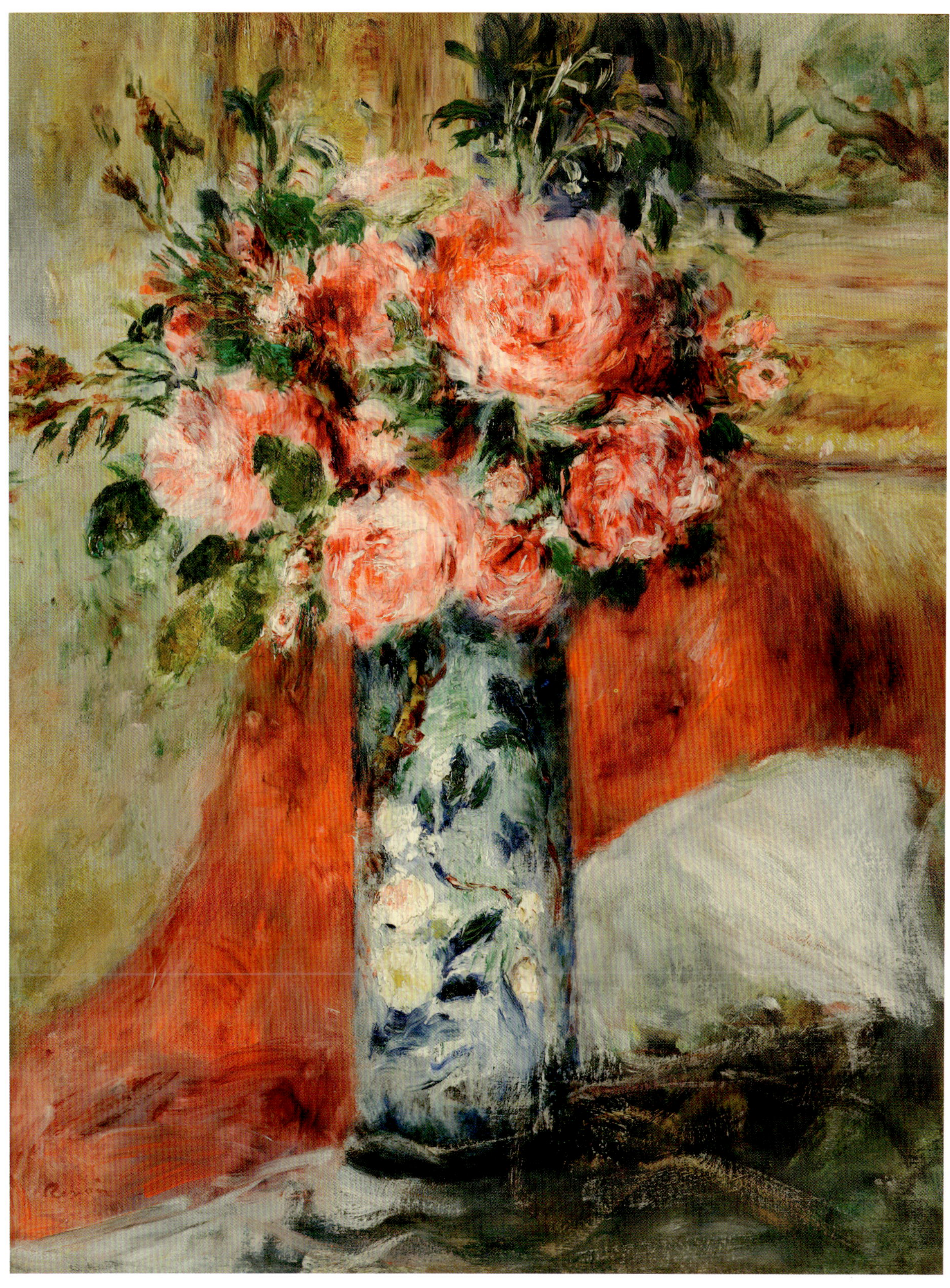

37 PIERRE-AUGUSTE RENOIR
(FRENCH, 1841–1919)

Roses and Peonies in a Vase, 1876

Oil on canvas, 23⅞ × 20¼ in. (60.6 × 51.4 cm)
Private Collection, Dallas

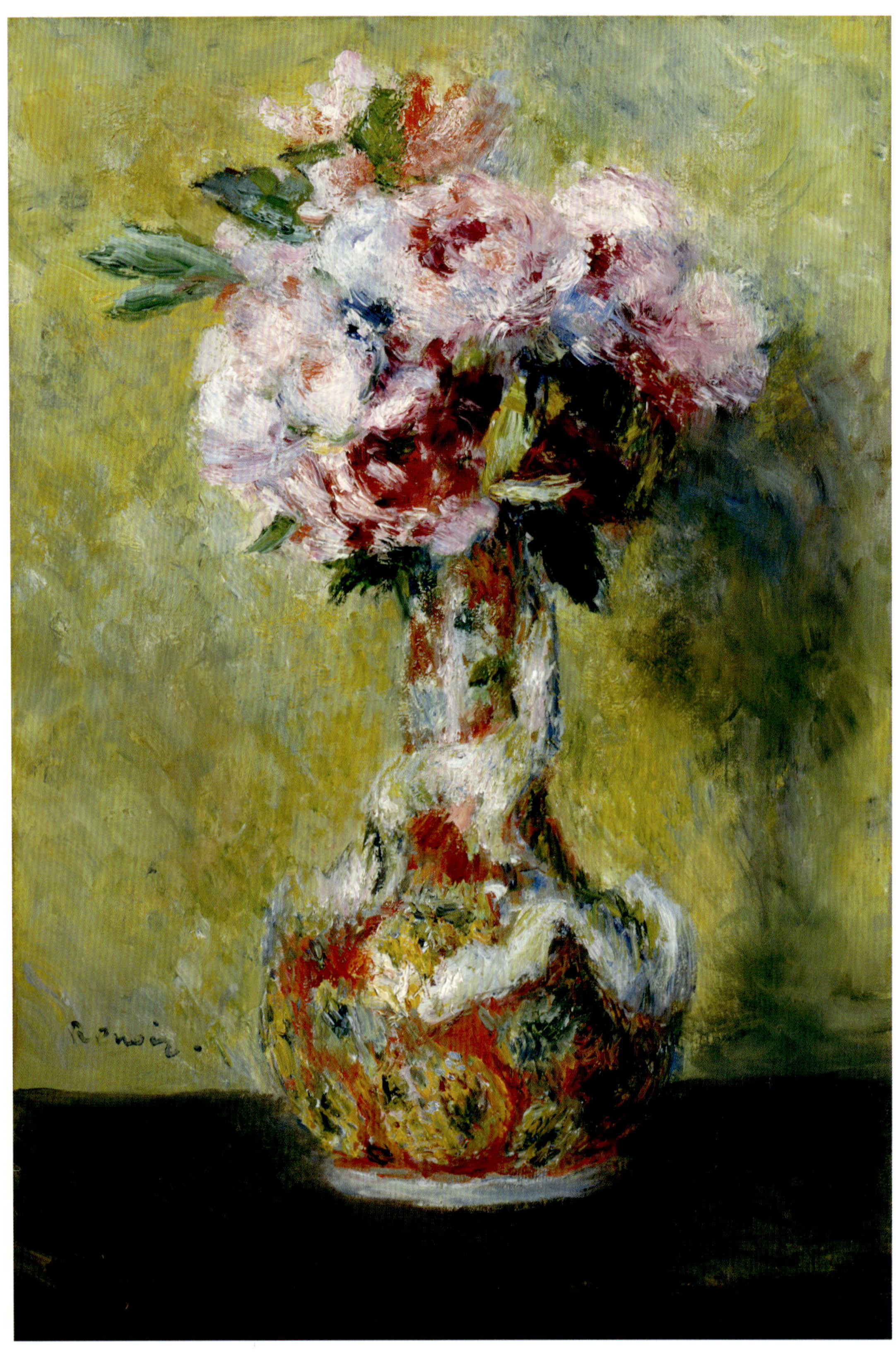

38 PIERRE-AUGUSTE RENOIR
(FRENCH, 1841–1919)

Bouquet in a Vase, 1878

Oil on canvas, 18¾ × 13 in. (47.63 × 33.02 cm)
Indianapolis Museum of Art, The Lockton Collection, 70.80

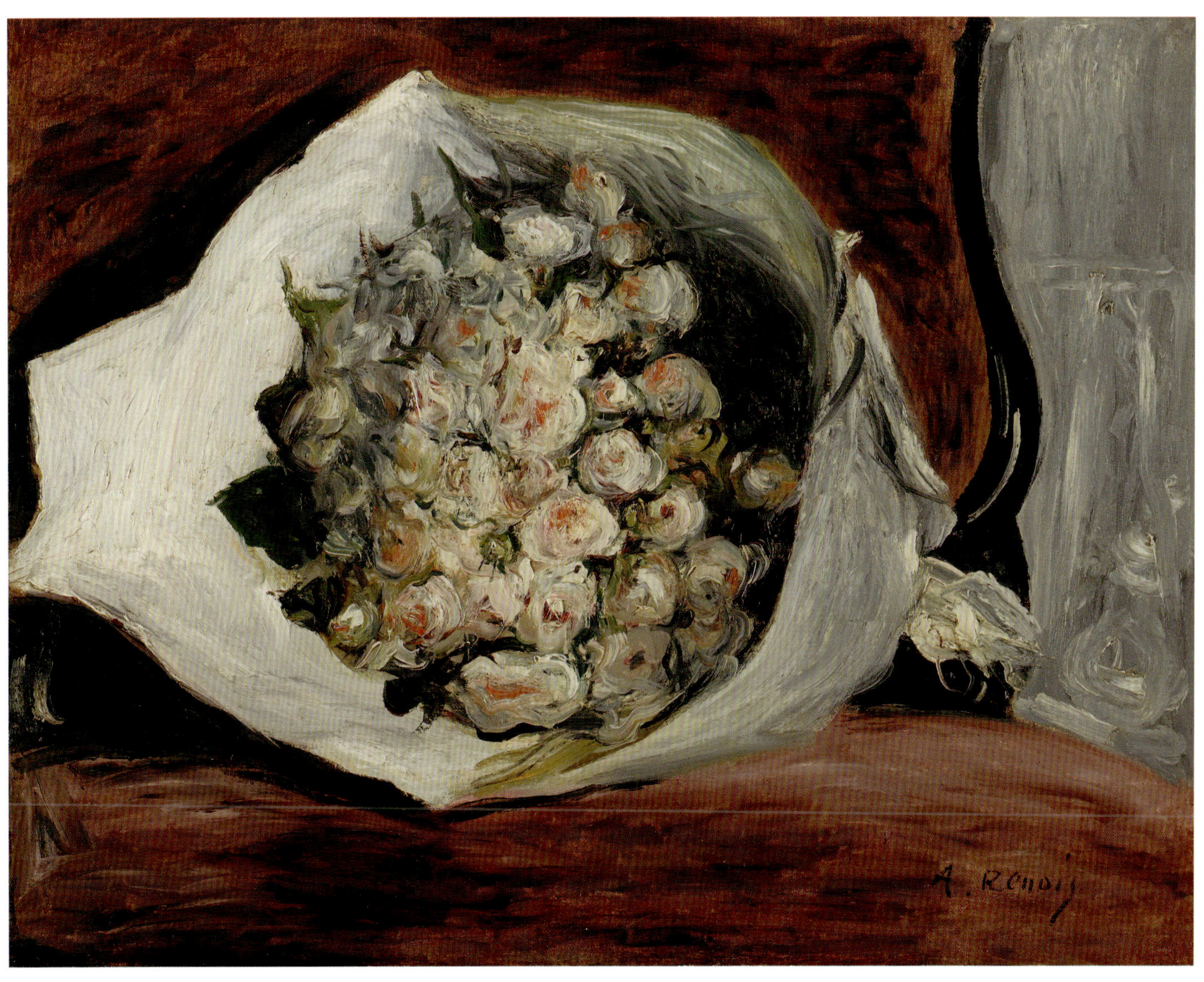

39 PIERRE-AUGUSTE RENOIR
(FRENCH, 1841–1919)

Bouquet in a Loge, ca. 1878–80

Oil on canvas, 15¾ × 20⅛ in. (40 × 51 cm)
Musée de l'Orangerie, Paris, RF 1960-20

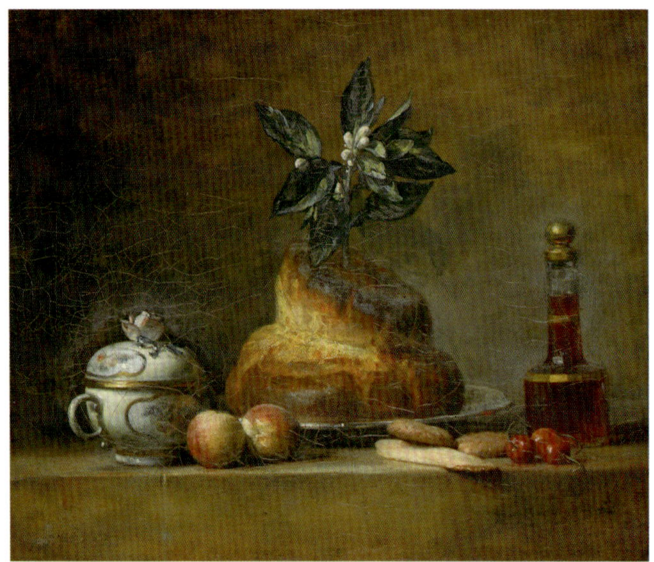

FIG. 63 Jean-Siméon Chardin, *The Brioche*, 1763, oil on canvas. Musée du Louvre, Paris. Legacy of Dr. Louis La Caze, MI 1038

THE EARLY YEARS OF IMPRESSIONIST STILL-LIFE painting were characterized by a variety of often idiosyncratic experiments, but Édouard Manet's still lifes remained consistent touchstones for his contemporaries. Importantly, they offered other artists a modernist response to Jean-Siméon Chardin's legacy, which had reemerged in the 1850s and 1860s as a potent source of painterly inspiration—one that Manet continued to mine throughout the 1870s. His series of paintings reprising Chardin's *The Brioche* (fig. 63), such as *Still Life with Brioche* (cat. no. 40), presents a modern iteration of the informal, seemingly offhand arrangement of the eighteenth-century prototype, in which a sprig of orange blossoms is introduced as the loaf's elegant decorative finial.

Manet returned to flower painting with great intensity in 1882. His renewed interest was at least in part dictated by personal concerns: his health was rapidly failing, and by that year he was only able to work on paintings of relatively small scale, mainly portraits of his close friends and pictures of the bouquets they brought to his bedside. In *Flowers in a Crystal Vase* (cat. no. 41), Manet plays with the contrast between zones of painterly immediacy and areas of pictorial restraint; the wet-in-wet technique Manet used for the flowers registers the confident speed with which he captured the small bouquet, while in adjoining areas of the canvas, bare ground shows through. This approach is used to particular effect to suggest the transparency of the short, heavy vase, its contours deftly carved out with the gray pigment that is also used to describe the neutral ground. This still life must have been painted sometime before the end of 1882, because Manet gave it as a New Year's gift in January 1883.

Vase of White Lilacs and Roses (cat. no. 42) was likely one of the last still lifes in this series; the inclusion of lilacs indicates that it was painted in the spring of 1883, shortly before Manet's death at the end of April. The thick, octagonal vase containing the bouquet is placed at the center of the marble tabletop, in front of a somber and hastily painted background that seems almost to brush against the feathery forms of the lilacs. Color is largely concentrated at the center of the bouquet, where

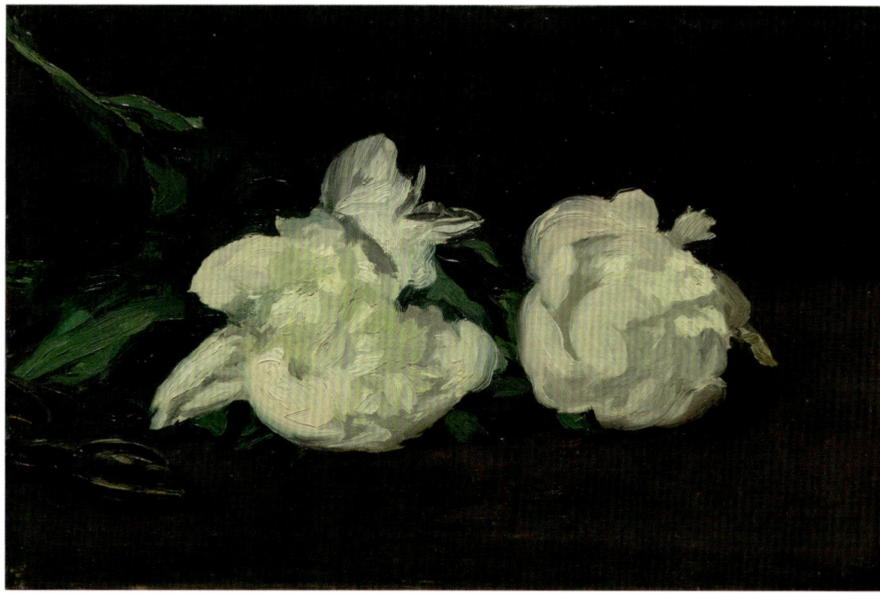

FIG. 64 Édouard Manet, *Branch of White Peonies*, 1864, oil on canvas. Musée d'Orsay, Paris, RF 1995

three pink roses and a bright sprig of greenery stand out against the subdued surroundings.

Two Roses on a Tablecloth (cat. no. 43), the smallest of Manet's final flower paintings, could serve as an emblem of the artist's maxim that "concision in art is a necessity as well as an elegance."[1] Here the "setting" is summarized by a simple horizon line suggesting the edge of the surface (linen tablecloth? marble table?) on which the two stems rest. The picture reprises one of Manet's earlier flower paintings, *Branch of White Peonies* of 1864 (fig. 64), but refuses that work's visual sensuality. The sparing brushwork, washed-out palette, and minimalist setting contribute to the elegiac tone that presides over this extraordinary final series of floral still lifes.

The opening years of the 1880s seemed to witness a new consensus about flower painting's importance as an autonomous site of formal experimentation and artistic dialogue. This was evident in Manet's quiet and very personal exploration of the genre but also in the growing enthusiasm of the Impressionists to exhibit such works. The first six Impressionist exhibitions, held between 1874 and 1881, had included only twenty-three floral still lifes, and more than half of those were painted by a mediocre specialist in the genre, Charles Tillot.[2] However, the seventh Impressionist exhibition, in 1882, featured *eleven* floral still lifes, including major examples by Paul Gauguin, Claude Monet, and Pierre-Auguste Renoir (Tillot quit the field that year).[3] Although landscapes still dominated the exhibition and figure paintings attracted the lion's share of critical attention, the new visibility of flower subjects that year was a remarkable change. This moment can be seen in retrospect as a high-water mark for serious collective interest in the genre's possibilities to convey formal, thematic, and even narrative complexity.

Gauguin's *Still Life with Peonies* (cat. no. 44) is an example of the artist's novel approach to the genre during the early 1880s. It was his first painting to include glimpses of other contemporary works of art, in this case a pastel by Degas (a gift from the older artist in exchange for one of Gauguin's recent still lifes) and an unidentified Impressionist landscape, also from Gauguin's collection. The prominent dedication in the upper left corner to Gauguin's brother-in-law Theodore Gad is a reminder that still lifes, like bouquets themselves, often served as gifts; the same year, Gauguin gave a floral still life to his close friend Émile Schuffenecker.

Although Mary Cassatt often incorporated floral motifs and bouquets into the well-appointed interiors of her modern genre scenes, she rarely painted independent floral subjects. Her artistic ambition perhaps led her to avoid a genre to which many female artists had historically been confined, but she joined fellow Impressionists in pursuing new experiments in floral still life during the early 1880s. Her *Lilacs in a Window* (cat. no. 45) shows an informal bouquet of the early spring blossoms, clearly picked from the garden rather than purchased from the florist, casually arranged in a double-handled vase placed on the window sill. The setting is not, to all appearances, one of Cassatt's comfortable Parisian interiors but rather a greenhouse or conservatory, with ivy growing abundantly on the exterior wall and the windows propped open to let in the fresh spring air. Though Gustave Caillebotte made a series of formally audacious decorative panels depicting flowers in his greenhouses at Petit Gennevilliers, near Argentuil, in the 1890s, Cassatt's suggestion of this new "modern interior" is far more ambiguous, focusing not on the setting but rather on the evocation of a particular kind of compositional informality and a dazzling optical transparency.

Caillebotte did not send any floral still lifes to the 1882 exhibition, but he painted nine flower subjects between 1881 and 1883, initiating a life-long practice of the genre. He had acquired his Petit Gennevilliers property in 1881 and was quickly occupied in laying out its gardens and greenhouses. While his new involvement in gardening may have been one impetus for his embrace of floral still life in these years, his close relationship with Monet (with whom he shared a Paris studio in 1882) may have been another. He would have had the opportunity to see the important series of still lifes that Monet had been working on since 1878. Although some of these are quite conventional in format (see for instance fig. 26) and even reminiscent of those that Monet, Renoir, and Bazille had painted in the 1860s, others are assertively experimental, signaling Monet's growing interest in translating the immediacy of perception through quick, spontaneous brushwork. In *Vase of Peonies* (cat. no. 46), the bouquet's setting is greatly minimized, and the action of Monet's virtuosic brush becomes the focus of the viewer's attention. The brushstroke's one-to-one relationship to the flower petal, particularly apparent in those scattered on the table's surface, sets up a perceptual dance between the still life itself and the materiality of its representation. John House has written that Monet's still lifes of this period "systematically undermined" the pervasive Chardin tradition, in which the objects of still lifes were presented in clear, orderly groupings and firmly grounded on a support or surface. "Monet played down the physicality of the objects," House noted, "in favour of emphasising their optical effect."[4] Monet's studio mate, Caillebotte, acquired a painting of chrysanthemums from this series for his own collection, lending it to the 1882 exhibition.

The floral still lifes Caillebotte made in the early 1880s, though, little resemble Monet's lush and extravagantly colorful bouquets. Rather, they suggest the influence of Manet's final paintings, particularly in works such as *Yellow Roses in a Vase* (cat. no. 47), a spare composition of a bouquet on a marble tabletop against a scumbled black ground. This work might almost have been intended as homage to the floral still lifes that Manet was painting the same year. Caillebotte's overblown bouquet scatters rose petals, each one deftly built with just a few brushstrokes of thickly applied paint, across the marble surface. The intensity of color in the central floral motif suggests Caillebotte's familiarity with the complex surfaces of Monet's recent flower paintings, while the dramatic, tilted perspective of the table reflects Caillebotte's own interest in the unfamiliar pictorial space of Japanese prints. The artist retained this painting throughout his life, and it was purchased at his postmortem sale by Edgar Degas, who likewise kept it until his own death. HMacD

1. Quoted in Gordon and Forge 1999, 30.
2. See Berson 1996, vol. 2:3–175.
3. Ibid., 179–97.
4. House 1986, 42.

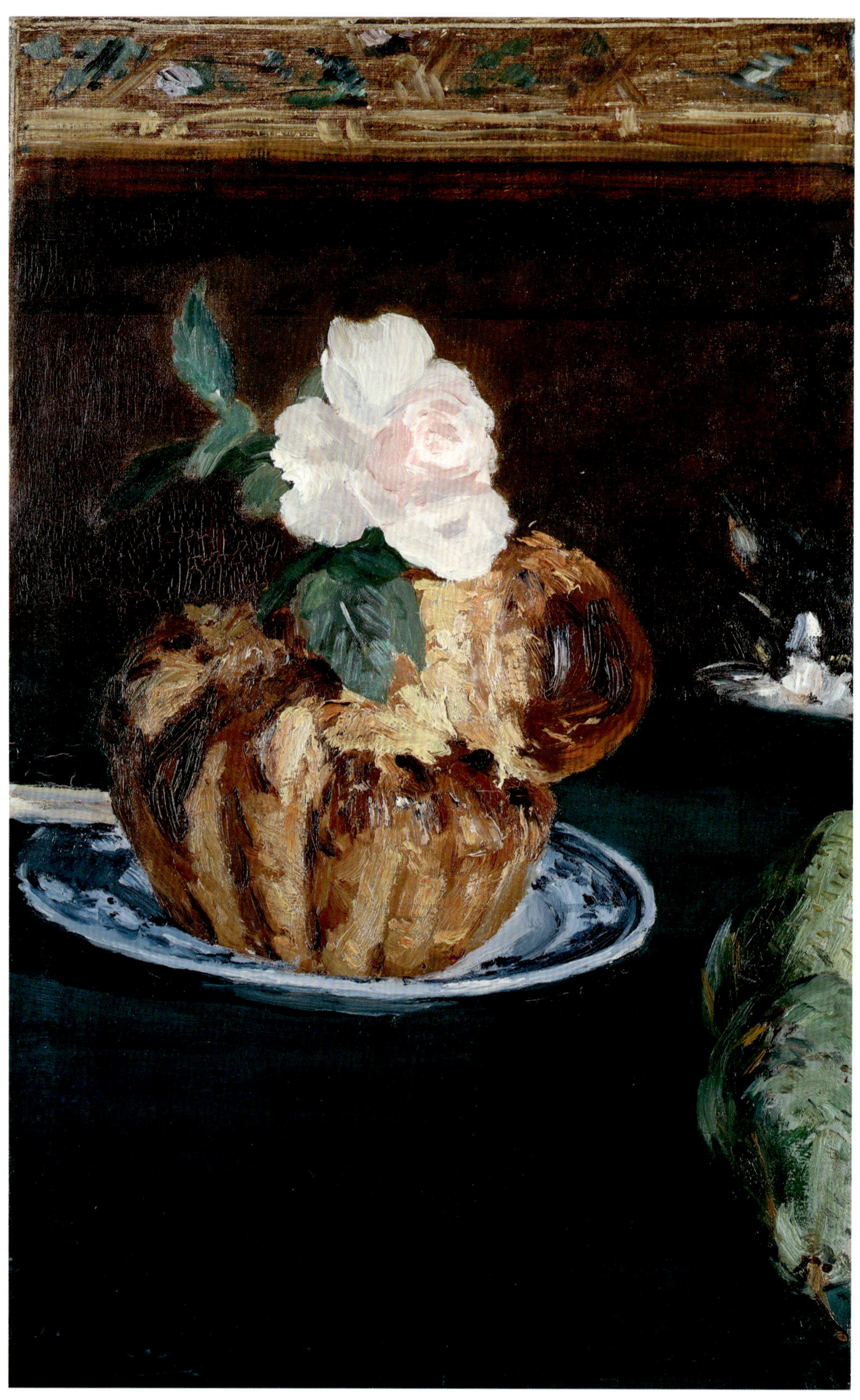

40 ÉDOUARD MANET
(FRENCH, 1832–1883)

Still Life with Brioche, 1880

Oil on canvas, 21¾ × 13⅞ in. (55 × 35 cm)
Carnegie Museum of Art, Pittsburgh, William R. Scott, Jr., Fund, 84.8

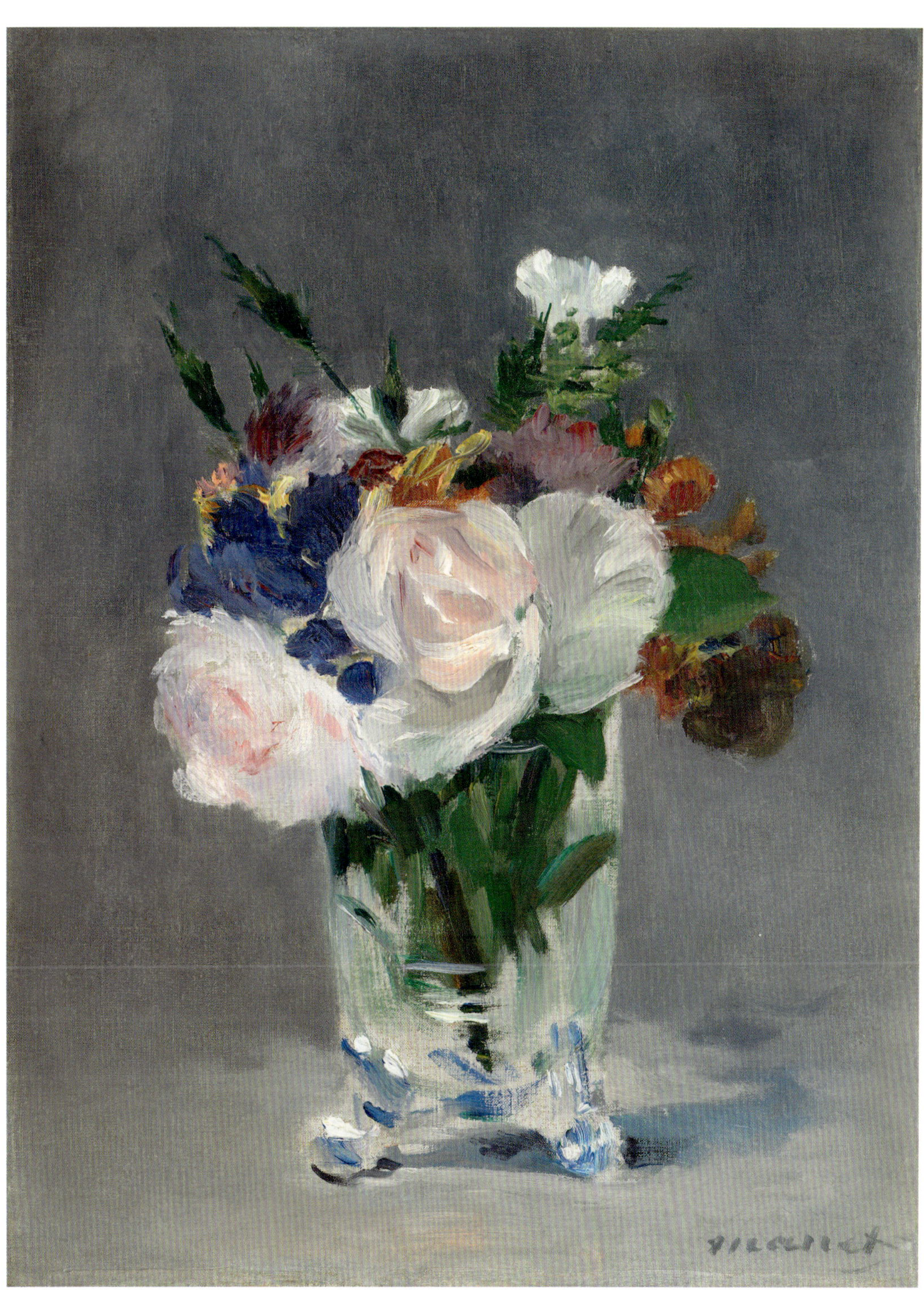

41 ÉDOUARD MANET
(FRENCH, 1832–1883)

Flowers in a Crystal Vase, ca. 1882

Oil on canvas, 12⅞ × 9⅝ in. (32.7 × 24.5 cm)
National Gallery of Art, Washington, D.C., Ailsa Mellon Bruce Collection, 1970.17.37

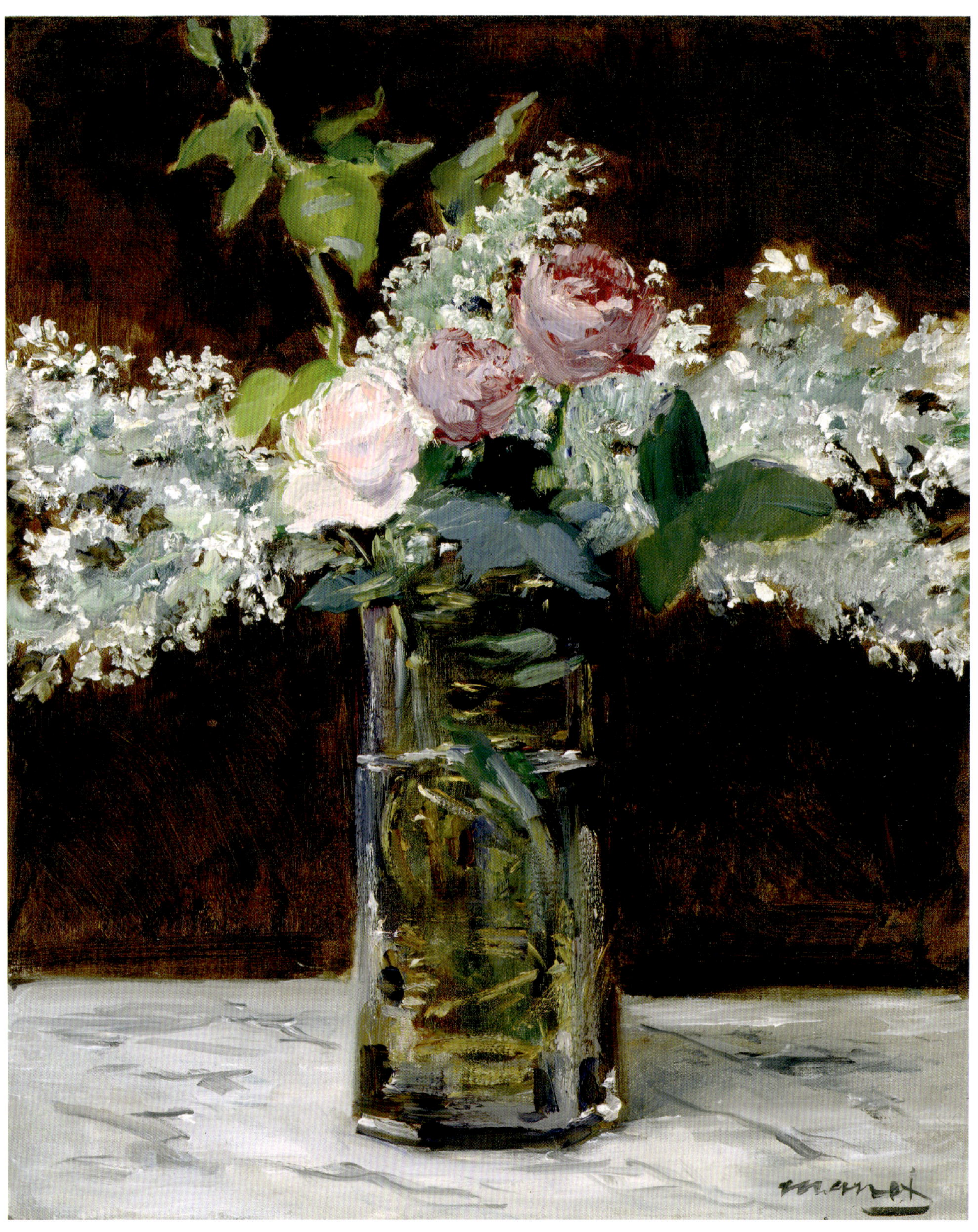

42 ÉDOUARD MANET
(FRENCH, 1832–1883)

Vase of White Lilacs and Roses, 1883

Oil on canvas, 22 × 18⅛ in. (55.9 × 46 cm)
Dallas Museum of Art, The Wendy and Emery Reves Collection, 1985.R.34

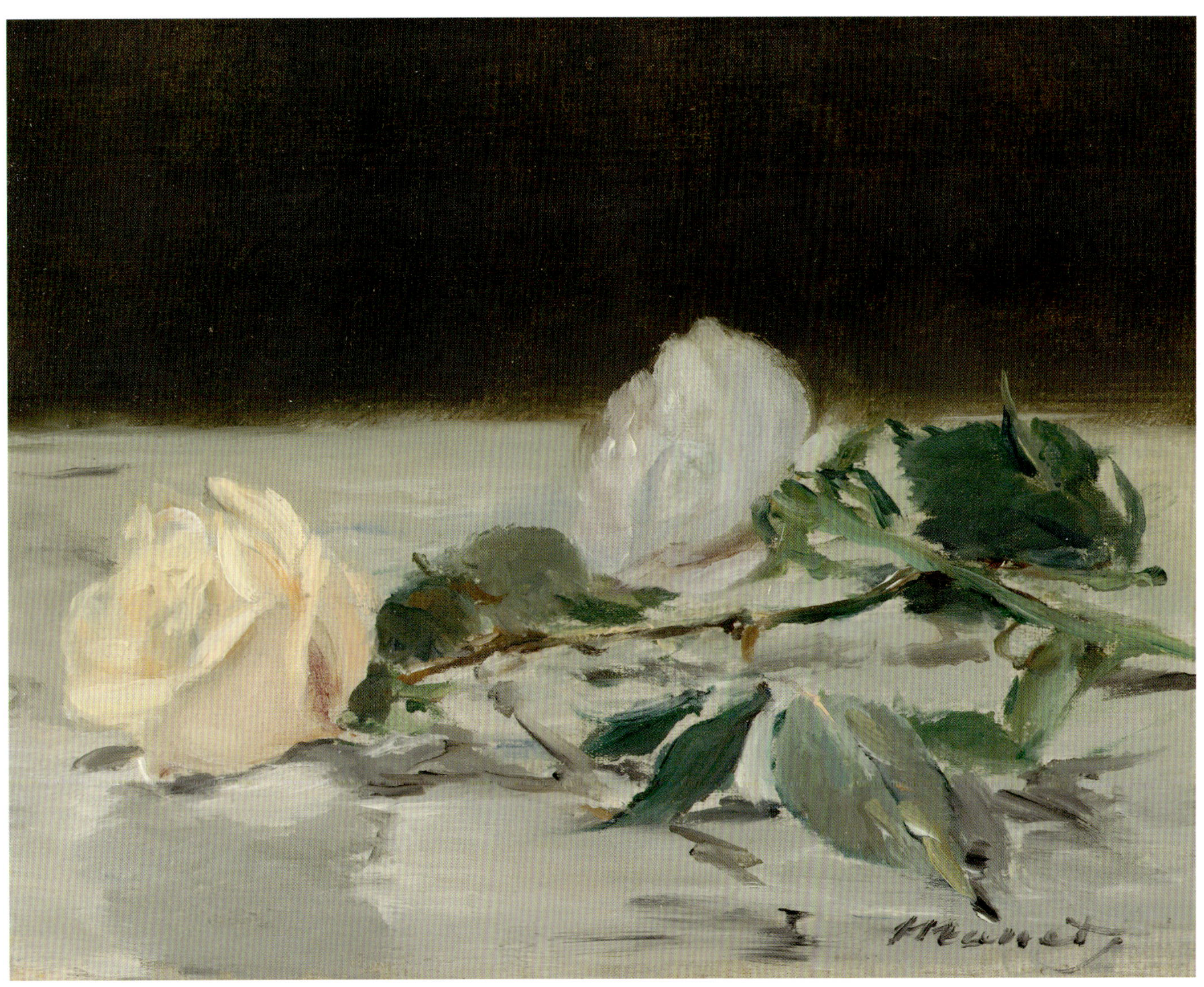

43 ÉDOUARD MANET
(FRENCH, 1832–1883)

Two Roses on a Tablecloth, 1882–83

Oil on canvas, 7⅝ × 9½ in. (18 × 24 cm)
Museum of Modern Art, New York, The William S. Paley Collection, 1990, SPC 17.1990

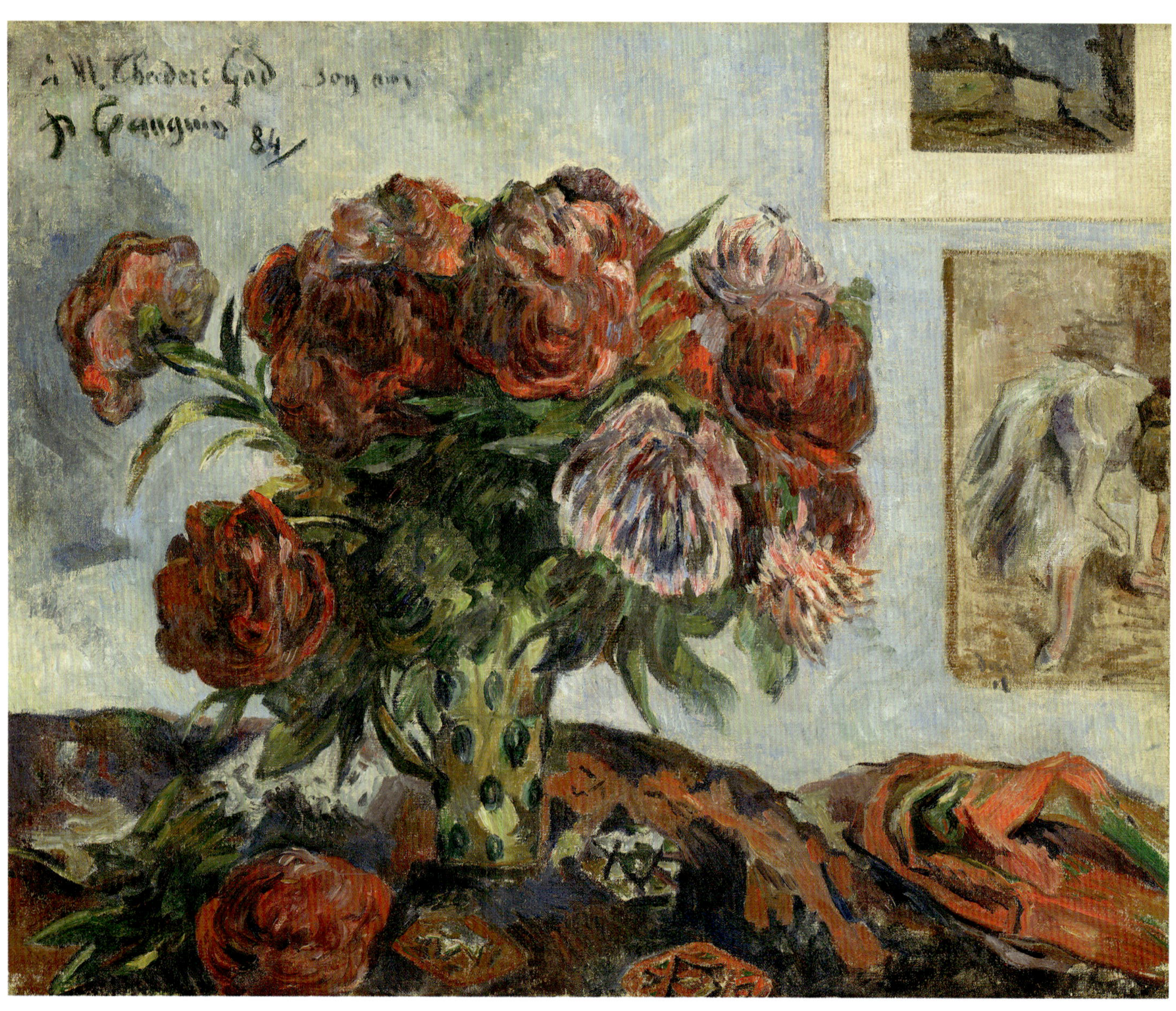

44 PAUL GAUGUIN

(FRENCH, 1848–1903)

Still Life with Peonies, 1884

Oil on canvas, 23½ × 28¾ in. (59.7 × 73 cm)
National Gallery of Art, Washington, D.C., Collection of Mr. and Mrs. Paul Mellon, 1995.47.10

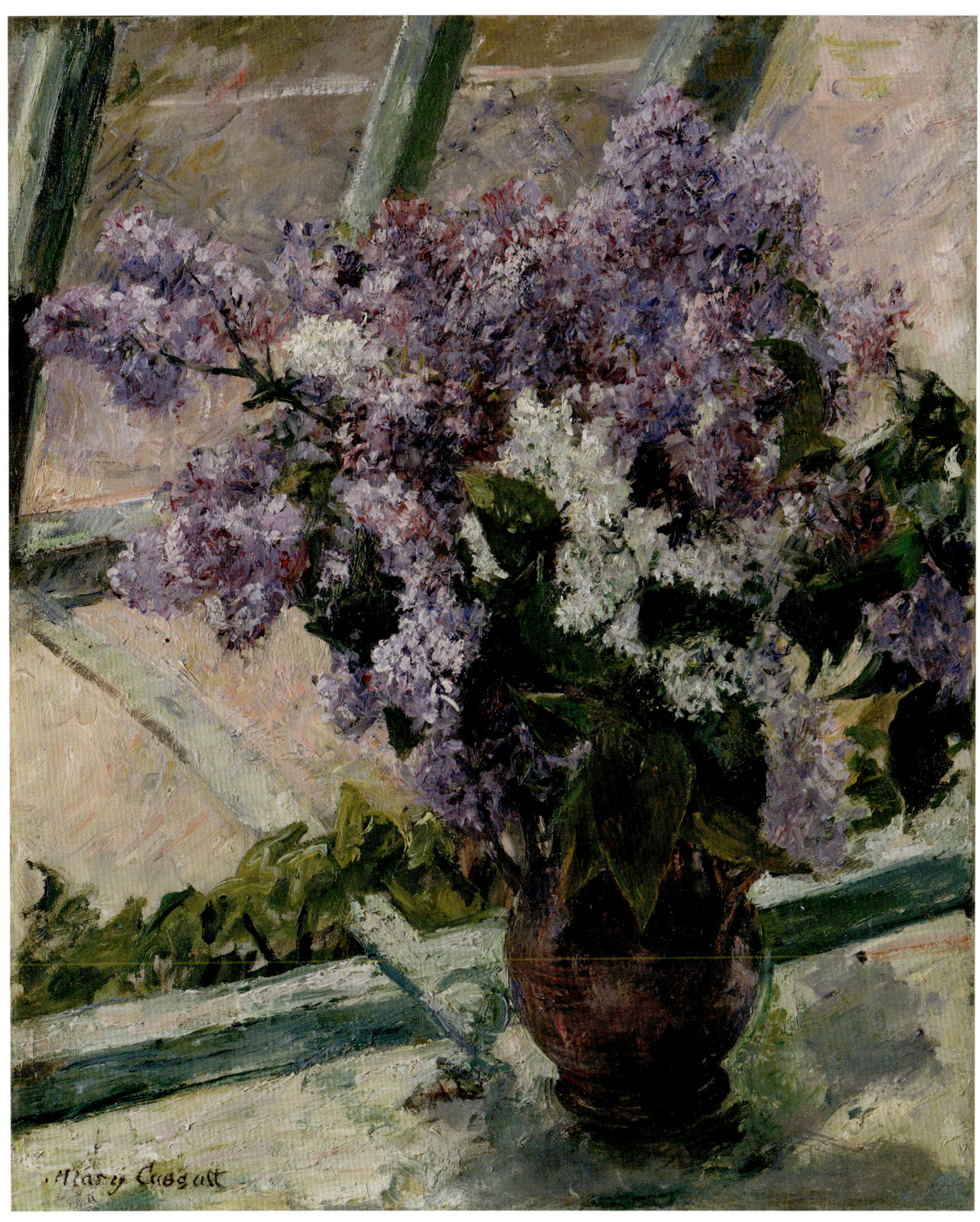

45 MARY CASSATT

(AMERICAN, 1844–1926; ACTIVE IN FRANCE)

Lilacs in a Window, ca. 1880–83

Oil on canvas, 24³⁄₁₆ × 20⅛ in. (61.5 × 51.1 cm)
Metropolitan Museum of Art, New York, Partial and Promised Gift of Mr. and Mrs. Douglas Dillon, 1997, 1997.207

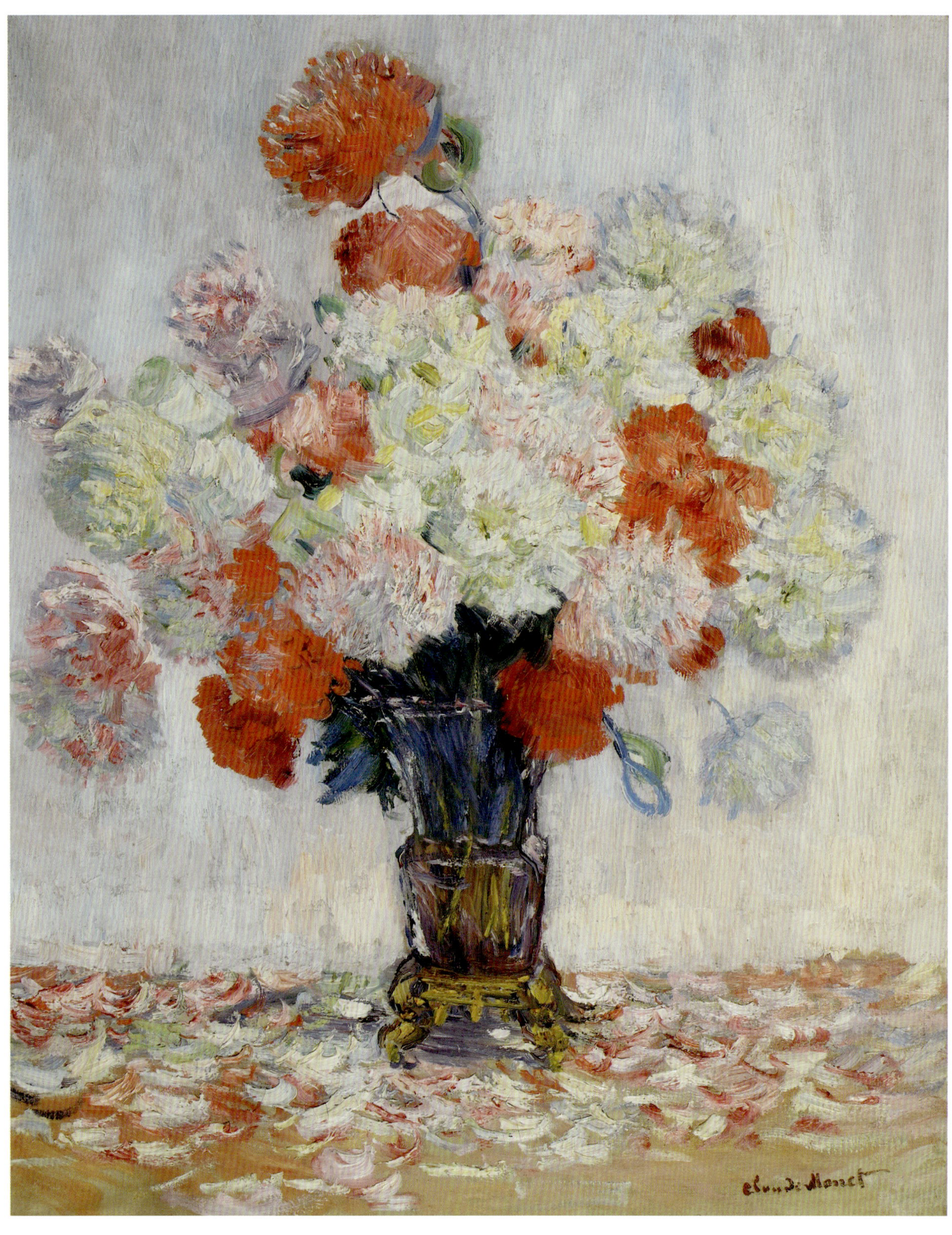

46
CLAUDE MONET
(FRENCH, 1840–1926)

Vase of Peonies, 1882

Oil on canvas, 39⅜ × 31⅞ in. (100.01 × 80.96 cm)
Private Collection

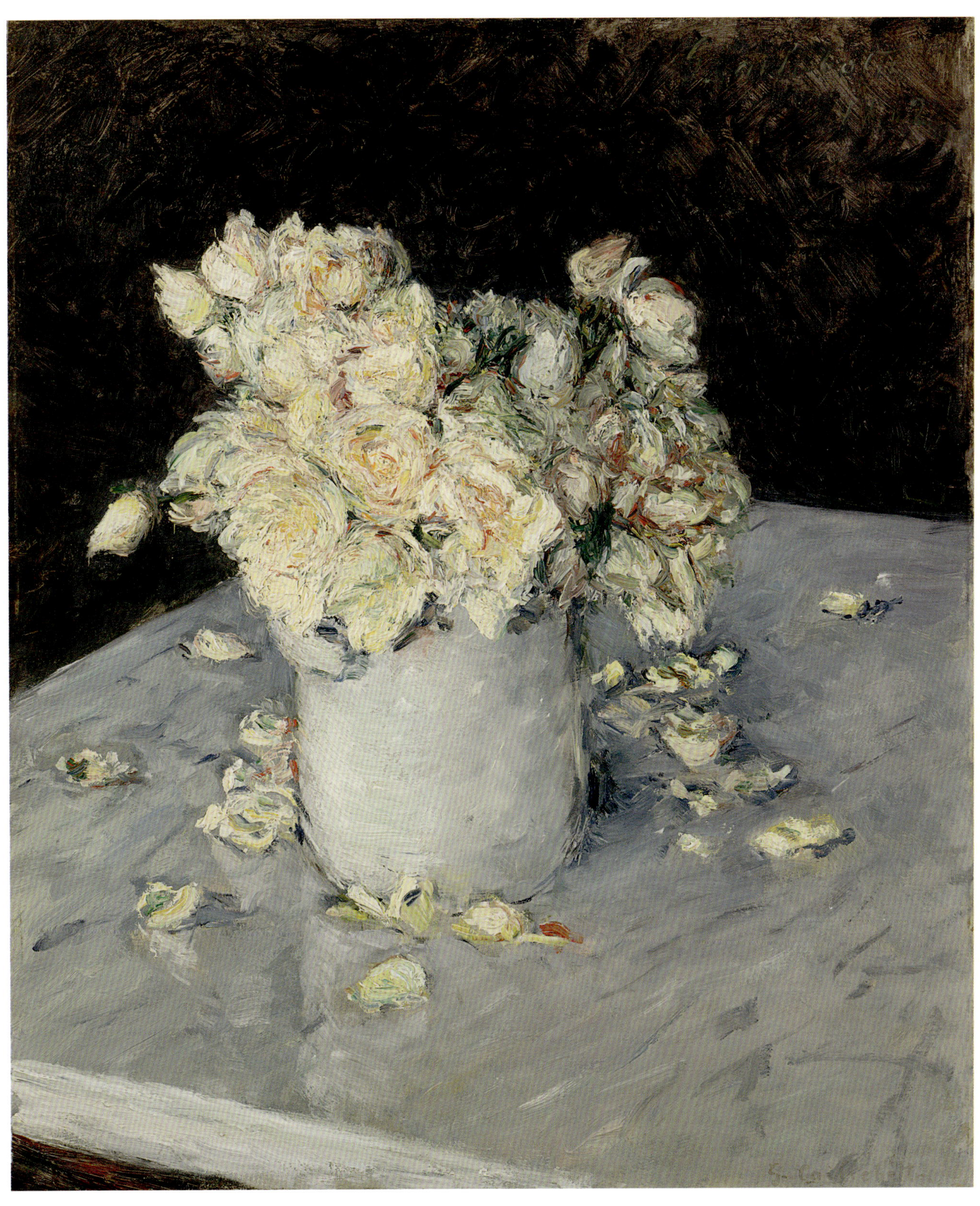

47 GUSTAVE CAILLEBOTTE

(FRENCH, 1848–1894)

Yellow Roses in a Vase, 1882

Oil on canvas, 21 × 18¼ in. (53.34 × 46.36 cm)

Dallas Museum of Art, The Eugene and Margaret McDermott Art Fund, Inc., in honor of Janet Kendall Forsythe, 2010.13.McD

AFTER IMPRESSIONISM: VAN GOGH AND THE EXPERIMENTS OF THE 1890S

IN 1886, SHORTLY BEFORE THE FINAL IMPRESSIONIST exhibition, the young Dutch artist Vincent van Gogh arrived in Paris. "There is much to be seen here," he wrote to his friend, British artist Horace Mann Livens, "for instance, Delacroix, to name only one master. In Antwerp I did not even know what the Impressionists were, now I have seen them and though *not* being one of the club yet I have much admired certain Impressionists' pictures."[1] Van Gogh arrived at a moment when the Parisian avant-garde was in the midst of a profound transformation, spurred in part by the emergence of new artistic movements, such as Neo-Impressionism and Symbolism, but also by the growing appreciation for distinctively individual work, such as that of Paul Cézanne.

In *The Blue Vase* (cat. no. 48), Cézanne's maturity as a still-life painter is evident. Even in the description of the flowers, the elusive subject that had defeated his laborious brush in the 1870s, he seems to be on firmer ground, allowing the (paper?) blossoms to take a leading role in the painting's chromatic and structural composition and not troubling with a great deal of specificity. The vase of flowers seems remarkably robust, with the convincing solidity of its presence fraying only where it encounters its surroundings and Cézanne is pressed to delineate the relationship between vase and plate, or foliage and wall.

Cézanne's still lifes had gained a formidable reputation among certain segments of the French avant-garde by the 1880s, but the practice of an artist like van Gogh illustrates the many different models available to a young still-life painter at the time.[2] As noted, van Gogh was already looking at Eugène Delacroix and the Impressionists soon after his arrival in Paris, but that summer he was also studying Édouard Manet. In June, he and his brother Theo saw *Vase of Peonies on a Pedestal* (see fig. 37), Manet's most important flower painting of the 1860s, when it was sold at auction. As he later recalled to Theo: "Do you remember that one day at the Hôtel Drouot we saw a quite extraordinary Manet, some large pink peonies and their green leaves on a light background? As much in harmony and as much a *flower* as anything you like, and yet painted in

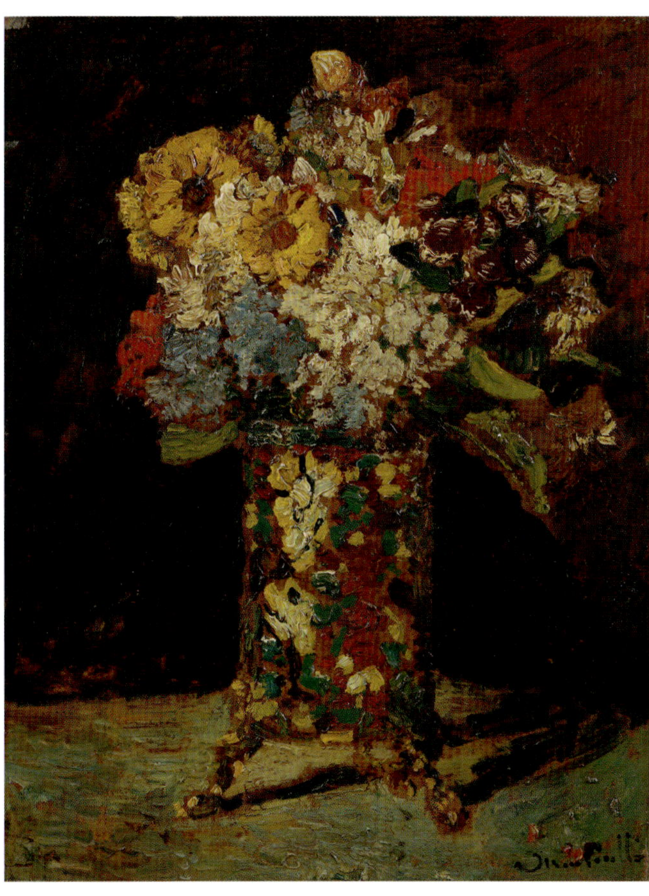

FIG. 65 Adolphe Monticelli, *Flower Still Life*, 1875, oil on canvas. Van Gogh Museum, Amsterdam

solid, thick impasto. . . . That's what I'd call simplicity of technique."[3]

Van Gogh was clearly impressed by Manet's virtuoso brushwork, but in the large series of flower paintings he made over the following months, he did not emulate it directly, experimenting first with the heavy, almost encrusted impasto of the recently deceased painter Adolphe Monticelli (fig. 65), whom van Gogh saw as the true heir to Delacroix's intense commitment to color. Van Gogh's central preoccupation in the series of floral still lifes he began in 1886 was color, whether working with the brilliant, jewel-like tones of *Bowl with Zinnias and Other Flowers* (cat. no. 49) or a refined palette of closely related hues, as in *Vase with Carnations* (cat. no. 50). In his letter to Livens, which dates to September or October of 1886, van Gogh described his floral still lifes as "a series of colour studies" in which he sought out "oppositions of blue with orange, red and green, yellow and violet, seeking THE BROKEN AND NEUTRAL TONES to harmonise brutal extremes. Trying to render intense COLOUR and not a grey harmony."[4] In this passage, van Gogh was alluding to the ambitious paintings he then had underway, works like *Vase with Cornflowers and Poppies* (cat. no. 51), the largest canvas of this series. His use of complementary colors and reference to "broken tones" suggest that he saw his floral still lifes as participating in some way in the emerging Neo-Impressionist project, even as his open brushwork little resembled the tightly controlled pointillism of Georges Seurat or Paul Signac. More important then to van Gogh's practice was the exercise of learning to describe form with color and abandoning the "grey harmonies" of the paintings he had made before coming to Paris. He reported to his sister the following year that his lengthy engagement with floral still life in 1886 had accustomed him to seeing color in his subjects, a study that he then carried over to his landscapes and portraits.[5]

Still life, though, remained an important genre to van Gogh on its own terms. During the winter of 1887–88, in Paris, he adopted an unusual vantage point in a number of his still lifes, painting small, prosaic arrangements of fruit or onions from above and close-up. After moving

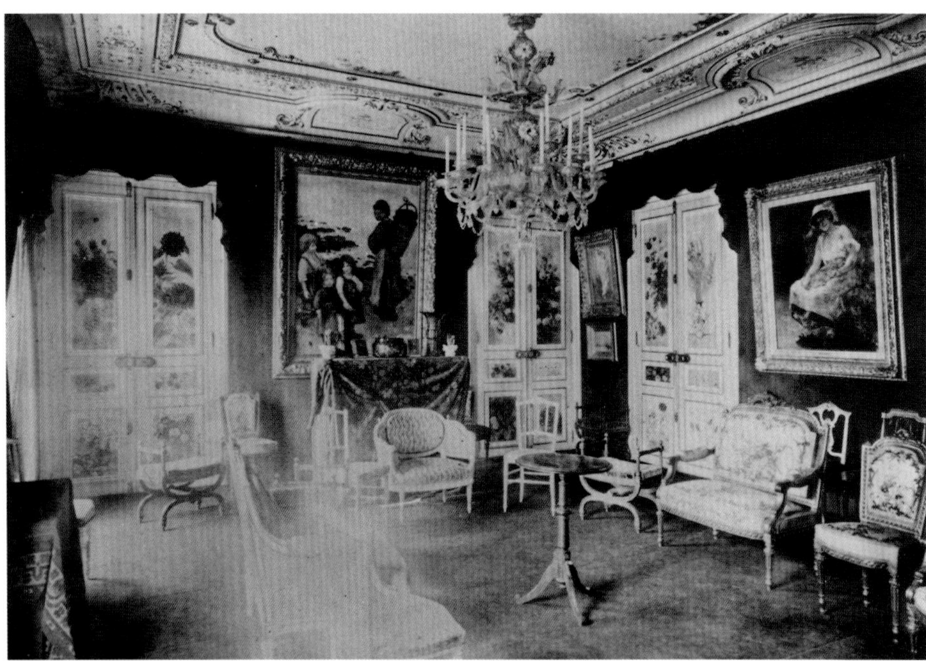

FIG. 66 The salon in Paul Durand-Ruel's Paris apartment, decorated with Monet's still-life panels. Archives Durand-Ruel

to Arles in the south of France that spring, van Gogh shifted his attention to landscape painting, but he continued to make several close-up still lifes of pointedly humble subjects, such as potatoes. Similarly, in *Daisies, Arles* (cat. no. 52), painted in the summer of 1888, the colorful bouquets of 1886 are replaced by an unassuming, even weed-like plant blooming with modest white flowers. In the summer of 1889, while van Gogh was recuperating from the mental breakdown he had suffered in Arles, Theo counseled him to emulate Delacroix by using flower painting as a kind of mental release. During the final months of his life, while under the care of Dr. Paul-Ferdinand Gachet, van Gogh was able to study flower paintings in Gachet's own collection, including "two fine bouquets by Cézanne."[6] It may have been the example of a work like Cézanne's *Small Delft Vase with Flowers* (see fig. 33) that prompted van Gogh's *Vase of Flowers* (cat. no. 53), a tightly cropped still life of a bulbous and even clumsy bouquet that is reminiscent of the oddly conceived flowers and heavily painted forms in Gachet's Cézanne.

The extent of van Gogh's familiarity with the contemporary floral still lifes by the artists of the Impressionist circle is uncertain. He mentioned in a letter to Theo in 1888 that he had never had a chance to see a work by Gustave Caillebotte, but the strong formal similarities between a work like van Gogh's *Vase with Cornflowers and Poppies* and Caillebotte's nearly contemporaneous *Vase of Gladiolas* (cat. no. 54) suggest that, at the very least, both artists were looking at similar models, perhaps the more formally audacious of Claude Monet's floral still lifes from the early 1880s, such as *Vase of Peonies* (cat. no. 46). Later in the decade, Monet continued to produce floral still lifes, but principally in the context of a decorative project for the salon of the Impressionists' art dealer Paul Durand-Ruel (fig. 66). Monet's painted door panels featuring vignettes of flowers and fruit were an unusual modernist reimagining of the still-life decor that often embellished eighteenth-century interiors. Monet's flower paintings for Durand-Ruel were essentially decorative in character and allowed him to explore in a concentrated series a type of still life that he had first shown at the seventh Impressionist exhibition, in 1882, and continued to pursue throughout the decade: radically simplified compositions that abandoned any suggestion of a conventional domestic context in favor of shallow, neutral fields of color (cat. no. 55).

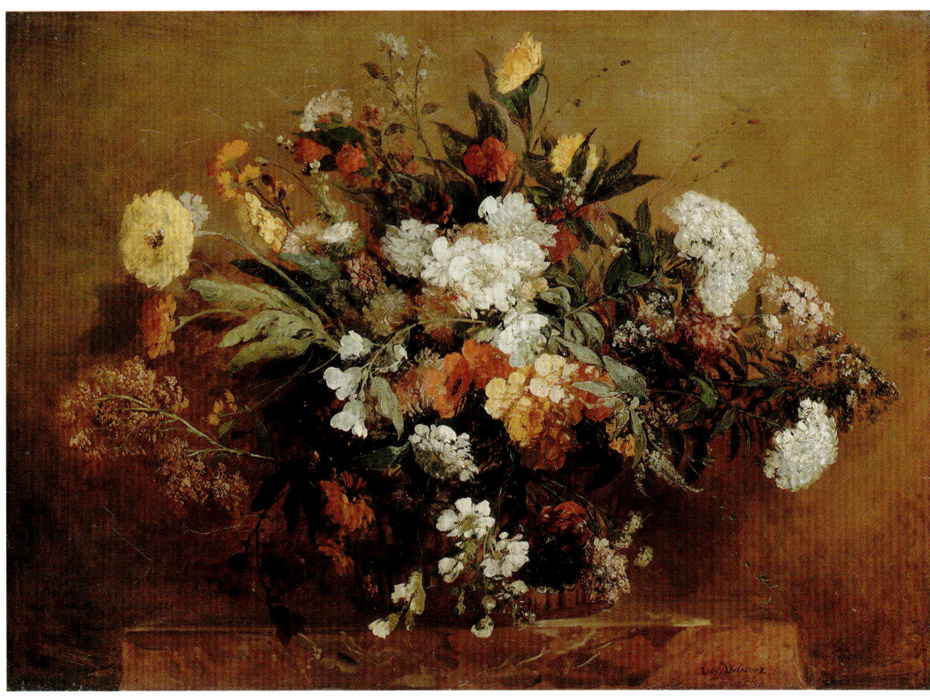

FIG. 67 Eugène Delacroix, *Bouquet*, ca. 1850, oil on canvas. Palais des Beaux-Arts, Lille, P.533

The move away from the domestic interior as a narrative or social context for the floral still life was widespread among modernist artists at the end of the nineteenth century, though Camille Pissarro retained the connection of the floral motif to the lived environment even in his late still lifes such as *Bouquet of Flowers* (cat. no. 56). Pissarro includes a glimpse of his own 1883 landscape, *Place Lafayette, Rouen* (Courtauld Gallery, London), and an apparently casually placed book (a feature in so many of the artist's flower paintings), on which he signs and dates the canvas.

Gauguin, too, who had been among the most innovative of the Impressionist artists in crafting intricate settings for his still lifes in the 1880s, tended to employ a nondescript, shallow space in the floral still lifes he painted in the late 1890s, after his definitive return to Tahiti in 1895. In *A Vase of Flowers* of 1896 (cat. no. 57), Gauguin's lush bouquet of tropical flowers evokes the compositional structure and subtle palette of Delacroix's floral still lifes (fig. 67), and indeed, Gauguin brought with him to Tahiti a photograph of the Delacroix flower painting that had belonged to his guardian and mentor, Gustave Arosa, and of which he had made a copy (see fig. 58). Gauguin sent *A Vase of Flowers* to his friend Daniel de Monfreid, who acted as the painter's agent in Paris and sold the canvas to Edgar Degas, a loyal admirer and collector of Gauguin's work. That same year, Gauguin wrote to Monfreid, asking him to send flower bulbs and seeds suitable for a hot climate: "I would like to embellish my little plantation, and as you know, I adore flowers."[7] Gauguin did not allude to the artistic (or commercial) possibilities of floral still life when he made this request, but by the time the irises, gladioli, and dahlias sent by Monfried had bloomed into "a veritable Eden" in the spring of 1899, Gauguin looked forward to making studies of flowers when his imagination for other work ran dry.[8] Later that year, however, when the Parisian dealer Ambroise Vollard wrote to Gauguin, offering to buy all of his new floral still lifes, the artist bristled and informed Vollard that he did not like to paint from nature, though when he did, he worked "without a model."[9] He added, "this isn't really a land of flowers."

The flowers from Monfreid are likely among those that appear in Gauguin's *Flowers and Cats* (cat. no. 58), painted the year of their first glorious spring bloom. Whether he worked directly from these natural models or from his memory of studying their complex forms,

Gauguin crafted a still life that is both more orthodox than his eccentric compositions of the 1880s and startlingly innovative in its decorative flatness and whimsical stylization. Although Gauguin sent the painting to Monfreid on consignment, hoping for another lucrative sale, it was eventually purchased by Vollard only after Gauguin's death, evidence that the dealer continued to see Gauguin's floral still lifes as among the most engaging and approachable of the artist's late work.

HMacD

1. Vincent van Gogh to Horace Mann Livens, September or October 1886, letter 569, Jansen et al. 2013.
2. See Przyblyski 1995, 283–84.
3. Vincent van Gogh to Theo van Gogh, August 24, 1888, letter 668, vangoghletters.org. The sale of this work took place in Paris on June 5, 1886.
4. Vincent van Gogh to Livens, September or October 1886, letter 569, ibid.
5. Vincent van Gogh to Willemien van Gogh, late October 1887, letter 574, ibid.
6. For comment on Delacroix, see Theo van Gogh to Vincent van Gogh, June 16, 1889, letter 781, ibid. For mention of Gachet's Cézanne paintings, see Vincent van Gogh to Theo van Gogh and Jo van Gogh-Bonger, May 20, 1890, letter 873, ibid.
7. "je voudrais embellir ma petite plantation, et comme vous le savez, j'adore les fleurs." Quoted in Fonsmark 1995, 181. Author's translation.
8. Quoted in ibid.
9. "Vous me parlez de fleurs peintes, je ne sais vraiment pas lesquelles malgré le petit nombre que j'en ai fait: et cela tient (comme vous avez pu le voir sans doute) que je ne suis pas un peintre d'après nature—aujourd'hui moins qu'avant. Tout chez moi se passe en ma folle imagination. Et quand je suis fatigué de faire des figures (ma prédilection) je commence une nature morte que je termine d'ailleurs sans modèle. Puis ici ce n'est vraiment pas le pays des fleurs." Quoted in ibid., 182. Author's translation.

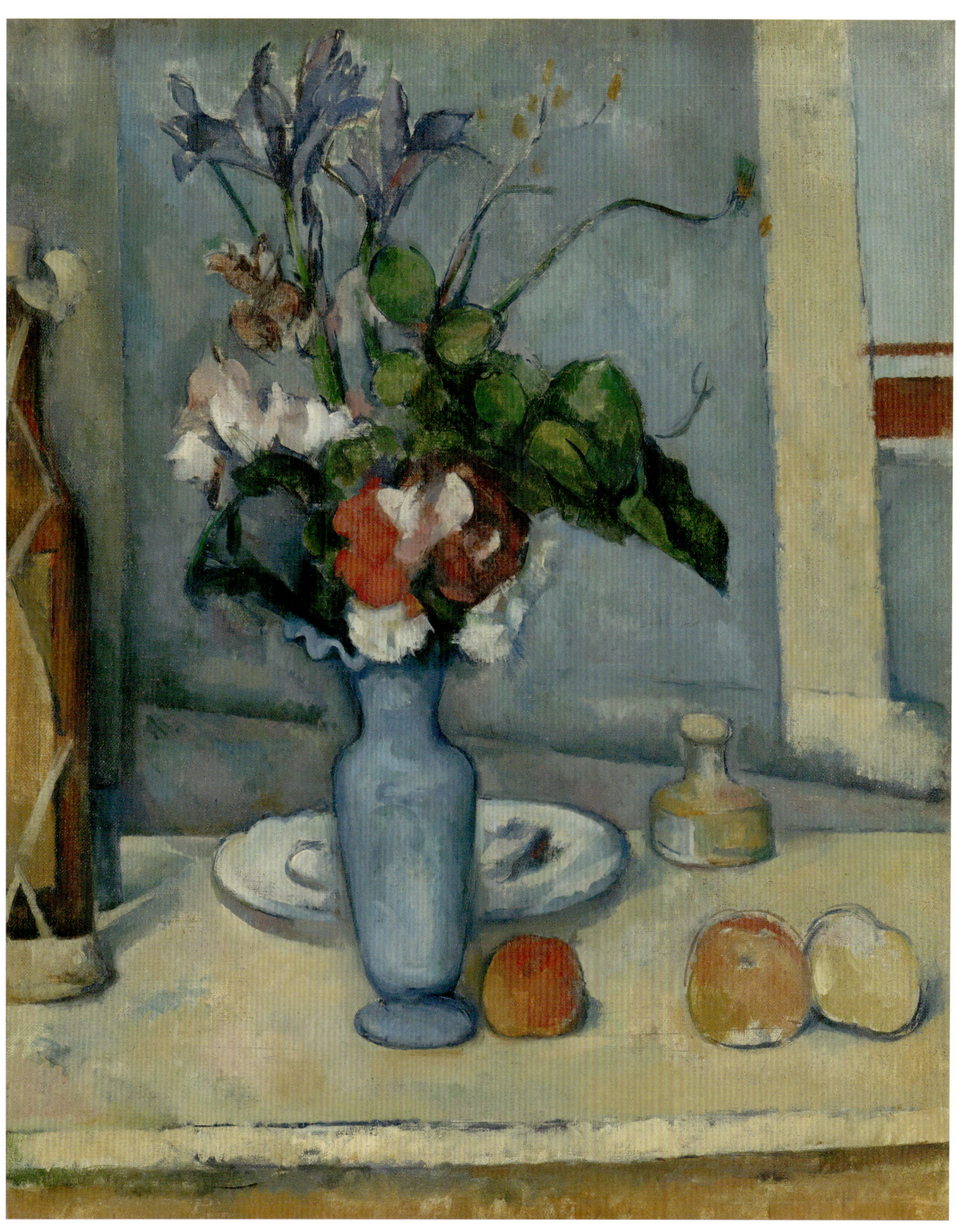

48
PAUL CÉZANNE
(FRENCH, 1839–1906)

The Blue Vase, ca. 1889–90

Oil on canvas, 24 × 19 11/16 in. (61 × 50 cm)
Musée d'Orsay, Paris, Bequest of Comte Isaac de Camondo, 1911, RF 1973

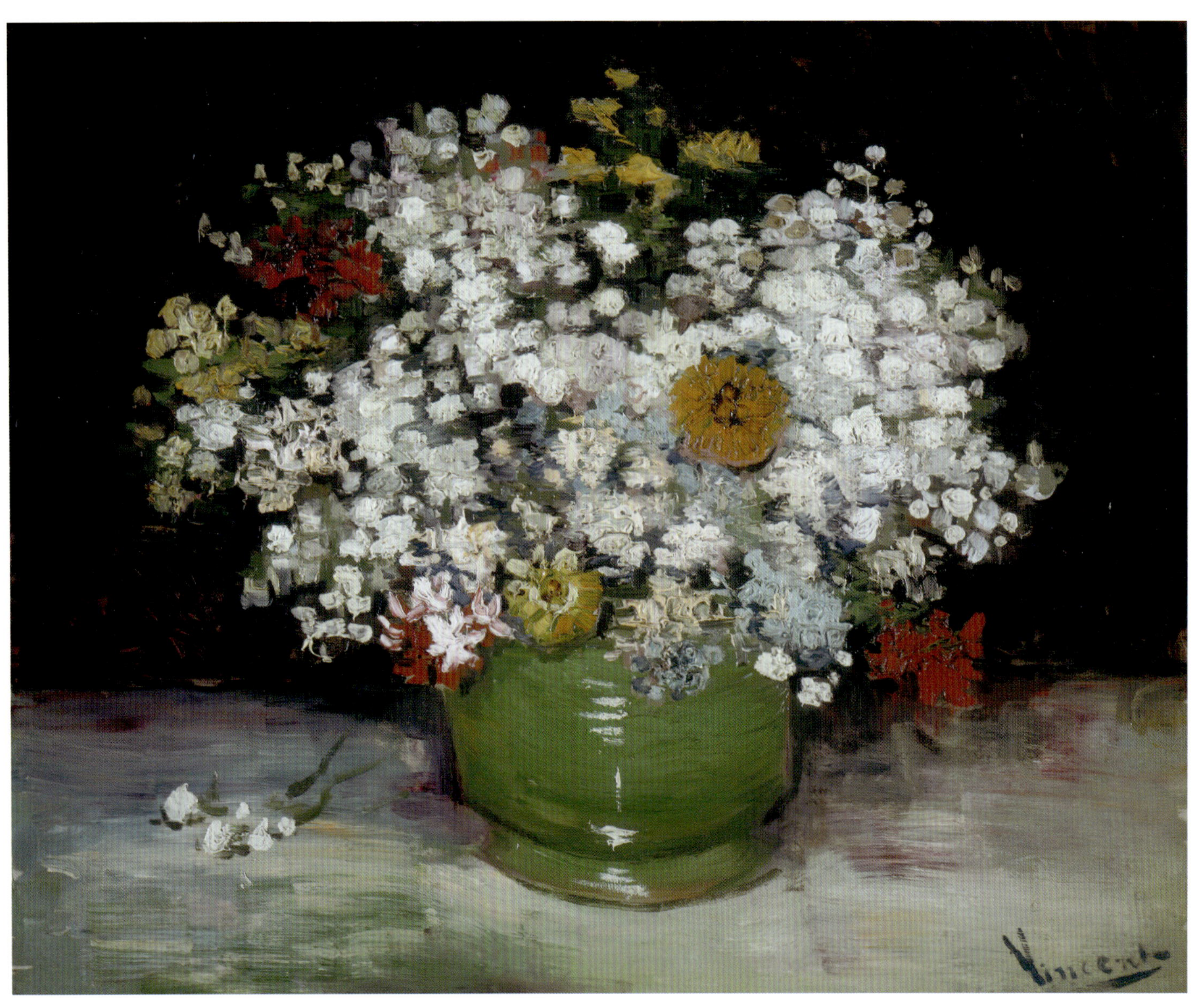

49 VINCENT VAN GOGH
(DUTCH, 1853–1890; ACTIVE IN FRANCE)

Bowl with Zinnias and Other Flowers, 1886

Oil on canvas, 19¾ × 24 1/16 in. (50.2 × 61 cm)
National Gallery of Canada, Ottawa, Purchased 1951, 5808

Dallas and Richmond only

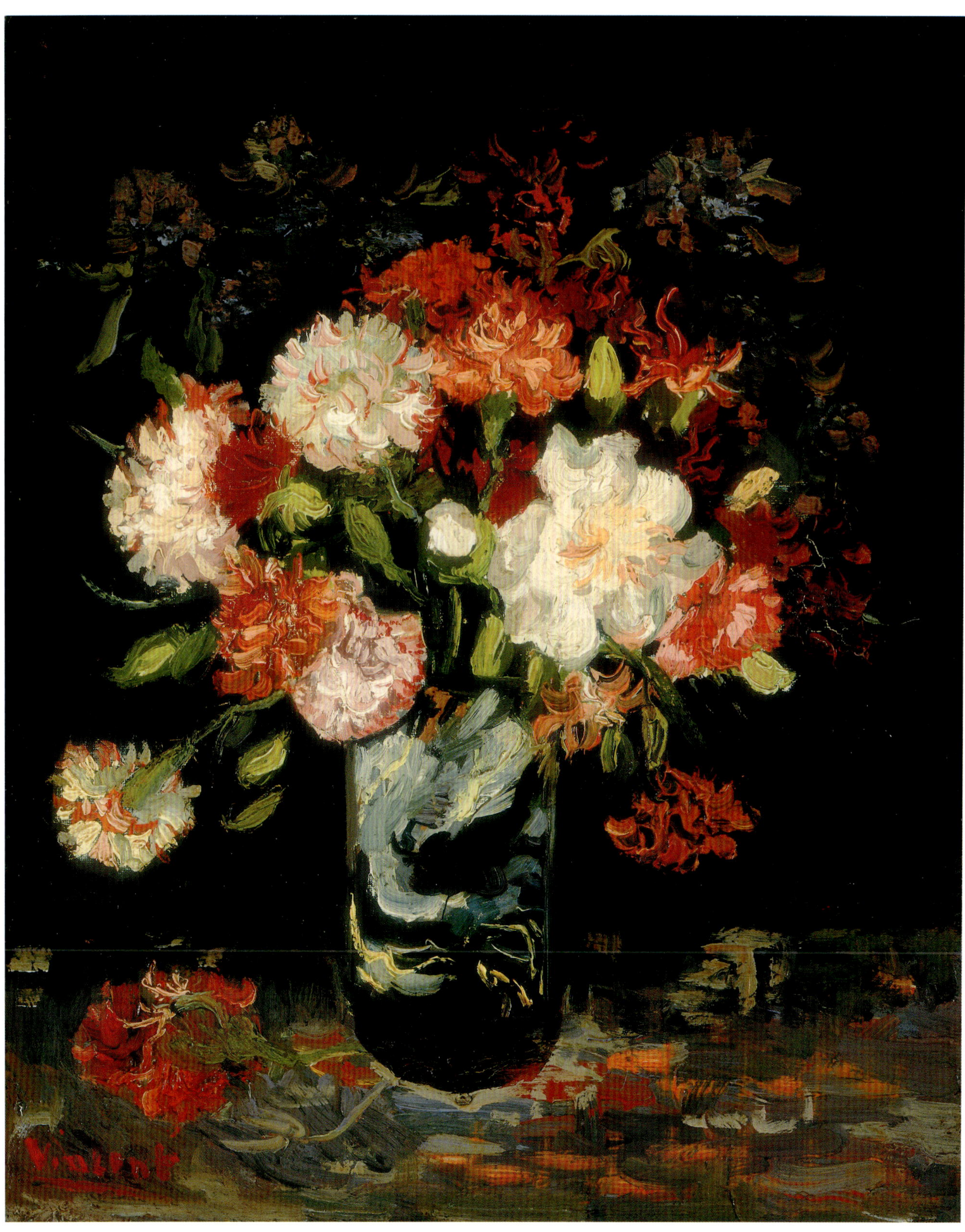

50 VINCENT VAN GOGH
(DUTCH, 1853–1890; ACTIVE IN FRANCE)

Vase with Carnations, summer 1886

Oil on canvas, 18⅛ × 14¾ in. (46 × 37.5 cm)
Collection Stedelijk Museum, Amsterdam, purchased with the generous support of the Vereniging van Hadendaagse Kunstaankopen, A2235

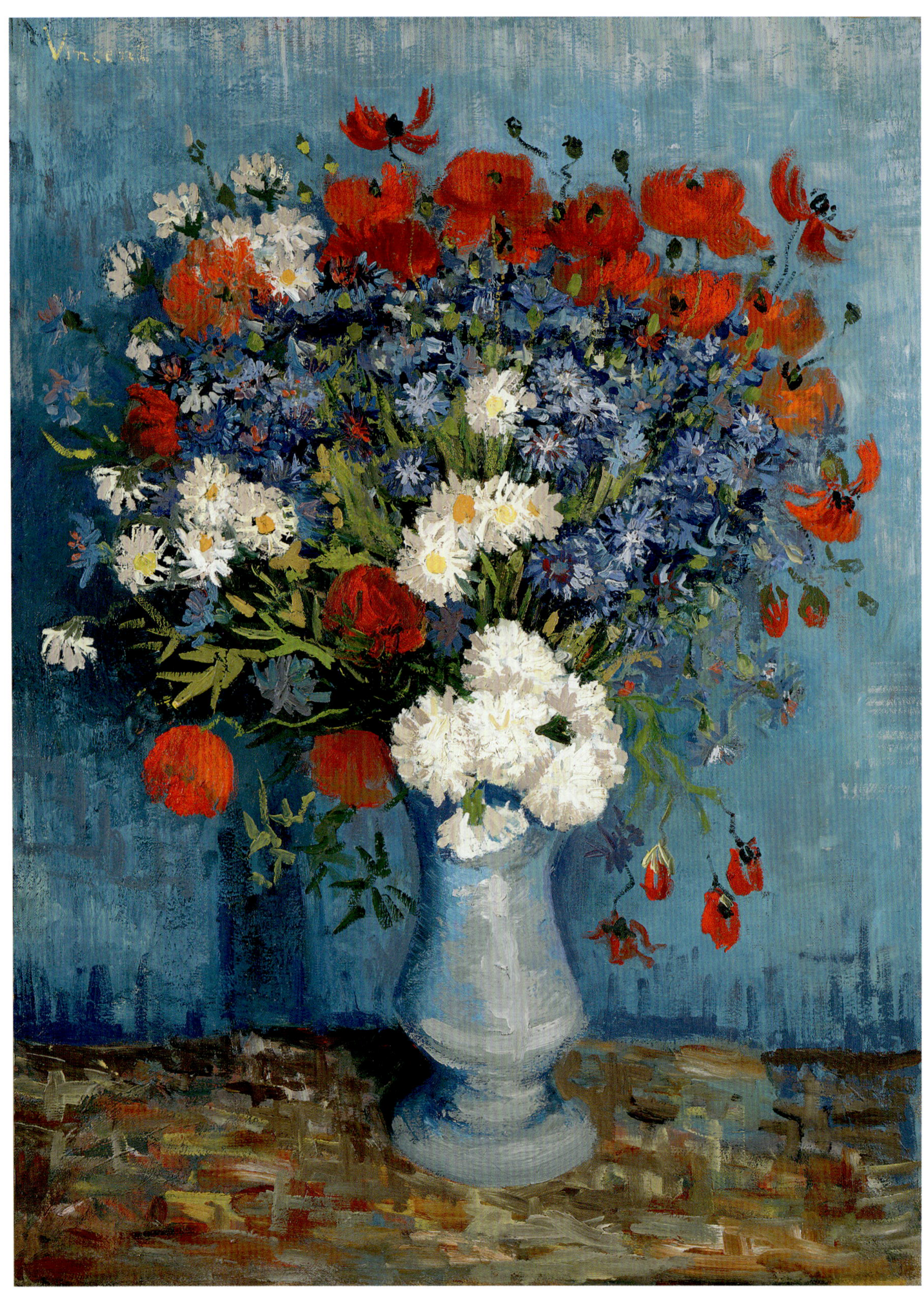

51 VINCENT VAN GOGH
(DUTCH, 1853–1890; ACTIVE IN FRANCE)

Vase with Cornflowers and Poppies, 1887

Oil on canvas, 31½ × 26⅜ in. (80 × 67 cm)
Triton Collection Foundation

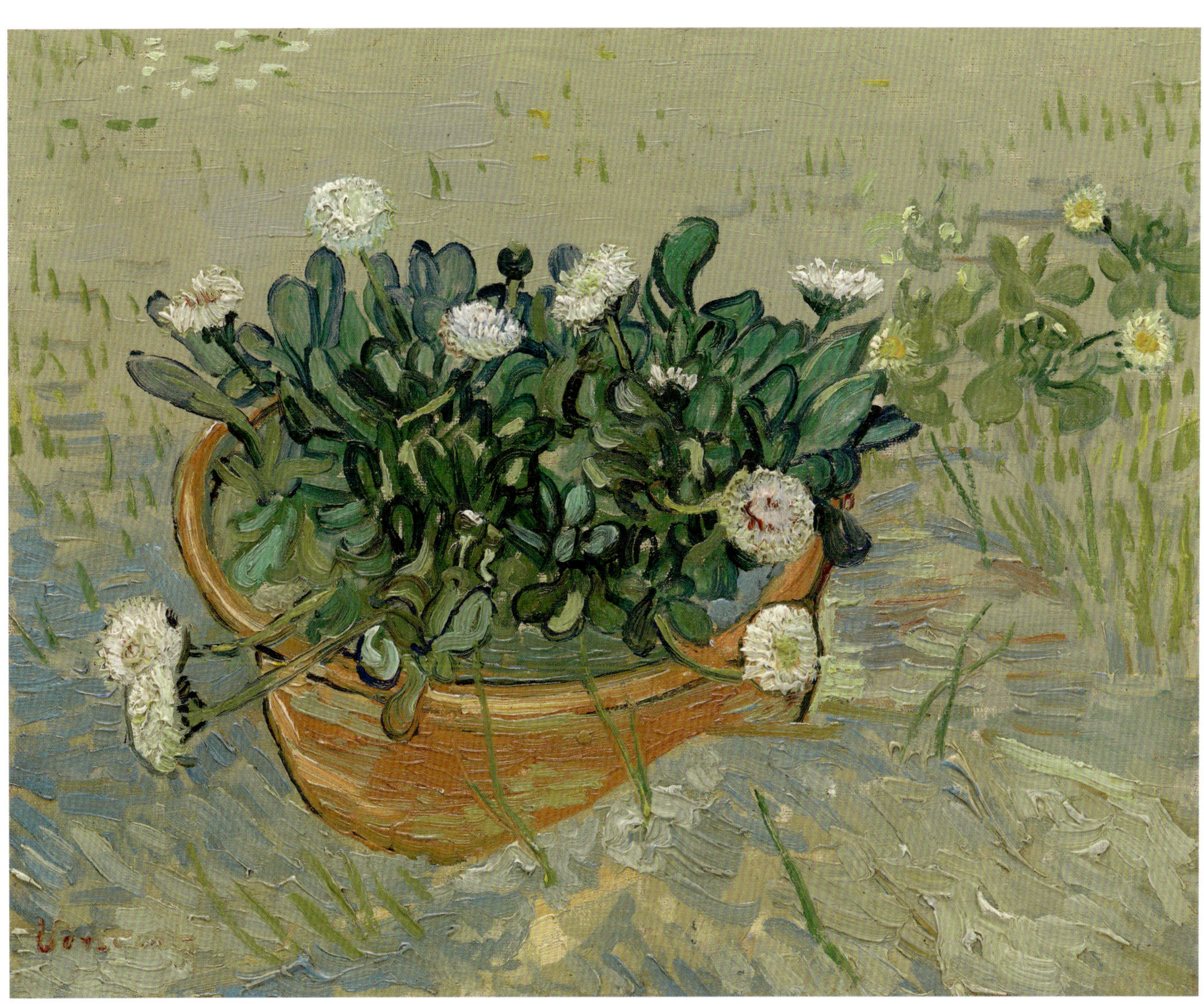

52 VINCENT VAN GOGH
(DUTCH, 1853–1890; ACTIVE IN FRANCE)

Daisies, Arles, 1888

Oil on canvas, 13 × 16½ in. (33 × 42 cm)
Virginia Museum of Fine Arts, Richmond, Collection of Mr. and Mrs. Paul Mellon, 2014.207

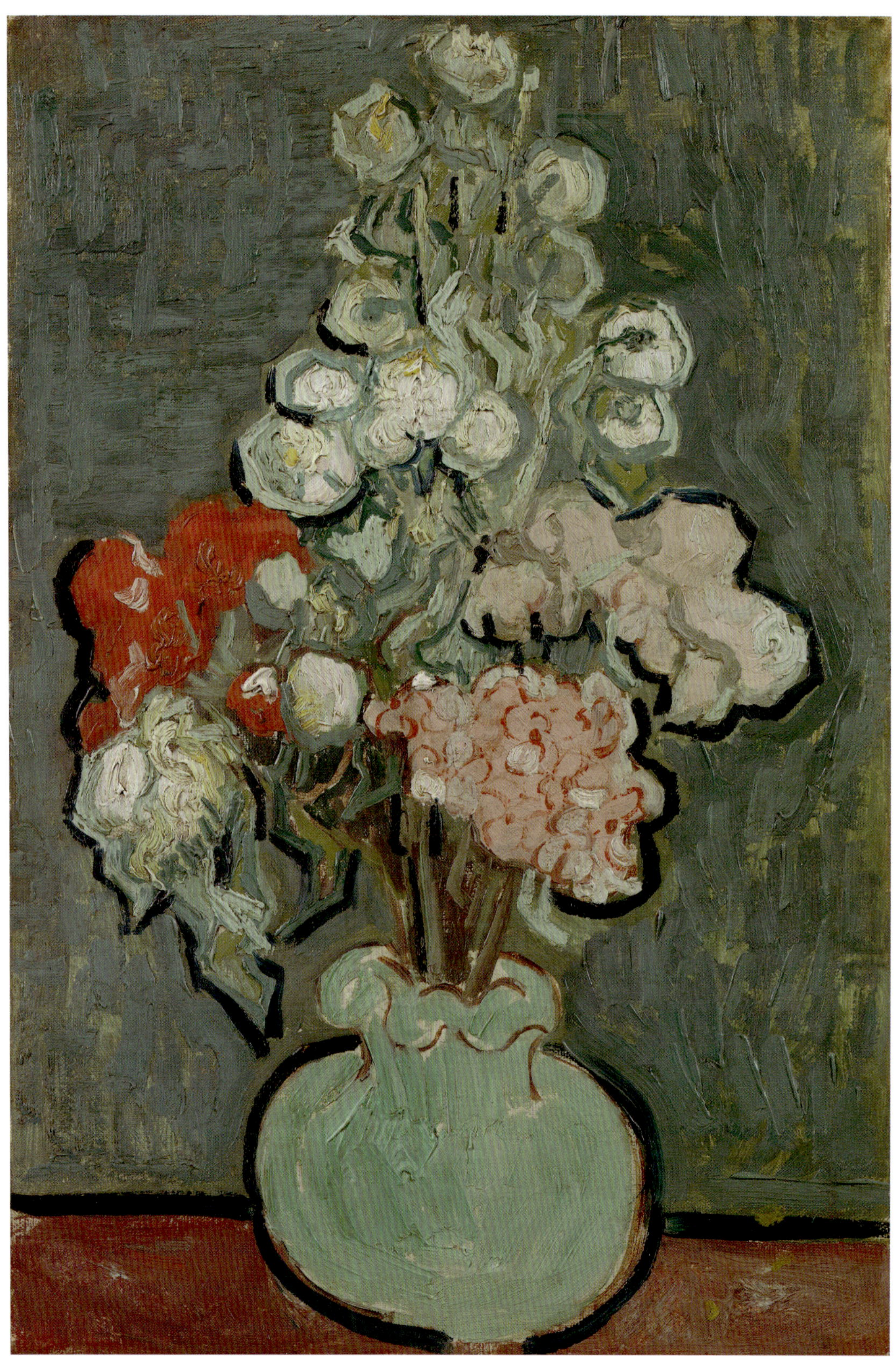

53 VINCENT VAN GOGH
(DUTCH, 1853–1890; ACTIVE IN FRANCE)

Vase of Flowers, summer 1890

Oil on canvas, 16⁹⁄₁₆ × 11⁷⁄₁₆ in. (42 × 29 cm)
Van Gogh Museum, Amsterdam (Vincent van Gogh Foundation), S109V/1962

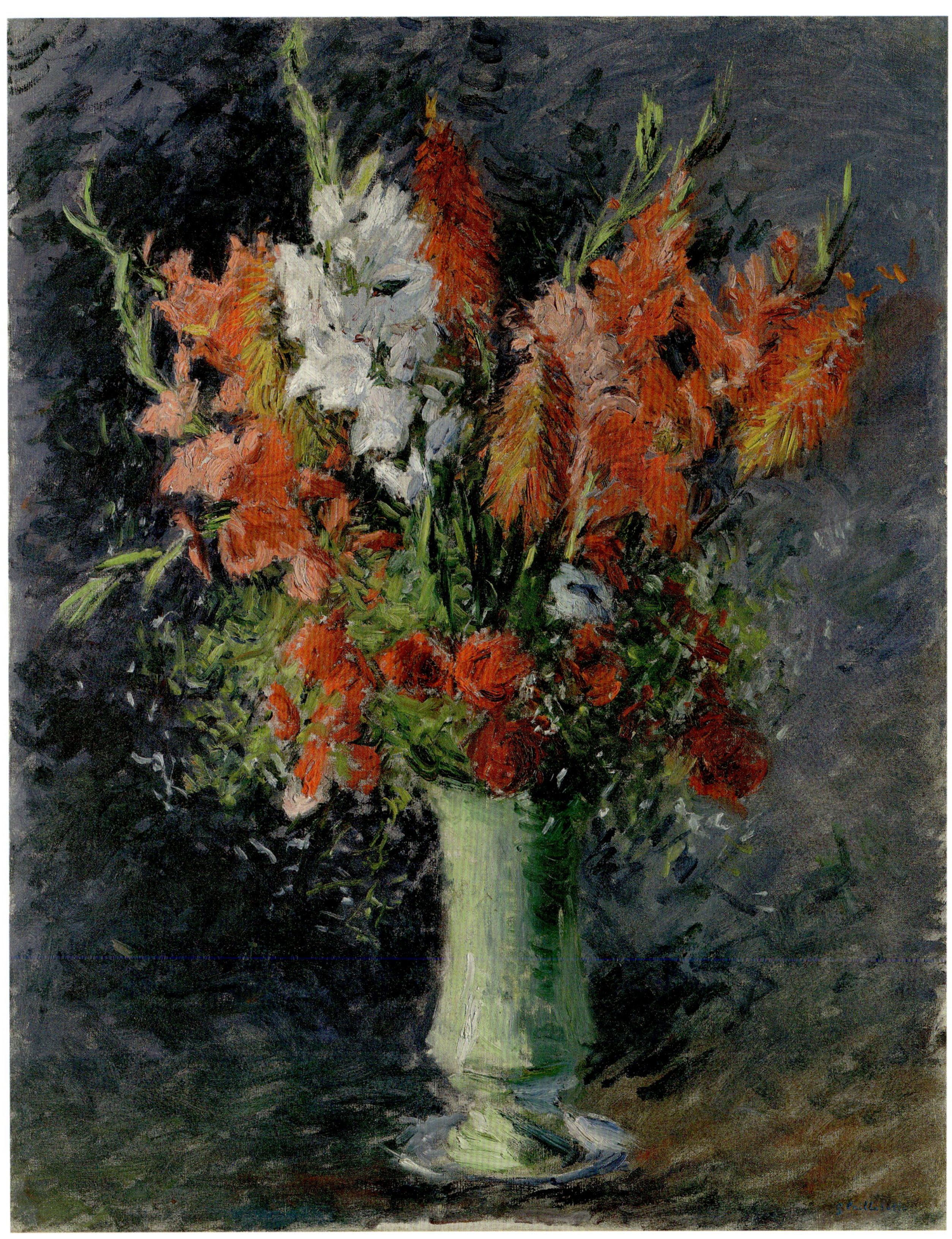

54 GUSTAVE CAILLEBOTTE
(FRENCH, 1848–1894)

Vase of Gladiolas, 1887–88

Oil on canvas, 31⅞ × 25⅝ in. (81 × 65.1 cm)
The Lawrence J. Ellison Art Collection

Dallas and Richmond only

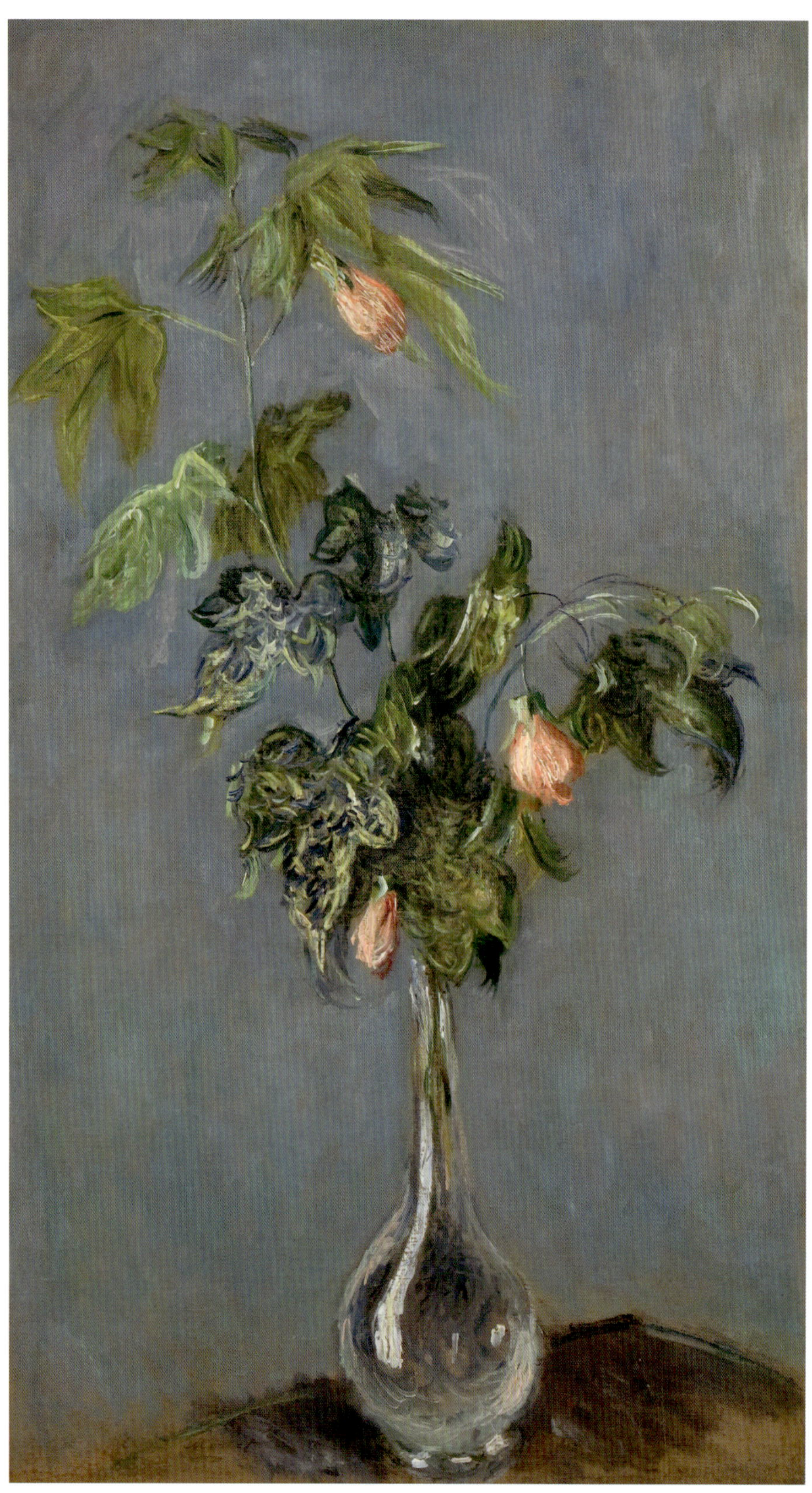

55 CLAUDE MONET
(FRENCH, 1840–1926)

Flowers in a Vase, 1888

Oil on canvas, 32½ × 17¾ in. (80 × 45.1 cm)
Philadelphia Museum of Art, Bequest of Charlotte Dorrance Wright, 1978, 1978-1-23

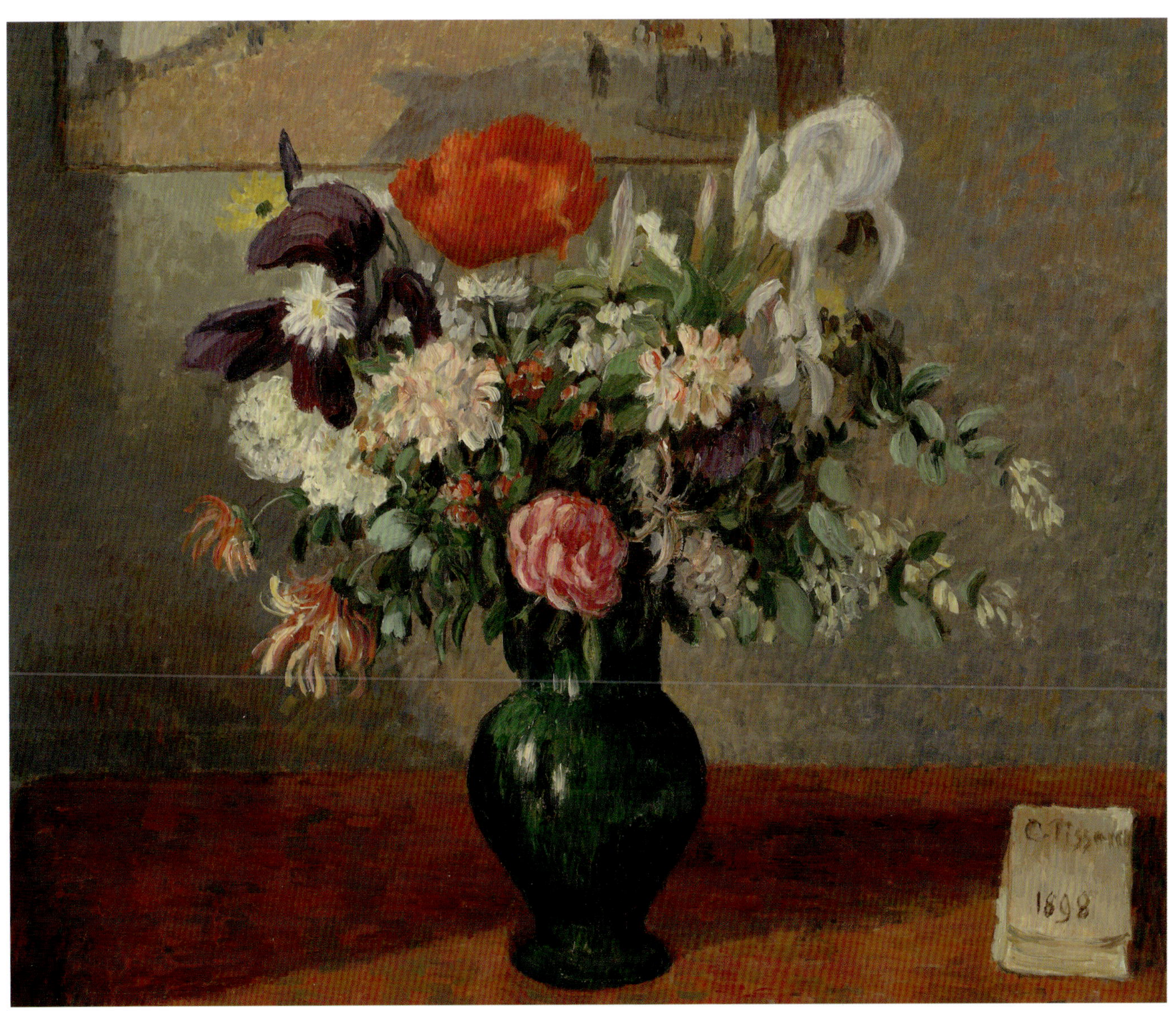

56 CAMILLE PISSARRO
(FRENCH, 1831–1903)

Bouquet of Flowers, ca. 1898

Oil on canvas, 21¼ × 25¾ in. (54 × 65.41 cm)
Fine Arts Museums of San Francisco, Bequest of Marco F. Hellman, 1974.6

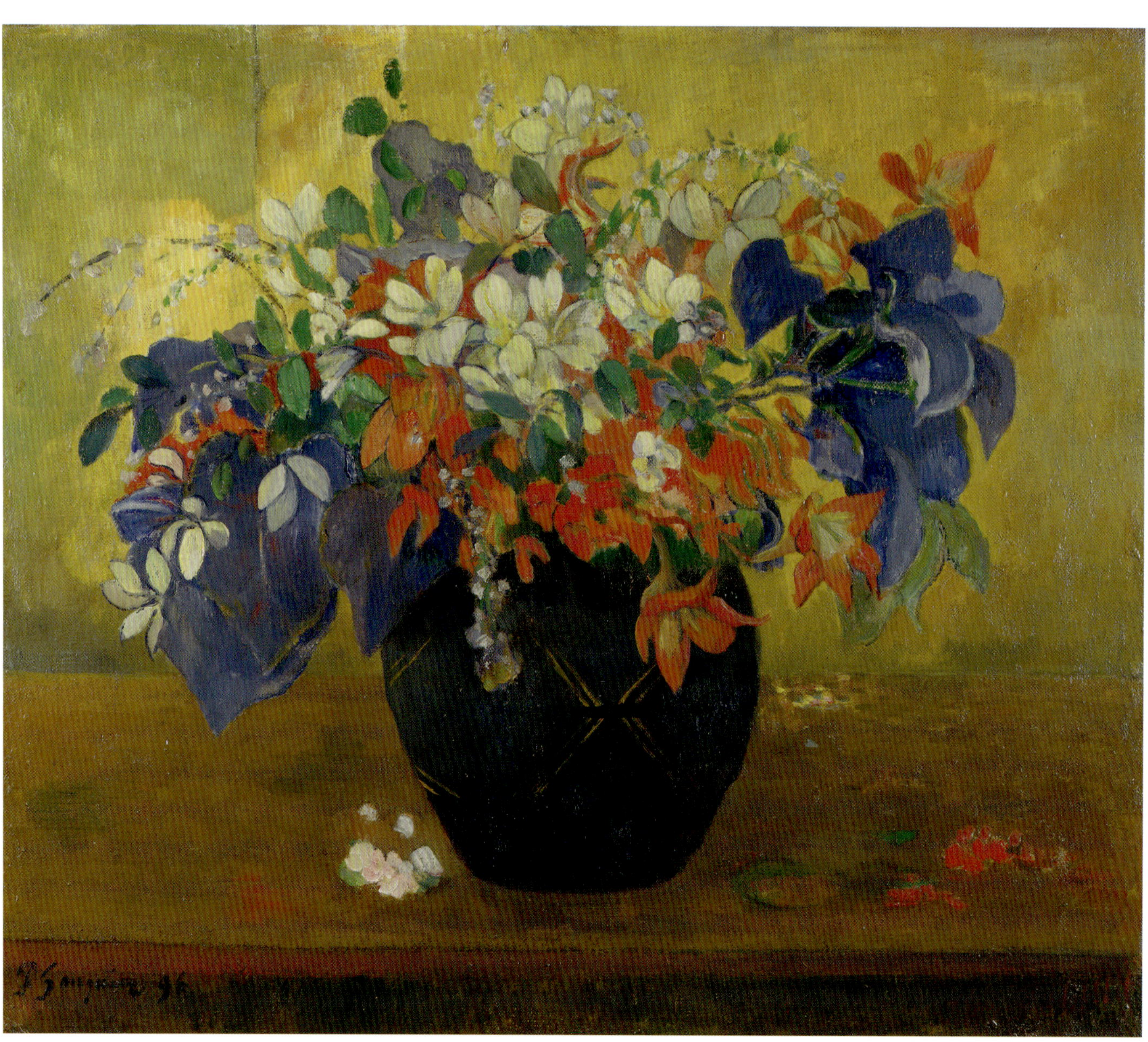

57 PAUL GAUGUIN
(FRENCH, 1848–1903)

A Vase of Flowers, 1896

Oil on canvas, 25³⁄₁₆ × 29⅛ in. (64 × 74 cm)
The National Gallery, London, Bought 1918, NG 3289

Dallas only

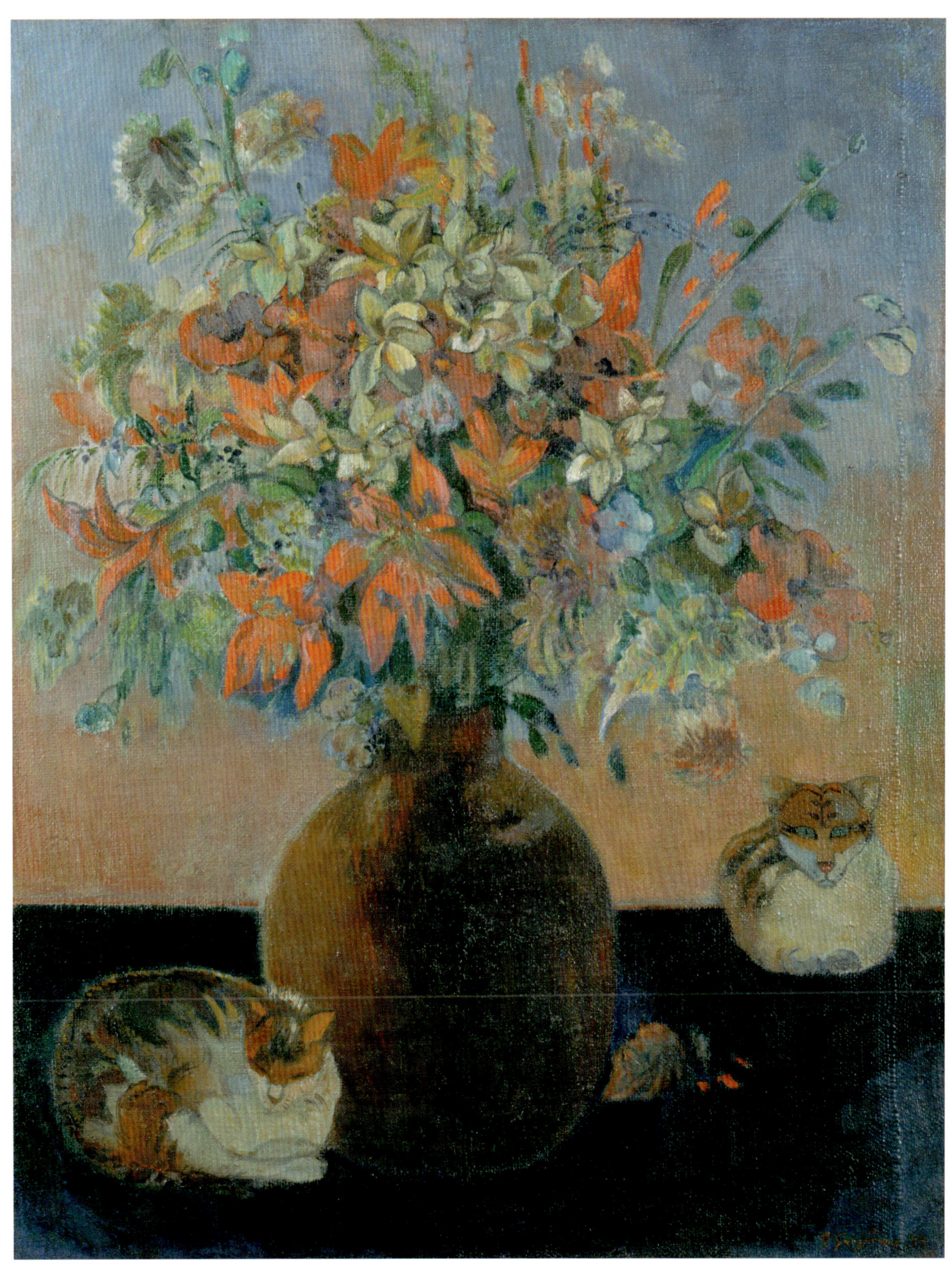

58
PAUL GAUGUIN
(FRENCH, 1848–1903)

Flowers and Cats, 1899

Oil on canvas, 36¼ × 27¹⁵⁄₁₆ in. (92 × 71 cm)
Ny Carlsberg Glyptotek, Copenhagen, MIN 1835

Dallas and Richmond only

IN THE 1920S, THE ART DEALER AMBROISE VOLLARD championed a failed effort to convince Louvre authorities to hang one of Paul Cézanne's modernist still lifes side by side with an iconic still-life painting by Chardin.[1] The mid-nineteenth-century revival of the nearly forgotten eighteenth-century master had come full circle, with his now canonical status used to anoint Cézanne as a modern icon of French still life. Vollard's unrealized project recalls an earlier tribute to Cézanne, Maurice Denis's *Homage to Cézanne* (fig. 68), a painting of a group of avant-garde artists in Vollard's shop, gathered around a Cézanne still life that had once been the centerpiece of Paul Gauguin's art collection. During the quarter century between these two attempts to formalize Cézanne's status as the archetypal still-life painter of the late nineteenth century, a group of younger artists continued to pursue their own very personal reappraisals of the floral still life, often in close dialogue with the French tradition.

One of these artists was Odilon Redon, whom Denis includes in his *Homage to Cézanne*, standing at far left, the apparent focus of the others' attention. Denis's

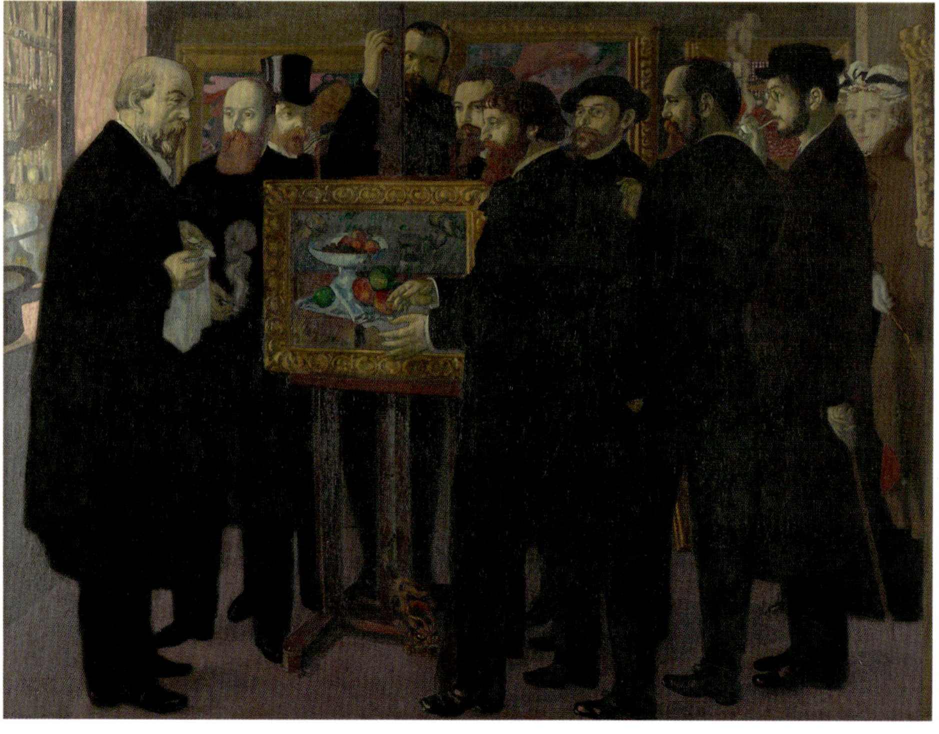

FIG. 68 Maurice Denis, *Homage to Cézanne*, 1900, oil on canvas. Musée d'Orsay, Paris, RF 1977 137

journal reveals that his first idea for this work was to "make a painting of Redon in Vollard's shop, surrounded by Vuillard, Bonnard, etc."[2] In other words, he envisioned a portrait of Odilon Redon in a contemporary artistic milieu, surrounded by younger artists of the Nabi circle, more or less in the model of Henri Fantin-Latour's *Homage to Delacroix* (see fig. 17). The conjunction of genres and motifs is curious, given Redon's lack of personal engagement with Cézanne's project, but by bringing the central protagonists together under the banner of still life, Denis signals Redon's deep roots in the genre.

Redon, who was born in 1840 and began to study art in Paris in 1864, had been a witness to, and occasional participant in, the most important developments of the French avant-garde over the second half of the nineteenth century. But, he remained at one remove from the center of modernism by his disavowal, since the 1860s, of both color and oil painting, preferring to work for some thirty years in monochrome charcoal drawings and lithographs, a body of work he called his *noirs*. Before abandoning oil painting, Redon had made a number of sensitive floral still lifes, and even in the *noirs* he continued to explore his interest in organic and botanical themes (fig. 69). This fascination dated back to Redon's youth in Bordeaux, where his most important intellectual mentor was the Darwinian botanist Armand Clavaud. Clavaud's scientific research was concerned with the frontier between the plant and animal worlds, and his ideas sparked Redon's visual imagination, giving rise to highly idiosyncratic floral imagery.

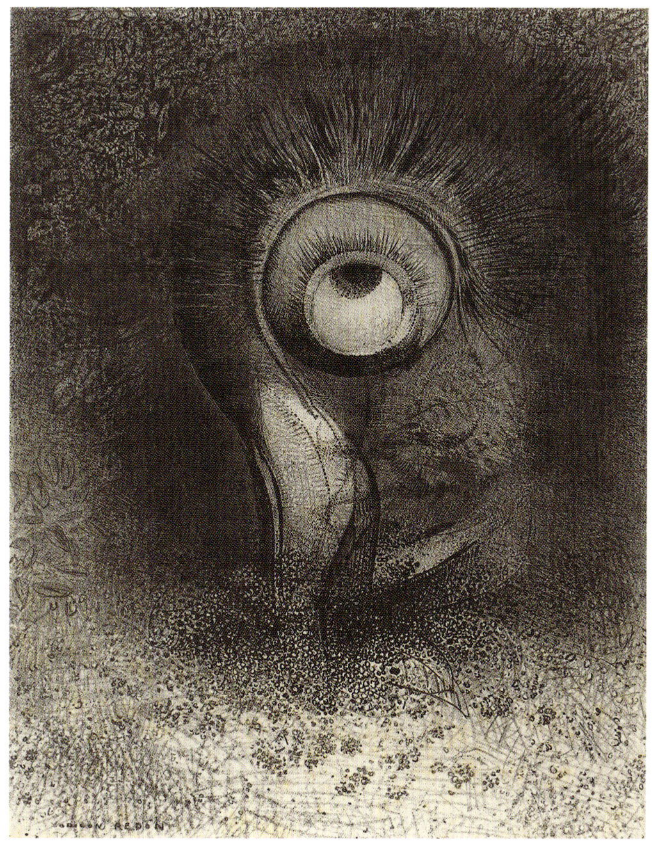

FIG. 69 Odilon Redon, *There was perhaps a first vision attempted in the flower* (Il y eut peut-être une vision première essayée dans la fleur), 1883, lithograph. National Gallery of Art, Washington, D.C., Rosenwald Collection, 1951.10.459

In the early 1890s, Redon slowly began to reintroduce color into his work, first in pastels and then in oil paintings. By the turn of the twentieth century, he was working almost exclusively in color. This transformation had gone hand in hand with his return to floral still life, which played a central role in his practice and exhibition strategy after 1900. Redon's *Vase of Flowers* (cat. no. 59) is typical of his work from the period. In the absence of any firm suggestion of a setting, or even of pictorial space, the vase and bouquet seem to hover in a color-washed void. The bouquet itself is rather conventional, but at lower left the plant forms reappear in a startling, swollen form. The disquieting nature of many of Redon's still lifes was seized on in one review of the Salon d'Automne of 1905, where Redon had been given his own retrospective alongside those devoted posthumously to Cézanne and Gauguin. The critic described Redon as "a painter of flowers as they are seen in dreams. They do not flourish under the gardener's hose, under the rays of the sun. Their middays are moonlight, and water from unhallowed springs has given them the strength to live."[3]

After a decade of critical and commercial success with his flower paintings, Redon sometimes felt they had come to dominate his artistic identity and wrote, "everything that leaves my studio from now on must carry their traces."[4] He translated his floral imagery into innovative suites of decorative painting and sought to vary his formula for exhibition pictures by experimenting with unusual vessels and containers or with provocative compositions. In *Green Plant in an Urn* (cat. no. 60), Redon playfully inverts the floral still life's expected hierarchy of vase, foliage, and flower. In 1913, when he was invited to participate in the Armory Show in New York, Redon sent thirty-six of his recent paintings, including *Etruscan Vase with Flowers* (cat. no. 61). The decorative flatness of the bouquet—which combines palm fronds with artificial or imaginary flowers—is amplified by the zones of stippling that fill the canvas around the flowers and by Redon's unusual matte tempera medium. The so-called Etruscan vase (though likely based on a modern Greek-style vase) is a reminder of the contemporary association between Etruscan style and an expressive primitivism, most famously expressed in Vaslav Nijinsky's 1912 ballet *Afternoon of a Faun*.[5]

Much like Redon, Pierre Bonnard had an early interest in floral still life, but he abandoned the genre for part of his subsequent career, returning to it only in his mid-forties. Associated with the Nabi avant-garde, Bonnard had been accorded a prominent place in Denis's *Homage to Cézanne*, appearing at far right. By 1910, however, when he took up floral still-life painting again, he was working in a highly individual style, somewhere "between intimacy and decoration," as he described it.[6] In some ways, Bonnard's floral still life can be read as a late chapter in the Impressionist project, though, like Gauguin, he worked from memory rather than direct observation. His bouquets set in crowded interiors, dense with the material of modern domesticity, have a kind of optical complexity that reflects the slow method by which they were built up in the studio (cat. no. 62).

Bonnard struggled with working from a natural motif and recalled that when trying to paint a bouquet "directly, scrupulously," he entirely lost his way in the details.[7] By making only sketches and watercolors from the motif, he was able to maintain a frame of reference for his memory while working through the long process of translating the subject to canvas. In one floral still life from around 1912 (cat. no. 63), a bouquet of wildflowers sprawls from the spout of a short, flared pitcher. The choice of flowers—poppies and Queen Anne's lace—creates a highly provisional bouquet, guaranteed to last no more than a few hours. In his much lengthier task of rendering the image, Bonnard lavished particular attention on the zone where the pitcher is reflected in the polished surface of the table. The same vessel, a favorite of Bonnard's, appears in a later still life, *Pitcher with Flowers* (cat. no. 64), but its handle has been broken off, confirming that this rather freely worked canvas dates to later in the artist's oeuvre.

Henri Matisse began making floral still lifes around the same time that Redon and Bonnard returned to the practice, and like them, he sustained his interest in the genre over the rest of his life, even as his stylistic and formal concerns changed radically. He painted *Parrot Tulips* (cat. no. 65) in the spring of 1905 with the divided brushstroke and pure, brilliant color of late Neo-Impressionist painting, reflecting his personal and professional affiliations with Paul Signac and Henri-Edmond Cross during this period (the painting is, in fact, based on a bouquet that was given to Matisse by Cross's wife). When it was exhibited in Paris that summer, it earned the admiration of the critic Louis Vauxcelles, who did not anticipate that the rigors of the Neo-Impressionist technique could produce "such beautiful effects of light, of volume, and of vibration. His gold and purple tulips are striking."[8]

By the next year, Matisse had already changed gears and was working in a Fauve mode. *Flowers* (cat. no. 66), with its evacuated space and open fields of chromatic experimentation, bears an unexpected resemblance to the contemporary works of Redon. More than a decade later, when Matisse painted the majestic *Bouquet* (cat. no. 67), he was in the midst of yet another intense period of transformation, moving away from an exploration of austere linear compositions that sometimes verged on abstraction to a rediscovery of naturalism and organic forms. Matisse described this evolution as one of inner struggle: "a will to rhythmic abstraction was battling with my natural, innate desire for rich, warm, generous colors and forms, in which the arabesque strove to establish its supremacy. From this duality

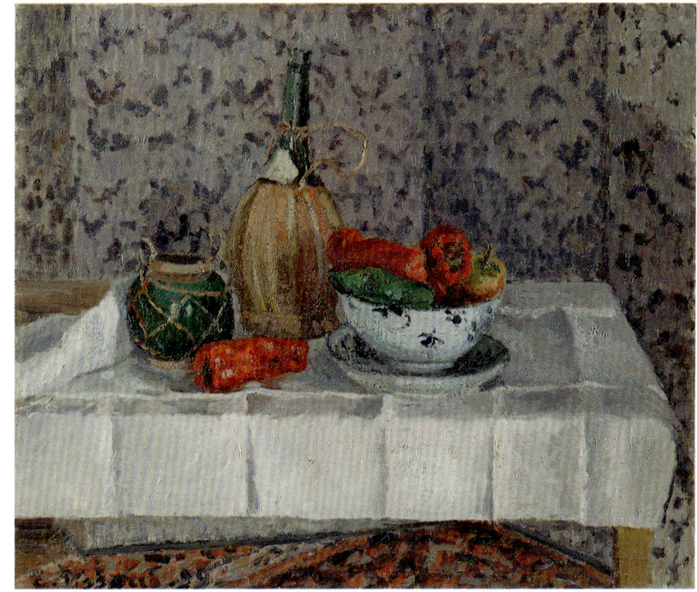

FIG. 70 Camille Pissarro, *Still Life with Spanish Peppers*, 1899, oil on canvas. Pauline Allen Gill Foundation

issued works that, overcoming my inner constraints, were realized in the union of [these two] poles."[9]

In the next decade, following his move to Nice, still life again became a sustained preoccupation, and between 1924 and 1925 Matisse painted a series of fifteen large still lifes, some of flowers and some of fruit. In *Still Life: Bouquet and Compotier* (cat. no. 68), the artist used a richly patterned folding screen as the backdrop to the arrangement, initiating a disorienting spatial ballet. The pictorial ambiguity that arises where the bouquet's botanical forms meet the quasi-floral motifs on the screen is evidence that Matisse was continuing to think through the questions posed by the still lifes of Cézanne, his "god of painting," as well as the spatial puzzles of Pissarro's late still lifes (fig. 70).

Henri Matisse's search for pictorial balance and order—what he called "a translucent setting for the mind"—is perfectly conveyed by his *Still Life with Pascal's "Pensées"* (cat. no. 69), in which the presence of the famous book of meditations by the seventeenth-century Jansenist philosopher Blaise Pascal underscores the artist's metaphysical intent. Pascal's views on the relationship between nature, humans, and the divine were a profound inspiration for a great many French modernist painters. The imagination, Pascal declared, "will sooner exhaust the power of conception than nature that of supplying material for conception. The whole visible world is only an imperceptible atom in the ample bosom of nature. No idea approaches it."[10] Matisse shared his attachment to Pascal's philosophy with other modernist painters of flowers. In a touching anecdote, Odilon Redon's son reported that his father, in his later years, "liked to begin his day deep in the garden, reading a few pages of Pascal, his favorite author. . . . My mother, during this time, prepared with care—and with love—his model: a grand vase of flowers."[11]

HMacD

1. See Przyblyski 1995, 283 and 289n14.
2. "Faire un tableau de Redon dans la boutique de Vollard, entouré de Vuillard, Bonnard, etc." See Cogeval 2011, 68.
3. Quoted in Stevens 1994, 297.
4. Quoted in Sharp 1994, 278.
5. The painting was exhibited at Carroll Galleries in New York under the title *Etruscan Vase* in 1915, two years after the work's first public exhibition, at the Armory Show (where, however, it was not included in the catalogue). The title's early association with the painting, and at the very gallery where Redon's widow would consign the work the following year, suggests that it may have been selected by the artist, or at the very least that the vase appeared "Etruscan" in style to his contemporaries. For the early exhibition history of *Etruscan Vase with Flowers*, see: http://www.metmuseum.org/Collections/search-the-collections/437381?rpp=20&pg=1&ao=on&ft=redon&pos=3.
6. Bonnard to George Besson, quoted in Munck 2009, 61.
7. Cited in Amory 2009, 5.
8. "Je n'avais pas cru, je l'avoue, que Monsieur Matisse, de qui j'ai cru devoir critiquer avec une amicable vivacité la récente incursion chez les néo-impressionistes, pût, grâce à l'exclusif procédé du point, obtenir d'aussi beaux effets de lumière, de volume, et de vibration. Ses tulips d'or et de pourpre sont éclatantes." Vauxcelles 1905, quoted in Fourcade et al. 1993, 423. Author's translation.
9. Quoted in Elderfield 2010, 310.
10. Pascal (1958) 2003, 16.
11. "Là se levant de bonne heure, mon père aimait commencer sa journée au fond du jardin, à lire quelques pages de Pascal—son auteur favori . . . Ma mere pendant ce temps, préparait avec soin—et amour—son modèle: un grand vase de fleurs." Quoted in Cogeval 2011, 420. Author's translation.

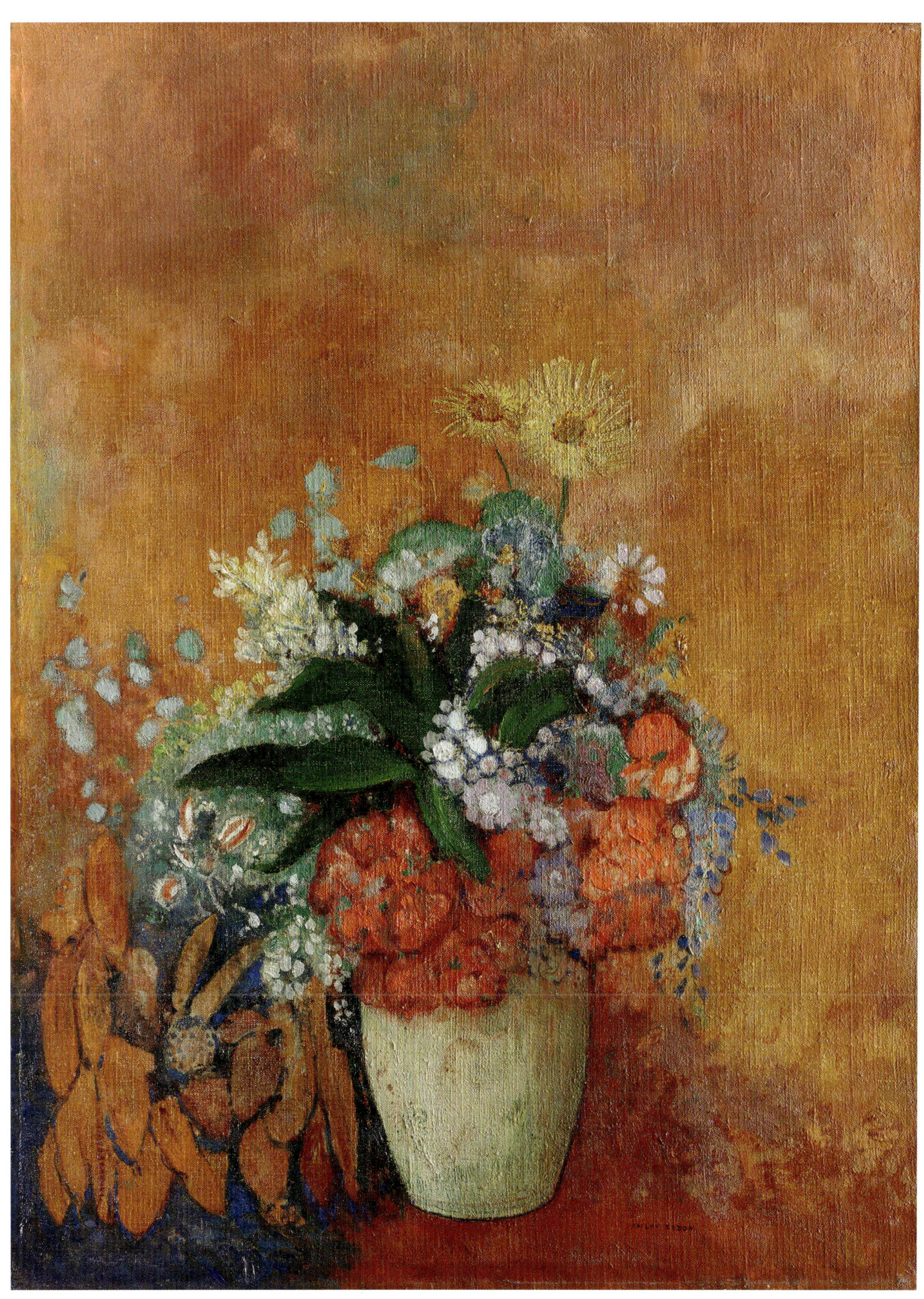

59 ODILON REDON

(FRENCH, 1840–1916)

Vase of Flowers, ca. 1905

Oil on fabric, 28$\frac{11}{16}$ × 23$\frac{3}{16}$ in. (73 × 59 cm)

Cleveland Museum of Art, Gift of Roberta Holden Bole, 1935.233

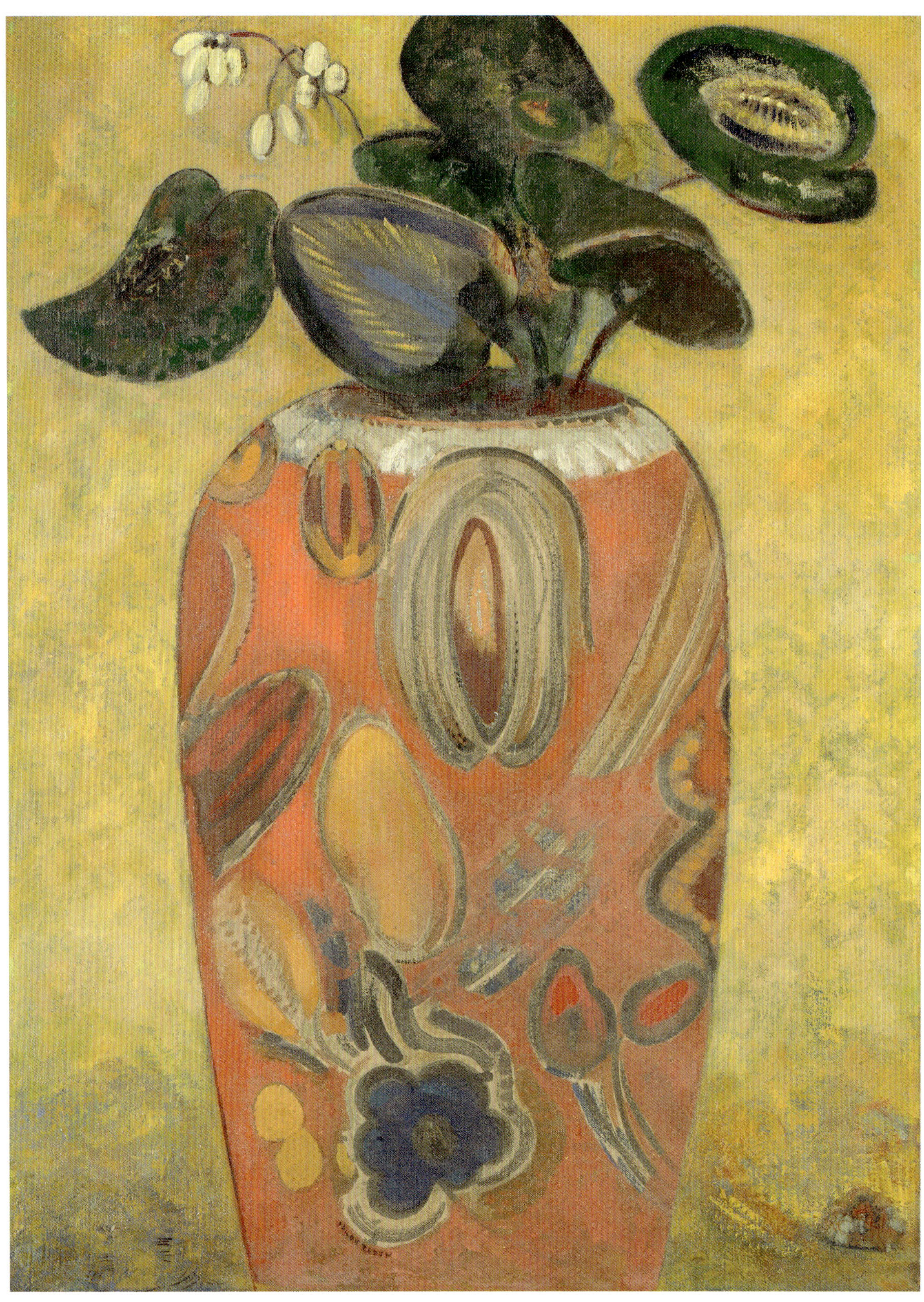

60
ODILON REDON
(FRENCH, 1840–1916)

Green Plant in an Urn, ca. 1910–11

Oil on canvas, 33½ × 23⅝ in. (85 × 60 cm)
Musée d'Orsay, Paris, Bequest of Mme Arï Redon in accordance with the wishes of her husband, the artist's son, 1984, RF 1984 44

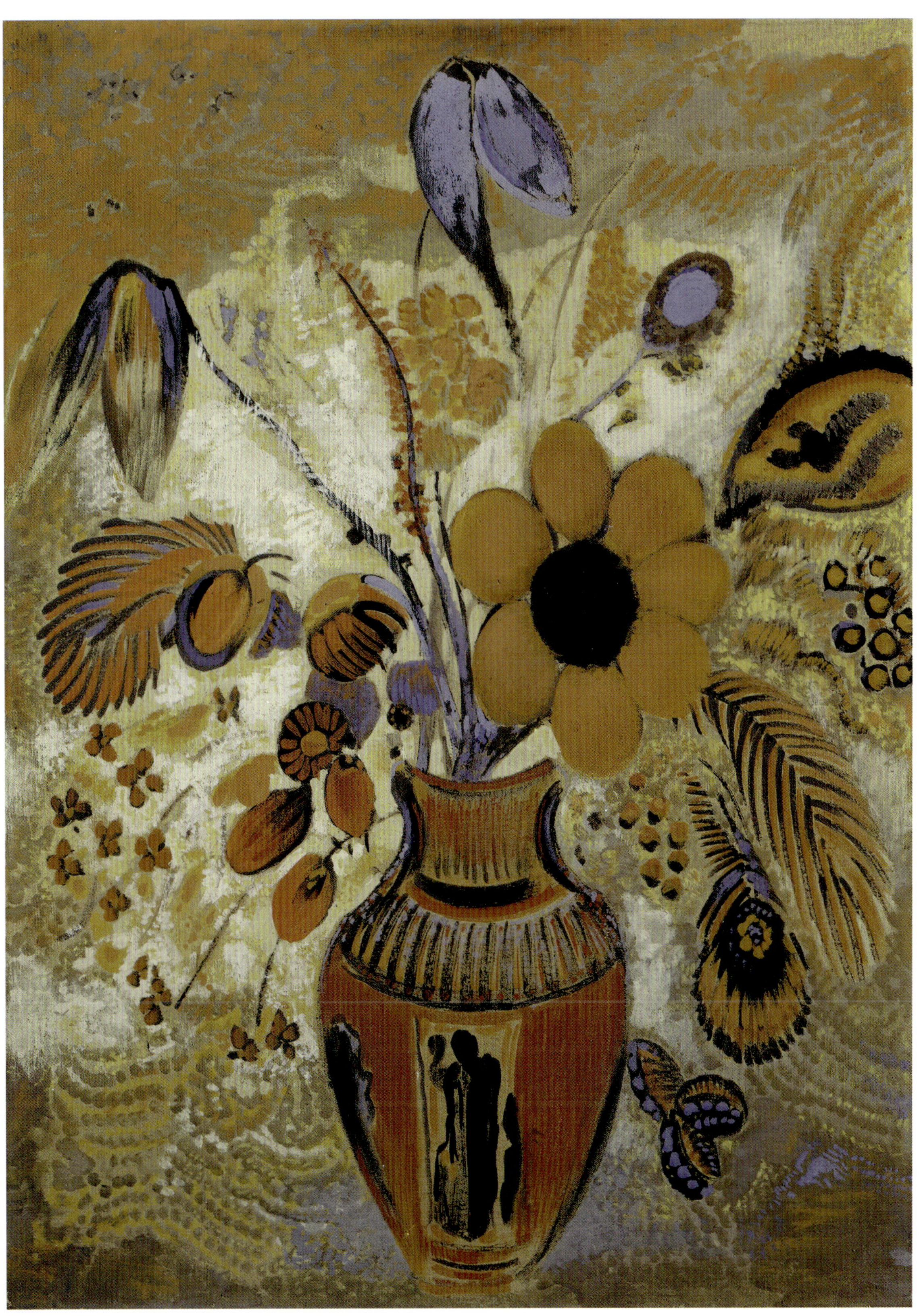

61
ODILON REDON
(FRENCH, 1840–1916)

Etruscan Vase with Flowers, 1900–10

Tempera on canvas, 32 × 23¼ in. (81.3 × 59.1 cm)
Metropolitan Museum of Art, New York, Maria DeWitt Jesup Fund, 1951; acquired from the Museum of Modern Art, Lillie P. Bliss Collection, 53.140.5

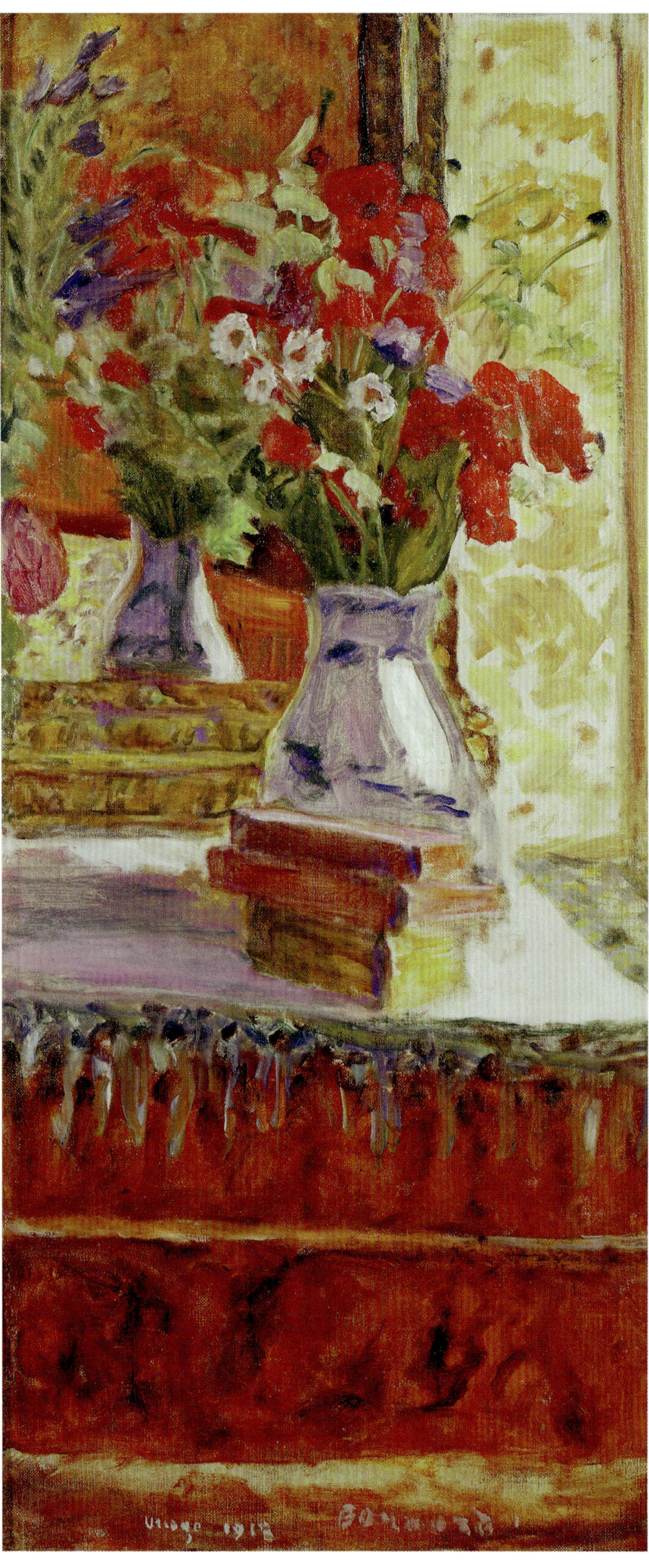

62
PIERRE BONNARD
(FRENCH, 1867–1947)

The Poppies, 1918

Oil on canvas, 27¾ × 12¼ in. (70.5 × 31 cm)
Musée National d'Art Moderne, Paris (AM.4530.P), on deposit at the Musée des Beaux-Arts et d'Archéologie de Besançon (Db.970.1.20)

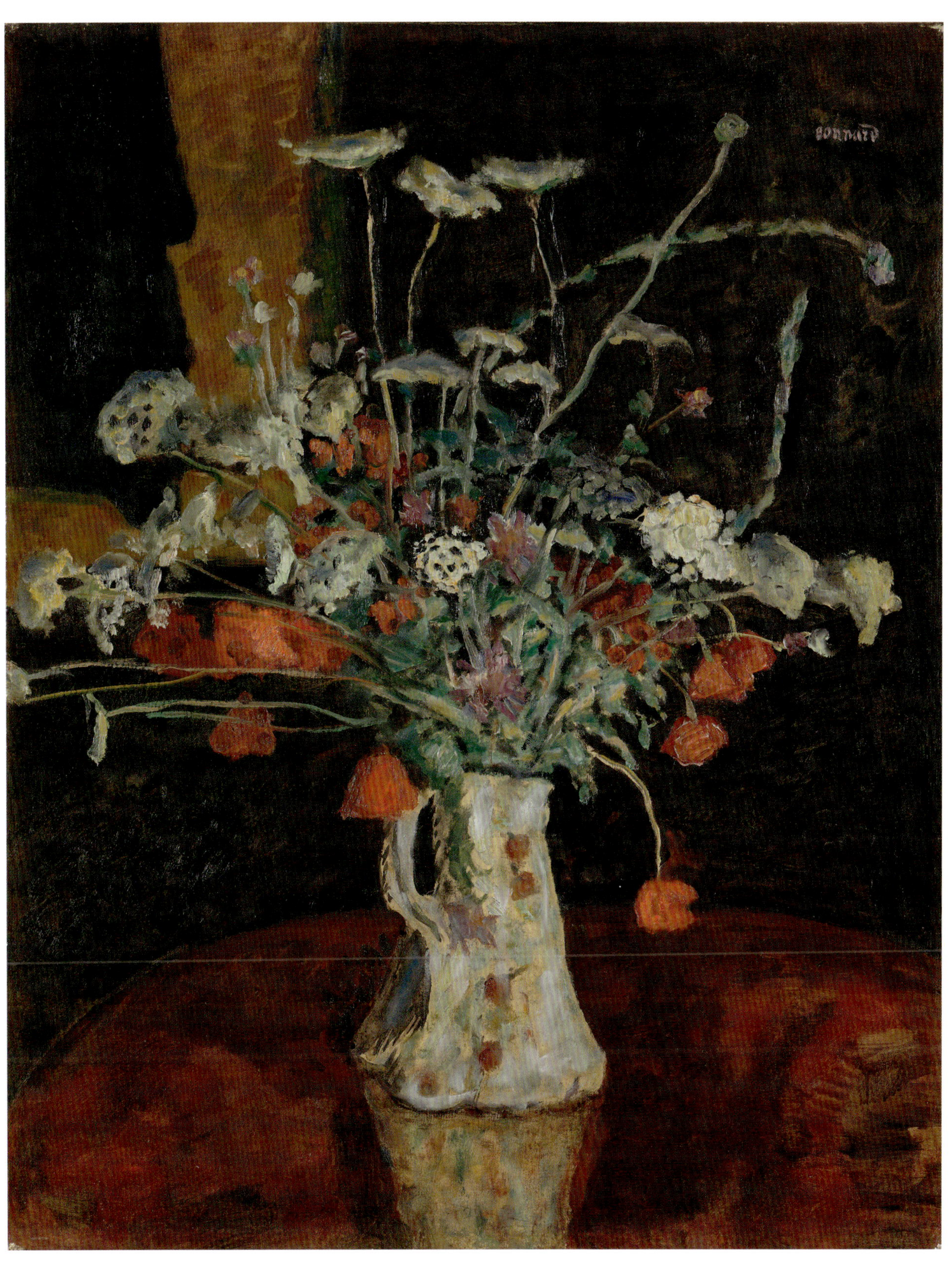

63 PIERRE BONNARD
(FRENCH, 1867–1947)

Wildflowers, Queen Anne's Lace, and Poppies, 1912

Oil on canvas, 30¾ × 24½ in. (78.1 × 62.2 cm)
Private Collection

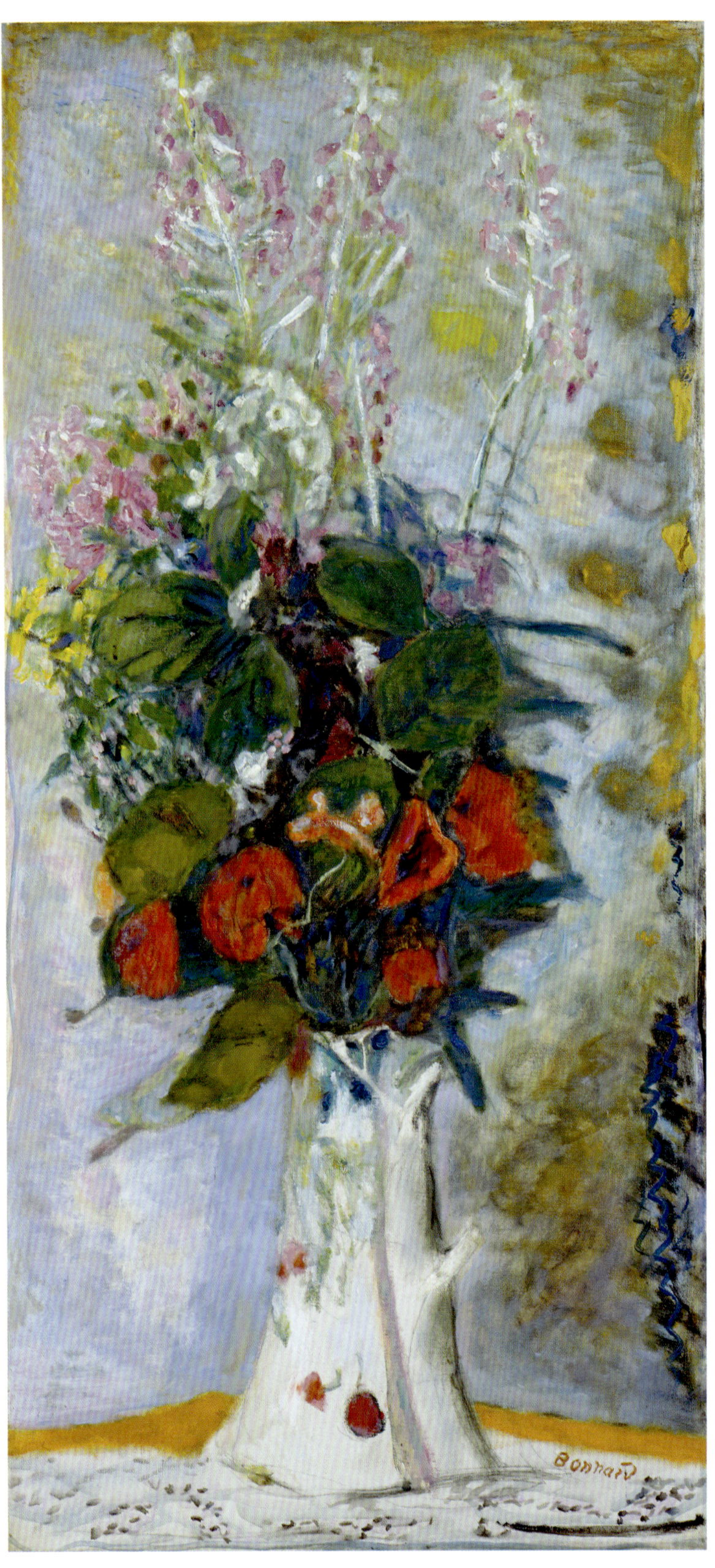

64 PIERRE BONNARD
(FRENCH, 1867–1947)

Pitcher with Flowers, 1935

Oil on canvas, 37½ × 17⅝ in. (95.3 × 44.8 cm)
Dallas Museum of Art, The Wendy and Emery Reves Collection, 1985.R.3

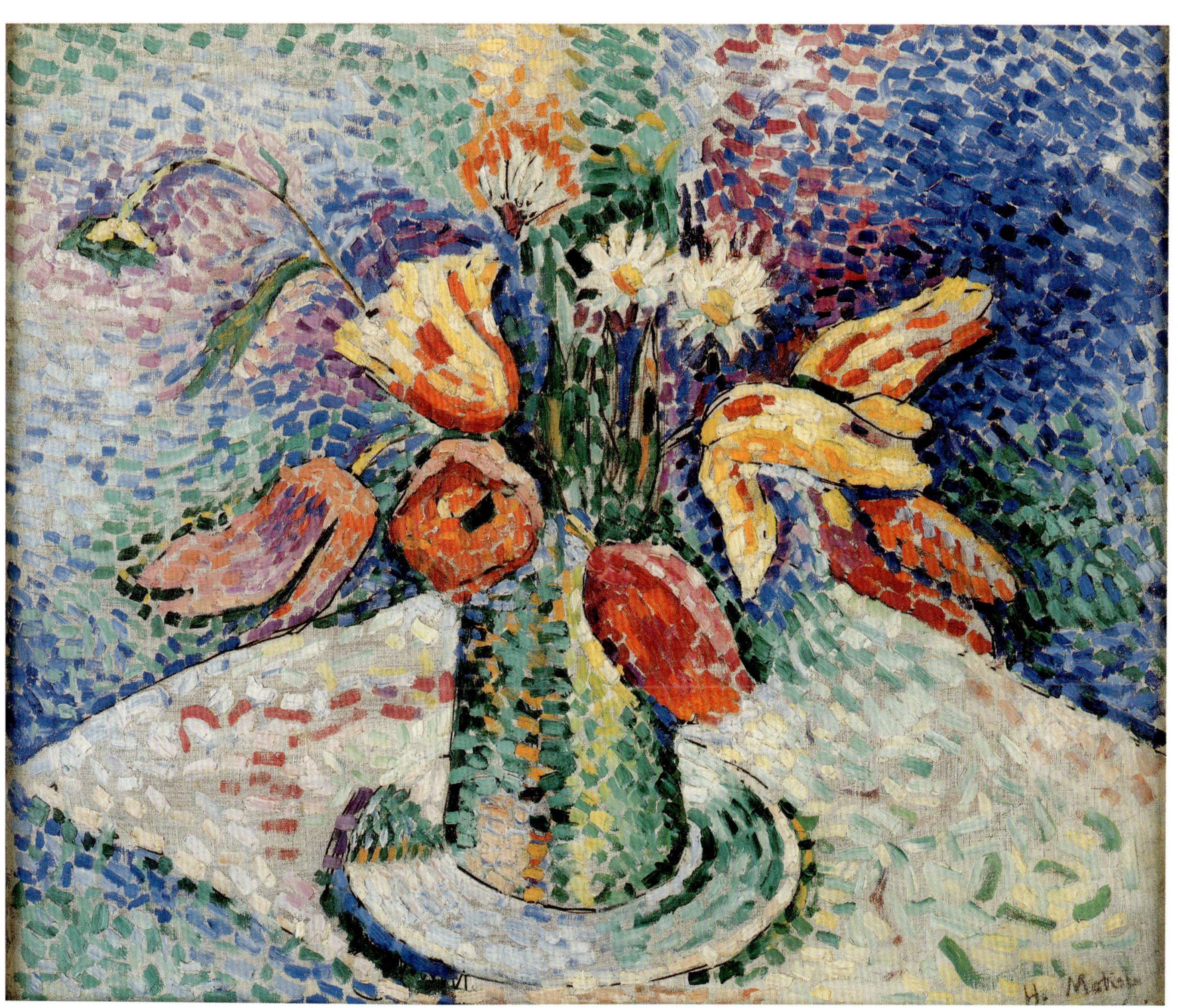

65 HENRI MATISSE
(FRENCH, 1869–1954)

Parrot Tulips, 1905

Oil on canvas, 18⅛ × 21$\frac{11}{16}$ in. (46 × 55 cm)
Albertina, Vienna, Batliner Collection, GE81DL

Dallas only

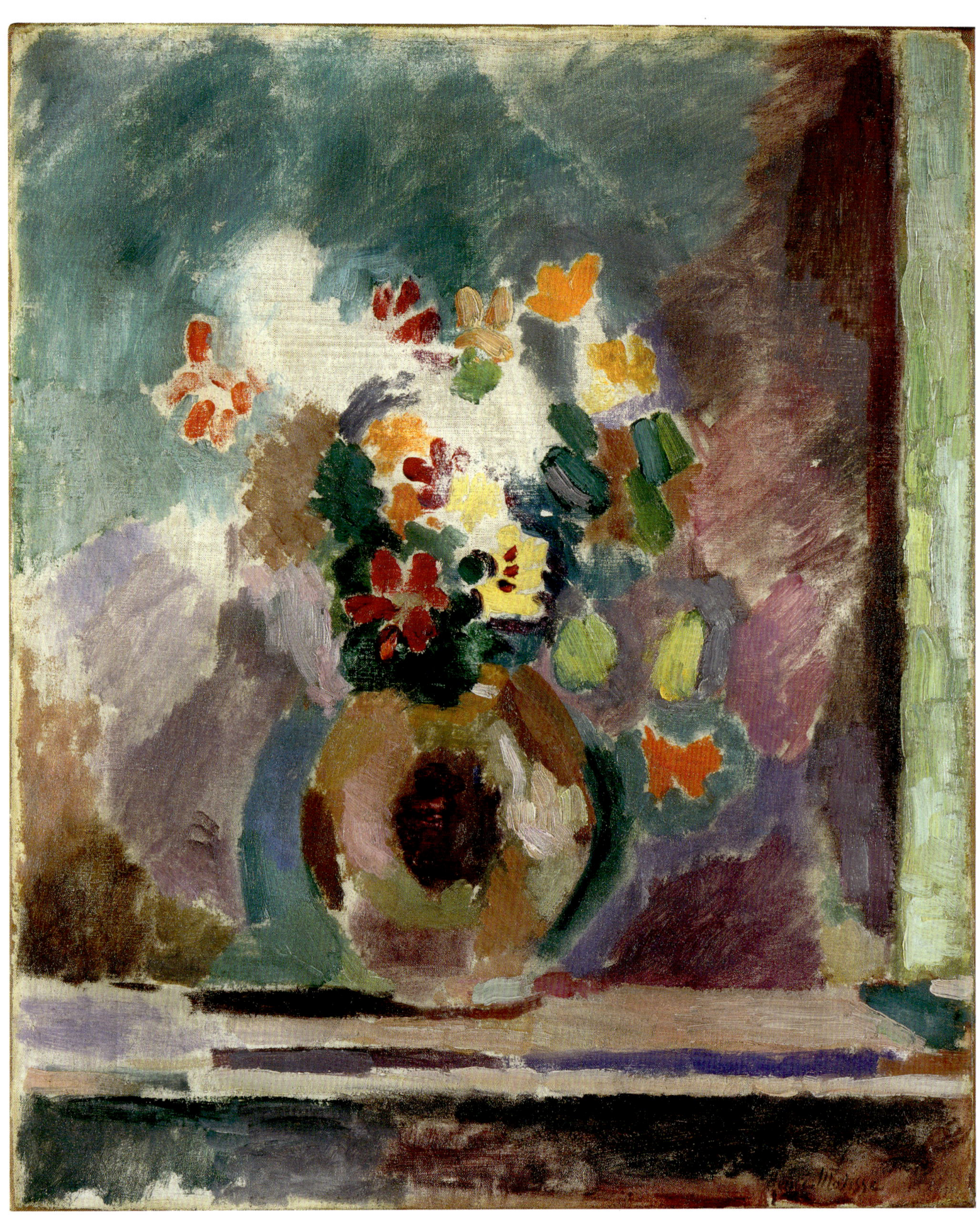

66

HENRI MATISSE

(FRENCH, 1869–1954)

Flowers, 1906

Oil on canvas, 21⅝ × 18⅛ in. (54.9 × 46 cm)

Brooklyn Museum, Gift of Marion Gans Pomeroy, 61.243

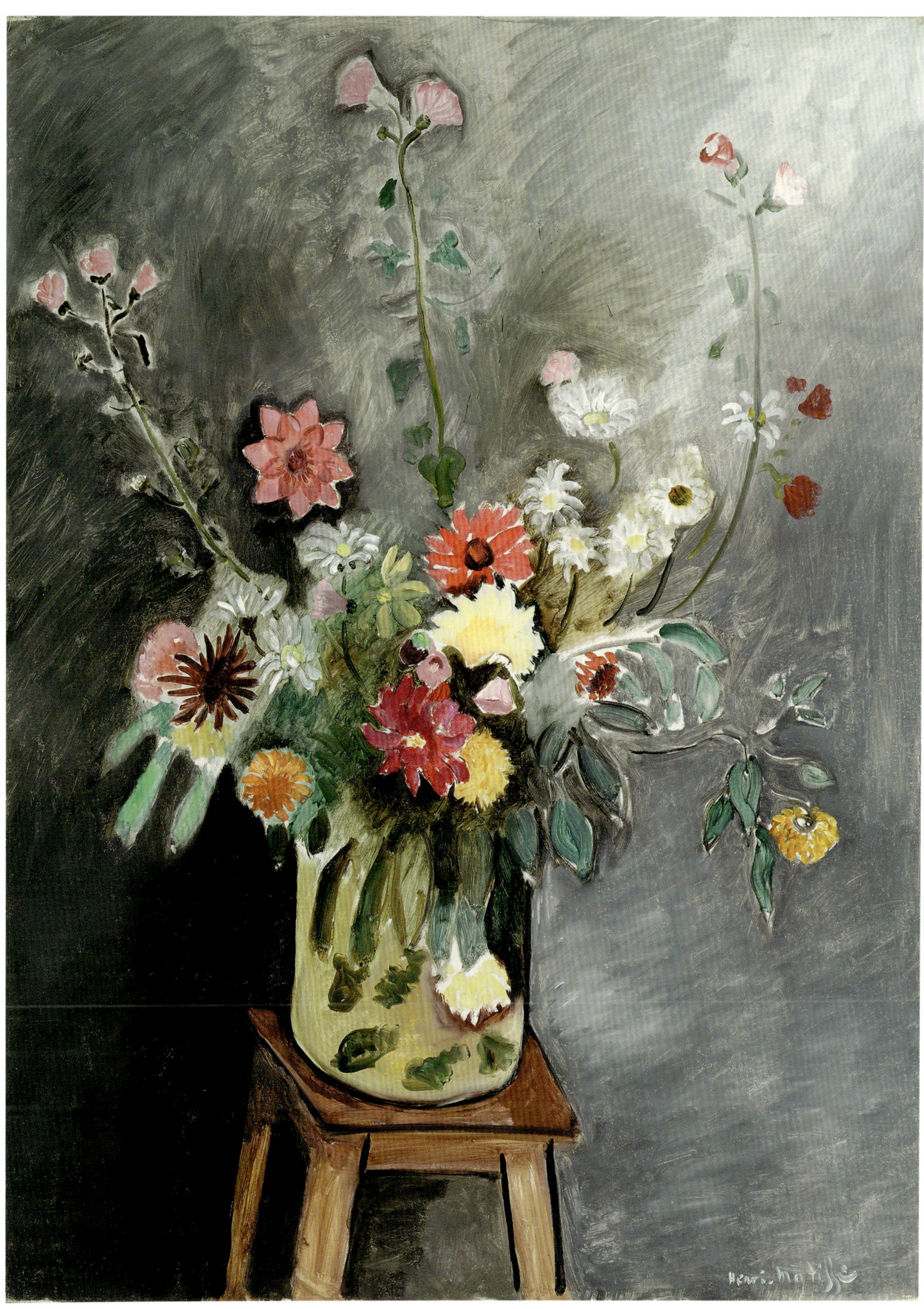

67

HENRI MATISSE
(FRENCH, 1869–1954)

Bouquet, 1916–17

Oil on canvas, 55 × 40¼ in.
San Diego Museum of Art, Gift of M. A. Wertheimer from the collection of his late wife, Annetta Salz Wertheimer, 1934.77

Dallas and Richmond only

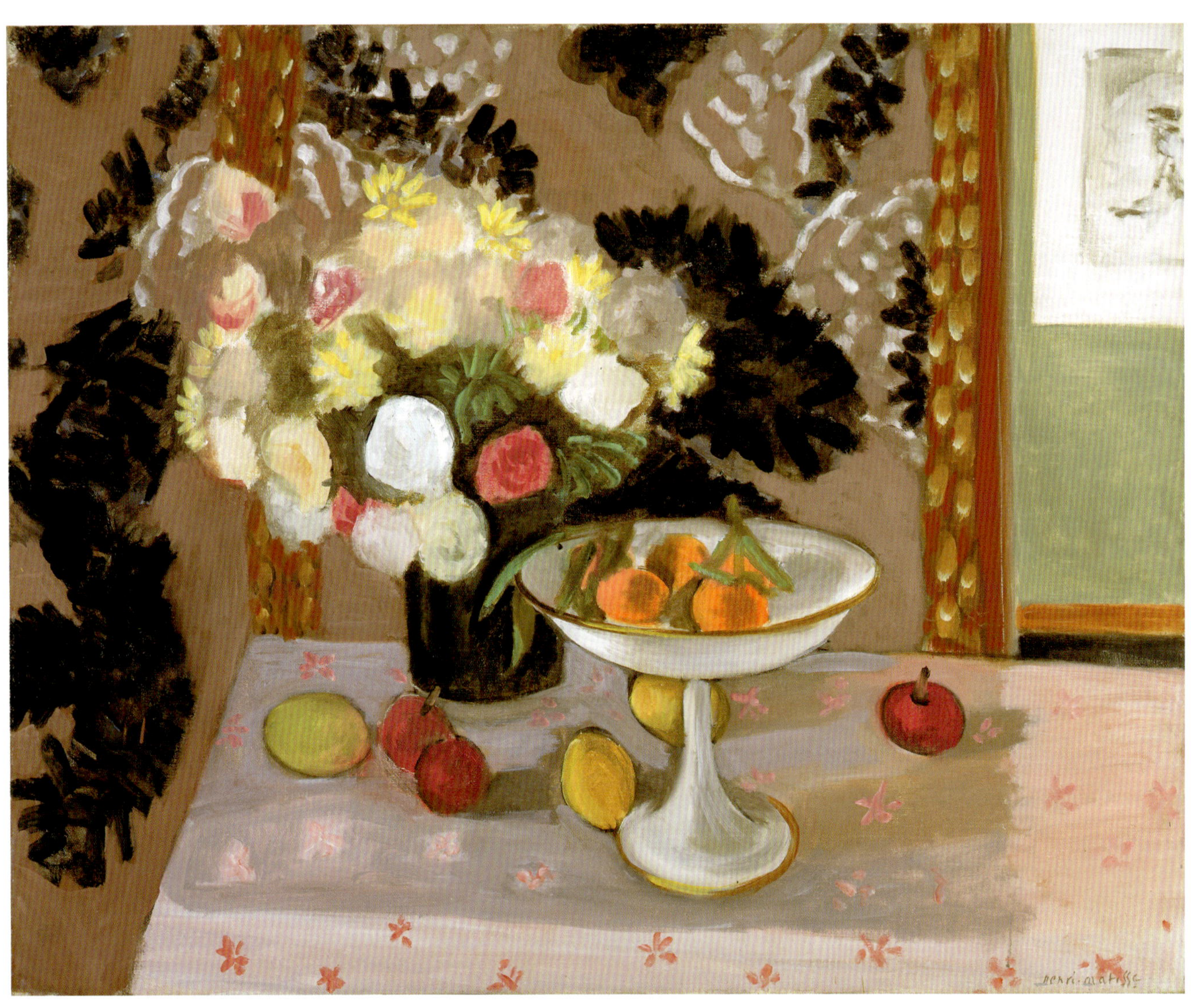

68
HENRI MATISSE
(FRENCH, 1869–1954)

Still Life: Bouquet and Compotier, 1924

Oil on canvas, 29¼ × 36½ in. (74.3 × 92.7 cm)
Dallas Museum of Art, The Eugene and Margaret McDermott Art Fund, Inc., in honor of Dr. Bryan Williams, 2002.19.McD

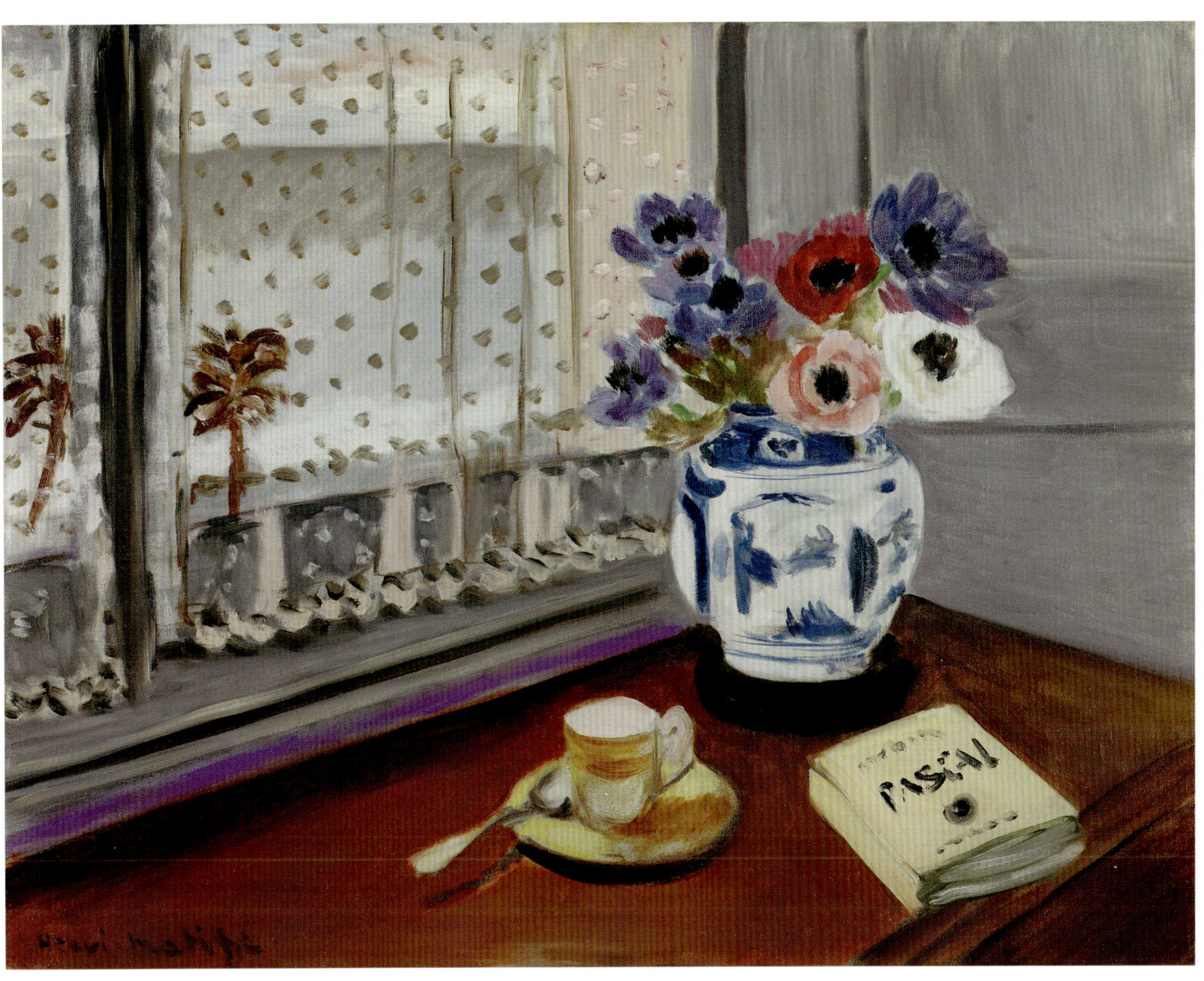

69 HENRI MATISSE
(FRENCH, 1869–1954)

Still Life with Pascal's "Pensées," 1924

Oil on canvas, 19¼ × 25⅛ in. (48.9 × 63.82 cm)
Minneapolis Institute of Arts, Gift of Ruth and Bruce Dayton, 2010.37

BIBLIOGRAPHY

Abélès 1987
Abélès, Luce. *Fantin-Latour,* Coin de Table*: Verlaine, Rimbaud et les vilains bonshommes*. Exh. cat. Paris: Réunion des musées nationaux in association with Musée d'Orsay, 1987.

Amory 2009
Amory, Dita, ed. *Pierre Bonnard: The Late Still Lifes and Interiors*. Exh. cat. New Haven: Yale University Press in conjunction with Metropolitan Museum of Art, New York, 2009.

Apollinaire 1956
Apollinaire, Guillaume. *Oeuvres poétiques*. Paris: Gallimard, 1956.

Arnoux et al. 2011
Arnoux, Mathilde, Thomas W. Gaehtgens, and Anne Tempelaere-Panzani, eds. *Correspondance entre Henri Fantin-Latour et Otto Scholderer (1858–1902)*. Paris: Éditions de la Maison des sciences de l'homme, 2011.

Bailey et al. 2003
Bailey, Colin B., Philip Conisbee, and Thomas W. Gaehtgens. *The Age of Watteau, Chardin and Fragonard: Masterpieces of French Genre Painting*. Edited by Colin B. Bailey. New Haven: Yale University Press in association with National Gallery of Canada, Ottawa, and National Gallery of Art, Washington, D.C., 2003.

Barker 1969
Barker, Richard J. "The Conseil General des Manufactures under Napoleon (1810–1814)." *French Historical Studies* 6, no. 2 (Autumn, 1969): 185–213.

Barrera 1856
Barrera, Le P. *Bouquet à la vierge Marie composé de trente et une fleurs*. Perpignan: Imprimerie de Mademoiselle Antoinette Tastu, 1856.

Baudelaire 1965
Baudelaire, Charles. "The Salon of 1845." In *Art in Paris, 1845–1862: Salons and Other Exhibitions Reviewed by Charles Baudelaire*, edited and translated by Jonathan Mayne. London: Phaidon, 1965.

Baudelaire (1857) 1993
Baudelaire, Charles. *Les Fleurs du mal*. Translated by James McGowan. Oxford, UK: Oxford University Press, 1993. Originally published 1857, Paris.

Béghain 2007
Béghain, Patrice. "Oublier Baudelaire." In *Le Temps de la peinture: Lyon 1800–1914*, edited by Sylvie Ramond et al., 6–7. Exh. cat. Lyon: Fage and Musée des Beaux-Arts de Lyon, 2007.

Béghain 2011
Béghain, Patrice. *Une histoire de la peinture à Lyon: de 1482 à nos jours*. Lyon: Stephane Bachès, 2011.

Berhaut and Pietri 1994
Berhaut, Marie, and Sophie Pietri 1994. *Gustave Caillebotte, sa vie et son œuvre: Catalogue raisonné des peintures et pastels*. Rev. ed. Paris: Wildenstein Institute in association with Bibliothèque des arts, 1994.

Berson 1996
Berson, Ruth. *The New Painting: Impressionism, 1874–1886: Documentation*. Vol. 2. San Francisco: Fine Arts Museums of San Francisco, 1996.

Blanc 1867
Blanc, Charles. *Grammaire des arts du dessin: Architecture, sculpture, peinture*. Paris: J. Renouard, Libraire-Éditeur, 1867.

Blanche 1921
Blanche, Jacques-Emile. "Les Dames de la Grande-Rue." In *Propos de peintre*. Paris: Émile-Paul Frères, 1921.

Bleichmar 2008
Bleichmar, Daniela. "Training the Naturalist's Eye in the Eighteenth Century: Perfect Global Visions and Local Blind Spots." In *Visualizing the Unseen, Imagining the Unknown, Perfecting the Natural: Art and Science in the 18th and 19th Centuries*, edited by Andrew Graciano, 1–24. Cambridge, UK: Cambridge Scholars Publishing, 2008.

Bleichmar 2012
Bleichmar, Daniela. *Visible Empire: Botanical Expeditions and Visual Culture in the Hispanic Enlightenment*. Chicago: University of Chicago Press, 2012.

Blunt 1994
Blunt, Wilfrid. *The Art of Botanical Illustration: An Illustrated History*. Revised and enlarged by William T. Stearn. Woodbridge, Suffolk: Antique Collectors Club, 1994.

Bodelsen 1968
Bodelsen, Merete. "Early Impressionist Sales 1874–94 in the Light of Some Unpublished 'Procès-Verbaux'." *The Burlington Magazine* 110, no. 783 (1968): 331–49.

Boggs 1999
Boggs, Jean Sutherland, and Gail Feigenbaum. *Degas and New Orleans: A French Impressionist in America*. Exh. cat. New Orleans: New Orleans Museum of Art in conjunction with Ordrupgaard Museum, Copenhagen, 1999.

Bonniot 1986
Bonniot, Roger. *Gustave Courbet en Saintonge: Scènes de la vie artistique en province sous le second empire*. 2nd ed. Semussac, France: La Saintonge littéraire, 1986.

Boulay 1834
Boulay, Édouard. *Le Mois de Marie, fleurs poétiques à la Sainte Vierge*. Lyon: Chez Périsse Frères, 1834.

Brettell and Fonsmark 2005
Brettell, Richard R., and Anne-Birgitte Fonsmark, eds. *Gauguin and Impressionism*. Exh. cat. New Haven: Yale University Press in conjunction with Kimbell Art Museum, Fort Worth, and Ordrupgaard Museum, Copenhagen, 2005.

Buchaniec 2010
Buchaniec, Nicolas. *Salons de province: Les expositions artistiques dans le Nord de la France, 1870–1914*. Rennes: Presses universitaires de Rennes, 2010.

Cailleux 1849
Cailleux, Léon. "Salon de 1849." *Le Temps*, June 28–29, 1849, feuilleton, article III.

Clairet et al. 1997
Clairet, Alain, Delphine Montalant, and Yves Rouart. *Berthe Morisot, 1841–1895: Catalogue raisonné de l'œuvre peint*. Montolivet: Cera, 1997.

Cogeval 2011
Cogeval, Guy. "Vuillard versus Redon: Fleurs de rêve et rêve de fleurs." In *Odilon Redon, Prince du Rêve, 1840–1916*, edited by Rodolphe Rapetti. Exh. cat. Paris: Éditions de la Réunions des musées nationaux–Grand Palais in association with Musée d'Orsay, 2011.

Courbet 1996
Courbet, Gustave. *Correspondance de Courbet*. Edited by Petra ten-Doesschate Chu. Paris: Flammarion, 1996.

D'Alessandro and Elderfield 2010
D'Alessandro, Stephanie, and John Elderfield, eds. *Matisse: Radical Invention, 1913–1917*. New Haven: Yale University Press in conjunction with Art Institute of Chicago and Museum of Modern Art, New York, 2010.

Dauberville and Dauberville 2007
Dauberville, Guy-Patrice, and Michel Dauberville. *Renoir: Catalogue raisonné des tableaux, pastels, dessins et aquarelles, 1858–1881*. 4 vols. Paris: Bernheim-Jeune, 2007.

Daulte 1959
Daulte, François. *Alfred Sisley: Catalogue raisonné de l'œuvre peint*. Lausanne: Éditions Durand-Ruel, 1959.

Delacroix 1936
Delacroix, Eugène. *Correspondance générale d'Eugène Delacroix, 1838–1849*. Edited by André Joubin. 5 vols. Paris: Plon, 1936.

Delacroix 1970
Delacroix, Eugène. *Eugène Delacroix, Selected Letters, 1813–1863*. Edited and translated by Jean Stewart. Boston: Museum of Fine Arts Publications, 1970.

Démoris 2000
Démoris, René. "Chardin and the Far Side of Illusion." In *Chardin*, edited by Pierre Rosenburg et al., 99–109. Exh. cat. New Haven and London: Yale University Press in association with Royal Academy of Arts, London, and Metropolitan Museum of Art, New York, 2000.

Desbordes-Valmore 1830
Desbordes-Valmore, Marceline. *Poésies*. 2 vols. Paris: Boulland, 1830.

Desbuissons 2008
Desbuissons, Frédérique. "Courbet's Materialism." *Oxford Art Journal* 31, no. 2 (2008): 251–60.

***Dessins du XVIe au XIXe Siècle* 1984**
Dessins du XVIe au XIXe siècle du Musée des arts décoratifs de Lyon. Exh. cat. Lyon: Sézanne in association with Musée historique des Tissus et des arts décoratifs, 1984.

Diderot 1798
Diderot, Denis. "Le Salon de 1765, Essai sur la peinture." In *Oeuvres de Denis Diderot, publiées sur les manuscrits de l'auteur*, compiled by Jacques-André Naigenon. Vol. 13. Paris: Chez Desray et Deterville, 1798.

Diderot (1759–81) 1975–83
Diderot, Denis. *Salons*. Edited by Jean Seznec and Jean Adhémar. 2nd ed. 3 vols. Oxford: Clarendon Press, 1975–83. Originally published 1759–81.

Druick and Hoog 1982
Druick, Douglas, and Michel Hoog. *Fantin-Latour*. Exh. cat. Paris: Réunion des musées nationaux, 1982.

Druick and Hoog 1983
Druick, Douglas, and Michel Hoog. *Fantin-Latour*. Exh. cat. Ottawa: National Gallery of Canada, 1983.

Druick 1994
Druick, Douglas W., ed. *Odilon Redon, Prince of Dreams, 1840–1916*. Exh. cat. Chicago: Art Institute of Chicago in association with Abrams, 1994.

Duranty (1876) 1986
Duranty, Louis Emile Edmond. "La Nouvelle peinture: A Propos du groupe d'artistes qui exposent dans les galleries Durand-Ruel." 1876. Reprinted and translated in *The New Painting: Impressionism 1874–1886*, 37–47, edited by Charles S. Moffett. San Francisco: Fine Arts Museums of San Francisco, 1986.

Dussol 1997
Dussol, Dominique. *Art et bourgeoisie: La Société des amis des arts de Bordeaux, 1851–1939*. Bordeaux: Le Festin, 1997.

***Explication des ouvrages* 1863**
Explication des ouvrages de peinture et de sculpture exposés dans les salles de la Mairie [de Saintes] au profit des Pauvres: 160 tableaux signés Corot, Courbet, Auguin, Pradelles. Paris: Imprimerie d'Alexandre Hus, 1863.

Faré 1962
Faré, Michel. *La Nature Morte en France: Son histoire et son évolution du XVIIe au XXe siécle*. Geneva: P. Cailler, 1962.

Faré 1979
Faré, Michel. *Peintres de fleurs en France du XVIIe aux XIXe siècles*. Paris: Musée du Petit Palais, 1979.

Faré and Faré 1976
Faré, Michel, and Fabrice Faré. *La Vie silencieuse en France: La Nature Morte au XVIIIe siècle*. Fribourg: Office du livre, 1976.

Félibien 1668
Félibien, André. Preface to *Conférences de l'Academie royale de peinture et de sculpture, pendant l'année 1667*, n.p. Paris: F. Léonard, 1668.

Fernier 1978
Fernier, Robert. *La vie et l'oeuvre de Gustave Courbet: catalogue raisonné*. Paris: Bibliothèque des arts, 1978.

Fonsmark 1995
Fonsmark, Anne-Birgitte, ed. *Manet, Gauguin, Rodin: Chefs-d'œuvre de la Ny Carlsberg Glyptotek de Copenhague*. Paris: Réunions des musées nationaux in association with the Musée d'Orsay, 1995.

Foucault 1994
Foucault, Michel. *The Order of Things: An Archaeology of the Human Sciences*. New York: Vintage Books, 1994.

Fourcade et al 1993
Fourcade, Dominique, Yve-Alain Bois, and Isabelle Monod-Fontaine et al. *Henri Matisse 1904–1917*. Exh. cat. Paris: Centre Georges Pompidou.

Freedberg 1994
Freedberg, David. "The Failure of Colour." In *Sight and Insight: Essays on Art and Culture in Honour of E. H. Gombrich at 85*, edited by John Onians, 245–62. London: Phaidon, 1994.

Gautier 1849
Gautier, Théophile. "Salon de 1849." *La Presse* (August 1, 1849).

Gifu Museum of Fine Arts 1990
Gifu Museum of Fine Arts. *La gloire de Lyon: la peinture de l'Ecole lyonnaise du XIXe siècle*. Exh. cat. Gifu: Museum of Fine Arts in conjunction with Tsukuba Museum of Art, Ibaraki, and Fukuyama Museum of Art, Hiroshima, 1990.

Goncourt and Goncourt 1863
Goncourt, Edmond de, and Jules de Goncourt. "Chardin." *Gazette des Beaux-Arts* 15 (December 1863): 514–23.

Goncourt and Goncourt (1856–75) 1948
Goncourt, Edmond de, and Jules de Goncourt. *French Eighteenth-Century Painters*. Translated by Robin Ironside. Ithaca: Cornell University Press, 1948. Originally published 1856–75, Paris.

Goncourt and Goncourt 1902
Goncourt, Edmond de, and Jules de Goncourt. *Renée Mauperin*. Translated by Alys Hallard. New York: P. F. Collier and Son, 1902.

Gordon and Forge 1999
Gordon, Robert, and Andrew Forge. *The Last Flowers of Manet*. Translated by Richard Howard. New York: Abrams, 1999.

Grafe 2007
Grafe, Étienne. "Le Salon des fleurs au musée de Lyon." In *Le Temps de la peinture: Lyon 1800–1914*, edited by Sylvie Ramond et al., 36–47. Exh. cat. Lyon: Fage and Musée des Beaux-Arts de Lyon, 2007.

Green 1999
Green, Nicholas. "Circuits of Production, Circuits of Consumption: The Case of Mid-Nineteenth-Century French Art Dealing." *Art Journal*, no. 1 (Spring 1999): 29–34.

Guégan 2011
Guégan, Stéphane, ed. *Manet inventeur du moderne*. Exh. cat. Paris: Gallimard in association with Musée d'Orsay, 2011.

Hardouin-Fugier 1978
Hardouin-Fugier, Elisabeth. "Baudelaire et Simon Saint-Jean." *Bulletin Baudelarien* (1978).

Hardouin-Fugier 1980
Hardouin-Fugier, Elisabeth. *Simon Saint-Jean: 1808–1860*. Translated by Étienne Grafe. Leigh-on-Sea: F. Lewis, 1980.

Hardouin-Fugier 1981
Hardouin-Fugier, Elisabeth. *The Pupils of Redouté*. Translated by Étienne Grafe. Leigh-On-Sea: F. Lewis, 1981.

Hardouin-Fugier and Grafe 1979
Hardouin-Fugier, Elisabeth, and Étienne Grafe. *Peintures de fleurs de l'école lyonnaise, XIXe–XXe siècles*. Exh. cat. Lyon: Musée des beaux-arts, 1979.

Hardouin-Fugier and Grafe 1989
Hardouin-Fugier, Elisabeth, and Étienne Grafe. *French Flower Painters of the 19th Century: A Dictionary*. Edited by Peter Mitchell. London: P. Wilson, 1989.

Hardouin-Fugier and Grafe 1992
Hardouin-Fugier, Elisabeth, and Étienne Grafe. *Les peintres de fleurs en France: de Redouté à Redon*. Paris: Les Editions de l'amateur, 1992.

Hédouin 1816
Hédouin, Pierre. *Le Bouquet de Lys: Recueil de poésies sur les révolutions de 1814 et 1815*. Boulogne: Chez LeRoy-Berge, 1816.

House and Ingram 2011
House, Emma, and David Ingram. *Painting Flowers: Fantin-Latour and the Impressionists*. Exh. cat. Dublin: Bowes Museum, 2011.

House 1986
House, John. *Monet: Nature into Art*. New Haven and London: Yale University Press, 1986.

Jansen et al. 2013
Jansen, Leo, Hans Luijten, and Nienke Bakker, eds. *Vincent van Gogh: The Letters*. Amsterdam and The Hague: Van Gogh Museum and Huygens ING. http://vangoghletters.org.

Jobert 1998
Jobert, Barthélémy. *Delacroix*. Princeton: Princeton University Press, 1998.

Jullien 1909
Jullien, Adolphe. *Fantin-Latour, sa vie et ses amitiés, lettres inédites et souvenirs personnels*. Paris: Lucien Laveur, 1909.

Kahng 2002
Kahng, Eik. "Vallayer-Coster/Chardin." In *Anne Vallayer-Coster: Painter to the Court of Marie-Antoinette*, edited by Eik Kahng and Marianne Roland Michel, 39–57. Exh. cat. New Haven and London: Yale University Press in association with Dallas Museum of Art, 2002.

Kane 1989
Kane, Elizabeth. "Victoria Dubourg." *Woman's Art Journal* 9, no. 2 (1989): 15–21.

Kemp 1990
Kemp, Martin. "Taking It on Trust: Form and Meaning in Naturalistic Representation." *Archives of Natural History* 17 (1990): 127–88.

Kemp 1996
Kemp, Martin. "'Implanted in Our Natures': Humans, Plants, and the Stories of Art." In *Visions of Empire: Voyages, Botany, and Representations of Nature*, edited by David Philip Miller and Peter Hanns Reill, 197–229. Cambridge, UK: Cambridge University Press, 1996.

Koerner 1996
Koerner, Lisbet. "Carl Linnaeus in His Time and Place." In *Cultures of Natural History*, edited by Nicholas Jardine, James A. Secord, and Emma C. Spary, 145–62. Cambridge, UK: Cambridge University Press, 1996.

Gifu Museum of Art 1990
La gloire de Lyon: la peinture de l'Ecole lyonnaise du XIXe siècle. Exh. cat. Gifu: Museum of Fine Arts in conjunction with Tsukuba Museum of Art, Ibaraki, and Fukuyama Museum of Art, Hiroshima, 1990.

La Pinière 1864
La Pinière, Aglaé de. *Le Mois de la Vierge, fleurs poétiques offertes à Marie*. Nantes: Imprimerie Merson, 1864.

Lang 2000
Lang, Andrew. *Complete Poems of Andrew Lang*. Vol. 1. Xlibris Corporation, 2000.

Le Bihan et al. 2007
Le Bihan, Olivier, Dominique Dussol, and Marie Weber. *Alfred Smith (1854–1936): Un regard sur la vie moderne*. Exh. cat. Bordeaux: Éditions Somogy in association with Musée des Beaux-Arts de Bordeaux, 2007.

Le Foll 1997
Le Foll, Joséphine. *La Peinture de fleurs*. Paris: Hazan, 1997.

Leribault 2011
Leribault, Christophe. "'Le Romanticism, c'est le veritable art moderne': La fabrique de *L'Hommage*." In *Fantin-Latour, Manet, Baudelaire: L'Hommage à Delacroix*, 31–85. Exh. cat. Paris: Le Passage Paris–New York Editions in association with Musée du Louvre, 2011.

Leribault et al. 2012
Leribault, Christophe, Stéphane Guégan, and Michele Hannoosh. *Delacroix, Othoniel, Creten: Des fleurs en hiver*. Exh. cat. Paris: Le Passage Editions, 2012.

***Lettres pittoresques* 1777**
Lettres pittoresques à l'occasion des tableaux exposés au Salon en 1777. Paris: Gueffier, 1777.

Lourenço et al. 2009
Lourenço, Eduardo, Olivier Meslay, and Vincent Pomarède. *Henri Fantin-Latour (1836–1904)*. Translated by Marisa Moreno Berzosa. Exh. cat. Madrid and Lisbon: Museo Thyssen-Bornemisza and Museu Calouste Gulbenkian, 2009.

Loyrette 1994
Loyrette, Henri. "Still Life." In *Origins of Impressionism*, edited by Henri Loyrette and Gary Tinterow, 149–82. Exh. cat. New York: Metropolitan Museum of Art in association with Abrams, 1994.

MacDonald et al.
MacDonald, Margaret F., Patricia de Montfort, and Nigel Thorp, eds. *The Correspondence of James McNeill Whistler, 1855–1903*. Online edition. University of Glasgow. http://www.whistler.arts.gla.ac.uk/correspondence.

Mallarmé 1945
Mallarmé, Stéphane. *Oeuvres complètes*. Compiled and edited by Henri Mondor and G. Jean-Aubry. Paris: Gallimard, 1945.

Mallarmé 1982
Mallarmé, Stéphane. *Selected Poetry and Prose*. Translated by Mary Caws. New York: New Directions, 1982.

Mallarmé 2006
Mallarmé, Stéphane. *Collected Poems and Other Verse*. Translated by E. H. and A. M. Blackmore. Oxford: Oxford University Press, 2006.

Mauner 2000
Mauner, George. *Manet: The Still-Life Paintings*. Exh. cat. New York: Abrams in association with American Federation of Arts, 2000.

McCoubrey 1958
McCoubrey, John W. "Studies in French Still-Life Painting, Theory and Criticism: 1600–1860." PhD diss., New York University, 1958.

McCoubrey 1964
McCoubrey, John W. "The Revival of Chardin in French Still Life Painting." *The Art Bulletin* 46, no. 1 (March 1964): 40.

Mérat 1898
Mérat, Albert. *Poésies d'Albert Mérat, 1866–1873*. Compiled by Alphonse Lemerre. Paris: Lemerre, 1898.

Meslay 2009
Meslay, Olivier. "White Roses and Lily Branches." In *Henri Fantin-Latour (1836–1904)*, 234–36. Exh. cat. Lisbon: Museu Calouste Gulbenkian, 2009.

Michel 2002
Michel, Marianne Roland. "Vallayer in Her Time." In *Anne Vallayer-Coster: Painter to the Court of Marie-Antoinette*, edited by Eik Kahng and Marianne Roland Michel, 13–37. Exh. cat. New Haven and London: Yale University Press in association with Dallas Museum of Art, 2002.

Michel et al. 2002
Michel, Marianne Roland, et al. *The Floral Art of Pierre-Joseph Redouté*. Exh. cat. London: Frances Lincoln in association with Bruce Museum of Arts and Science and Kimbell Art Museum, 2002.

Miel 1817
Miel, François. *Essai sur le Salon de 1817 ou examen critique des principaux ouvrages dont l'exposition se compose . . . par Monsieur M****. Paris: Imprimerie de Didot le Jeune, 1817.

Mireur 1911–12
Mireur, Hippolyte. *Dictionnaire des ventes d'art faites en France et à l'étranger pendant les XVIIIe et XIXe siècles: Tableaux, dessins, estampes, aquarelles, miniatures, pastels, gouaches, sépias, fusains, émaux, éventails peints et vitraux*. 7 vols. Paris: C. de Vincenti, 1911–12.

Mitchell 1973
Mitchell, Peter. *Great Flower Painters: Four Centuries of Floral Art*. Woodstock, NY: Overlook Press, 1973.

Moreau-Nélaton 1901
Moreau-Nélaton, Étienne. "Un précurseur: Laurent Bouvier." *Art et décoration* 9 (1901): 166–72.

Munck 2009
Munck, Jacqueline. "'The Cat Drank All the Milk!': Bonnard's Continuous Presence." In *Pierre Bonnard: The Late Still Lifes and Interiors*, edited by Dita Amory. Exh. cat. New Haven: Yale University Press in conjunction with Metropolitan Museum of Art, New York, 2009.

Oudry (1752) 1861
Oudry, Jean-Baptiste. "Discours sur la pratique de la peinture et ses procédés principaux: Ébaucher, peindre à fond et retoucher." Delivered on December 2, 1752. Originally published in *Le Cabinet de l'amateur*, 1861, 107–17.

Pascal (1958) 2003
Pascal, Blaise. *Pensées*. Translated by W. F. Trotter. New York: Dutton, 1958. Reprint Mineola, New York: Dover Publications, 2003.

Patry 2007
Patry, Sylvie. "Victoria Dubourg: 'Femme supérieure et peintre de mérite'." In *Fantin-Latour de la réalite au rêve*, edited by Juliane Cosandier, Rudolf Koella, and Sylvie Wuhrmann. Exh. cat. Lausanne: Foundation de l'Hermitage and Bibliothèque des arts, 2007

Patry 2009
Patry, Sylvie. "Renoir et la décoration, *un plaisir sans pareil*." In *Renoir au XXe siècle*. Exh. cat. Paris: Gallimard in association with Réunion des musées nationaux, 2009.

Patry 2011
Patry, Sylvie. "Edouard Manet et les débuts du japonisme: remarques sur quelques portraits." In Arnauld Brejon de Lavergnée et al., *Édouard Manet (1832–1883)* Exh. cat. Nara-Ken: Nara Prefectural Museum of Art, 2011.

Patry 2012
Patry, Sylvie. "Renoir's Early Career: From Artisan to Painter." In *Renoir, between Bohemia and Bourgeoisie: The Early Years*, edited by Nina Zimmer, 53–76. Exh. cat. Basel: Hatje Cantz in conjunction with Kunstmuseum Basel, 2012.

Peisse 1849
Peisse, Louis. "Salon de 1849." *Le Constitutionnel*, July 8, 1849.

Pissarro and Snollaerts 2005
Pissarro, Joachim, and Claire Durand-Ruel Snollaerts. *Pissarro: Critical Catalogue of Paintings*. 3 vols. Paris: Wildenstein Institute, 2005.

Pliny 1980
Pliny (the Elder). *Natural History*. Translated by W. H. S. Jones. 2nd ed. 10 vols. Cambridge, Mass.: Harvard University Press in association with W. Heinemann, London, 1980.

Pomarède 1998
Pomarède, Vincent. *Delacroix: The Late Years*. Exh. cat. London: Thames and Hudson in association with Philadelphia Museum of Art, 1998.

Pradel 1815
Pradel, Eugène de. *Le Bouquet de violettes, ou la réunion des braves au café Montansier: Recueil de couplets, strophes, hymnes, odes et autres morceaux de poésie*. Paris: Marchands de nouveautés, 1815.

Proust 1903
Proust, Marcel. "La Cour aux lilas et l'atelier des roses." *Le Figaro*, May 11, 1903.

Przyblyski 1995
Przyblyski, Jeannene M. "Le Parti Pris des Choses: French Still Life and Modern Painting, 1848–1876." PhD diss., University of California, Berkeley, 1995.

Pugh 2004
Pugh, Anthony R. *The Growth of "A la recherche du temps perdu," 1909–1911*. Toronto: University of Toronto Press, 2004.

Rapetti et al. 2011
Rapetti, Rodolphe, ed. *Odilon Redon, prince du rêve, 1840–1916*. Exh. cat. Paris: Éditions de la Réunions des musées nationaux-Grand Palais in association with Musée d'Orsay, 2011.

Rathbone and Shackelford 2001
Rathbone, Eliza E., and George T. M. Shackelford. *Impressionist Still Life*. New York: Phillips Collection in association with Abrams, 2001.

Réunion des musées nationaux 1998
Réunion des musées nationaux. *Le Japonisme*. Exh. cat. Paris: Réunion des musées nationaux, 1988.

Rewald et al. 1996
Rewald, John, Walter Feilchenfeldt, and Jayne Warman. *The Paintings of Paul Cézanne: A Catalogue Raisonné*. 2 vols. New York: Harry N. Abrams, 1996.

Rimbaud 1954
Rimbaud, Arthur. *Oeuvres complètes*. Edited by Rolland de Renéville and Jules Mouquet. Paris: Gallimard, 1954.

Rimbaud 2008
Complete Works. Translated by Paul Schmidt. New York: Harper Perennial Modern Classics, 2008.

Rishel 1982
Rishel, Joseph J. "A Lyonnais Flower Piece by Antoine Berjon (1754–1843)." *Philadelphia Museum of Art Bulletin* 78, no. 336 (1982): 16–24.

Rix 1981
Rix, Martin. *The Art of the Botanist*. New York: Arch Cape Press, 1981.

Robaut and Chesneau 1885
Robaut, Albert, and Ernest Chesneau. *L'Oeuvre complet de Eugène Delacroix: Peintures, dessins, gravures, lithographies*. Paris: Charavay Frères, 1885.

Rochebrune 1999
Rochebrune, Marie-Laure de. "À propos de quelques objets de céramique et de verre dans la peinture de Chardin." In *Chardin*, edited by Pierre Rosenberg, 37–53. Exh. cat. Paris: Réunion des musées mationaux, 1999.

Ronsard 1938
Ronsard, Pierre de. *Continuation des Amours, Oeuvres completes*. Vol. 2. Paris: Gallimard, 1938.

Rouart and Wildenstein 1975
Rouart, Denis, and Daniel Wildenstein. *Édouard Manet: Catalogue raisonné*. Lausanne and Paris: Bibliothèque des arts, 1975.

Rubin 1994
Rubin, James H. *Manet's Silence and the Poetics of Bouquets*. London: Reaktion Books, 1994.

Samain 1911
Samain, Albert. *Au jardin de l'infante*. Paris: Mercure de France, 1911.

Saunders 1995
Saunders, Gill. *Picturing Plants: An Analytical History of Botanical Illustration*. Berkeley and London: University of California Press in association with Victoria and Albert Museum, London, 1995.

Scarron 1654
Scarron, Paul. *Les Oeuvres de Monsieur Scarron*. Paris: Chez Guillaume de Luynes, 1654.

Schulman 1995
Schulman, Michel. *Frédéric Bazille, 1841–1870: Catalogue raisonné: Peintures—dessins, pastels, aquarelles, sa vie, son oeuvre, sa correspondance*. Paris: Éditions de l'Amateur–Editions des catalogues raisonnés, 1995.

Sharp 1994
Sharp, Kevin. "Redon and the Marketplace after 1900." In *Odilon Redon, Prince of Dreams, 1840–1916*, edited by Douglas Druick. Exh. cat. Chicago: Art Institute of Chicago in association with Abrams, 1994.

Smith and Findlen 2002
Smith, Pamela H., and Paula Findlen. "Commerce and the Representation of Nature in Art and Science." In *Merchants and Marvels: Commerce, Science, and Art in Early Modern Europe*, edited by Pamela H. Smith and Paula Findlen, 1–25. New York: Routledge, 2002.

Soubiran 2007
Soubiran, Jean-Roger. "L'Exposition de 1863: Une experience singulière." In *Autour de Courbet en Saintonge*, edited by Gaby Scaon and Jean-Roger Soubiran, 91–115. Exh. cat. Bordeaux: Le Festin in association with Musée de l'Echevêché, 2007.

Sterling 1952
Sterling, Charles. *Nature Morte de l'antiquité à nos jours*. Paris: Pierre Tisné, 1952.

Stevens 1994
Stevens, Maryanne. "Artistic and Critical Position." In *Odilon Redon, Prince of Dreams, 1840–1916*, edited by Douglas Druick. Exh. cat. Chicago: Art Institute of Chicago in association with Abrams, 1994.

Syme 2010
Syme, Alison. *A Touch of Blossom: John Singer Sargent and the Queer Flora of Fin-de-Siècle Art*. University Park, Penn.: Penn State University Press, 2010.

Thoré 1860
Thoré, Théophile [W. Bürger, pseud.]. "Peintres d'objets quelconques." In Thoré, *Musées de la Hollande*. Vol. 2. Paris: Jules Renouard, 1860.

Thoré 1870
Thoré, Théophile [W. Bürger, pseud.]. "Salon de 1868." In *Salon de W. Bürger, 1861 à 1868*. Paris: Jules Renouard, 1870.

Tourneux 1877–82
Tourneux, Maurice, ed. *Correspondance littéraire, philosophique et critique par Grimm, Diderot, Raynal, Meister, etc.: Revue sur les textes originaux*. 16 vols. Paris: Garnier Frères, 1877–82.

van Druten 2013
van Druten, Terry. "Pierre-Joseph Redouté: A Life Between Science and Beauty." In *Pierre-Joseph Redouté: Botanical Artist to the Court of France*, edited by Terry van Druten, 8–23. Exh. cat. Rotterdam and Haarlem: nai010 publishers in association with Teylers Museum, 2013.

van Spaendonck
van Spaendonck, Gérard. *Fleurs dessinés d'après nature . . . recueil utile aux amateurs, aux jeunes artistes, aux élèves des écoles centrales et aux dessinateurs des manufactures*. Engraved by P. F. Le Grand. Paris: ca. 1800.

van Tilborgh 2008
van Tilborgh, Louis. *Vincent van Gogh et les tournesols*. Amsterdam: Fonds Mercator in association with Van Gogh Museum, 2008.

Vollard 1938
Vollard, Ambroise. *En écoutant Cézanne, Degas, Renoir*. Paris: Grasset, 1938.

Weisberg 1977
Weisberg, Gabriel P. "Fantin-Latour and Still Life Symbolism in *Un Atelier aux Batignolles*." *Gazette des Beaux-Arts* 90 (1977): 206–15.

Wheelock 1999
Wheelock, Arthur K. *From Botany to Bouquets: Flowers in Northern Art*. Exh. cat. Washington, D.C.: National Gallery of Art, 1999.

Wildenstein, A. 1996
Wildenstein, Alec. *Odilon Redon: Catalogue raisonné de l'oeuvre peint et dessiné*. 4 vols. Paris: Wildenstein Institute, 1996.

Wildenstein 1996
Wildenstein, Daniel. *Monet ou le triomphe de l'impressionnisme: Catalogue raisonné*. 4 vols. Cologne and Paris: Taschen in association with Wildenstein Institute, 1996.

Wildenstein 2002
Wildenstein, Daniel. *Gauguin: Savage in the Making—Catalogue Raisonné of the Paintings, 1873–1888*. 2 vols. Paris: Wildenstein Institute, 2002.

Williams 2001
Williams, Roger Lawrence. *Botanophilia in Eighteenth-Century France: The Spirit of the Enlightenment*. Dordrecht, Netherlands: Kluwer Academic Publishers, 2001.

Willsdon 2004
Willsdon, Clare A. P. *In the Gardens of Impressionism*. New York: Vendome, 2004.

Zola 1902
Zola, Émile. *His Masterpiece [L'Oeuvre]*. Translated by Ernest Alfred Vizetelly. London: Chatto and Windus, 1902.

Zola 1928
Zola, Emile. *Oeuvres complètes*. Edited by Maurice Le Blond. 50 vols. Paris: François Bernouard, 1928.

INDEX

Notes: Page references in *italics* denote illustrations. To distinguish them from paintings, texts have been annotated with the date of first publication.

This catalogue accompanies exhibitions at the following museums:

DALLAS MUSEUM OF ART, October 26, 2014–February 8, 2015

VIRGINIA MUSEUM OF FINE ARTS, March 21–June 21, 2015

DENVER ART MUSEUM, July 19–October 11, 2015

The exhibition was co-organized by the Dallas Museum of Art and the Virginia Museum of Fine Arts. This exhibition is supported by an indemnity from the Federal Council on the Arts and the Humanities.

This book is dedicated to the memory of Roslyn Mona Briskin Merling (1935–2014) and Donald John Edmond MacDonald (1943–2014).

Stacy Moore and Sally Curran, VMFA Project Editors
Rosalie West, Editor-in-Chief
vmfa.museum

Distributed by Yale University Press, New Haven and London
yalebooks.com/art

Produced by Marquand Books, Inc., Seattle
marquand.com

Designed by Susan E. Kelly
Composed and typeset by Marie Weiler in Whitman with heads in Filosofia and selected elements in Verlag
Proofread by Diana George
Indexed by Frances Bowles
Image management by iocolor, Seattle
Printed on Gold East matte artpaper
Printed and bound in China by C&C Offset Printing Co., Ltd.

Library of Congress Cataloging-in-Publication Data
Working among flowers : floral still-life painting in nineteenth-century France / Heather MacDonald and Mitchell Merling; with essays by Audrey Gay-Mazuel, Olivier Meslay, and Sylvie Patry.
pages cm
Includes bibliographical references.
ISBN 978-0-300-20950-1 (hardback)
1. Flowers in art—Exhibitions. 2. Painting, French—19th century—Exhibitions. 3. Art and society—France—History—19th century—Exhibitions. I. MacDonald, Heather (Heather Eleanor) author. Information and illusion. II. Merling, Mitchell Frank, author. Path to the modern floral still life. III. Patry, Sylvie, author. Impressionist flower paintings and the market. IV. Gay-Mazuel, Audrey, author. Ceramic containers in French nineteenth-century flower painting. V. Meslay, Olivier, author. A Time to bloom, a time to die.
ND1403.F85W67 2014
758'.420944074755451—dc23 2014015512

FRONT COVER Gustave Caillebotte, *Yellow Roses in a Vase*, cat. no. 47 (detail); FRONTISPIECE Frédéric Bazille, *Flowers*, cat. no. 22 (detail); PAGE IV Paul Cézanne, *The Blue Vase*, cat. no. 48 (detail); PAGE VIII Paul Gauguin, *Still Life with Peonies*, cat. no. 44 (detail); PAGE X Antoine Berjon, *Bouquet of Lilies and Roses in a Basket on a Chiffonier*, cat. no. 13 (detail); PAGES 72–73 Vincent van Gogh, *Daisies, Arles*, cat. no. 52 (detail); BACK COVER Vincent van Gogh, *Bowl with Zinnias and Other Flowers*, cat. no. 49

PHOTOGRAPHY CREDITS

Frontispiece, pp. 90, 105, 109 (left), © Musée de Grenoble (see also below p. 111); pp. iv, xvi, 2, 6, 8, 40, 44, 45 (left & right), 46 (left), 49 (left), 51, 53 (left), 80, 82, 93, 106, 124–25, 129, 147, 158, 164, © RMN-Grand Palais/Art Resource, NY (see also below pp. 16, 24ff., 36 [right], 53, 67, 76, 145) ; p. 5, Bridgeman Art Library; p. 16, © RMN-Grand Palais/Art Resource, NY, photo by Bulloz; p. 17, © Metropolitan Museum of Art. Image source: Art Resource, NY; p. 19, 81, 83, 87, © Fitzwilliam Museum, Cambridge, U.K.; p. 21, © By kind permission of the Trustees of the Wallace Collection; pp. 24, 46 (right), 47, 58, 64 (right), 65, 99, 130–31, © RMN-Grand Palais/Art Resource, NY, photo by Hervé Lewandowski; p. 33, Photo courtesy of Sotheby's, Inc., © 2014; p. 35, Bridgeman Art Library; p. 36 (right), © RMN-Grand Palais/Art Resource, NY, photo by Michèle Bellot; p. 42, © Montauban, Musée Ingres; p. 50 (left), © Yannick Blaise, Direction des Musées et du patrimoine culturel, Ville d'Aix-en-Provence; p. 53 (right), © RMN-Grand Palais/Art Resource, NY, photo by Gérard Blot; p. 61, Photo by Hugo Maertens; p. 63, Adoc-photos/Art Resource, NY; p. 67, © RMN-Grand Palais/Art Resource, NY, photo by Patrice Schmidt; pp. 72–73, Photo by Travis Fullerton, VMFA; p. 76, © RMN-Grand Palais/Art Resource, NY, photo by Daniel Arnaudet/Jean Schormans; pp. 84, 86, 94, © Musées de la Ville de Rouen; pp. 89, 92, 95–97, © Lyon MBA, Photo Alain Basset; p. 104, © CSG CIC Glasgow Museums and Libraries Collections; p. 107, Photo © 2014 Museum of Fine Arts, Boston; p. 111, Musée de Grenoble, Gianni Dagli Orti/The Art Archive at Art Resource, NY; p. 112, Photo: Jamison Miller; p. 137, Digital Image © Museum of Modern Art/Licensed by SCALA/Art Resource, NY; p. 140, Courtesy Ober Fine Art, LLC; p. 144, © Durand-Ruel & Cie; p. 145, © RMN-Grand Palais/Art Resource, NY, photo by René-Gabriel Ojéda; p. 153, © Christie's Images Limited 2014; p. 157, Photo by Ole Haupt; p. 165, © Metropolitan Museum of Art. Image source: Art Resource, NY; p. 166, Erich Lessing/Art Resource, NY; pp. 169–173, © 2014 Succession H. Matisse/Artists Rights Society (ARS), New York